Adolescent Development
The Essential Readings

Edited by Gerald Adams

BLACKWELL
Publishers

Copyright © Blackwell Publishers 2000
Editorial matter and organization copyright © Gerald Adams,
Darwin Muir and Alan Slater 2000

First published 2000

2 4 6 8 10 9 7 5 3 1

Blackwell Publishers Ltd
108 Cowley Road
Oxford OX4 1JF
UK

Blackwell Publishers Inc.
350 Main Street
Malden, Massachusetts 02148
USA

British Library Cataloguing in Publication Data

A CIP catalogue record for this book is available from the British Library.

Library of Congress Cataloging-in-Publication Data has been applied for.

ISBN 0 631 21742 8 (hbk)
ISBN 0 631 21743 6 (pbk)

Typeset in 10½ on 13 pt Photina
by Best-set Typesetter Ltd., Hong Kong
Printed in Great Britain by T J International, Cornwall.

This book is printed on acid-free paper

Adolescent Development

Essential Readings in Developmental Psychology

Series Editors: Darwin Muir and Alan Slater
Queen's University, Kingston, Ontario, and the University of Exeter

In this brand new series of nine books, Darwin Muir and Alan Slater, together with a team of expert editors, bring together selections of readings illustrating important methodological, empirical, and theoretical issues in the area of developmental psychology. Volumes in the series and their editors are listed below:

• *Infant Development*	Darwin Muir and Alan Slater
• *Childhood Social Development*	Wendy Craig
• *Childhood Cognitive Development*	Kang Lee
• *Adolescent Development*	Gerald Adams
• *The Psychology of Aging*	William Gekoski
• *The Nature–Nurture Debate*	Steven Ceci and Wendy Williams
• *Educational Development*	Charles Desforges
• *Language Development*	Elizabeth Bates
• *Developmental Disorders*	Darwin Muir, Alan Slater, Wendy Williams, and Steven Ceci

Each book is introduced by the volume editor with a rationale behind the chosen papers. Each reading is then introduced and contextualized within the individual subject debate as well as within the wider context of developmental psychology. A selection of further reading is also assigned, making each volume an ideal teaching resource for both classroom and individual study settings.

Contents

Acknowledgments

The authors and publishers gratefully acknowledge the following for permission to reproduce copyright material:

Adams, G. R., Abraham, K. G. & Markstrom, C. A. "The relations among identity development, self-consciousness, and self-focusing during middle and late adolescence", *Developmental Psychology*, 23(2) 1987. Copyright (c) 1987 by the American Psychological Association. Reprinted with permission.

Bingham, C. R. & Crockett, L. J. "Longitudinal adjustment patterns of boys and girls experiencing early, middle and late sexual intercourse", *Developmental Psychology* 32(4) 1996. Copyright (c) 1996 by the American Psychological Association. Reprinted with permission.

Carlo, G., Koller, S. H., Eisenberg, N., Da Silva, M. S. & Frohlich, C. B. "A cross-national study on the relations among prosocial moral reasoning, gender role orientation, and prosocial behaviors", *Developmental Psychology* 32(2) 1996. Copyright (c) 1996 by the American Psychological Association. Reprinted with permission.

Côté, J. E. "Was Mead wrong about coming of age in Samoa? An analysis of the Mead/Freedman controversy for Scholars of Adolescence and Human Development", *Journal of Youth and Adolescence* 21(5) 1992. Reprinted by permission of Plenum Publishing Corporation, New York.

D'Angelo, L. L., Weinberger, D. A. & Feldman, S. S. "Like father, like son? Predicting male adolescents' adjustment from parents' distress and self-restraint", *Developmental Psychology* 31(6) 1995. Copyright (c) 1995 by the American Psychological Association. Reprinted with permission.

Gavin, L. A. & Furman, W. "Adolescent girls' relationship with mothers and best friends", *Child Development* 67, 1996.

Kim, K. & Smith, P. K. "Retrospective survey of parental marital relations and child reproductive development", *International Journal of Behavioural Development* 22(4) 1998. Reprinted by permission of the International Society for the Study of Behavioural Development.

Larson, R. "The High School 'junior theme': as an adolescent rite of passage", *Journal of Youth and Adolescence* 17(4) 1988. Reprinted by permission of Plenum Publishing Corporation, New York.

Leone, C. M., & Richards, M. H. "Classwork and homework in early adolescence: the ecology of achievement", *Journal of Youth and Adolescence* 18(6) 1989. Reprinted by permission of Plenum Publishing Corporation, New York.

Loeber, R., Russo, M. F., Stouthamer-Loeber, M., & Lahey, B. B. "Internalizing problems and their relation to the development of disruptive behaviors in adolescence", *Journal of Research on Adolescence* 4(4) 1994. Reprinted by permission of Lawrence Erlbaum Associates, Inc., Mahwah, N. J.

Mortimer, J. T., Finch, M., Shanahan, M. & Ryu, S. "Work experience, mental health, and behavioral adjustment in adolescence", *Journal of Research on Adolescence* 2(1) 1992. Reprinted by permission of Lawrence Erlbaum Associates, Inc., Mahwah, N. J.

Thompson, R. L., & Larson, R. "Social context and the subjective experience of different types of rock music", *Journal of Youth and Adolescence* 24(6) 1995. Reprinted by permission of Plenum Publishing Corporation, New York.

Windle, M., Miller-Tutzauer, C., & Domenico, D. "Alcohol use, suicidal behavior, and risky activities among adolescents", *Journal of Research on Adolescence* 2(4) 1992. Reprinted by permission of Lawrence Erlbaum Associates, Inc., Mahwah, N. J.

The publishers apologize for any errors or omissions in the above list and would be grateful to be notified of any corrections that should be incorporated in the next edition or reprint of this book.

Introduction

Gerald Adams

A recent Canadian magazine printed a lead article on adolescents. The general theme was that while Generation X adolescents (1980s teens) were portrayed (wrongly) as slackers with little ambition, the Echo Generation adolescents (1990s teens) hold higher expectations for their education, work potential, and buying power. After all, for most North American and European youth, the economy has improved in the 1990s and stock markets around the world have been jingling with profit taking most everywhere (outside of Asia, Africa, and South America).

Advertisers have quickly recognized the buying power of the growing numbers of adolescents. They divide teenagers into two groups. Tweens are the 9–14 year-olds who buy merchandise to look, dress, and act like teenagers. Teens are 15–20 year-olds who buy things to dress, act, and appear like adults. The market focuses on the teen years because the younger set of tweens want to be teens and teens set the standards. So teenagers provide the buying power and creative energy for the pop culture, personal services, entertainment, and even educational and training systems.

Entertainment centers and businesses have emerged as the new focal point for teenage interactions. These settings also provide a crossroad for adolescent consumer behavior. Nowhere else than at the Megaplex, with its multi-screen movies, blinking lights, video games, fast-food, and mingling crowds can one see so many types of teenagers – ravers, skaters, punks, jocks, tough guys, nerds, and more. Youth move around, mixing and conversing, playing video games, gossiping, teasing, flirting and such. If you want to know how to look and act "cool" it isn't found in the school or mall anymore . . . go watch tweens and teens at the Megaplex. And if you wish to observe what adolescents think about and do, watch the latest teenage soap on television, or go to the movies and watch those high school antic movies that keep coming and coming, year after year. Watch out though because you can get "dumber and dumber."

No longer can a nation, state, province or community ignore the power of youth. They not only bring energy to a community, its schools, and institutions, but also the buying power that drives products that even adults want to purchase (mostly to fool themselves into thinking they are still young and youthful). Once the power of influence was exclusively from adult to child or adolescent. Now influence is shared mutually between adult and adolescent. The anthropologist Margaret Mead (1980) has even suggested that we are becoming a world where adolescents are coming to hold power and information that the adult must seek and emulate. I have, on more than one occasion, seen this when parents buy a computer for the family and they have to ask the child or adolescent how to use it.

There are many reasons to study the adolescent years. I found this age interesting because there are so many changes and transitions occurring. The body undergoes a second and dramatic growth period (like that of infancy). The body changes, sexuality emerges, and social stigma and social influences around sexuality unfold. The mind undergoes major transitions and is able to engage in analytic and metaphoric reasoning. Social context broadens to include not only family and school, but work, peers, community, and much more. School transitions occur with entry into junior high, high school, and again in college or apprenticeships. A combination of biological, psychological, and social influences merge into one big dynamic influence on adolescent behavior and youth. There is so much to observe, to be fascinated with, to analyze and understand, about the adolescent years. Since I am a student of change and development I have found the world of adolescence a wonderful place to study and discover. I think if you join me in this Twlight Zone know as Adolescence you too will find it a wonderful place to observe, analyze, and discover the nature of human beings, at a time when they face so many transitions and potential for growth.

My career has been one of scientist and I have studied adolescence and youth for more than 30 years. I have been teaching courses on adolescence for 25 of those years. And I have always done so with an eye to what we can learn from sociology, psychology, and anthropology. However, the most dominant energy in the study of adolescence comes from developmental psychology. Developmental psychologists are interested in how people differ (e.g., males versus females) and how they grow and mature (develop). Either they look for increases or decreases in behavior or they identify stages or phases of growth and development. Each of these perspectives offers us considerable insight into the nature of adolescence. From sociology we often learn how context influences human behavior. Most often we find that the "social address" or characteristics of the family (parental education, family income) or neighborhood (poor or well-to-do), even the quality of the local school, provide the context for individual socialization and successes or failures. In recent years the context is thought to offer financial or social (parent-child interaction) capital that allows for certain forms of development. That is, financial capital offers the capacity for the family to purchase educational opportunities and other resources for the child's enrichment, with efficient and productive parenting giving the child capital (such as good communication skills) that facilitate a child's success in school. Finally, anthropologists often look at culture and the distinctions that exist between and within cultures which influence behavior. As an interdisciplinary scholar, I have used all of these perspectives to shape my thinking and interests. I hope they will influence you too.

In particular, what I have learned from reading widely about adolescence is that there are three components that should be considered when constructing an understanding of the nature of human experience. These components include the person, the context, and the occasions. The *person* involves the characteristics, attributes, or features of the self. Gender, physical characteristics, group membership, or family role (son or daughter) are person variables. For example, a given study may be undertaken to see how adolescents of various ethnic heritage differ as person variables on feelings, behaviors, or thoughts. Other examples would be studies comparing females versus males, high achieving students versus low achieving students, or delinquent versus non-delinquent youth. The *context* variable focuses on either the context itself or differences in behaviors that occur between contexts. Sometimes we are interested, for example, in how adolescents behave within their family. We might examine and compare behaviors by the adolescent with only his/her father versus his/her mother or sibling. Other times scholars investigate how an adolescent behaves at home versus in school or at work. In addition to person and context, we often are interested in *occasion*. The most frequently used version of occasion includes comparisons between chronological age or time (measured as years). That is, we observe a youth at age 14, again at 15, and maybe yet again at 16 years of age. Of course, occasions refer to repeated assessments on the same measure over multiple occasions. Sometimes occasion is based on age (14 versus 15 versus 16) and other times just on repeated times that are often very close in intervals (such as minutes, hours or days). Another way is to compare samples of 14 year-olds in consecutive years (e.g., 1998, 1999, and 2000). This involves obtaining new samples each year who are 14 years old and then comparing them for the differences. If 14 year-old tweens in 1998 report different behaviors than in the year 2000, the difference is attributed to historical or cultural shifts. If there are differences between behaviors for when adolescents are 14, 15, and 16, we refer to this as development.

I have introduced you to the scholastic reason I have studied adolescence. And I have suggested that we can view adolescents from features of the person, context, and occasion. In fact, I hope you look for these three components in each of the readings to see when one or more are used or when the interaction (person × context, or person × occasion) is the focus of the study. But I have another reason for studying adolescents. This reason deals with the personal need to help adolescents experience this stage of life in a positive and productive way. I want to understand the nature of adolescence, its progressions and regressions, so that I can help teenagers and young adults have a happy, healthy, and productive transition from childhood to adulthood.

My own applied professional experiences with teenagers (beyond the personal experience of raising four adolescent daughters, who tried hard to drive me crazy, but failed, or so I want them to think) focused initially on work with difficult teens who were under court order to work on correcting problem behavior. I found I tried hard to help these troubled youths, and mostly they tried hard not to change. In time, my frustrations drove me to turn my attention instead to the concept and issues of primary prevention. After many years of teaching about prevention and serving on an editorial board for the *Journal of Primary Prevention*, I now believe that while treatment for the many problems that emerge during adolescence is necessary, it is not sufficient to promote wider health among teenage populations. Instead of spending time and resources on problems once they emerge, I believe more resources should be put into prevention. A few pennies for every dollar spent on intervention can reduce the risks of problems for many adolescents who are on the verge or at-risk for a social problem. However, to build strong primary prevention programs we need good applied science to show us how or why problems emerge and give us guidance on what factors need to be considered in building prevention programs.

So I have selected 14 articles that include research on person, context, and occasion. These essays or research reports are useful to understand the nature of adolescence. However, the readings can also be informative to the practitioner who wishes to build prevention programs or create policy. I urge you to read each article with an eye to what are the person, context, and occasion components of each study. But I hope you won't stop there. Consider how each study gives some suggestions for prevention or policy.

For each article I have prepared a brief introduction to guide your reading. Mostly, the introduction provides a rationale for why a particular article was selected. I will share with you some fascination I have for either the research area or the article and get you "primed" to read the article with the enthusiasm that you already bring to a course on adolescent development. So now you enter the Twilight Zone of Adolescence. I hope you get hooked on this stage of life like I am. Maybe you will be the graduate student who one day takes my job when I retire and your introduction to the study of adolescence began with a reading of this book. So here we go on our journey together. I am so pleased to be your guide.

Reference

Mead, M. 1980: *Culture and commitment: a study of the generation gap*. Garden City, NY: Natural History Press.

Suggested Reading

Bloom, M. 1996: *Primary prevention practices*. Issues in Children's and Families' Lives (Vol 5). Thousand Oaks, CA: Sage Publications, Inc.

Albee, G. W., and Gullotta, T. P. (Eds.) 1997: *Primary Prevention Works*. Issues in Children's and Families' Lives (Vol 6). Thousand Oaks, CA: Sage Publications, Inc.

Part I

Theories of Adolescent Development

In the course of time a few individuals, whose careers have included writing about the nature of adolescence, came to be recognized as great theoreticians. As an introduction to several of the highly influential theorists in the study of adolescence, Michael Berzonsky has written an essay on theories of adolescence.

Theories of Adolescence

Introduction

There are, at times, great individuals who capture the attention of the scientific community through their descriptive writings. These women and men have an insight about the world that provides both compelling descriptive and profound analytic portraits of the human experience. Often such scholars provide the very theory that is used to drive research questions or to help explain and understand research findings.

Rather than offer a glimpse at a scholar or two that have provided us with a descriptive story of adolescence, I have asked a fellow scholar and friend to write a brief summary of some of the points that several key theorists have provided in their writing. This account will give you an opportunity to consider several profound thoughts that have come from key theorists' minds. But this reading is only a glimpse, since our journey together is to cover so much of what is written and studied about adolescence.

Look for how the various theorists have included various forms of person, context, and occasion variables in their writing. Berzonsky's introduction will give you a sense of how several eminent women and men have broadly examined and portrayed the adolescent experience. Most of the thoughts of these theorists have driven and continue to drive many of the explanations for research findings that emerge to this day.

I am constantly amazed at how some people grasp the complexity of adolescent life and write about it with a style that retains our interest for years. I was introduced to the field of adolescent development by a professor that helped train me in the 1960s. The theories of Erik H. Erikson and Peter Blos were among the first I read in their raw, original, and challenging books. These two men baited the intellectual hook, by providing interesting ways to think of adolescence, and through my reading I was caught in the Twilight Zone of Adolescence. I became a student of adolescent development. If you find any of the theories of adolescence of interest, do some extra reading. Perhaps you could look at some of the original writings, or at the additional reading I've suggested below.

So go to it and see if theories of adolescence become of interest to you. I'm certain you will find some interesting ideas in the following reading by Michael Berzonsky.

Suggested reading

Muuss, R. E. (1996): *Theories of adolescence*. Sixth Edition. New York: McGraw Hill.

ONE

Theories of Adolescence

Michael D. Berzonsky

The academic discipline of adolescent psychology originated in the twentieth century. Of course, people made distinctions among children, youth, and adults before the modern era. Plato (427–347 BC), for instance, suggested that because boys were so excitable they should not be allowed to drink wine until they were at least 18 years of age. Since rational thinking developed during the teens, Plato (1921) advocated that mathematical and scientific instruction should be emphasized during that phase of life. Aristotle (384–322 BC) divided the preadult period into three segments: infancy (first 7 years), young childhood (from 7 to puberty), and young adulthood (puberty to 21). Aristotle (1941) viewed adolescents as being impulsive, moody, and controlled by their passions; he stressed the need for adolescents to learn volitional self-control. Although the term *adolescence* first appeared in the fifteenth century (Muuss, 1988), the publication of G. Stanley Hall's two-volume work entitled *Adolescence* (1904) marked the onset of adolescent psychology as a scientific academic discipline.

In this chapter we consider some theories of adolescence that have had a major influence during the past century. Specifically we will consider five somewhat distinctive types of theories: 1) biological views; 2) cultural views; 3) psychoanalytic views; 4) psychosocial views; and 5) cognitive views.

Biological Views: G. Stanley Hall

Granville Stanley Hall (1844–1924) is the acknowledged father of adolescent psychology. Although few contemporary people have heard of
Hall and his theoretical contributions, early in the twentieth century he
was one of the most eminent psychologists in the United States. His
awards and achievements include: earning the first Ph.D. in psychology
awarded in the United States; founding the first psychology laboratory;
being one of the founders and the first president of the American Psychology Association; serving as the first president of Clarke University.

Ontogeny recapitulates phylogeny

Hall's two-volume work on adolescence proffered a recapitulation view
of human development. He suggested that during their individual life
spans (ontogenetic development) people briefly re-enacted (recapitulated) evolutionary changes that the species had experienced (phyloge-
netic development). Collectively all the people alive today represent the
end point of an evolutionary process – phylogenetically the human
species has evolved from simpler life forms. These evolutionary changes
then were briefly recapitulated during the ontogenetic development of
subsequent generations. For instance, creeping and crawling in infancy
was considered to be a replay of a primitive animal-like era in human
evolutionary history. The unruly, obnoxious, and undisciplined behavior of junior high school students reflected a more barbaric and savage
human epoch (Berzonsky, 1981).

Adolescence, however, marked a "rebirth." Humans, according to
Hall (1904) were born first as members of the animal kingdom with
selfish drives, needs, and survival concerns. During adolescence they
were "reborn" as members of a civilized species concerned with social
responsibility and the rights and welfare of others. Being altruistic and
socially responsible sometimes required one to sacrifice and frustrate
personal wants and needs. According to Hall (1904), this internal struggle between self-interest and social good resulted in an intensive period
of *Sturm und Drang* (storm and stress). Normal adolescence was seen
to be characterized by emotional upheavals and extensive stress and
turmoil: exaggerated emotional swings from being exuberant and
euphoric to suddenly becoming indifferent or melancholy.

Although Hall (1904) did identify many of the major dimensions of adolescent development – e.g., intellectual development, sexual development, physical and mental diseases, adolescent crime and antisocial behaviors, physical and motor development, and the like – the major emphasis was placed on the hypothesis that adolescence was universally an extraordinarily turbulent and stressful period of life. Evidence about adolescents obtained in America and other Western cultures generally supported the storm and stress hypothesis. However, in the 1920s anthropologists began to study adolescents in non-Western cultures. The findings they reported led to the development of cultural theories.

Cultural Theories: Margaret Mead and Ruth Benedict

In the 1920s and 1930s a number of anthropological studies (e.g., Malinowski, 1927; Mead, 1928, 1935) revealed that adolescent behaviors varied considerably from culture to culture. As an anthropology student, Margaret Mead's (1901–1978) doctoral dissertation was designed to test Stanley Hall's hypothesis that adolescence is universally a period of storm and stress. Her dissertation work was conducted in Samoa, a small island in the South Pacific. The findings she reported indicated that Samoan adolescents experienced few problems and difficulties; in fact little significance or fanfare was associated with the adolescent transition (Mead, 1928). (Freeman (1983) has challenged the reliability and validity of Mead's findings in Samoa; compare however, Côté (1994) for an alternative critique.)

These and other anthropological findings (see Muuss, 1988) led to a view known as *cultural relativism*; the way adolescents act and the problems they experience are relative to the cultural circumstances within which they live and develop. Accordingly, there is not *a* single cultural theory of adolescence, there is a different micro-theory for each culture. One anthropologist, Ruth Benedict (1887–1948), did develop a more macro-cultural theory of adolescence.

Cultural continuities and discontinuities

Benedict's (1938) review of cultural studies of adolescence revealed that specific adolescent behaviors and problems did vary from culture to culture. However, in some cultures, like American and Western cultures, adolescence was a stressful and tumultuous time of life. In other cultures, the transition from childhood to adulthood was less problematic and stressful. Benedict asked a macro-question: what characteristics and aspects do stress-provoking cultures seem to share and how do they differ systematically from cultures in which adolescence is relatively tranquil and non-problematic?

Her answer focused on the manner in which socialization, instruction, and rearing occurred. In non-stressful cultures, training and socialization was relatively gradual and continuous. Consider, for instance, a girl growing up in a traditional setting – one where her mother does not work outside of the home – who will herself assume that same traditional role when she subsequently becomes an adult. The games she plays as a child, her responsibilities helping her mother with the cooking and cleaning or taking care of younger siblings, are all gradual and continuous training and preparation for the role she will assume when she becomes an adult. When it is time to make the transition to an adult role, she is well prepared and experiences little turmoil or difficulty. In contrast, Benedict (1938) found that the training and instruction for youth in cultures in which adolescence is stressful tends to be discontinuous. There is a sharp break or distinction between what one does and learns as a child and the role one is expected to assume as an adult. For instance, a distinction is made between the responsible work that adults do and the non-responsible play of children (Benedict, 1938). Of course, children may have chores or even part-time jobs like a paper route, but that is rarely seen as preparation relevant to their "real" life's work. In fact, with most Western adolescents, instruction and education take place in artificial learning contexts – schools – which bear little resemblance to the contexts within which they will work as adults. (School-based instruction is most likely more continuous for students who go to an adult career in education.) Two other themes emphasized by Benedict (1938) were whether or not there were sharp discontinuities between cultural expectations for submission in childhood and dominance in adulthood and cultural expectations about sexual behavior.

Postfigurative and prefigurative cultures

Do such cultural findings indicate that by instituting more continuous education practices, Western cultures could reduce the amount of turmoil and stress that Western adolescents experience? Mead (1970) argued that even though there is a relationship between adolescent stress and instructional practices, one does not necessarily cause the other: the nature of the culture within which adolescents live moderates the relationship.

Mead (1970) identified three types of cultures: postfigurative; cofigurative; and prefigurative. We will only consider the two extremes. A figure is a representation; it stands for something else. The question Mead asked is: what represents the type of world today's adolescents will live in when they become adults? In a postfigurative culture the past represents the future – it is a relatively stable, tradition-oriented culture with limited technological and social change. Within a postfigurative culture, effective continuous instruction is possible because teachers and parents know *specifically* what adolescents need to learn and be able to do in order to become successful adults. Adolescents need to learn the same skills, knowledge, and values that the current generation of adults possess because the world adolescents will live in in the future will be virtually the same as the world their parents and teachers grew up in.

In contrast, prefigurative cultures are marked by rapid social and technological change. (Cofigurative cultures are characterized by moderate change.) Parents and teachers may still be interested in continuously preparing adolescents for adulthood, but they don't know the *specific* knowledge and skills that will be required because cultural demands, problems, and opportunities are constantly changing. Effective education within a prefigurative culture involves teaching students how to think, how to evaluate, how to solve problems, and how to effectively adapt rather than teaching them specifically what to think, what to value, what to do, and what to believe (Berzonsky, 1981).

Psychoanalytic Theory: Sigmund Freud

Psychoanalytic theory did not develop as a reaction to or outgrowth of cultural theories. Sigmund Freud (1856–1939) was a contemporary of G. Stanley Hall. He began his scholarly activities in the late nineteenth century and in 1899 he published his first great work, *The Interpretation of Dreams* (first published 1899, see Freud, 1953). Of course psychoanalytic theory is more than an explanation of adolescent development; it is a comprehensive framework that attempts to account for virtually all aspects of human personality and behavior. Classical psychoanalytic theory emphasized the role that childhood experiences play in adult personality; few significant changes in personality were said to occur during adolescence. Sigmund Freud's daughter Anna and other neo-Freudians have elaborated classical psychoanalytic theoretical principles and applied them to changes and developments that occur during adolescence.

Freud's structural theory

According to Freud, the mature personality is composed of three structures: id, ego, and superego (C. S. Hall, 1954). Virtually all behavior is an interactive product of the three structures. The id is the primary system and plays a major role in the development of the others.

The id refers collectively to the basic urges, drives, and needs people are born with – it operates according to the *pleasure principle*. Immediate gratification is the primary aim of the id. This can occur via motor activity – getting a sandwich when you are hungry – or *wish fulfillment*: thinking about eating a lobster dinner rather than actually consuming it! If every time people were hungry they merely generated mental images of food and didn't actually eat, they would not survive very long. Consequently, thinking driven by the id is irrational and is referred to as *primary-process thinking*.

The ego refers collectively to the control, regulatory, rational, and inhibitory aspects of personality. It follows the *reality principle* and attempts to take into account the demands and consequences of reality as well as personal wants and needs. The aim of the ego, however, is not to curb the id; it attempts to maximize pleasure by considering long-term as well as short-term implications and consequences of actions. Thinking governed by the ego is referred to as *secondary-process thinking*; it is logical, rational, and reality-based, whereas primary-process thinking is emotional, self-serving, and subjective. Aspects of ego strength include: frustration tolerance, delay of gratification, logical thinking, reality testing, and defensive control of conscious access to ideas (see Berzonsky, 1981).

The superego consists collectively of the values, standards, restrictions, and principles that people use to guide and evaluate their behavior. It consists of two components, the *conscience* and the *ego ideal*. The former contains restrictions and prohibitions – what one *should not* do – whereas the latter specifies the goal one *ought* to aspire to and how one ideally should act.

In the mature personality the ego serves as the central integrative structure. It considers conflicting demands made by the id, superego, and physical and social reality and attempts to work out reasonable compromises. The ego of a well-adjusted person manages to maintain a relative balance among these influences.

Freud's development theory

In the development theory, Freud (1915, 1923) explained how and why these personality structures emerged. Five psychosexual stages were specified.

In the *oral stage* infants are "pure" id – a bundle of needs, urges, and impulses whose aim is instant gratification. In the *anal stage*, somewhere around the second year of life, children are expected to begin exercising self-control including toilet training. This intrapsychic conflict leads to the emergence of the ego; the personality structure that attempts to rationally regulate the impulsive nature of the id.

In the *phallic stage*, children are said to experience an *Oedipal complex*. (In females this is referred to as an *Electra complex*.) Freud maintained that a child experienced a strong incestuous love attachment to the opposite-sexed parent. For instance, a boy is in love with his mother, but she already has a lover – his father. Thus a classical love triangle emerges: two "men" vying for the same woman; hostility and anger are directed toward the same-sexed parental rival. Of course the boy's thinking is dominated by the primary process; it is subjective and self-serving rather than logical and reality based. As he develops ego strength, however, he comes to realize how precarious his situation is: castration anxiety (or penis envy for girls) leads to a repression of Oedipal feelings and brings about a strong identification with the father. This identification process is fear based and is known as *introjection*. It involves an attempt to become like the same-sexed parent and internalize his (or her) goals, values, attitudes, and so forth; it results in the emergence of the superego.

During the preadolescent stage of *latency*, all three personality components have emerged and a relative balance is being established. The onset of puberty marks the onset of the *genital stage* and the beginning of adolescence. The id is re-energized and sexual needs and fantasies become more personally salient and clash with explicit societal expectations and restrictions as well as those of the superego. The ego-id-superego equilibrium established during latency is destabilized producing a state of stress, turmoil, and emotional turbulence. According to Freud the previously repressed Oedipal feelings once again resurface and influence adolescent behavior. For instance, initial "crushes" of adolescent love should tend toward real or imagined images of the opposite-sexed parent. Generational conflict may be driven by a need to successfully compete with the previously feared same-sexed parent or a parental substitute. According to the Freudian view, adolescent behaviors and problems are not necessarily the result of contemporaneous factors and influences; adolescents may be acting out unresolved Oedipal feelings and intrapsychic conflicts that have been repressed since childhood.

Sigmund Freud placed a limited emphasis on adolescent development. Although intrapsychic upheaval accompanied puberty, personality development was considered to be determined by the way previous conflicts had been negotiated. His daughter, Anna, however, focused on developmental changes that continued to occur during adolescence. In particular, Anna Freud (1946, 1972) indicated that emotional turmoil during adolescence may be desirable. Emotional turmoil indicated that adolescents were in the process of restructuring their personalities on a more personal or individualized basis. The absence of storm and stress was not necessarily positive; it may imply that adolescents are defining themselves exclusively in terms of the parental introjects acquired during childhood. Although submissiveness and conformity may be convenient for parents, it may signal a reluctance to grow up and establish autonomy (A. Freud, 1972). Too much stress and turmoil, of course, will be maladaptive; the complete absence of stress however may not be adaptive. Anna Freud (1946) also emphasized two defensive maneuvers that are especially characteristic of adolescence: *intellectualization* and *asceticism*. Asceticism is complete self-denial and restraint, say, in reaction to unfamiliar sexual thoughts and feelings. This "solution" is not an adaptive compromise between the id, reality, and the superego; it is a rigid and inflexible defensive tactic. Intellectualization involves dealing with personal problems and conflicts on an abstract, philosophic plane. It enables adolescents to "distance" themselves from personal emotion-laden issues, thereby gaining a more realistic perspective. Also intellectualization provides practice in abstract thinking and hypothesis generation and testing which leads to advanced intellectual development (see Berzonsky, 1981).

Psychosocial Theory: Erik Erikson

Erik Erikson (1902–1995) was psychoanalyzed and trained by Anna Freud and certified as a lay analyst by the Vienna Psychoanalytic Institute. His views reflect his psychoanalytic training, but he placed much greater emphasis on social environmental influences. According to classical Freudian theory, development is completed by at least adolescence and ego development is defensive in nature; the ego emerges in order to control and regulate the id. In contrast, Erikson (1950) emphasizes the autonomous or conflict-free development of an adaptive ego. Erikson postulates that human beings have a need to integrate and synthesize past and present experiences, as well as a need to satisfy their basic biological needs. Optimal personality functioning requires establishing a consolidated sense of ego identity – a perceived sense of inner self-sameness and self-continuity. According to Erikson (1968, p. 92) personality develops through eight life-span stages governed by the epigenetic principle that "states that anything that grows has a ground plan, and that out of this ground plan the parts arise, each part having its time of special ascendancy, until all parts have arisen to form a functioning whole."

Each stage is characterized by a normative conflict that must be negotiated. These bipolar crises may stem from intrapsychic conflicts but the adaptive effectiveness of a resolution depends on the quality of the social relationship within which it occurs. Ideally resolutions should not be totally one-sided; having too much initiative or being arrogant, for instance, may be maladaptive.

The stages are assumed to build upon one another in a cumulative manner; personality becomes increasingly differentiated and hierarchically organized. Achieving ego identity during adolescence is the theoretical linchpin; it is the basis for integrating previous developments and it serves as the foundation upon which subsequent progress will be based. The names of each stage reflect the psychosocial crisis that ascends during that time of life.

Stage 1: Trust versus mistrust (infancy). Infants are dominated by biological needs and impulses. The extent to which they develop a sense of trust (or mistrust) in themselves, others, and the world in general depends on the quality and consistency of the relationship they have with primary care givers.

Stage 2: Autonomy versus doubt and shame (early childhood). How successfully children react to social demands for self-regulation and bodily control (toilet training) will influence feelings of self-efficacy versus self-doubt.

Stage 3: Initiative versus guilt (preschool age). Now children begin to actively explore and intrude upon their environment. Will engaging in self-initiated activities produce a sense of guilt? Or will they feel justified in planning and asserting control over their activities?

Stage 4: Industry versus inferiority (school age). In stage 4 children typically participate in some sort of formal instruction or training. Being able to master tasks and skills valued by teachers and the larger society is the focal crisis at this stage.

Stage 5: Identity and diffusion (adolescence). This is the pivotal concept in Erikson's theory, the stage when adolescents actively attempt to integrate their experiences in an attempt to construct a stable sense of personal identity. Although this process is psychosocial in nature, reality testing and the acquisition of credible self-knowledge are highlighted. At this stage, despite a lifetime of changes, adolescents need to be able to see themselves as products of their previous experiences – to achieve an adaptive sense of identity they need to experience a unified sense of spatial and temporal self-continuity. Positive resolutions of prior crises – being trusting, autonomous, willful, and industrious – facilitate the process of identity formation, whereas previous failures may lead to identity diffusion.

Erikson's theory deals with developmental changes that occur after adolescence. However, the three adult stages – briefly sketched below – are directly influenced by the identity achieved during adolescence.

Stage 6: Intimacy versus isolation (young adulthood). During stage 6, young adults must be willing and able to unite their identity with another's. Since open and honest disclosure and reciprocal mutuality make one vulnerable, a firm sense of identity is a necessary prerequisite for intimacy.

Stage 7: Generativity versus stagnation (middle adulthood). This is the stage in life when people strive to realize the identity they have constructed and shared with select others. During stage 7 people become concerned with generating and producing offspring, artefacts, ideas, products, and so forth that exemplify and reflect the identity they have achieved.

Stage 8: Integrity versus despair (maturity). The final stage focuses on how the end or fulfillment of one's life cycle is subjectively evaluated. As people become aware of their own mortality, do they feel despair and fear? Or do they view their inevitable death philosophically and perceive the completion and meaningfulness of their life within a larger perspective?

The identity status paradigm

Identity formation during adolescence is the keystone of Erikson's theory of psychosocial personality development. Most research on Eriksonian identity has been inspired by the identity status paradigm formulated by Jim Marcia (1966). Drawing on the Eriksonian criteria of self-exploration and commitment, Marcia identified four identity statuses or types:

1 *Identity achievers.* Adolescents who have experienced an extensive period of soul searching and who have committed themselves to a set of goals, values, and life choices.
2 *Identity moratoriums.* Adolescents who are currently engaged in active self-exploration but have not yet formed stable personal commitments.
3 *Identity foreclosurers.* Adolescents who have adopted goals, values, and other commitments from parents or significant others in a relatively automatic fashion without having engaged in extensive self-exploration.
4 *Identity diffusers.* Adolescents who lack firm commitments and who are not currently in the process of active self-exploration.

Research indicates that at least within a university setting – what Erikson terms an institutionalized moratorium – identity achievers are generally the most effective and successful, especially more so than their diffuse counterparts (see Berzonsky and Adams, 2000). Moratorium adolescents typically rank second to achievers in status comparisons, but they are highly anxious and variable in their behavior (Berzonsky,

1981). Foreclosed adolescents can be effective and goal-oriented, especially in highly structured contexts, but they tend to be the most rigid and inflexible of the status types (Marcia, 1966).

Cognitive Theory: Jean Piaget

Jean Piaget's (1896–1980) formal training was in biology. After receiving his Ph.D. in biology, he accepted a position as a research assistant in the laboratory of Alfred Binet who was studying standardized intelligence testing. During this work Piaget began to realize that mistakes and wrong answers did not always occur randomly; systematic errors could provide insight into how children and adolescents were thinking about problems. In contrast to the other theorists we have already considered, Piaget did not emphasize social or emotional influences on adolescent behavior: he viewed adolescents as intuitive scientists actively attempting to construct an understanding of their world.

Adaptation: structure and function

Drawing on his biological training, Piaget (1950) viewed cognition and intellectual activity as means by which adolescents adapt in everyday life. Cognitive *structures* refer to the internal organization of mental units people use to comprehend the world. For instance, when you look at this book you "see" a three-dimensional object, yet the array of information on your retina is two-dimensional. Some mental unit or cognitive structure (also referred to as a schema or scheme) enables you – with minimal mental effort – to transform the stimulus array into the "book" you perceive. According to Piaget, these structures are constantly being refined, revised, and improved as adolescents develop; cognitive structures are what develop according to Piagetian theory. The more differentiated and integrated adolescents' cognitive structures are the more effectively and efficiently they can solve problems and adapt to changing environmental demands.

Cognitive *functioning*, according to Piaget, involves an ongoing interchange between *assimilation* – fitting problems and information into existing cognitive structures – and *accommodation* – modifying and revising cognitive structures when they are ineffective or unsuccessful.

When an adolescent is unable to use an existing structure to solve a problem, an unpleasant state of disequilibrium occurs (Piaget, 1950). Disequilibrium or cognitive conflict is the process that produces cognitive development by inducing revisions in the existing structures.

Cognitive stages

According to Piaget, cognitive development proceeds through four qualitatively different stages; each stage reflects a different type of structural organization. The *sensori-motor* stage occurs in infancy. Reflexes and motor schemes (strategies) predominate during this stage. In the *preoperational stage* children are beginning to mentally represent actions – think about pouring milk from a carton into a glass without actually doing it – but those mental actions are rigid and inflexible. These mental representations will eventually constitute the "parts" from which cognitive structures will emerge. In the *concrete-operational stage* mental actions are fully internalized and transformable – a concrete operator can *mentally* break an egg, scramble, and fry it and then, mentally un-fry, un-scramble, un-break and boil the egg. Piagetian theory postulates that concrete operators have mental structures that enable them to think and solve problems in a logical and rational manner whereas children at the preoperational and sensori-motor stages do not. There are, however, limitations to concrete operations. The major limitation is that because concrete-operational structures reflect internalized actions they are still tied to reality: concrete operators have difficulty reasoning with purely hypothetical ideas, especially ones that lead to conclusions that are contrary to fact (Inhelder and Piaget, 1958).

Formal operational reasoning

Formal operational thinking emerges during adolescence. Concrete reasoners *describe what* has occurred, whereas formal operators go beyond description and attempt to *explain why* things happened – the adolescent operates as an intuitive scientist (Inhelder and Piaget, 1958). One aspect of formal reasoning has to do with the *relationship between reality and possibility*. For concrete reasoners they are one and the same; what happened is the only thing possible. Formal-operational adolescents, however, think in terms of the broader realm of hypothetical possibilities; what actually happened is just a subset of possible outcomes. They know that what happened may be a quirk of chance rather than a reliable indicator of what typically occurs or will occur in the future. In addition, formal adolescents engage in *hypothetical-deductive reasoning* in order to test and verify the possible explanations or hypotheses they generate. For instance, when attempting to figure out what influences the period of a pendulum (Inhelder and Piaget, 1958), an adolescent may consider a number of possibilities: the weight of the bob, the length of the string, the height of its release, and the degree of force used to push it. However, to effectively test one possibility, say the weight of the bob, without confounding the results, the adolescent has to systematically vary the weight while simultaneously holding the other variables constant. This requires logical structures that have not emerged at the concrete operational stage (Inhelder and Piaget, 1958). Other aspects of formal reasoning include being able to think about the combined or interactive effects of multiple variables and being able to think metacognitively – think about one's own thinking process (Berzonsky, 1981).

Extensions of formal operational thinking

Once adolescents are able to think formally it has implications for many areas of their lives. For instance, if you were to ask concrete reasoners why they read fictional literature, they might tell you because it was assigned, it's a pleasant distraction, or because it is enjoyable. Formal reasoners, however, realize that even though the work is fictional and didn't actually happen, it could have happened – perhaps it should have happened. By definition a classical fictional work is more prototypic – a better example – of aspects of the human condition than events and incidents that have actually occurred in the lives of particular people. Thus generation after generation of adolescents have read Shakespeare's fictional accounts and benefited from them because of how they portray aspects of the human predicament such as jealousy, tragedy, greed, and the like.

Concrete reasoners view moral dilemmas in terms of *what is*; what the law specifies or which behaviors are punished or rewarded. In contrast, formal reasoners focus on how one *ought* to behave or should act whether or not people actually behave in that fashion (Kohlberg, 1976). According to Kohlberg's (1976) view formal reasoners are able to use postconventional moral reasoning; they define morality in terms of a personal obligation to abide by contractual commitments. To do that adolescents must understand the relativistic nature of rules and laws, but realize the need for contractual agreements to protect individual rights. Although formal operations are necessary for adolescents to use postconventional moral reasoning, not all formal operational adolescents will use postconventional moral reasoning.

According to Elkind (1967) a negative byproduct associated with the emergence of formal reasoning is a conceptual egocentrism. In Piagetian theory, egocentrism means being tied to one's own view point. For instance, preoperational egocentrism is tied to a personal *perceptual* perspective. If I held up my right hand, a preoperational child facing me would say that it is my left hand because from her perceptual vantage point it is on her left side. (Transformable concrete-operational structures make it possible to mentally rotate the perceptual image 180 degrees and realize that it is my right hand.) Adolescents, according to Elkind (1967), are tied to their own *conceptual perspective*. Formal operations enable them to think about their own thinking (metacognition) and consequently they are aware other people think as well. Since adolescents undergoing pubertal, social, physical, and other changes are constantly self-preoccupied, they assume that the thoughts of others are preoccupied with them as well; they are tied to their own *conceptual* perspective. This gives rise to an *imaginary audience*; a self-constructed audience that scrutinizes their every move, purchase, and imperfection (Elkind, 1967). Since, from their perspective, they alone receive this constant attention, they generate a *personal fable* about their importance, uniqueness, and invulnerability (Elkind, 1967). With increasing social interactions and comparisons the imaginary audience should be replaced by a more realistic one.

Summary

The five types of theories reviewed in this chapter provide an overview of the dominant influences in adolescent psychology during the twentieth century. The theories differ in terms of which aspects of the adolescent are emphasized, including cultural experiences, sexuality, psychosocial influences, cognition and reasoning, identity, and so on. They also differ in terms of the factors or combinations of factors postulated as causal influences, such as biological evolution, cultural learning, disequilibrium, intrapsychic conflict, psychosocial conflict, and so forth. Clearly no single theory has been able to completely capture the developing adolescent across different cultural and historical contexts.

References

Aristotle (1941). Ethica Nicomachea. In R. McKeon (Ed.), *The basic works of Aristotle*. New York: Random House.

Benedict, R. (1938). Continuities and discontinuities in cultural conditioning. *Psychiatry, 1,* 161–167.

Berzonsky, M. D. (1981). *Adolescent development*. New York: Macmillan.

Berzonsky, M. D., & Adams, G. R. (2000). The identity-status paradigm: Still useful after thirty-five years. *Developmental Review*.

Côté, J. E. (1994). *Adolescent storm and stress: An evaluation of the Mead–Freeman controversy*. Hillsdale, NJ: Lawrence Erlbaum.

Elkind, D. (1967). Egocentrism in adolescence. *Child Development, 38,* 1025–1038.

Erikson, E. H. (1950). *Childhood and society*. New York: Norton.

Erikson, E. H. (1968). *Identity: Youth and crisis*. New York: Norton.

Freeman, D. (1983). *Margaret Mead and Samoa: The making and unmaking of an anthropological myth*. Cambridge, MA: Harvard University Press.

Freud, A. (1946). *The ego and mechanisms of defense*. New York: International Universities Press.

Freud, A. (1972). Adolescence. In J. F. Rosenblith, W. Allinsmith, & J. P. Williams (Eds.). *The causes of behavior* (3rd ed.), pp. 317–323. Boston: Allyn & Bacon.

Freud, S. (1915). *Instincts and their vicissitudes*. In *Collected papers*, Vol. XIV. London: Hogarth Press.

Freud, S. (1923). *The ego and the id*. London: Hogarth Press.

Freud, S. (1953). *The interpretation of dreams*. London: Hogarth. (First German edition, 1900.)

Hall, C. S. (1954). *A primer of Freudian psychology*. New York: New American Library.

Hall, G. S. (1904). *Adolescence*. 2 vols. New York: Appleton.

Inhelder, B., & Piaget, J. (1958). *The growth of logical thinking*. New York: Basic Books.

Kohlberg, L. (1976). Moral stages and moralization: The cognitive-developmental approach. In T. Lickona (Ed.). *Moral development and behavior: Theory, research, and social issues* (pp. 31–53). New York: Holt, Rinehart & Winston.

Malinowski, B. (1927). *Sex and repression in savage society*. New York: Harcourt Brace.

Marcia, J. E. (1966). Development and validation of ego identity status. *Journal of Personality and Social Psychology, 3,* 551–558.

Mead, M. (1928). *Coming of age in Samoa*. New York: Dell.

Mead, M. (1935). *Sex and temperament in three primitive societies*. New York: New American Library.

Mead, M. (1970). *Culture and commitment*. New York: Doubleday.

Muuss, R. E. (1988). *Theories of adolescence* (3rd ed.). New York: Random House.

Piaget, J. (1950). *Psychology of intelligence*. London: Kegan Paul.

Plato. (1921). *The republic*. Oxford: Clarendon Press.

Part II

Development of Self

Individual differences and developmental patterns of the self are hall-marks of adolescent development. Research reports on aspects of individual development are included in this section.

Retrospective Survey of Parental Marital Relations and Child Reproductive Development

Introduction

It is all too easy to think of adolescence as a stage of life that is set off from that of infancy and childhood. Often popular writers of the day will talk of adolescence as being disconnected from childhood – a whole different kind of "beast." A few years back I worked with a colleague and a team of editors to explore the transition from childhood to adolescence (Montemayor et al., 1990). We were interested in knowing how much continuity versus discontinuity there is between these two stages of life. The question we put to several contributors of the book was: is adolescence a distinctively different period of life from that of childhood? Or as the title of the book reveals, is adolescence a transitional period? In the end several conclusions were drawn.

In the final chapter Montemayor and Flannery (1990) concluded that biological contributions do influence the physiology, actions, and feelings of teenagers. However, the size of some effects is not as dramatic and universal as some people suggest. Likewise, the role of context can be widely observed as a major factor in the nature and outcome of the transition from childhood to adolescence. Contexts interact to influence behavior, different family or educational structures predict different developmental trajectories, and one context can diminish a positive effect of another. Further, these authors conclude that adolescents are not just reactive to environments. They also influence environments. New abilities, emerging talents, new physical and social strengths influence the environment as the environment is influencing the adolescent. In their conclusion Montemayor and Flannery (1990) write:

> based on the evidence presented in this volume, both continuity and change characterize the transition from childhood to adolescence . . . Adolescents are different from children in almost every characteristic that has been examined, but the origins for most of those differences are found in childhood . . . Differences between adolescents and children emerge gradually rather than suddenly, although puberty and the transition out of elementary school affect adolescent behavior (p. 300).

This conclusion suggests there are many person and context influences and that we can expect person × context interactions.

For the first research report I have selected a study that explores the association between early childhood family environments, the onset of puberty, and reproductive development. This is a retrospective study where individuals report on the experiences in their life at earlier times. This technique has its limitations, but it is suggestive of what we might find if we were able to follow children from infancy to adulthood. The results are presented based on several kinds of statistical analyses. Do not get anxious because you might not fully understand how they were computed. Focus instead on the findings in figure 2.1 and 2.2 and the associations between various actions or events that occur at various times in the life cycle. I should say, however, the larger the beta, be it positive or negative, the stronger the association between two things.

What interests me with this retrospective study is the attempt to identify what happens for both girls and boys. More often, the focus of study on adolescent sexuality and biological processes deals just with girls. The authors of the report tell you why. Likewise, it is very rare for us to find a study of this nature from childhood to young adulthood. Finally, this study provides an interesting set of figures that makes us think more about how childhood experiences might influence even biological aspects of the self, let alone social behaviors.

See if you can find how this study uses person, context, and occasion in its research design. Think how a study like this could be improved. Are there any policy implications about families and children that would come to mind after reading this report?

Here we go again on our journey. In this phase of the journey we shall look at how parents can affect the production of sperm or the onset of menarche and what that might mean in regards to dating and the frequency of sexual experience. It is scary to think that how mothers and fathers treat us might be carried on to our reproductive development. Read the article and see if you agree that our parents are even contributors to the frequency of our sex life. This is the Twilight Zone of Adolescence and once again we enter this amazingly interesting world.

References

Montemayor, R., Adams, G. R., and Gullotta, T. P. (Eds.) (1990). *From childhood to adolescence: a transitional period?* Advances in Adolescent Development Vol. 2. Newbury Park, CA: Sage Publications, Inc.

Montemayor, R., and Flannery, D. J. (1990). Making the transition from childhood to early adolescence. In R. Montemayor et al. (Eds.). *From childhood to adolescence: a transitional period?* Advances in Adolescent Development Vol. 2 (pp. 291–301). Newbury Park, CA: Sage Publications, Inc.

Suggested reading

Katchadourian, H. (1990). Sexuality. In S. S. Feldman, and G. R. Elliott (Eds.). *At the threshold: the developing adolescent* (pp. 330–351). Cambridge, MA: Harvard University Press.

Downs, A. C., and Hillje, L. S. (1993). Historical and theoretical perspectives on adolescent sexuality: an overview. In T. P. Gullotta, G. R. Adams, and R. Montemayor (Eds.). *Adolescent sexuality.* Advances in Adolescent Development Vol. 5 (pp. 1–33). Newbury Park, CA: Sage Publications, Inc.

TWO

Retrospective Survey of Parental Marital Relations and Child Reproductive Development

Kenneth Kim and Peter K. Smith

Draper and Harpending (1982) hypothesised that father absence in early childhood could have culture-specific consequences on behavioural development. Barkow (1984) predicted that father-absent girls would develop early menarche. Based on their findings, Hulanicka (1986, 1989), Steinberg (1988, 1989), and Surbey (1988, 1990) independently suggested that social stress (and stress related to father absence) in the childhood family environment could hasten the onset of puberty. These studies and other previous research have reported associations between childhood familial stressors and adolescent reproductive behaviour and also between the timing of puberty and this behaviour. Draper and Belsky (1990), Belsky et al. (1991), and Steinberg and Belsky (1996) went further to hypothesise that the timing of puberty (via the central nervous system [CNS] and hormonal mechanisms) would be linked with both these antecedent stressors and post-pubertal reproductive behaviour in a developmental trajectory.

Belsky et al. (1991) hypothesised that the first 5 to 7 years in the family enable a child to assess the availability of resources, durability of pair bonds, and reliability of others as a basis to develop his/her reproductive strategy. Children from families with adequate resources, durable parental bonds, and adequate parenting would delay the onset of puberty and sexual activity and would incline toward stable pair bonds. Children from families with scarce or unpredictable resources, unstable parental bonds, and familial mistrust would reduce the age of pubertal onset, accelerate sexual activity, and would incline toward a succession of unstable pair bonds. In girls, internalising symptoms would reduce the rate of metabolism, accumulate fat via weight gain, and stimulate earlier menarche, whereas in boys externalising symptoms would stimulate earlier pubertal onset via androgenic hormonal (i.e. testosterone) mechanisms. In effect, the characteristics of the family environment would prepare children for the similar environment that they would likely encounter as adults.

Environmental conditions indicative of stress (e.g. reduced socioeconomic conditions, inadequate nutrition, increased sibling size) have more often been associated with delayed rather than accelerated puberty in past research (see Adams, 1981, for a review). In the cross-cultural and clinical literature, life event stressors and chronic difficulties have been associated with distress and depression which become psychosomatised in a culture-specific pattern to physiological dysfunction (Lumsden, 1991). In childhood, such stressors could induce a culture-specific form of depression, loss of appetite, less weight gain, and, hence, delayed puberty. Childhood socioenvironmental stress could also be linked to delayed puberty via the CNS–hypothalamic-pituitary-adrenal axis (HPA) system and the hormone, cortisol (Flinn and England, 1995). In contrast, in the Belsky et al. (1991) reformulation of theory, stress is linked to environmental conditions to the extent to which reproductive strategy operates within these conditions. For example, the stress of father absence or family disruption could accelerate early puberty, within environmental constraints such as reduced socioeconomic conditions associated with delayed puberty directly (or indirectly via increased sibling size) from inadequate housing and nutrition. Belsky et al. (1991) consider early puberty to be an evolutionarily adapted response which is elicited in environments with unpredictable or scarce resources. The proximate causes are the effects of perceived psychosocial stress on the CNS and endocrine system which induce early puberty. Although moderate levels of stress elicit early puberty as an adaptive response in this manner, severe levels of stress delay puberty by directly inhibiting the CNS-endocrine system, to minimise the risks of reproduction.

Available research has provided inconsistent support for the Belsky et al. (1991) theory. Childhood life events, such as family or life event-related stress, divorce/father absence, parent-child conflict, parent-child emotional distance, and behavioural autonomy, have been associated with early puberty in women and men to a limited extent (see Kim, 1997; Kim et al., 1997, for reviews). Limited support for the psychosocial stress predictors of puberty in women, concurrent and subsequent to the theoretical development of the Belsky et al. (1991) theory, has been provided by Steinberg (1988, 1989), Surbey (1988, 1990), Ellis (1991), Moffitt et al. (1992), Wierson et al. (1993), Campbell and Udry (1995), and Graber et al. (1995). All these have been longitudinal studies except Surbey (1988, 1990). Of these studies, only Steinberg (1988, 1989) and Ellis (1991) included data for men, and only Ellis (1991) reported significant, albeit limited, results.

Few reports have considered the onset of puberty in relation to both pre-pubertal stressors and post-pubertal reproductive behaviour. An exception is Leek (1991), who carried out a cross-sectional self-report survey of English women ($n = 139$). Leek found that a group of women who reported earlier menarche, earlier intercourse, increased intercourse frequency, and more partners reported more negative experiences in childhood family life (these included a more tense family environment and more distant relations with mothers or siblings) than a comparison group of women. A direct attempt to test aspects of the Belsky et al. (1991) theory of childhood family environment and adult reproductive strategy was reported by Kim et al. (1997) with a retrospective survey sample of participants ($n = 380$; 197 women and 183 men) aged 16 to 19 from southern Italy. Subsequently, Kim and Smith (1998) reported, with more detailed retrospective survey data, results with a younger adolescent pubertal sample of daughters ($n = 28$) aged 12 to 15 and their mothers ($n = 21$) from northern England. In both samples, although there were many nonsignificant results, all significant findings supported the Belsky et al. (1991) theory in that earlier puberty was associated with more childhood psychosocial stress and earlier/more extensive reproductive behaviour.

But there are alternative interpretations for these findings to that of Belsky et al. (1991). These include the possibility that early puberty could be influenced as a physiological side-effect of childhood psychosocial stress (Hulanicka, 1986, 1989). It could also be influenced by developmental maturation rates in the fetal stage (Coe et al., 1988), infancy (Liestol, 1982; Mills et al., 1986), or childhood (Ellison, 1982).

Finally, early puberty and reproductive life history could be due in part to intergenerational transmission of genetic characteristics (Kim and Smith, 1998; Leek, 1991; Rushton, 1984, 1985). Evidence for such an inheritance of characteristics comes from concordance between monozygotic versus dizygotic twins. Such studies have been reported for parent-child conflict in adolescence (Reiss, 1995); life events from childhood to adolescence (Thapar and McGuffin, 1996); internalising or externalising symptoms in childhood (Edelbrock et al., 1995; Gjone et al., 1996; Hewitt et al., 1992; Silberg et al., 1994); menarcheal timing in sisters (Meyer et al., 1991; Treloar and Martin, 1990); pubertal growth and weight gain rates (Fischbein, 1977); testosterone level in brothers (Meikle et al., 1987); age at first sexual intercourse (Martin et al., 1977); parental care and overprotection of offspring (Pérusse et al., 1994); and divorce rates (McGue and Lykken, 1992), linked to personality traits (Jockin et al., 1996). In addition, studies have related menarcheal timing between mothers and daughters (Campbell and Udry, 1995; Chern et al., 1980; Damon et al., 1969; Graber et al., 1995; Kaur and Singh, 1981; Kim and Smith, 1998; Surbey, 1988, 1990). In sum, these data indicate that an inherited component must form a part of the explanation of age at puberty and reproductive life history.

The present report attempted to examine further the Belsky et al. (1991) theory with a third sample from a central Canadian urban population. It addressed a limitation of the previous samples (Kim et al., 1997; Kim and Smith 1998), which had relatively moderate rates of sexual activity. The present results enable further consideration of the Belsky et al. theory with another cross-national sample, within the limitations of retrospective self-report data (see Discussion section). The hypotheses tested include whether earlier puberty would be associated with: (1) childhood father absence; (2) more parental marital and parent-child stress/conflict and more childhood behavioural symptoms; and (3) earlier/extensive reproductive behaviour. Although such results would support the Belsky et al. (1991) theory, they would not preclude alternative interpretations based on lifestyle factors (e.g. effect of childhood overweight on early puberty), or inherited parental characteristics. In particular, the latter view often predicts the same findings on different attributed causal mechanisms (i.e. stress-dependent vs. inherited life history developmental trajectory).

For the dependent measures of puberty, age at menarche and sper-marche were self-reported for women and men, respectively. Although menarche is observed as the first menses, or menstruation period, spermarche (emission of spermatozoa) was estimated by age at first emission of seminal fluid via first ejaculation (e.g. from masturbation or nocturnal seminal emission). Menarche, as a mid-pubertal event (relative to age 15 or 16 at adult stature), occurs after the peak growth spurt; however, spermarche, as a relatively early-pubertal event (relative to age 17 or 18 at adult stature), occurs before the peak growth spurt when the secondary sexual characteristics are at an early stage of development (Nielsen et al., 1986). None the less, spermarche remains the least ambiguous marker of male puberty and functionally the most proper analogue to menarche in women; both represent indicators of reproductive potential, specifically ovulation in women and spermatogenesis in men (although the initial onset of the endocrine changes of puberty begins several years previous to either menarche or spermarche).

Method

Sample

The sample ($n = 357$) consisted of 268 post-menarcheal women (median age = 20 years 2 months; mean age = 20 years 6 months) and 89 post-spermarcheal men (median age = 20 years 1 month; mean age = 20 years 6 months) aged 18 to 24 from an undergraduate university student population in Toronto, Canada. The sample was heterogeneous in ethnic/racial terms; Caucasian ($n = 257$), oriental ($n = 33$), Indian-subcontinental ($n = 26$), African-continental ($n = 25$), and mixed race category ($n = 4$), with 12 ambiguous or missing responses. It was predominantly from lower-middle to middle class backgrounds. Questionnaire data were collected in January 1995 of all students in selected undergraduate lecture theatre sessions and classroom tutorials at York University. Prior to data entry, a small proportion of questionnaires was discarded (less than 10 per cent) due to incomplete data for childhood family structure history, puberty (menarche/spermarche), or other questionnaire items. Further details of sample characteristics and data collection have been reported elsewhere (Kim, 1997).

Measures

A retrospective self-report questionnaire was used to obtain data on family composition of all household members from birth to age 16 (as previously used in Kim et al., 1997). Data also were obtained for childhood family life indicators, which used single 7-point scales with 4 as the average (mid-point) value. These measures for the intervals *birth to age 7* and *age 8 to 11* were quality of family life (1 = very stressful, 7 = very unstressful); parental marital relations (1 = very unhappy, 7 = very happy); parental marital conflict and parent-self conflict (1 = high conflict, 7 = low conflict); parental care of self (1 = rejecting, 7 = accepting); and parent-self emotional distance (1 = very distant, 7 = very close). Additional measures for the interval *age 8 to 11* were behavioural autonomy (1 = not independent, 7 = independent); aggressiveness (1 = aggressive, 7 = not aggressive); unruliness (1 = not obedient, 7 = obedient); anxiousness (1 = anxious–worrying, 7 = not anxious–not worrying); and depression (1 = sad–depressed, 7 = happy–not depressed). Finally, data were obtained for developmental timing in years and months for menarche (age at first menstruation), spermarche (estimated by age at first seminal emission), age at first dating of the opposite sex, frequency of boyfriends/girlfriends, incidence of having had sexual intercourse, age at first intercourse, age of first intercourse partner, and frequency of intercourse partners. Further details of measures have been reported elsewhere (Kim, 1997).

Results

Age at menarche and spermarche

For women, the reported age at menarche ranged from 8 years 6 months to 16 years 10 months (median = 12 years 6 months; mean = 12 years 11 months, SD = 14.7 months). The mean value is close to the mean of 13 years 0 months for southern Ontario (inclusive of Toronto) reported by Surbey (1988, 1990). For men, the reported age at spermarche ranged from 9 years 6 months to 18 years 6 months (median = 13 years 6 months; mean = 13 years 8 months, SD = 19.3 months). No comparable reports for spermarche were found for Canada. The reported

incidence of sexual intercourse was 158/252 or 63 per cent of women
(which excluded 16 missing responses) and 66/87 or 74 per cent of men
(which excluded 2 missing responses). Heterosexual reports charac-
terised all respondents; the absence of reported nonheterosexual activity could be related to the missing responses. Prior to analyses, all age
data were converted into months.

Antecedents of puberty and post-pubertal
reproductive behaviour

The effect of childhood father absence (of at least one year) on pubertal
onset was tested with independent group *t*-tests. This test qualified
the: (1) presence of the mother in both the father absent versus present groups; (2) absence of the father and the stepfather before
menarche/spermarche in the father absent group; and (3) absence of all
other genetically unrelated household members, such as adopted
siblings, family friends, and boarders/lodgers before menarche/sper-
marche in both groups. In women, the test result was nonsignificant for
the 18 (vs. 208) cases with father absence (vs. presence). However, in
men father absence before spermarche was associated with earlier spermarche ($n = 6$, mean = 12 years 6 months, SD = 10.7) than those with
father presence ($n = 72$, mean = 13 years 6 months, SD = 16.4) [$t(7.12)$
$= -2.54, P < 0.05$].

The effects of family life stressors were then tested on age at puberty
and, similarly, age at puberty on post-pubertal reproductive behaviour.
Analyses consisted of linear regression correlations between dichotomous, interval, and ratio predictor variables with interval and ratio predicted variables. These were supplemented by simple monotonic
curvilinear regressions from transformed predictors for possible better
fit to data, with a few exceptions which consisted of a monotonic
S-curve and a nonmonotonic cubic curve.

For all tests with developmental timing overlap between predictor and
predicted measures, individual cases in which the predictor measure
exceeded the predicted measure were excluded from analyses to prevent
the confound in the directionality of interpretation between the independent and dependent measures. For example, when pre-pubertal
measures for the interval *birth to age 11* or *age 8 to 11* predicted for
puberty, cases of puberty before *age 11 years 0 months* were excluded

from analyses. Similarly, when puberty predicted for age at dating, cases of dating before puberty were excluded from analyses. These results are summarised in table 2.1 for women and table 2.2 for men.

For women (table 2.1), earlier menarche was associated with more unhappiness in parental marital relations in early childhood (birth to age 7) and throughout childhood (birth to age 11) (mean of birth to age 7 and age 8 to 11); more parental marital conflict in early childhood (birth to age 7); more behavioural independence from mother or father in late childhood (age 8 to 11); and less anxiousness or internalising symptoms (mean of anxiousness and depression) in late childhood (age 8 to 11). Nonsignificant measures included those for quality of family life, conflict with mother or father, mother or father care of self, and distance from mother or father. Externalising symptoms measures were also nonsignificant. Of the post-pubertal measures, earlier menarche was associated with earlier age at dating men and having had more boyfriends. Age at menarche was not associated with likelihood of having had sexual intercourse, age at first intercourse, age of first intercourse partner, and frequency of intercourse partners.

For men (table 2.2), earlier spermarche was associated with more stress in quality of family life in early childhood (birth to age 7); more unhappiness in parental marital relations in early childhood (birth to age 7); more parental marital conflict in early childhood (birth to age 7); and more behavioural independence from mother or father in late childhood (age 8 to 11). Nonsignificant measures included those for conflict with mother or father, mother or father care of self, distance from mother or father, and externalising symptoms measures. Internalising symptoms measures were also nonsignificant. Of the post-pubertal measures, earlier spermarche was associated with earlier age at dating women, having had more girlfriends, and also earlier age at first sexual intercourse. Age at spermarche was not associated with likelihood of having had intercourse, age of first intercourse partner, and frequency of intercourse partners.

Multivariate regression models of the developmental trajectory

The results for the childhood, pubertal, and post-pubertal measures were then considered together to examine evidence for links in the

Table 2.1 Summary of results for women

Independent	Dependent	Result
Parental marital relations birth–7	Menarche	$n = 259$; $F(1,257) = 3.90$, beta = 0.12, adjusted $r^2 = 0.01$, $r^2 = 0.01$, $P < 0.05$
Parental marital relations birth–11	Menarche[1]	$n = 233$; $F(1,231) = 4.01$, beta = −0.13, adjusted $r^2 = 0.01$, $r^2 = 0.02$, $P < 0.05$
Parental marital conflict birth–7	Menarche[2]	$n = 258$; $F(1,256) = 3.85$, beta = −0.12, adjusted $r^2 = 0.01$, $r^2 = 0.01$, $P = 0.05$
Independence from mother age 8–11	Menarche[3]	$n = 253$; $F(1,251) = 4.61$, beta = −0.13, adjusted $r^2 = 0.01$, $r^2 = 0.02$, $P < 0.05$
Independence from father age 8–11	Menarche	$n = 238$; $F(1,236) = 4.27$, beta = −0.13, adjusted $r^2 = 0.01$, $r^2 = 0.02$, $P < 0.05$
Anxiousness age 8–11	Menarche[4]	$n = 252$; $F(1,250) = 4.43$, beta = 0.13, adjusted $r^2 = 0.01$, $r^2 = 0.02$, $P < 0.05$
Anxiousness/depression age 8–11	Menarche[5]	$n = 252$; $F(1,250) = 4.12$, beta = 0.13, adjusted $r^2 = 0.01$, $r^2 = 0.02$, $P < 0.05$
Menarche	Age at dating men	$n = 211$; $F(1,209) = 14.95$, beta = 0.26, adjusted $r^2 = 0.06$, $r^2 = 0.07$, $P = 0.0001$
Menarche	Frequency of boyfriends[6]	$n = 211$; $F(1,209) = 3.89$, beta = 0.14, adjusted $r^2 = 0.01$, $r^2 = 0.02$, $P = 0.05$

Note: Predictor (curvillinear) estimates: *predictor variable* = ×
[1] $×^6$ *monotonic concave upward: reverse-coded 7-point scale*
[2] *Monotonic concave upward to 1 to 3 (< mid-point) and concave downward to 5 to 7 (> mid-point); reverse-coded 7-point scale*
[3] *Linear 1 to 4 (midpoint) and $×^2$ monotonic concave upward 5 to 7 in 7-point scale*
[4] $×^3$ *monotonic concave downward; reverse-coded 7-point scale*
[5] $×^2$ *monotonic concave downward; reverse-coded 7-point scale*
[6] $×^4$ *monotonic concave downward (inverse of menarche *23,500 = same mean of menarche); dependent coded as 0, 1, 2, 3, >3*

Table 2.2 Summary of results for men

Independent	Dependent	Result
Quality of family life *birth–7*	Spermarche[1]	$n = 87$; $F(3,83) = 4.09$, adjusted $r^2 = 0.10$, $r^2 = 0.13$, $P < 0.01$
Parental marital relations *birth–7*	Spermarche	$n = 85$; $F(1,83) = 3.94$, beta = 0.21, adjusted $r^2 = 0.03$, $r^2 = 0.05$, $P = 0.05$
Parental marital conflict *birth–7*	Spermarche[2]	$n = 85$; $F(1,83) = 6.53$, beta = −0.27, adjusted $r^2 = 0.06$, $r^2 = 0.07$, $P = 0.01$
Independence from mother *age 8–11*	Spermarche[3]	$n = 86$; $F(1,84) = 4.05$, beta = 0.21, adjusted $r^2 = 0.03$, $r^2 = 0.05$, $P < 0.05$
Independence from father *age 8–11*	Spermarche[4]	$n = 79$; $F(1,77) = 4.00$, beta = −0.22, adjusted $r^2 = 0.04$, $r^2 = 0.05$, $P < 0.05$
Spermarche	Age at dating women	$n = 58$; $F(1,56) = 25.10$, beta = 0.56, adjusted $r^2 = 0.30$, $r^2 = 0.31$, $P = 0.0000$
Spermarche	Frequency of girlfriends[5]	$n = 61$; $F(1,60) = 5.51$, beta = −0.29, adjusted $r^2 = 0.07$, $r^2 = 0.08$, $P < 0.05$
Spermarche	Age at first intercourse	$n = 60$; $F(1,58) = 5.30$, beta = 0.29, adjusted $r^2 = 0.07$, $r^2 = 0.08$, $P < 0.05$

Note: Predictor (curvilinear) estimates; *predictor variable* = ×

[1] *Non-monotonic cubic curve (earliest spermarche at 1 = maximum stress in 7-point scale)*
[2] *Monotonic concave downward S-curve (earliest spermarche at 1 = maximum conflict in 7-point scale)*
[3] ×[4] *monotonic concave downward; reverse-coded 7-point scale*
[4] ×[2] *monotonic concave upward*
[5] ×[2] *monotonic concave upward*

developmental trajectories consistent with Belsky et al. (1991). Simple path models were derived from backward variable deletion ordinary least squares (OLS) multiple regressions. These models included the final target dependent variable, frequency of intercourse partners (range: 0 to 30 partners for women, mean = 2.10, SD = 3.68; 0 to 21 partners for men, mean = 3.38, SD = 4.62); this necessitated the exclusion of the measures age at first intercourse and age of first intercourse partner, in order not to exclude those who have not had intercourse from the analyses. In these analyses the predictor variables at each successive stage were controlled for, because all such controls, once added, were maintained throughout to enable these path models to be interpreted as developmental stage models.

For women (figure 2.1) the predictors of parental marital relations in early childhood (birth to age 7) ($n = 234$, $F = 4.72$, beta = -0.14, $p < 0.05$) and independence from father in late childhood (age 8 to 11) ($n = 234$, $F = 3.79$, beta = -0.13, $p = 0.05$) were entered in the multiple regression in the first stage to predict for menarche. When these predictors together with menarche were entered in the next stage, parental marital relations in early childhood (birth to age 7) ($n = 181$, $F = 3.86$, beta = -0.14, $p = 0.05$) and menarche ($n = 181$, $F = 14.41$, beta = 0.27, $p < 0.0005$) predicted for age at dating men. When these four predictors were entered in the next stage, only age at dating men [$n = 168$, $F(1,166) = 26.86$, beta = -0.37, adjusted $r^2 = 0.13$, $r^2 = 0.14$, $p = 0.0000$] predicted for frequency of boyfriends. In the final stage when all five of these predictors were entered in the model, only frequency of boyfriends [$n = 153$, $F(1,151) = 24.06$, beta = 0.37, adjusted $r^2 = 0.13$, $r^2 = 0.14$, $p = 0.0000$] predicted for frequency of sexual intercourse partners. In sum, for women, three paths were found in the results: (1) increased parental marital unhappiness (birth to age 7), earlier menarche, earlier age at dating men, more boyfriends, more intercourse partners; (2) increased parental marital unhappiness (birth to age 7), earlier age at dating men, more boyfriends, more intercourse partners; and (3) increased independence from father (age 8 to 11), earlier menarche, earlier age at dating men, more boyfriends, more intercourse partners.

For men (figure 2.2) the predictors entered in the multiple regression in the first stage to predict for spermarche were parental marital relations in early childhood (birth to age 7) ($n = 73$, $F = 4.31$, beta = -0.22, $p < 0.05$), independence from mother in late childhood (age 8 to 11)

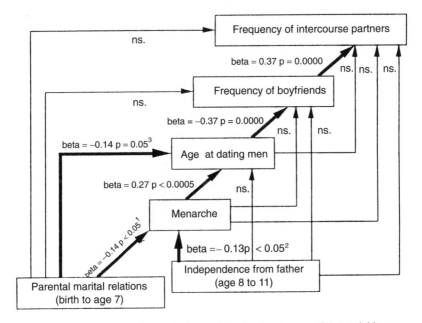

Predictor (dichotomous and monotonic curvilinear) estimates: predictor variable = x
[1] x [4]concave upward; reverse-coded 7-point scale
[2] x[3]concave upward
[3] indicator variable-coded: 1 = values 1 to 3 (below midpoint) vs.
0 = values to 7 in 7-point scale

Procedure: backward variable deletion

Figure 2.1 Women: OLS multiple regression beta weight coefficients

($n = 73$, $F = 6.48$, beta $= -0.26$, $p = 0.01$), and the dichotomous indicator variable-coded predictor father absence (birth to before spermarche) coded as present for father absence before spermarche with its reference category of father presence throughout spermarche ($n = 73$, $F = 4.45$, beta $= -0.22$, $p < 0.05$). When these predictors together with spermarche were entered in the next stage, independence from mother in late childhood (age 8 to 11) ($n = 48$, $F = 4.18$, beta $= -0.27$, $p < 0.05$) and spermarche ($n = 48$, $F = 5.21$, beta $= 0.31$, $p < 0.05$) predicted for age at dating women. When these five predictors were entered in the next stage, only age at dating women [$n = 45$, $F(1,47) = 23.32$, beta $= -0.58$, adjusted $r^2 = 0.32$, $r^2 = 0.33$, $p = 0.0000$] predicted for frequency of girlfriends. In the final stage when all six of these predictors were

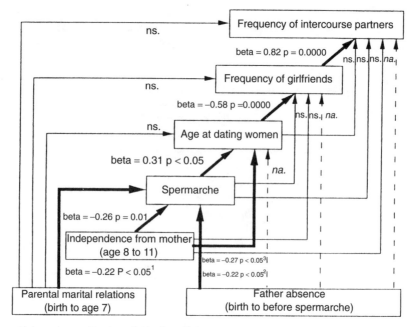

Note: na. = result not available (insufficient data)

Predictor (dichotomous and monotonic curvilinear) estimates: predictor variable = ×
[1] × [3]concave upward: reverse-coded 7-point scale
[2] indicator variable-coded 1 = father absence before spermarche vs.
  0 = father presence
[3] × [3]concave upward

Procedure: backward variable deletion

Figure 2.2 Men: OLS multiple regression beta weight coefficients

entered in the model, only frequency of girlfriends [$n = 40$, $F(1,41) = 85.56$, beta = 0.82, adjusted $r^2 = 0.67$, $r^2 = 0.68$, $p = 0.0000$] predicted for frequency of sexual intercourse partners. In these results it should be qualified that there were too few (less than four) cases of father absence after prediction for spermarche to be considered as valid predictors of the post-pubertal targets. In sum, for men four paths were found in the results: (1) increased parental marital unhappiness (birth to age 7), earlier spermarche, earlier age at dating women, more girlfriends, more intercourse partners; (2) father absence (birth to before spermarche), earlier spermarche, earlier age at dating women, more girlfriends, more intercourse partners; (3) increased independence from mother (age 8 to 11), earlier spermarche, earlier age at dating women, more girlfriends, more intercourse partners; and (4) increased independence from mother (age 8 to 11), earlier age at dating women, more girlfriends, more intercourse partners.

Discussion

This report tested aspects of the Belsky et al. (1991) theory that childhood psychosocial stressors would be associated with early age at puberty and early/extensive reproductive behaviour. These results have provided some support for the hypotheses advanced by Belsky et al. (1991), with a central Canadian sample, similarly to the previous results with southern Italian (Kim et al., 1997) and younger, pubertal northern English (Kim and Smith, 1998) samples.

A notable nonsignificant finding in women was the lack of earlier menarche being associated with childhood father absence before menarche, though it should be added that there were only 18 such cases. However, some of the other findings for women supported the similar findings of previous research: more parental marital conflict and early menarche (Wierson et al., 1993); more parental permissiveness and early puberty (Steinberg, 1988, 1989); more self-governance from parents and early puberty (Ellis, 1991); and more behavioural autonomy and early puberty (Kracke and Silbereisen, 1996).

Some of the current findings also confirmed the results from the previous Italian (Kim et al., 1997) and pubertal English (Kim and Smith, 1998) samples. Common findings supporting the Belsky et al. (1991) hypotheses included more parental marital unhappiness and more independence from both mother and father measures and early menarche with the Italian sample. In contrast, conflict with and distance from father measures were not associated with menarche in all these samples. Early menarche was associated with more conflict with and distance from mother in both the Italian and English samples, more rejection from mother in the English sample, and more rejection from father in the Italian sample. However, the only parent-child relations associated with early menarche in the Canadian sample were more independence from parents (which were also associated with early menarche in the Italian sample). These results suggest that in these Canadian women, more parental marital conflict and parental unhappiness in early child-hood (birth to age 7) could lead to more independence from parents in late childhood (age 8 to 11) which then lead to early puberty. This pattern is in contrast to the Italian and English women in which their relations with their mothers, and to a lesser extent, fathers in the Italian sample, seem more involved in age at puberty than in the Canadian women.

Another contrast occurs in the results for anxiousness (age 8 to 11) and internalising symptoms (anxiousness/depression) (age 8 to 11). In the English sample these were associated with early menarche, as pre-dicted by Belsky et al. (1991). However, in the Canadian sample they were associated with *late* menarche, opposite to these predictions. These latter findings are also not consistent with those of Graber et al. (1995) who provided the first support for this aspect of the Belsky et al. (1991) theory, in that more internalising symptoms, as well as more body weight but not body fat, in women were associated with early menar-che. Taken together, it seems possible that moderate rates of internalis-ing symptoms could reduce self-esteem, and, as a compensatory effect, induce early puberty and post-pubertal reproductive behaviour, whereas severe rates, particularly of depression, could lead to reduced appetite, less weight gain, hence, less gain of body fat, and delayed menarche.

Of the post-pubertal measures, in all samples early menarche was associated with early age at dating men, and it was also asso-ciated with having had more boyfriends in the Canadian and English samples. Early menarche being associated with early age at dating men is consistent with much of the previous research (Aro and Taipale, 1987; Magnusson et al., 1985, 1986; Phinney et al., 1990; Presser, 1978).

The path results for women demonstrated that the predictors, increased parental marital unhappiness (birth to age 7) and increased independence from father (age 8 to 11) each linked early puberty to post-pubertal reproductive behaviour. However, early menarche did not predict for increased frequency of boyfriends or intercourse partners but was only indirectly linked to them, although early age at menarche did predict for early age at dating men. In these results, the path of increased independence from father (age 8 to 11) to earlier menarche, earlier age at dating men, more boyfriends, and more intercourse partners could conceivably be an effect of an earlier developmental trajectory from genetic transmission of maternal characteristics linked by inherited early menarcheal timing from the mother. Alternatively, or in conjunction with the previous possibility, this pattern could result from a stress-related early childhood environment, from increased parental marital unhappiness in early childhood (birth to age 7). This would be consistent with Belsky et al. (1991), though this too could be due to inheritance of personality traits likely to cause marital problems and dissatisfaction with future husbands.

In contrast to women, childhood father absence in men was associated with earlier spermarche. Some other findings for men supported the findings of previous research: more independence in childhood (age 6 to 10) and early age at peak height velocity in pubertal growth (Goodson and Jamison, 1987); more self-governance from father and early puberty (Ellis, 1991); and more behavioural autonomy from parents and early puberty (Kracke and Silbereisen, 1996). In contrast, only one of these findings confirmed the results from the previous Italian sample (Kim et al., 1997), in which more parental marital conflict was associated with early spermarche. In neither sample was conflict with or rejection from parents or distance from mother measures associated with spermarche. Although more distance from father and more externalising symptoms were associated with early spermarche in the Italian sample, it was more stress in quality of family life, parental marital unhappiness, and independence from parents which were associated with early spermarche in the Canadian sample. In these Canadian men, as with the women, more parental marital conflict and parental unhappiness in early childhood (birth to age 7) could lead to more independence from parents in late childhood (age 8 to 11) which then lead to early puberty.

Of the post-pubertal measures, early spermarche was associated with early age at dating women and having had more girlfriends in the Canadian and Italian samples, whereas it was also associated with younger age at first sexual intercourse in the Canadian sample. Consistent with the latter is a report by Zabin et al. (1986) with a US African-American sample of 13- to 18-year-olds. They found an association between early age at first nocturnal emission of seminal fluid (which follows spermarche) and early age at first intercourse. Early puberty in men being associated with early sexual behaviour is consistent with much of the previous research (Capaldi et al., 1996; Crockett and Petersen, 1987; Flannery et al., 1993; Halpern et al., 1993; Hulanicka, 1996).

The path results for men demonstrated that the predictors, increased parental marital unhappiness (birth to age 7), father absence (birth to before spermarche), and increased independence from mother (age 8 to 11) each linked early puberty to post-pubertal reproductive behaviour. Although early age at spermarche predicted for early age at dating women, early spermarche did not predict for increased frequency of girlfriends or intercourse partners but was only indirectly linked to them. The path of increased independence from mother (age 8 to 11) to earlier spermarche, earlier age at dating women, more girlfriends, and more intercourse partners could (similarly to the argument for women) be an effect of an earlier developmental trajectory from genetic transmission of paternal characteristics linked by inherited early spermarcheal timing from the father. Alternatively, or in conjunction with this, the pattern could result from a stress-related early childhood environment. One possibility is increased parental marital unhappiness in early childhood (birth to age 7). This would be consistent with Belsky et al. (1991), though this could be due to inheritance of personality traits likely to cause marital problems and dissatisfaction with future wives. Another possibility is father absence throughout childhood (birth to before spermarche), though this too could be due to inheritance of personality traits likely to cause conflict with future wives, hence separation/divorce and father absence. Consistent with Belsky et al. (1991), it is possible that father absence during the son's childhood, linked by early spermarche, could lead to adoption of an opportunistic post-pubertal quantity reproductive strategy, that is, increased frequency of intercourse partners.

References

Adams, J. F. (1981). Earlier menarche, greater height and weight: A stimulation-stress factor hypothesis. *Genetic Psychology Monographs, 104,* 3–22.

Aro, H., & Taipale, V. (1987). The impact of timing of puberty on psychosomatic symptoms among fourteen- to sixteen-year-old Finnish Girls. *Child Development, 58,* 261–268.

Barkow, J. H. (1984). The distance between genes and culture. *Journal of Anthropological Research, 40,* 367–379.

Belsky, J., Steinberg, L., & Draper, P. (1991). Childhood experience, interpersonal development, & reproductive strategy: An evolutionary theory of socialization. *Child Development, 62,* 647–670.

Campbell, B. C., & Udry, J. R. (1995). Stress and age at menarche of mothers and daughters. *Journal of Biosocial Science, 27,* 127–134.

Capaldi, D. M., Crosby, L., & Stoolmiller, M. (1996). Predicting the timing of first sexual intercourse for at-risk adolescent males. *Child Development, 67,* 344–359.

Chern, M. M., Gatewood, L. C., & Anderson, V. E. (1980). The inheritance of menstrual traits. In A. J. Dan, E. A. Graham, and C. P. Beecher (Eds.), *The menstrual cycle: A synthesis of interdisciplinary research* (pp. 123–130). New York: Springer.

Coe, C. L., Hayashi, K. T., & Levine, S. (1988). Hormones and behavior at puberty: Activation or concatenation. In M. R. Gunnar and W. A. Collins (Eds.), *The Minnesota Symposia on Child Psychology: Vol. 21. Development during the transition to adolescence* (pp. 17–41). Hillsdale, NJ: Erlbaum.

Crockett, L. J., & Petersen, A. C. (1987). Pubertal status and psychosocial development: Findings from the early adolescence study. In R. M. Lerner and T. T. Foch (Eds.), *Biological-psychosocial interactions in early adolescence* (pp. 173–188). Hillsdale, NJ: Erlbaum.

Damon, A., Damon, S. T., Reed, R. B., & Valadian, I. (1969). Age of menarche of mothers and daughters, with a note on accuracy of recall. *Human Biology, 41,* 161–175.

Draper, P., & Belsky, J. (1990). Personality development in evolutionary perspective. *Journal of Personality, 58,* 141–161.

Draper, P., and Harpending, H. (1982). Father absence and reproductive strategy: An evolutionary perspective. *Journal of Anthropological Research, 38,* 255–273.

Edelbrock, C., Rende, R., Plomin, R., & Thompson, L. A. (1995). A twin study of competence and problem behavior in childhood and early adolescence. *Journal of Child Psychology and Psychiatry, 36,* 775–785.

Ellis, N. B. (1991). An extension of the Steinberg accelerating hypothesis. *Journal of Early Adolescence, 11,* 221–235.

Ellison, P. T. (1982). Skeletal growth, fatness, and menarcheal age: A comparison of two hypotheses. *Human Biology, 54,* 269–281.

Fischbein, S. (1977). Intra-pair similarity in physical growth of monozygotic and of dizygotic twins during puberty. *Annals of Human Biology, 4,* 417–430.

Flannery, D. J., Rowe, D. C., & Gulley, B. L. (1993). Impact of pubertal status, timing, and age on adolescent sexual experience and delinquency. *Journal of Adolescent Research, 8,* 21–40.

Flinn, M. V., & England, B. G. (1995). Childhood stress and family environment. *Current Anthropology, 36,* 854–866.

Gjone, H., Stevenson, J., Sundet, J. M., & Eilertsen, D. E. (1996). Changes in heritability across increasing levels of behavior problems in young twins. *Behavior Genetics, 26,* 419–426.

Goodson, C. S., & Jamison, P. L. (1987). The relative rate of maturation and its psychological effect. *Journal of Biosocial Science, 19*, 73–88.

Graber, J. A., Brooks-Gunn, J., & Warren, M. P. (1995). The antecedents of menarcheal age: Heredity, family environment, and stressful life events. *Child Development, 66*, 346–359.

Halpern, C. T., Udry, J. R., Campbell, B. C., & Suchindran, C. (1993). Testosterone and pubertal development as predictors of sexual activity: A panel analysis of adolescent males. *Psychosomatic Medicine, 55*, 436–447.

Hewitt, J. K., Silberg, J. L., Neale, M. C., Eaves, L. J., & Erickson, M. (1992). The analysis of parental ratings of children's behavior using LISREL. *Behavior Genetics, 22*, 293–317.

Hulanicka, B. (1986). Effects of psychologic and emotional factors on age at menarche. *Materialy i Prace Antropologiczne, 107*, 45–80.

Hulanicka, B. (1989). Age at menarche of girls from disturbed families. *Humanbiologia Budapest, 19*, 173–177.

Hulanicka, B. (1996). Self-assessment of maturation rate at adolescence in adult males. In B. É. Bodzsár and C. Susanne (Eds.), *Studies in human biology* (pp. 247–253). Budapest: Eötvös University Press.

Jockin, V., McGue, M., & Lykken, D. T. (1996). Personality and divorce: A genetic analysis. *Journal of Personality and Social Psychology, 71*, 288–299.

Kaur, D. P., & Singh, R. (1981). Parent-adult offspring correlations and heritability of body measurements in a rural Indian population. *Annals of Human Biology, 8*, 333–339.

Kim, K. (1997). *Family structure, puberty, and reproductive development.* Unpublished PhD thesis, University of Sheffield, Sheffield, UK.

Kim, K., & Smith, P. K. (1998). Childhood stress, behavioural symptoms, and mother-daughter pubertal development. *Journal of Adolescence, 21*, 231–240.

Kim, K., Smith, P. K., & Palermiti, A. L. (1997). Conflict in chilhood and reproductive development. *Evolution and Human Behavior, 18*, 109–142.

Kracke, B., & Silbereisen, R. K. (1996, May). *Behavioral autonomy and pubertal maturation.* Paper presented at the Fifth Biennial Conference of the European Association for Research on Adolescence, Liège, Belgium. May 11–15.

Leek, M. M. (1991). *Genetic narcissism in the family unit: Genetic similarity theory as an extension of Hamilton's rule into the human domain.* Unpublished PhD thesis, University of Sheffield, Sheffield, UK.

Liestol, K. (1982). Social conditions and menarcheal age: The importance of early years of life. *Annals of Human Biology, 9*, 521–537.

Lumsden, D. P. (1991). The awakened brain: From Wright's psychozoology to Barkow's selfless persons [Commentary]. *Behavioral and Brain Sciences, 14*, 311–312.

Magnusson, D., Stattin, H., & Allen, V. L. (1985). Biological maturation and social development: A longitudinal study of some adjustment processes from mid-adolescence to adulthood. *Journal of Youth and Adolescence, 14*, 267–283.

Magnusson, D., Stattin, H., & Allen, V. L. (1986). Differential maturation among girls and its relations to social adjustment: A longitudinal perspective. In P. Baltes, D. Featherman, and R. Lerner (Eds.), *Life span development and behavior* (Vol. 7, pp. 74–101). Hillsdale, NJ: Erlbaum.

Martin, N. G., Eaves, L. J., & Eysenck, H. J. (1977). Genetical, environmental and personality factors influencing the age of first sexual intercourse in twins. *Journal of Biosocial Science, 9*, 91–97.

McGue, M., & Lykken, D. T. (1992). Genetic influence on risk of divorce. *Psychological Science, 3*, 368–373.

Meikle, A. W., Bishop, D. T., Stringham, J. D., & West, D. W. (1987). Quantifying genetic and nongenetic factors that determine plasma sex steroid variation in normal male twins. *Metabolism, 35*, 1090–1095.

Meyer, J. M., Eaves, L. J., Heath, A. C., & Martin, N. G. (1991). Estimating genetic influences on the age-at-menarche: A survival analysis approach. *American Journal of Medical Genetics, 39*, 148–154.

Mills, J. L., Shiono, P. H., Shapiro, L. R., Crawford, P. B., & Rhodes, G. G. (1986). Early growth predicts timing of puberty in boys: Results of a 14-year nutrition and growth study. *Journal of Pediatrics, 109*, 543–547.

Moffitt, T. E., Caspi, A., Belsky, J., & Silva, P. A. (1992). Childhood experience and the onset of menarche: A test of a sociobiological model. *Child Development, 63*, 47–58.

Nielsen, C. T., Skakkebæk, N. E., Richardson, D. W., Darling, J. A. B., Hunter, W. M., Jørgensen, M., Nielsen, A., Ingerslev, O., Keiding, N., & Müller, J. (1986). Onset of the release of spermatozoa (spermarche) in boys in relation to age, testicular growth, pubic hair, and height. *Journal of Clinical Endocrinology and Metabolism, 62*, 532–535.

Pérusse, D., Neale, M. C., Heath, A. C., & Eaves, L. J. (1994). Human parental behavior: Evidence for genetic influence and potential implication for gene-culture transmission. *Behavior Genetics, 24*, 327–335.

Phinney, V. G., Jensen, L. C., Olsen, J. A., & Cundick, B. (1990). The relationship between early development and psychosexual behaviors in adolescent females. *Adolescence, 25*, 321–332.

Presser, H. B. (1978). Age at menarche, socio-sexual behavior, and fertility. *Social Biology, 25*, 94–101.

Reiss, D. (1995). Genetic influence on family systems: Implications for development. *Journal of Marriage and the Family, 57*, 543–560.

Rushton, J. P. (1984). Sociobiology: Toward a theory of individual and group differences in personality and social behavior. In J. R. Royce and L. P. Mos (Eds.), *Annals of theoretical psychology* (Vol. 2, pp. 1–48). New York, Plenum.

Rushton, J. P. (1985). Differential K theory: The sociobiology of individual and group differences. *Personality and Individual Differences, 6*, 441–452.

Silberg, J. L., Erickson, M. T., Meyer, J. M., Eaves, L. J., Rutter, M. L., & Hewitt, J. K. (1994). The Application of structural equation modeling to maternal ratings of twins' behavioral and emotional problems. *Journal of Consulting and Clinical Psychology, 62*, 510–521.

Steinberg, L. (1988). Reciprocal relation between parent-child distance and pubertal maturation. *Developmental Psychology, 24*, 122–128.

Steinberg, L. (1989). Pubertal maturation and parent-adolescent distance: An evolutionary perspective. In G. R. Adams, R. Montemayor, and T. P. Gullotta (Eds.), *Advances in adolescent development: An annual book series: Vol. 1. Biology of adolescent behavior and development* (pp. 71–97). Newbury Park, CA: Sage.

Steinberg, L., & Belsky, J. (1996). An evolutionary perspective on psychopathology in adolescence. In D. Cicchetti and S. L. Toth (Eds.), *Rochester Symposium on Developmental Psychology: Vol. 7. Adolescence: Opportunities and Challenges* (pp. 93–124). Woodbridge, Suffolk: University of Rochester Press.

Surbey, M. K. (1988). *The Timing of human menarche.* Unpublished PhD thesis, McMaster University, Hamilton, Ontario, Canada.

Surbey, M. K. (1990). Family composition, stress, and the timing of human menarche. In T. E. Ziegler and F. B. Bercovitch (Eds.), *Monographs in primatology: Vol. 13. Socioendocrinology of primate reproduction* (pp. 11–32). New York: Wiley-Liss.

Thapar, A., & McGuffin, P. (1996). Genetic influences on life events in childhood. *Psychological Medicine, 26*, 813–820.

Treloar, S. A., & Martin, N. G. (1990). Age at menarche as a fitness trait: Nonadditive genetic variance detected in a large twin sample. *American Journal of Human Genetics, 47*, 137–148.

Wierson, M., Long, P. J., & Forehand, R. L. (1993). Toward a new understanding of early menarche: The role of environmental stress in pubertal timing. *Adolescence, 28*, 913–924.

Zabin, L. S., Smith, E. A., Hirsch, M. B., & Hardy, J. B. (1986). Ages of physical maturation and first intercourse in Black teenage males and females. *Demography, 23*, 595–605.

A Cross-National Study on the Relations Among Prosocial Moral Reasoning, Gender Role Orientation, and Prosocial Behaviors

Introduction

One of the many developmental tasks of the adolescent is to construct self-regulation systems that guide moral judgments. These self-regulation systems include the development of prosocial moral reasoning where the needs of others are recognized as part of the adolescent's judgment about right and wrong. Too often we hear of teenagers who hurt someone and then when asked why they did it or how did they feel about it, simply report inadequate judgment about their actions and the effects of such actions for others. In affluent cultures where there are ample resources to help children and adolescents develop high standards of prosocial moral reasoning, there should be little excuse for society to fail any youth.

In the next reading you are introduced to a study that compares boys and girls and looks for differences or similarities between Brazilian and United States teenagers. Likewise, the investigators look for age differences in prosocial moral reasoning. In fact, this study demonstrates how, in a single study, you can include person, context, and occasion, in a single investigation.

Often we hear in common day discussions that girls are more mature than boys, or that boys have advantages over girls. I prefer to call this the *gender deficit hypothesis*. This study has addressed this issue in regards to prosocial moral reasoning. Look to see if girls or boys fare the best in this study. Also, look carefully to see if there are context or occasion differences.

Here we go again on another reading journey together. If you read carefully, once you have re-entered the Twilight Zone of Adolescence, you might find some small surprises in this study. Again, don't worry about the computational issues in the results section. Rather, read for the findings themselves. Again, look for any surprises that emerge from this published investigation.

Suggested reading

Walker, L. J. (1991). Sex differences in moral reasoning. In W. M. Kurtines, and J. L. Gewirtz (Eds.), *Handbook of moral behavior and development: Vol. 2. Research* (pp. 333–64). Hillsdale, NJ: Erlbaum.

THREE

A Cross-National Study on the Relations Among Prosocial Moral Reasoning, Gender Role Orientations, and Prosocial Behaviors

Gustavo Carlo, Silvia H. Koller,
Nancy Eisenberg, and Marcia S. Da
Silva and Claudia B. Frohlich

Children and adolescents often are faced with the decision to help others at some cost to themselves. Many times, these decisions are difficult because they arise in situations in which formal external guidelines are absent or unclear. Decisions in those contexts have been the focus of researchers interested in prosocial moral reasoning (i.e., reasoning about moral dilemmas in which one person's needs or desires conflict with those of needy others in a context in which the role of prohibitions, authorities' dictates, and formal obligations are minimal or absent; Eisenberg, 1986; see Rest, 1983).

According to Eisenberg (1986), developmental changes in prosocial moral reasoning are somewhat consistent with developmental changes in justice-oriented, Kohlbergian (Colby, Kohlberg et al., 1983) moral reasoning. This similarity is due to the role of cognition as a necessary but not sufficient factor for some types of moral reasoning. However,

Eisenberg (Eisenberg and Shell, 1986; Eisenberg et al., 1987) has argued and presented some supportive evidence that individuals' level of prosocial moral reasoning, within the limits of their sociocognitive competence, varies as a function of personal (e.g., sympathetic tendencies) and contextual (e.g., cost of helping) factors. Following this argument, social contextual factors such as culture might be expected to influence level of prosocial moral reasoning depending on the values and socialization emphases in the culture. Furthermore, because education and logical skills appear to be associated with level of moral reasoning (Colby et al., 1983; Eisenberg, 1986), differences in educational experiences may result in cross-cultural variations in prosocial moral reasoning (particularly at the highest levels).

Consistent with cognitive developmental theory, researchers frequently have found that the sophistication of moral judgment increases during adolescence, presumably due in part to an increase in perspective taking and reflective abstract cognitive skills (Colby et al., 1983; Eisenberg, 1986; Rest, 1983; Selman, 1980). In a series of longitudinal and cross-sectional studies on children and adolescents from the United States, Eisenberg and her colleagues have found several age-related changes in several types of prosocial moral reasoning (Eisenberg et al., 1995; Eisenberg et al., 1991). For example, when an interview measure of prosocial moral reasoning was used, judgments regarding gaining the approval of others and global, stereotyped notions about good or bad behaviors tended to increase in adolescence until between the ages of 13–14 and 15–16 years, and then decreased somewhat in frequency. In contrast, self-reflective perspective taking and internalized norms judgments tend to emerge in late childhood and increase through adolescence (Eisenberg et al., 1991; Eisenberg et al., 1995). In addition, researchers interested in the motives for prosocial behaviors have presented a pattern of findings that is similar and consistent with the aforementioned pattern. For example, intrinsic (e.g., internalized or other-oriented) motives for prosocial behavior appear to be relatively high during adolescence in industrialized European societies such as Germany, Italy, and Poland (Boehnke et al., 1989), as well as in other countries such as Israel (Bar-Tal et al., 1980; Raviv et al., 1980).

At present, there is relatively little cross-cultural research on prosocial moral reasoning. Nonetheless, some research suggests that the prosocial moral reasoning of elementary school children and adolescents is similar (although relatively small differences have been found) across various industrialized societies (Eisenberg, 1986; Eisenberg et al., 1985). For example, Israeli kibbutz children expressed more concern with the humaneness of recipients and internalized norms and laws than Anglo-Americans or Israeli city children (Fuchs et al., 1986). Furthermore, in one study on prosocial moral reasoning in a non-Western, non-industrialized culture, researchers found that adolescents from two Maisan coastal communities in Papua New Guinea verbalized virtually no higher-level internalized, stereotypic, or sympathetic moral reasoning (Eisenberg, 1986), although such reasoning is found in adolescents from Western and industrialized communities. Instead, the Papua New Guinea adolescents used substantial amounts of reasoning based on the needs of others, concern with assisting others connected with or liked by one's self, and pragmatic concerns. These types of reasoning presumably reflect the personal ties and interactions and the collectivist orientation of their society (Tietjen, 1986). In brief, prosocial moral reasoning appears to be similar in the few industrialized societies examined thus far. However, cultural factors do seem to influence the frequency and report of some types of reasoning across Western and non-Western societies.

Brazilians, particularly from the southern region, in many respects are perhaps the most Westernized people in Latin America (Poppino, 1973). The southern region of Brazil is the country's most populous region and is a center for manufacturing, agriculture, and technology. In this region, approximately 80 percent of the workforce earns more than the region's minimum wage, infant mortality rates are about a third lower than in the northeast region of Brazil, and most children stay in school at least through the fourth grade (Lang, 1988). According to Hofstede (1982), on the whole, Brazil ranks close to the United States on the masculinity–femininity dimension (i.e., relative importance of advancement, earnings, and recognition). In addition, some researchers (Haidt et al., 1993) have found that judgment of mores about specific affect-laden issues generally were comparable between individuals from this region of Brazil and a sample of individuals from the United States; social mores varied more as a function of socioeconomic status than culture. Nonetheless, there is evidence that Brazilian society is oriented toward collectivism (i.e., less personal time and freedom, more dependency on a system) and personal and interpersonal relationships to a greater degree than the majority of society in the United States (Botenmpo et al., 1990; Hofstede, 1982).

An emphasis on collectivism and interpersonal relationships in Brazilian society might be reflected in some modes of prosocial moral reasoning, including generalized reciprocity reasoning (i.e., the belief that helping would benefit everyone) or affectional relationship reasoning (i.e., consideration of the existing relationship with the needy individual). Presumably, some socialization practices in Brazil would be aimed at promoting and nurturing collectivism and personal ties and contact. Consistent with this notion, Biaggio (1976) found that Brazilians scored high on Kohlbergian Stage 3 (i.e., concern with interpersonal relationships) moral reasoning. However, note that generalized reciprocity reasoning, in contrast to Stage 3 in Kohlberg's moral reasoning scheme, is a high-level mode of prosocial moral reasoning. Moreover, there is some evidence (Botenmpo et al., 1990) that Brazilians (from Rio De Janeiro) may behave prosocially without much concern for self-presentation (i.e., they appear to be intrinsically motivated). In summary, we know little concerning the preferred modes of prosocial moral reasoning in Brazilians when compared directly to individuals from the United States. Consequently, it is difficult to predict whether generalized reciprocity and other high-level modes of prosocial moral reasoning would be more preferred by Brazilians or individuals from the United States.

Gender is another social category that has been linked to individual differences in prosocial moral reasoning. This issue is important in order to address claims (e.g., Gilligan, 1982) that there are cultural biases in moral reasoning. To date, however, the answer to this question remains relatively unclear (see Baumrind, 1986; Gilligan and Attanucci, 1988; Eisenberg et al., 1989; Walker, 1991). Eisenberg (Eisenberg et al., 1989) and others (Gilligan, 1982) have theorized that gender-specific socialization practices may lead to gender differences in care-oriented modes of moral reasoning. Indeed, in adolescence, girls sometimes have expressed more higher level, other-oriented modes of prosocial moral reasoning (e.g., perspective taking and internalized affect about consequences-type reasoning; Eisenberg et al., 1995), although this pattern seemed stronger in early rather than late adolescence (see Eisenberg et al., 1991; Eisenberg et al., 1995). Furthermore, adolescent girls have exhibited somewhat higher moral reasoning overall than have adolescent boys (Eisenberg et al., 1989; Eisenberg et al., 1995).

In research with a paper-and-pencil measure of prosocial moral reasoning, some gender differences also have been found. For example, girls from the United States score higher on internalized moral reasoning and lower on approval-oriented than do boys (Eisenberg et al., 1995) and also score higher than boys on stereotypic reasoning (Carlo et al., 1992). Because of the similarities between Anglo-American and Brazilian societies in gender roles (Hofstede, 1982), we anticipated that Brazilian adolescents might display gender differences similar to those in the US sample.

To date, most of the research on prosocial moral reasoning has been conducted using interview measures of moral reasoning. However, Carlo et al. (1992) recently introduced a paper-and-pencil measure of prosocial moral reasoning (the prosocial reasoning objective measure, or PROM) designed to examine prosocial moral reasoning in adolescence. As pointed out by these and other researchers (e.g., Gibbs et al., 1984; Kurtines and Pimm, 1983; Rest, 1983), paper-and-pencil measures of moral reasoning have been designed to assess the individual's ability to choose among alternative moral viewpoints, a skill that is related, but distinct from spontaneously producing, elaborating, and defending moral viewpoints (as in interview measures). Paper-and-pencil measures facilitate verification of standardized administration, enhance comparability of findings across studies, and may require less verbal skills than interview measures. The benefits of paper-and-pencil measures may be particularly evident when conducting studies in different countries and in applied settings.

In summary, based on social and economic similarities between specific regions of Brazil and the United States and on the cognitive prerequisites for prosocial moral reasoning, we hypothesized that the pattern of age-related changes in prosocial moral reasoning for Brazilian children and adolescents would be similar to that of US children and adolescents. Furthermore, girls were expected to score higher on other-oriented and internalized modes of prosocial moral reasoning (although no cultural differences in the pattern of gender differences were expected). In the first part of Study 1, the age- and gender-related patterns of prosocial moral reasoning in Brazilian children and adolescents were examined. In the second part, the moral reasoning of Brazilian adolescents (aged 11 to 15 years) was compared with the moral reasoning of a similar age group of Anglo-American adolescents (selected from the sample used in Carlo et al., 1992).

Study 1: Part 1

Method

Participants

The participants were 271 fifth- through tenth-grade children and adolescents (128 male, 143 female) from private schools in a predominantly White, middle-class community in a southern city (Porto Alegre) of Brazil. Six students left some items blank on the questionnaire and were dropped from the main analyses. Thus, there were 265 students (127 male, 138 female; *M* age = 14.6 years, *SD* = 1.9 years) in the final sample. Participation in the study was voluntary, and the students received no material compensation for participating.

Materials

The paper-and-pencil measure of prosocial moral reasoning (Carlo et al., 1992) was based on a previously developed (see Eisenberg et al., 1987) interview measure of prosocial moral reasoning. The PROM was translated into Portuguese and back into English by a researcher who is fluent in both Portuguese and English and who is an expert in moral development (Silvia H. Koller). Then the PROM was translated back into Portuguese, and the translation was confirmed by a fellow researcher who is fluent in both English and Portuguese. The PROM contained seven story dilemmas designed to invoke a conflict between the actor's needs, wants, and desires and those of another (or others). The dilemmas dealt with the following issues: (a) choosing to get an injured child's parents versus going to a friend's party, (b) keeping food after a flood versus giving some food to others who had none, (c) helping disabled children strengthen their legs by teaching them to swim versus practicing for a swimming contest to win prize money, (d) continuing to stay and play in one's own backyard versus going to try and stop a bully that is picking on a peer, (e) going to the beach with friends versus helping a peer to study for and pass a math test, (f) donating blood to a needy other versus losing time and money at work and school, and (g) helping a peer who is being teased versus risking rejection from peers.

The following is a sample story from the PROM (English version):

> One day Mary was going to a friend's party. On the way, she saw a girl who had fallen down and hurt her leg. The girl asked Mary to go to the girl's house and get her parents so the parents could come and take her to a doctor. But if Mary did run and get the girl's parents, Mary would be late to the party and miss the fun and social activities with her friends.

The order of the PROM stories was randomized for each student, the protagonists were the same gender as the student, and there was a practice story at the beginning. After reading each story, adolescents were first asked to indicate whether (a) the protagonist should help the needy other, (b) the protagonist should not help the needy other, or (c) they were unsure what the protagonist should do. Following this decision, the students were asked to rate the importance of six considerations pertaining to why the protagonist should or should not help the needy other in the story (on a 5-point scale; $1 = $ *not at all*, $5 = $ *greatly*). The PROM took each student about 15 to 20 min to complete.

A representative sampling of frequently reported prosocial moral reasoning choices was selected for each story. Each of the stories (there were seven stories) included one hedonistic item (Level 1 in Eisenberg's, 1986, schema, which included simple hedonistic or direct reciprocity reasoning; e.g., "It depends how much fun Mary expects the party to be and what sorts of things are happening at the party"; Cronbach's $\alpha = 0.61$), one needs-oriented item (Level 2; e.g., "It depends whether the girl really needs help or not"; $\alpha = 0.60$), one approval-oriented item (Level 3; e.g., "It depends whether Mary's parents and friends will think she did the right or she did the wrong thing"; $\alpha = 0.85$), and one stereotypic item (Level 3; e.g., "It depends if Mary thinks it's the decent thing to do or not"; $\alpha = 0.61$). In addition, each of the stories contained one item that reflected higher level reasoning (Levels 4 and 5; i.e., sympathetic, perspective taking, internalized affect, or abstract internalized reasoning; e.g., "It depends how Mary would feel about herself if she helped or not"; $\alpha = 0.61$). The sixth reasoning choice was a lie/nonsense item (e.g., "It depends whether Mary believes in people's values of metacognition or not").[1]

Procedure

All adolescents were administered a demographic questionnaire and the PROM. The session lasted about 20 to 30 min and was conducted in the classrooms (maximum group size of 30). Students then were carefully debriefed and thanked.

Scoring of the PROM

For each participant, PROM ratings that corresponded to one of the five types of prosocial moral reasoning were summed across the seven stories to obtain a frequency score. A frequency score also was obtained using the lie/nonsense items in the PROM; however, this scale was used only to assess whether students scored 2 standard deviations or higher on this scale (as suggested by Carlo et al., 1992), and no adolescents met this criterion.

As in prior studies (Carlo et al., 1992; Eisenberg et al., 1995), preliminary analyses using the frequency PROM scores suggested that there was a response bias in the use of the scale. Students tended to use either the lower or the higher ends of the PROM scale. Thus, the frequency PROM scores were transformed to proportion PROM scores (see Boehnke et al., 1989, for a similar procedure) by dividing each of the PROM scale scores (reflecting the five types of reasoning) by the sum of the PROM scale scores. Conceptually, the proportion scores reflect a participant's preference for a reasoning type in relation to the other reasoning types. In the subsequent analyses of the PROM, proportion scores were used rather than frequency scores.

Results

Table 3.1 presents the means and standard deviations for the PROM scales for Part 1. There were significant main effects of both age and gender on the first step for approval-oriented, stereotypic, and internalized moral reasoning, $Fs(2, 262) = 19.90, 12.44,$ and $6.51, p < 0.001,$ $p < 0.001,$ and $p < 0.005$ (R^2 changes $= 0.13, 0.09,$ and 0.05), respectively. Younger children and boys scored higher on approval-oriented reasoning, $ts(262) = -4.31$ and $-4.67, p < 0.001$ (standardized $Bs = -0.25$ and -0.27). In contrast, children scored higher on stereotypic and internalized reasoning as age increased, $ts(262) = 3.05$ and $2.69,$

Table 3.1 Means and standard deviations for prosocial moral reasoning by samples in Study 1

| Moral reasoning | Part 1 (n = 265) | | Part 2 | | | | | |
| | | | Brazil (n = 211) | | United States (n = 63) | | Total (n = 174) | |
	M	SD	M	SD	M	SD	M	SD
Hedonistic	0.18	0.03	0.18	0.03	0.17	0.04	0.18	0.03
Approval	0.15	0.05	0.15	0.05	0.14	0.05	0.15	0.05
Needs-oriented	0.21	0.03	0.23	0.04	0.22	0.04	0.21	0.03
Stereotyped	0.23	0.04	0.21	0.03	0.21	0.04	0.23	0.04
Internalized	0.24	0.03	0.24	0.03	0.26	0.04	0.24	0.04

Note: *The Brazilian sample in Part 2 is a subsample of the Brazilian sample in Part 1 selected to match the Anglo-American sample on age range*

$p < 0.005$ and $p < 0.01$ (standardized $Bs = 0.18$ and 0.16), respectively, and girls scored higher than boys on both stereotypic and internalized reasoning, $ts(262) = 4.00$ and 2.44, $ps < 0.001$ and 0.02 (standardized $Bs = 0.24$ and 0.15), respectively. There were no other significant main or interaction effects.

Study 1: Part 2

The second part of Study 1 was designed to directly compare age, gender, and cultural group differences in Brazilian and Anglo-American adolescents' ratings of prosocial moral reasoning.

Method

Participants

The Brazilian participants were 219 students (a subset of the sample from Study 1) matched to the US sample by age (selected if age range was from 141 to 198 months; 106 male, 113 female; *M* age = 14.2 years, *SD* = 1.5 years).

The students from the United States were 67 adolescent students (25 male, 42 female) from a prior published study on prosocial moral reasoning (Carlo et al., 1992). The US students were selected only if they were between 141 months and 198 months of age (2 students from the original sample were dropped on the basis of this criterion; for the final sample, *M* age = 14.2 years, *SD* = 1.7 years). Four students were dropped from some analyses because they left some items on the PROM unanswered. The students were predominantly White, middle-class, and from public junior high or high schools in Tempe, Arizona. The students received $10 (2 tenth graders received $20 in an effort to recruit more male students) to motivate voluntary participation.

Materials

The paper-and-pencil measure of prosocial moral reasoning (PROM; Carlo et al., 1992) was the same as described earlier. Although the Brazilians were administered all seven stories from the PROM (see Part 1), only the same five stories (the first five stories described earlier) that were administered to the US sample were used for analyses. The scoring procedures were the same as described previously. Two Brazilian boys scored 2 standard deviations above the mean on the lie/nonsense scale of the PROM and were dropped from subsequent analyses.

Procedure

As mentioned earlier, the Brazilian adolescents participated in an experimental session in which they completed a demographic information sheet and the PROM questionnaire. The session lasted about 30 min and was conducted in the classrooms (maximum group size of 30). The US adolescents participated in two experimental sessions (see Carlo et al., 1992), but only the demographic information and PROM questionnaire data from the first session were used in the present study. In this session, the demographic information and the PROM were administered before all other questionnaires were administered. In both the Brazilian and Anglo-American sessions, participating students were carefully debriefed and thanked.

Results

Table 3.1 presents the means and standard deviations for the PROM scales for the Brazilian sample, the US sample, and the total sample in Part 2. There were significant main effects of age and culture group on the first step for internalized reasoning, $F(3, 270) = 8.00$, $p < 0.001$ (R^2 change = 0.08). Older children and US children scored higher on internalized reasoning, $ts(270) = 2.71$ and 3.51, $ps < 0.01$ and 0.001 (standardized $Bs = 0.16$ and 0.21), respectively.

There also were significant main effects of age and gender on the first step for approval-oriented and stereotypic moral reasoning, $Fs(3, 270) = 13.81$ and 7.43, both $ps < 0.001$ (R^2 change = 0.13 and 0.08), respectively. Younger children and boys scored higher on approval-oriented reasoning, $ts(270) = -4.08$ and -4.75, $ps < 0.001$ (standardized $Bs = -0.23$ and -0.27), respectively. In contrast, older children and girls scored higher on stereotypic reasoning, $ts(270) = 2.56$ and 3.77, $ps < 0.01$ and 0.001 (standardized $Bs = 0.15$ and 0.22), respectively. There were no other significant main effects, and there were no significant two- or three-way interaction effects.

Discussion of Study 1

The present findings from both parts of Study 1 were generally consistent with the hypotheses and yielded several interesting findings. More specifically, the age, gender, and cultural group differences were generally consistent with prior findings from studies using children and adolescents from Western and non-Western, industrialized countries.

Of particular interest was the one cultural group difference on prosocial moral reasoning in Part 2. Children from the United States scored higher on internalized moral reasoning compared with Brazilian children. This finding is somewhat consistent with other researchers' findings that Brazilians score approximately one stage lower than Americans on Kohlbergian moral reasoning (Hutz et al., 1993). Because moral reasoning has been found to be significantly related to education and logical skills (Colby et al., 1983; Eisenberg, 1986), it may be that the culture difference was partly a function of these variables. Although children from both samples were recruited from schools, there may be differences in the degree to which the educational systems stress critical reasoning skills that may be necessary for developmentally sophisticated moral reasoning.

Despite the moderate sample size in this study, there were no differences between US and Brazilian adolescents in age or gender effects on prosocial moral reasoning (i.e., there were no significant interactions of age or gender with cultural group in Part 2). Indeed, consistent with Eisenberg et al.'s (1995) findings, approval-oriented reasoning declined with age whereas internalized reasoning increased with age (in Carlo et al., 1992, internalized reasoning increased with age particularly for male participants). In addition, stereotypic reasoning increased with age in both studies. This latter finding may not be surprising given that stereotypic reasoning appears to increase with age sometime in mid-adolescence (Eisenberg et al., 1991) before declining in frequency.

With regard to gender differences in prosocial moral reasoning, there were several findings of interest. Girls preferred stereotypic reasoning and rejected approval-oriented reasoning more than did boys. The former finding was consistent with the suggestion that girls, compared with boys, may be more exposed to global, traitlike verbalizations in socialization opportunities (Carlo et al., 1992). It was less clear why girls did not report more internalized moral reasoning than boys in Part 2 of Study 1 as in the first part and as in prior studies using the PROM (Eisenberg et al., 1995).

Note

1   Both the English and Portugese versions of the PROM may be obtained from Gustavo Carlo on request.

References

Bar-Tal, D., Raviv, A., & Lewis-Levin, T. (1980). The development of altruistic behavior: Empirical evidence. *Developmental Psychology, 16*, 516–524.

Baumrind, D. (1986). Sex differences in moral reasoning: Response to Walker's (1984) conclusion that there are none. *Child Development, 57*, 511–521.

Biaggio, A. M. B. (1976). A developmental study of moral judgment of Brazilian children and adolescents. *Interamerican Journal of Psychology, 10*, 71–78.

Boehnke, K., Silbereisen, R. K., Eisenberg, N., Reykowski, J., & Palmonari, A. (1989). Developmental pattern of prosocial motivation: A cross-national study. *Journal of Cross-Cultural Psychology, 20*, 219–243.

Botenmpo, R., Lobel, S., & Triandis, H. (1990). Compliance and value internalization in Brazil and the United States: Effects of allocentrism and anonymity. *Journal of Cross-Cultural Psychology, 21,* 200–213.

Carlo, G., Eisenberg, N., & Knight, G. P. (1992). An objective measure of prosocial moral reasoning. *Journal of Research on Adolescence, 2,* 331–349.

Colby, A., Kohlberg, L., Gibbs, J., & Lieberman, M. (1983). A longitudinal study of moral judgment. *Monographs of the Society for Research in Child Development, 48* (Serial No. 200).

Eisenberg, N. (1986). *Altruistic emotion, cognition and behavior.* Hillsdale, NJ: Erlbaum.

Eisenberg, N., Boehnke, K., Schuler, P., & Silbereisen, R. K. (1985). The development of prosocial behavior and cognitions in German children. *Journal of Cross-Cultural Psychology, 16,* 69–82.

Eisenberg, N., Carlo, G., Murphy, B., & Van Court, P. (1995). Prosocial development in late adolescence: A longitudinal study. *Child Development, 66,* 1179–1197.

Eisenberg, N., Fabes, R., & Shea, C. (1989). Gender differences in empathy and prosocial moral reasoning: Empirical investigations. In M. M. Brabeck (Ed.), *Who cares? Theory, research, and educational implications of the ethic of care* (pp. 127–143). New York: Praeger.

Eisenberg, N., Miller, P. A., Shell, R., McNalley, S., & Shea, C. (1991). Prosocial development in adolescence: A longitudinal study. *Developmental Psychology, 27,* 849–857.

Eisenberg, N., & Shell, R. (1986). The relation of prosocial moral judgment and behavior in children: The mediating role of cost. *Personality and Social Psychology Bulletin, 12,* 426–433.

Eisenberg, N., Shell, R., Pasternack, J., Lennon, R., Beller, R., & Mathy, R. M. (1987). Prosocial development in middle childhood: A longitudinal study. *Developmental Psychology, 23,* 712–718.

Fuchs, I., Eisenberg, N., Hertz-Lazarowitz, R., & Sharabany, R. (1986). Kibbutz, Israeli City, and American children's moral reasoning about prosocial moral conflicts. *Merrill-Palmer Quarterly, 32,* 37–50.

Gibbs, J. C., Arnold, K. D., Morgan, R. L., Schwartz, E. S., Gavaghan, M. P., & Tappan, M. B. (1984). Construction and validation of a multiple-choice measure of moral reasoning. *Child Development, 55,* 527–536.

Gilligan, C. (1982). *In a different voice: Psychological theory and women's development.* Cambridge, MA: Harvard University.

Gilligan, C., & Attanucci, J. (1988). Two moral orientations: Gender differences and similarities. *Merrill-Palmer Quarterly, 34,* 223–238.

Haidt, J., Koller, S. H., & Dias, M. G. (1993). Affect, culture, and morality, or is it wrong to eat your dog? *Journal of Personality and Social Psychology, 65,* 613–628.

Hofstede, G. (1982). Dimensions of national cultures. In R. Rath, H. S. Asthana, D. Sinha, & J. B. P. Sinha (Eds.), *Diversity and unity in cross-cultural psychology* (pp. 173–187). Lisse, The Netherlands: Swets & Zeitlinger.

Hutz, C. S., De Conti, L., & Vargas, S. (1993). Rules used by Brazilian students in systematic and nonsystematic reward allocation. *Journal of Social Psychology, 134,* 331–338.

Kurtines, W. M., & Pimm, J. B. (1983). The moral development scale: A Piagetian measure of moral judgement. *Educational and Psychological Measurement, 43,* 89–105.

Lang, J. (1988). *Inside development in Latin America: A report from the Dominican Republic, Columbia, and Brazil.* Chapel Hill: University of North Carolina Press.

Poppino, R. E. (1973). *Brazil: The land and people* (2nd ed.). New York: Oxford University Press.

Raviv, A., Bar-Tal, D., & Lewis-Levin, T. (1980). Motivations for donation behavior by boys of three different ages. *Child Development, 51,* 610–613.

Rest, J. (1983). Morality. In P. Mussen (Series Ed.) & J. H. Flavell, & E. Markman (Vol. Eds.), *Handbook of child psychology: Vol. 3. Cognitive development* (pp. 556–629). New York: Wiley.

Selman, R. (1980). *The growth of interpersonal understanding.* New York: Academic Press.

Tietjen, A. (1986). Prosocial reasoning among children and adults in a Papua New Guinea society. *Developmental Psychology, 22,* 861–868.

Walker, L. J. (1991). Sex differences in moral reasoning. In W. M. Kurtines, & J. L. Gewirtz (Eds.), *Handbook of moral behavior and development: Vol. 2. Research* (pp. 333–364). Hillsdale, NJ: Erlbaum.

The Relations Among Identity Development, Self-Consciousness, and Self-Focusing During Middle and Late Adolescence

Introduction

My own research program on adolescent development has focused on the study of identity. I think my interests in identity emerged when I was a teenager. I used to wonder a lot about what I might become. I came from a rather poor family and my father was usually gone. My mother raised my sister, brother, and me, doing the best she could. She worked long hours and we often took care of ourselves. Fortunately, we didn't get into too much trouble and we each found a good way of life. My brother is a businessman, my sister a nurse, and I became a teacher and scientist. But when I was an adolescent I simply couldn't decide if I should work hard and get a lot of education or do something like my father and become a truck driver or laborer. Fortunately, my mother used to say that it doesn't matter what you become as long as you are good at it. So I thought, questioned, searched, and found that I wanted to be a teacher. And here I am today, doing the very thing that I thought I would like to do.

I couldn't resist the opportunity to show you a little of my own work. I hope you won't see this as vanity. I just want to share with you some of what I have loved to study within adolescent development.

The research article I selected shows you a little of how the writings of Erik Erikson have influenced my research. You might recall from my earlier statements that Erikson was one of the first writers that hooked me on the study of adolescence. I hope, as you read my work, that you can see how I have used Erikson to investigate if there is an association between different types of adolescent identity and the state of identity-consciousness. In one study we used self-report measures of self-consciousness. In the other study we used a more experimental approach to test for self-consciousness or self-focusing behavior. We thought the use of both self-report and experimental evidence would strengthen our conclusions.

Again, look for person, context, and occasion dimensions in our research. Are all three of these factors found in or between the two studies? Hope you have fun with us in the Zone! Now get down to your reading and see our enthusiasm for Erikson. Maybe you'll see why he is one of my own personal role models.

Suggested reading

Adams, G. R., and Marshall, S. K. (1996). A developmental social psychology of identity: understanding the person-in-context. *Journal of Adolescence*, 19, 429–442.

FOUR

The Relations Among Identity Development, Self-Consciousness, and Self-Focusing During Middle and Late Adolescence

Gerald R. Adams, Kitty G. Abraham
and Carol Ann Markstrom

A growing body of research is emerging on the study of identity development in middle and late adolescence. Impetus for this research has come largely from Marcia's (1966) work in operationalizing Erikson's (1968) conceptions about identity into four distinct identity categories: diffusion, foreclosure, moratorium, and identity achievement. Adolescents are classified, on the basis of their reported experience of "crisis" and "commitment," into one of the four identity statuses. Identity crisis refers to a psychological process of self-awareness through the exploration of alternatives and a corresponding subjective discomfort that leads to an evaluation of attitudes, values, and behavior. Commitment (toward content of identity) is comprised of self-defined goals, values, or beliefs that provide an individual with purpose, meaning, and direction (Waterman, 1984). At one extreme, identity-achieved adolescents have experienced a crisis period and have established personal commitment, and, at the other extreme, diffused adolescents remain role-confused or disorganized as to commitment and appear uncompelled to ameliorate this psychological state. Adolescents classified as moratorium are experiencing a crisis and are seeking personal commitments; foreclosed adolescents have made commitments without first experiencing crisis (i.e., they have adopted wholesale the commitments of others, usually parents, without testing the fit of these commitments for themselves).

Much of the research on identity formation has focused on classification and prediction of individual differences between the four basic identity statuses (see Marcia, 1980, for a review). Findings reveal that as comparisons are made between less advanced (diffusion, foreclosure) and more advanced (moratorium, identity achievement) identity statuses, corresponding psychological profiles on measures of personality characteristics (such as moral development and locus of control, among others) reflect a parallel pattern of less advanced, or undifferentiated to more advanced or highly differentiated, psychological states (e.g., see Waterman, 1984). Several developmentalists interested in the study of intraindividual similarities and differences perspectives have suggested that patterns of growth from less to higher differentiated identity development are paralleled by corresponding changes in cognitive or social–cognitive development, reflecting increasing maturity in thinking processes (e.g., see Waterman, 1984). Thus, previous research suggests that identity formation may be associated with important thinking and social–cognitive processes (Waterman, 1984).

However, little attention has been given to Erikson's (1968) discussion of the potential nature and quality of the social–cognitive process of self-awareness and self-consciousness proposed to be associated with various stages in the identity-formation process. Erikson proposes that adolescence is associated with ego processes reflecting a state of "identity-consciousness." More specifically, in his theory of the epigenesis of identity formation, he theorizes that undue self-consciousness is the by-product of identity confusion in late adolescence and that positive-identity formation is optimally related to self-certainty, social- and self-assurance, psychological confidence, and a sense of well-being. Indeed, Erikson maintains that severe identity confusion is accompanied by a highly self-conscious and possibly destructive self-preoccupation that manifests itself in overall shame, narcissism, and continual self-testing. Conversely, identity achievement is accompanied by a psychological state of inner assurance, self-direction, and self-certainty. Self-awareness preoccupation, at the more general conceptual level, involves a self-focusing process of centering on the self within the context of others. As such, self-focusing may have little association with an emotional connotation and merely reflects a cognitive focus on the self. In contrast, self-consciousness may include an affective component wherein self-awareness is associated with a conscious process that includes an emotional state of discomfort and self-perceived exposure or vulnerability. Although both self-focusing and self-consciousness are implied in Erikson's writing, self-consciousness is the primary form of self-awareness that is proposed to be associated with identity formation.

Accordingly, we hypothesized that identity-achieved adolescents would be likely to perceive themselves with self-assurance and would anticipate that others would also view their commitments positively and within the context of alternatives; therefore, they would be unselfconsciously willing to reveal themselves to others. In contrast, adolescents who had not undergone the ideal identity-formation process, or had not completed the process of making a self-definition (i.e., diffused, foreclosed, or moratorium youths), would be likely to view themselves negatively and, therefore, be more self-conscious and less willing to reveal information about the self to others. These two hypotheses are supported by studies summarized by Marcia (1980) and Waterman (1984) in which (a) identity-achieved individuals are described as having a high acceptance of self, a stable self-definition, emotional stability, and the capacity for interpersonal perspective-taking, and (b) diffused persons are described as role-confused and as having deep feelings of guilt and rejection.

Study 1

Method

Subjects

The sample consisted of 9th through 12th-grade adolescents attending a high school in the southwestern United States. Of a total of 1,204 students enrolled at the school, 1,076 (89 percent) were in attendance on the designated data-collection day. The majority of these students consisted of two dominant ethnic heritages: Anglo-American and Mexican-American. Because previous research (Abraham, 1983, 1986) has indicated differences in identity development according to ethnic heritages, it was included as a factor in the first study. Eighty-two students who could not be classified into one of the two ethnic heritages (Native Americans, $n = 51$; Blacks, $n = 21$; Orientals, $n = 10$) were eliminated from the sample. One hundred and twenty-four other students who chose not to participate in the study were also self-eliminated from the sample.

The final sample included 870 students: 445 males and 425 females. The distribution by grade was 231 ninth graders (112 males and 119 females), 255 tenth graders (128 males and 127 females), 236 eleventh graders (126 males and 110 females) and 148 twelfth graders (76 males and 72 females). One hundred and sixty of the adolescents were Mexican-American (18.4 percent) and 710 were Anglo-American (81.6 percent). There was a similar proportion of Mexican-American and Anglo-American students at each grade level. Of the 870 students, 773 could be classified into ideological identity-status categories and 767 could be classified into interpersonal identity-status categories. Demographic data completed by the subjects indicated that 50 percent of the subjects' fathers and 62 percent of the subjects' mothers had a high school degree, vocational training (or both), or less education. A greater proportion of Anglo-American fathers and mothers than of Mexican-American fathers and mothers had a college degree (54 percent of Anglo-American fathers compared with 33 percent of Mexican-American fathers, and 41 percent of Anglo-American mothers compared with 24 percent of Mexican-American mothers).

Measures

Ego-identity status. The Extended Measure of Ego Identity Status (EOM-EIS; Grotevant and Adams, 1984) consists of 64 items reflecting the presence or absence of crisis and commitment in both ideological and interpersonal content realms. The ideological or instrumental realm includes content areas of occupation, religion, politics, and philosophical life-style; the interpersonal realm includes the content areas of friendship, dating, recreation, and sex roles. There are two diffusion, two foreclosure, two moratorium, and two identity-achievement items for each of the four ideological and each of the four interpersonal content areas. Raw scale scores for diffusion, foreclosure, moratorium, and identity achievement are derived by summing responses to the appropriate items (1 = *strongly disagree*, 6 = *strongly agree*). Subjects may then be classified into an ideological identity status, or an interpersonal identity status (or both) separately by using scoring rules derived in the development of the EOM-EIS prototype scale (Adams et al., 1979).

Self-consciousness. Self-consciousness, as a measure of self-awareness with negative emotional connotations, was measured using the Elkind and Bowen (1979) assessment of the Imaginary Audience Scale (IAS). The Imaginary Audience Scale consists of 12 items designed to measure adolescents' degree of willingness to reveal themselves to others. Six of the items describe potentially embarrassing situations of a momentary sort, such as going to a party with a grease spot on one's clothes. These items make up the Transient Self Scale. Six other items describe potentially self-revealing situations, such as presenting a report before one's class. These items make up the Abiding Self Scale. For each of the 12 items, subjects chose one of three possible reactions to the situations: (a) an unwillingness to participate (2 points), (b) indifference (1 point), and (c) willingness to participate (no points). For both the Transient Self Scale and the Abiding Self Scale, the range of scores is 0 to 12. Lower scores reflect greater willingness of subjects to expose the transient and the abiding self to others. Evidence on reliability and validity for the IAS has been provided in several studies (Adams and Jones, 1981, 1982; Anolik, 1981; Elkind and Bowen, 1979; Gossens, 1984; Riley et al., 1984).

Procedure

Adolescents were administered the EOM-EIS and the IAS by classroom teachers who had been previously trained by the experimenter to administer the tests. Standard instructions for the tests were read aloud and explained to the adolescents by the teachers. Students did not write their names on their test forms and were assured of anonymity and confidentiality.

Results

Ideological identity status

A significant one-way ANOVA ($p < 0.001$) was observed for comparisons among the four identity statuses for abiding and transient

Table 4.1 Abiding self scale and transient self scale means and standard deviations for individuals classified in ideological-identity status categories

Scale	Identity status			
	Diffusion (*n* = 82)	Foreclosure (*n* = 84)	Moratorium (*n* = 514)	Achievement (*n* = 99)
Abiding self				
M	6.57	6.26	6.44	5.31
SD	2.35	2.44	2.41	2.34
Transient self				
M	4.72	5.84	5.33	4.64
SD	2.65	3.14	2.71	2.34

self-consciousness. Identity-achieved adolescents were significantly less self-conscious (i.e., more inclined to reveal themselves to others) than were diffused, foreclosed, and moratorium adolescents (see table 4.1). Individual mean comparisons (Scheffé tests) revealed that identity-achieved subjects were different from moratorium subjects on both abiding self ($p < 0.01$) and transient self ($p < 0.05$) and from foreclosure subjects on both abiding self ($p < 0.01$) and transient self ($p < 0.01$), but were significantly different from diffusion subjects on abiding self only ($p < 0.01$).

Interpersonal identity status

No significant differences were observed from the one-way ANOVA for interpersonal identity on the abiding or transient self of the Imaginary Audience Scale.

Discussion

The purpose of the first study was to explore the possible intraindividual similarity in development between identity status and self-consciousness in adolescence. The findings suggest that, where ideological development is concerned, identity achievement, rather than diffusion, foreclosure, or moratorium, is associated with decreased self-consciousness. Apparently, the very undergoing of the identity process (i.e., exploring a variety of ideological alternatives, trying them out, and subsequently making commitments to those values and life styles that fit one's personality best) is a corequisite for the development of a sense of self that is highly self-satisfying, that engenders an anticipation of approval by others, and that minimizes anxiety or emotional uneasiness at being the focus of attention in potentially embarrassing or self-revealing situations. Where interpersonal-identity development is concerned, however, the undergoing of the complete identity process (i.e., crisis and commitment) does not appear to predict decreased self-consciousness. Such a finding currently remains unclear and warrants further examination.

Study 2

Method

Subjects

The subjects were 10 males and 10 females, who were identified as being either diffused, foreclosed, in moratorium, or identity-achieved, from a larger sample of 462 subjects. The 80 subjects in the four identity statuses for the ideological domain were different from the 80 subjects for the interpersonal domain. All subjects ($n = 160$) were between 18 and 20 years of age and were enrolled in a college in the western United States.

Procedures and Measures

All subjects completed the EOM-EIS (Grotevant and Adams, 1984) in large classroom settings. Upon selection for the study, they were given the Self-as-Target Questionnaire (Fenigstein, 1984) to complete at home and were asked to return it to their instructor the following day.

The Self-as-Target Questionnaire consists of eight interactional situations in which scenarios are provided about a social event with two alternatives of how the subject might think or act. Subjects were asked to indicate which choice best agreed with their own likely conduct or perceptions. Each of the two choices reflected a self-relevant and nonself-relevant option. The final score from the scenarios resulted in a self-as-target score ranging from 0 to 8. The internal consistency of the items in this study was high ($\alpha = 0.79$) and odd–even reliabilities were excellent ($r = 0.89$).

Approximately three weeks later subjects were asked to complete the laboratory portion of the study within a small group context (10 subjects per group). Using the procedure reported by Fenigstein (1984) to measure susceptibility to the inclusion of seeing oneself as the object of other persons' interest or actions, a measure of the estimation of the likelihood that an event was targeted toward the subject was obtained during the group sessions. Upon arrival subjects were seated in a row of 10 chairs. After completing some bogus experimental forms, it was announced that the experimenter wished to engage in a demonstration and that a volunteer was required. The experimenter then indicated that one of the subjects for participation in the demonstration had already been chosen earlier. No other information was provided about the nature of the demonstration. Eye contact was made one time with each subject and then the experimenter avoided further direct visual contact. Contact was made for approximately 20 s to assure that the subject was likely to perceive being seen by the experimenter, but excessive contact was avoided to create a condition of heightened self-awareness. As Greenwald (1980) has indicated, overperception of the self as a target is a cognitive bias reflecting self-referencing and a corresponding form of self-consciousness. As such, self-referencing should be measurable by the degree to which a person perceives being chosen (self-focused) above chance level in a demonstration context. Therefore, subjects were asked to indicate what was the likelihood on a scale of 0 percent to 100 percent that they had been chosen as the person for the demonstration.

Results

Separate analyses were computed for the identity status domains of ideology or instrumental and interpersonal (social-role) content. A 2×4 (Sex × Identity Status) ANOVA was computed on the dependent measures derived from the Self-as-Target Questionnaire and the likelihood estimate from the demonstration experiment. Significant main effects were observed for both the ideology and interpersonal domains for the identity-status factor ($ps < 0.01$). The interaction and main effect for sex were nonsignificant. The means for the full interaction are

Table 4.2 Association (mean scores) between ideological and interpersonal identity and responses to the Self-as-Target Questionnaire

Group	Identity status			
	Diffusion	Foreclosure	Moratorium	Achievement
		Ideology		
Males	4.2	4.6	3.2	1.3
Females	4.7	3.9	4.4	1.9
Combined	4.4_a	4.2_a	3.8_a	1.6_b
		Interpersonal		
Males	4.7	3.8	2.9	1.7
Females	4.9	3.5	3.6	1.2
Combined	4.8_a	3.6_b	3.2_b	1.4_c

Note: n = 80. Means with shared subscripts are not significantly different; means with different subscripts are significantly different (ps < 0.05 or greater)

Table 4.3 Association between ideological and interpersonal identity and a behavioral estimate of the illusion of Self-as-Target (self-consciousness)

Group	Identity status			
	Diffusion	Foreclosure	Moratorium	Achievement
		Ideology		
Males	22.1	17.8	19.7	10.1
Females	29.5	21.3	19.6	9.3
Combined	25.7_a	19.5_b	19.6_b	9.7_c
		Interpersonal		
Males	33.0	18.7	18.1	11.2
Females	31.2	17.4	17.9	8.7
Combined	32.1_a	18.1_b	18.0_b	9.9_c

Note: n = 80. Identity = status figures for male and female groups are percentages; identity = status figures for combined group are mean scores. Means with shared subscripts are not significantly different; means with different subscripts are significantly different (ps < 0.05)

summarized for both measures in tables 4.2 and 4.3. For the self-focus score from the questionnaire, identity-achieved adolescents were significantly less likely to report self-referencing (focusing) than youths from other identity statuses for both ideological and interpersonal identity. On ideological identity, the diffused, moratorium, and foreclosed youths did not differ in their degree of reported self-focusing; however, for interpersonal identity, diffused youths were significantly more self-focused than foreclosed or moratorium peers. On the behavioral estimate, diffused adolescents were most likely to be self-referencing and identity-achieved youths were most likely to be least self-focused (with foreclosed and moratorium youths falling between the two extremes). Finally, as a concurrent validity check between the two measures of self-focus in this study, a correlation was computed between the raw scores. The correlation for the Self-as-Target Questionnaire and Behavioral Estimate of Being a Target was $r = 0.59$ ($p < 0.05$).

Discussion

The second study replicates and extends the first because it was consistently observed that identity-achieved late adolescents were the least self-focused among the four identity-status comparisons for both self-report and behavioral estimates in a laboratory context. The effect also appears to hold for both ideological and interpersonal forms of identity. Furthermore, some evidence suggests that diffused youths overestimate the importance of self as a target of attention by others. Given other studies that suggest that this over-focus on the self is associated with a cognitive bias in the attribution of causality and ineffective perspective taking (see Greenwald, 1980), these findings may account for why diffused youths are unlikely to have mature and intimate social relations. Likewise, given that they are the least self-focused, identity-achieved youths may have more intimate and involved social relations because of their self-certainty and assurance.

References

Abraham, K. G. (1983). The relation between identity status and locus of control among rural high school students. *Journal of Early Adolescence, 3,* 257–264.

Abraham, K. G. (1986). Ego-identity differences among Anglo-American and Mexican-American adolescents. *Journal of Adolescence, 9,* 151–166.

Adams, G. R., & Jones, R. (1981). Imaginary audience behavior: A validation study. *Journal of Early Adolescence, 1,* 1–10.

Adams, G. R., & Jones, R. (1982). Adolescent egocentrism: Exploration into possible contributions of parent–child relations. *Journal of Youth and Adolescence, 11,* 25–31.

Adams, G. R., Shea, J. A., & Fitch, S. A. (1979). Toward the development of an objective assessment of ego-identity status. *Journal of Youth and Adolescence, 2,* 223–237.

Anolik, S. A. (1981). Imaginary audience behavior and perceptions of parents among delinquent and nondelinquent adolescents. *Journal of Youth and Adolescence, 10,* 443–454.

Elkind, D., & Bowen, R. (1979). Imaginary audience behavior in children and adolescents. *Developmental Psychology, 15,* 38–44.

Erikson, E. H. (1968). *Identity: Youth and crisis.* New York: Norton.

Fenigstein, A. (1984). Self-consciousness and the overperception of self as a target. *Journal of Personality and Social Psychology, 47,* 860–870.

Gossens, L. (1984). Imaginary audience behavior as a function of age, sex and formal operational thinking. *International Journal of Behavioral Development, 7,* 77–93.

Greenwald, A. G. (1980). The totalitarian ego: Fabrication and revision of personal history. *American Psychologist, 35,* 603–618.

Grotevant, H. D., & Adams, G. R. (1984). Development of an objective measure to assess ego identity in adolescence: Validation and replication. *Journal of Youth and Adolescence, 13,* 419–438.

Marcia, J. E. (1966). Development and validation of ego-identity status. *Journal of Personality and Social Psychology, 5,* 551–558.

Marcia, J. E. (1980). Identity in adolescence. In J. Adelson, (Ed.), *Handbook of adolescent psychology.* New York: Wiley.

Riley, T., Adams, G. R., & Nielsen, E. (1984). Adolescent egocentrism: The association between imaginary audience behavior, cognitive development, parental support and rejection. *Journal of Youth and Adolescence, 13,* 401–417.

Waterman, A. S. (1984). *The psychology of individualism.* New York: Praeger.

Classwork and Homework in Early Adolescence: The Ecology of Achievement

Introduction

Each decade a new report comes out on children's and adolescents' achievement. International comparisons are made on adolescents' performance on various tests of achievement or intelligence, or average marks or grades. Mostly, it is reported that academic performance has either declined or remained primarily stable. Then a flurry of magazine articles and editorials in newspapers blame the kids, the schools, or the parents. Sometimes an insightful article is written about the shortcomings of society and its contribution to teenagers' floundering or failures.

As I helped to raise my daughters, schoolwork was always considered important. I can recall helping my children to understand ideas or to discipline their use of time. I can also recall some pretty serious arguments about how much TV they should watch or how much time they should spend studying and reading. I wouldn't let my kids say that they were doing poorly because of bad teaching. I would say, as my mother said to me, if it is worth learning or doing, then you can find a way to understand it.

But when report after report says we aren't doing enough in our schools and that parents need to help discipline their adolescents to study more, it is time to look at the "ecology of achievement." To do just this I selected for your reading a very innovative study that used a combination of methods. But most importantly in the report by Leone and Richards you will be introduced to a technique called the Experience Sampling Method. This method allowed the investigators to measure the amount of time young adolescents spend doing classwork and homework, how they felt about the experience while actually doing it, and who were their companions (if any) while doing homework.

We often think that homework increases achievement. And we typically assume that while kids are in school they are working and learning. But are these common sense truths or are they myths? Go with me into the Zone and find the answers to these questions. While you are there, look to see if there is use of person, context, and occasion in the report you are reading. When you finish the report and return from the Zone, ask yourself if what was observed in a sample in the midwestern region of the United States fits your own recollections and feelings. If there is congruity between what you experienced and felt with the facts and observations reported by the investigators of the report, do you think there are policy implications? What might they be?

Suggested reading

Jencks, C., Smith, M., Acland, H., Jo Bane, M., Cohen, D., Gintis, H., Heyns, B., and Michelson, S. (1972). *Inequality: a reassessment of the effect of family and schooling in America*. New York: Basic Books, Inc.

FIVE

Classwork and Homework in Early Adolescence: The Ecology of Achievement

Carla M. Leone and
Maryse H. Richards

Introduction

While all experiences influence children's development, school is one of the few activities specifically intended to do so: education is designed to socialize children to become productive contributors to society. Despite this intent, the recent government investigation, *A Nation at Risk* (National Commission on Excellence in Education, 1983), indicated that US schools may not be adequately preparing children for today's society, especially in comparison to the educational preparation of students from other industrialized nations. In particular, the report questioned the amount of time US school children currently spend on schoolwork, including both classwork and homework.

The present study investigates both the amount of time young adolescents spend doing schoolwork, and the quality of this time: students' companions while doing homework and their inner subjective experience during both classwork and homework. The relationship between these variables and students' academic performance is also examined, since academic performance is one measure of how well students are adapting to societal expectations.

Consistent with the recommendations of the *A Nation at Risk* report, academic performance has been found to be related to the amount of time spent on classwork (Wahlberg and Frederick, 1982). Results of a recent meta-analysis of previous studies (Paschal et al., 1984) and of a national longitudinal study (Keith and Page, 1985) also indicated that the amount of time spent on homework is positively related to achievement.

Despite the apparent benefits of increased schoolwork time, evidence indicates that US children spend relatively little time doing classwork and homework – substantially less than students from other industrialized countries (Csikszentmihalyi and Larson, 1984). The length of the school day and year in the typical US school is shorter than in many other nations (Karweit, 1984). Moreover, two recent classroom observation studies (McIntyre et al., 1983; Sanford and Evertson, 1983) found that of currently available class time, US young adolescents were "engaged" or "on-task" for only 72–77 percent of the time. Finally, recent estimates of amount of time spent on homework vary from 2.3 hours per week for 5th and 6th graders (Timmer et al., 1985) to 5.9 hours per week for 7th and 8th graders (Patton et al., 1983). The present study will attempt to confirm these previous estimates of time spent on classwork and homework, using an alternative measure of time use.

While the amount of time spent on schoolwork is clearly important, the quality of experience during these activities may also affect the socialization process. An angry, resentful student reluctantly doing homework alone in his or her bedroom is likely to be having a very different learning experience than a student in a more positive mood doing homework with a supportive parent. However, it appears that only two studies have investigated the circumstances in which adolescents do homework or how these variables relate to students' academic performance. In the first, reading achievement was found unrelated to the presence of distractors such as music or TV during study (Patton et al., 1983), while the other provided case study data that suggested that the quality of family interaction can either enhance or interfere with homework's effectiveness (McDermott et al., 1984). Both studies called for additional research on the contexts in which homework is done.

Subjective experience, as assessed with one-time measures of attitudes toward school or achievement motivation (e.g., Ugurolglu and

Wahlberg, 1979), has been found to be significantly related to achievement. However, such one-time measures reveal little about students' actual immediate experience while engaged in school-work. In contrast, a relatively new measure, the Experience Sampling Method (Csikszentmihalyi and Larson, 1987), is designed to assess feelings during ongoing daily life rather than in retrospect. The Experience Sampling Method allows an immediate assessment of moods during the activity itself, rather than in retrospect. In a previous study using this measure (Csikszentmihalyi and Larson, 1984), high school students were found to experience more negative affect, lower arousal, and less motivation when doing classwork and homework as compared to other daily activities. The latter study and a previous analysis of the present sample (Leone, 1989) both reported that students' overall daily subjective experience was related to their academic performance.

Building on this previous literature, the present report provides a detailed examination of moments in young adolescents' daily lives when they reported doing classwork or homework. Utilizing the Experience Sampling Method to obtain information unavailable through conventional methods of assessment, the study investigates the quantity and quality of time young adolescents spend engaged in learning activities. To examine the socializing influence of school, the study identifies age differences in these variables and investigates their relationship to students' academic performance.

Method

Sample

The sample consisted of 401 public school students in Grades 5–9 who were randomly selected and agreed to participate in a larger study of early adolescence. The sample was stratified by grade and sex, and was drawn equally from two suburban communities: one an urban, working-class, blue-collar community, and the other an outlying, middle to upper middle-class, white-collar community. The final sample represents 75 percent of the total number of randomly selected students ($n = 532$) who were invited to participate in the study.

Measures

Experience Sampling Method

The Experience Sampling Method was used to assess the three major independent variables of the study: the amount of time spent on schoolwork, the environmental contexts in which homework was done, and students' inner experience (moods, attention, and motivation) while doing classwork and homework. Participants carried an electronic pager for one week and filled out brief self-reports when signaled randomly every 2 hours during the day between 7.30 a.m. and 9.30 p.m.

The self-report items assessed what the respondents were thinking, what they were doing, where they were, and who they were with when signaled. The adolescents were also asked to rate the following aspects of their experience when signaled: their affect (three items such as happy–unhappy, on a 7-point scale), their arousal (three items such as strong–weak, on a 7-point scale), their motivation or desire to be doing the activity (one item, 10-point scale), and how well they were paying attention (one item, 10-point scale).

These subjective experience variables were standardized in order to examine students' experience during classwork and homework relative to their own overall experience, or to control for individual differences in overall experience. Thus standardized scores allowed us to focus on the differential experience during a particular activity as opposed to the overall experience of the individuals. To do so, z scores were calculated for each pager response by subtracting each person's average score and dividing by each person's standard deviation. These measures have been used in several previous studies and have been found to have adequate psychometric properties (Csikszentmihalyi and Larson, 1987).

Students were coded as doing classwork only if they reported a classwork activity in response to the question "What were you doing?" Thus classwork excludes times when students were in a classroom but reported doing something other than classwork. In addition, only academic classes were included in the present analysis: participation in vocation classes, art, physical education, etc. was not included as classwork.[1] "Homework" was coded if students reported doing academic assignments outside of school *or* if they reported "doing homework" while in school.

Academic performance

Students' current academic performance was assessed by computing their academic grade point average (GPA) and then controlling for the influence of their previous performance, school, grade level, and sex. GPAs were computed from report card grades in academic subjects only (see note 1) for the quarter students participated and the preceding three quarters. Previous performance was controlled in order to assess the degree to which subjects were currently achieving at a level consistent with their demonstrated potential. Composite percentile scores on standardized achievement tests were used as the measure of previous performance, with the Survey of Basic Skills (SBS; Science Research Associates, 1985) used for 5th–8th grades and the Comprehensive Test of Basic Skills (CTBS, McGraw-Hill, 1982) used for 9th graders. Finally, school, grade level, and sex were controlled to adjust for potential differences in grading practices based on school, and differing norms by grade and gender.

Following the procedure proposed by Thorndike (1963), a regression equation was computed using test scores, school, grade level, and gender to predict actual GPA scores. Residual scores for each student, representing the variance in GPA *not* accounted for by the control variables (Leone, 1988), provided the measure of academic performance.

Because individual students each had very few responses in which they reported doing homework, the correlation between each student's homework time and academic performance was not useful; therefore, students were divided into groups based on their academic performance, and the time use of overall groups was compared. Students whose residual score was more than one standard deviation below the mean residual score (zero) were classified as "underachievers" ($n = 57$), those with a residual score within one standard deviation of the mean were classified as "congruent achievers" ($n = 253$), and those with a residual score more than one standard deviation above the mean were classified as "overachievers"[2] ($n = 45$; Thorndike, 1963; Yule, 1973). Preliminary analyses revealed that underachievers' actual GPAs ranged from (the equivalent of) 0.0 to 3.0, with an average of 1.5; actual GPAs for congruent achievers ranged from 1.0 to 3.5 with an average of 2.5; and overachievers' actual GPAs ranged from 2.0 to 4.0 with an average of 3.5.

Results

Time spent on classwork and homework

Students reported spending 15.5 percent of their waking time or approximately $15\frac{1}{2}$ hours per week doing classwork, and 6.4 percent of their time or $6\frac{1}{2}$ hours per week doing homework (table 5.1). As students reported being in an academic class approximately 21 hours per week, results indicate that they were actually doing classwork for 71 percent of the time they were in academic classes. These findings are quite consistent with the previous findings described earlier (McIntyre et al., 1983; Patton et al., 1983; Sanford and Evertson, 1983).

Tests of the standard error of the differences between proportions (Loether and McTavish, 1974) were conducted to identify significant differences between groups. Results revealed that both time spent on classwork and time spent on homework decreased significantly with age for girls but remained fairly stable across age groups for boys (table 5.1). Thus, although time spent on schoolwork might be expected to increase as students move into more advanced grades, present findings reveal an opposite pattern.

Overall, girls spent significantly more time on homework and significantly less time on classwork than did boys. The former finding is consistent with previous studies (Timmer et al., 1985), but the latter finding was unexpected. In addition, the sex difference in homework was reversed for 9th graders, as 9th-grade boys reported doing homework significantly more often than did 9th-grade girls.

Time spent on learning activities was expected to be significantly related to children's academic performance after controlling for their previous performance and other variables. Tests of the standard error of the difference between proportions revealed that, contrary to expectations, time spent doing classwork was unrelated to academic performance. However, as expected, similar tests revealed that time spent on homework was positively associated with school performance, as shown in figure 5.1. Students in the highest achievement group (overachievers) reported doing homework significantly more often than did students in the other two groups[3] ($p < 0.05$). Moreover, while homework decreased with age for underachievers and congruent achievers ($p < 0.05$), overachievers of all age groups spent similar amounts of time doing

Table 5.1 Percent of time spent on schoolwork[a]

	Girls				Boys			
	Grade				Grade			
	5 and 6	7 and 8	9	Total	5 and 6	7 and 8	9	Total
Total number of self-reports	3,038.0	3,294.0	1,448.0	7,780.0	3,000.0	2,947.0	1,149.0	7,096.0
Classwork	16.6	14.5	12.1[bc]	14.9	16.3	16.0	15.4[d]	16.0[d]
Homework	7.3	7.4	5.1[bc]	6.9	6.2[d]	5.3[d]	6.5[d]	5.9[d]

[a] Table shows the percentage of time participants reported doing each activity, based on the total number of self-reports (n = 14,876)
[b] Significantly different (p < 0.05) from the next youngest age group, based on the standard error of the difference between proportions
[c] Significantly different (p < 0.05) from the 5th and 6th graders
[d] Significantly different (p < 0.05) from the girls

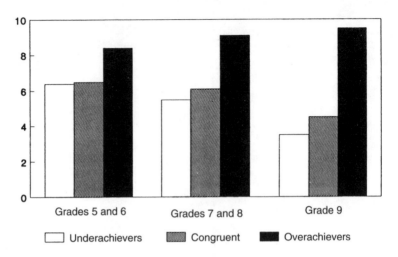

Figure 5.1 Percent of time spent on homework by achievement group
and grade

homework. Hence, it appears that the age trend toward disengagement
from schoolwork applies only to the lower achieving groups.

Overall, these results reveal that students spend relatively little time
engaged in the learning activities intended to prepare them to function
productively in society. Moreover, although time spent on homework
appears to enhance learning, time spent doing homework did not
increase with age and in fact was found to decrease with age for girls.

Companions during homework

In addition to the quantity of time spent on homework, the present
study was designed to examine the quality of this time, including the
contexts in which students do homework. Students' companions during
homework were expected to affect their experience of homework and
thus, presumably, their academic performance.

Students' companions during homework were found to differ considerably by age and sex (table 5.2). On the average, girls reported doing
approximately one-third of their homework alone and slightly less than
one-third with a family member, with the remaining portion divided
roughly equally between homework done in class and with friends. This

Table 5.2 Percent of time spent doing homework with different companions[a]

	Girls				Boys			
	Grade				Grade			
	5 and 6	7 and 8	9	Total	5 and 6	7 and 8	9	Total
Number of self-reports during homework	204.0	229.0	67.0	503.0	174.0	147.0	68.0	389.0
Companions								
Alone	30.9	38.1	40.3	35.4	29.1	44.5	57.4[cd]	39.8
With a parent	7.8	7.3	4.5[bc]	7.2	7.4	5.6	14.7[bcd]	8.0
With other family members	27.5	15.9[b]	26.9[b]	22.1	29.1	11.3[b]	4.4[bcd]	18.3
In class	19.1	28.4[b]	13.4[b]	22.5	30.9[d]	31.4	17.6[bc]	28.8
With friends	14.7	10.4	14.9	12.8	3.4[d]	7.2	5.9[d]	5.1
Total	100.0	100.0	100.0	100.0	100.0	100.0	100.0	100.0

[a] Table shows the percentage of time participants reported being with different companions, of the total number of self-reports in which they reported doing homework (n = 889)

[b] Significantly different (p < 0.05) from the next youngest age group, based on the standard error of the difference between proportions

[c] Significantly different (p < 0.05) from the 5th and 6th graders

[d] Significantly different (p < 0.05) from the girls

pattern was quite stable across age groups for girls, with two exceptions: (1) 7th- and 8th-grade girls did more homework in class and less with families relative to older and younger girls, and (2) there was a trend ($p < 0.10$) toward older girls doing homework alone more often than younger girls, again based on tests of the standard error of the differences between proportions.

In contrast to the fairly stable pattern across age groups for girls, tests of the standard error of the differences between proportions revealed that boys' companions during homework differed substantially by grade. For 5th and 6th graders, boys' homework companions were similar to those of girls (described above), except that the boys did a much greater percentage of homework in class and rarely did homework with friends. However, older boys did homework alone more often than younger boys, so that by 9th grade boys reported spending well over half their homework time alone, considerably more than the percentage for 9th-grade girls. Older boys were also more likely to do homework with one parent than were younger boys and girls of all age groups. Lastly, as homework done alone or with one parent increased for boys, homework done in class or with other family members significantly decreased.

To determine if certain homework companions were associated with better academic performance, the companions typically reported by students in the three achievement groups were compared. There were no significant differences between groups on homework done alone, in class, or with friends. However, adequate and overachievers were found to be significantly more likely to do homework with family members than were underachievers[4] (table 5.3). Overachievers also reported doing homework alone with a parent significantly more often than did students in the two lower groups.[5] Since grade and sex differences in GPA were controlled, the differences in homework companions between achievement groups cannot be explained by the grade and sex differences in homework companions; rather, the differences appear to reflect a true relationship between companions during homework and school performance.

These findings extend considerably previous studies that have focused only on the amount of time spent on homework. Overall, young adolescents were found to do homework primarily alone or in class, although homework done with family members was associated with better academic performance.

Table 5.3 Percent of time spent with different homework companions by achievement group

	Underachievers	Adequate achievers	Overachievers
Number of students	57.0	253.0	45.0
Number of self-reports during homework[a]	81.0	519.0	141.0
Companions			
Alone	43.2	38.0	37.0
With a parent	6.1	5.2	13.3[bc]
With other family members	9.9	20.4[b]	18.7[c]
In class	29.6	26.6	22.1
With friends	11.1	9.8	8.9
Total	100.0	100.0	100.0

[a] *Due to missing achievement data, 148 of the total of 889 "homework" pager responses were excluded from this analysis*
[b] *Significantly different ($p < 0.05$) from the next lowest group, based on the standard error of the difference between proportions*
[c] *Significantly different ($p < 0.05$) from the underachievers*

Subjective experience during classwork and homework

Lastly, the present study proposed that adolescents' inner subjective experience during schoolwork would also affect their school performance. Subjective experience during classwork and homework as compared to other activities was examined first, followed by a comparison of experience during different homework contexts.

Subjective experience during classwork and homework vs. other activities

Three-way analyses of variance revealed no significant interactions between type of activity and grade or sex, for any of the four subjective experience variables (affect, arousal, motivation, and attention), but significant main effects for type of activity emerged for all four variables. However, since this analysis was based on an *n* of 14,876 self-reports, it was unclear whether the highly significant differences reflected meaningful differences. Therefore, mean *z* scores were computed for each subject for each of the four experience variables (affect, activation, motivation, and attention) in each of the four activities (homework, classwork, maintenance, and leisure), to allow comparisons based on an *n* of 401 students. Separate paired *t* tests were then conducted, based on an *n* of 401 students, in which mean subjective experience during homework was compared to mean experience during each of the other three activities.

Results are presented in table 5.4. Affect, arousal, and motivation during homework differed significantly from the same variables during classwork, maintenance, and leisure. Thus, regardless of their age or sex, students' moods while doing homework were strikingly lower than those during any other activity, including classwork.

The relationship between relative subjective experience and academic performance was then examined. Contrary to predictions, *z* scores of subjective experience during classwork and homework did not differ significantly by achievement group. Thus, results indicated that underachievers, adequate achievers, and overachievers all felt similarly negative during homework relative to their experience during other activities.

Subjective experience while doing homework with different companions

Students of all ages reported the highest relative levels of affect and arousal when doing homework with friends and the lowest levels when doing homework alone (table 5.5), consistent with the overall relationship between companions and subjective states. However, it is notable that students were most attentive to homework when completing it with a parent and least attentive when doing so with friends, although this difference did not quite attain significance. These findings appear to partially explain why children who did homework with their parents were found to earn better grades: working with parents may lead to better attention without the more negative experience involved in doing homework alone.

In sum, both the amount of time spent on homework and the contexts in which students did homework were found to vary with grade

Table 5.4 Subjective experience by activity[a]

	Activity				Tests		
	(1) Homework	(2) Classwork	(3) Maintenance	(4) Leisure	T_{1-2}	T_{1-3}	T_{1-4}
Affect[c]	−0.30	0.00	−0.06	0.07	−5.94[b]	−4.93[b]	−7.69[b]
Arousal	−0.32	−0.07	−0.06	0.10	−5.22[b]	−5.28[b]	−9.02[b]
Attention	−0.07	−0.09	−0.13	0.11	0.37	1.12	−3.80[b]
Motivation	−0.64	−0.61	0.09	0.29	−0.57	14.91[b]	−19.63[b]

[a] *Mean subjective experience z scores were computed for each subject for each of the four activities. For this analysis, results are therefore based on an n of 401 subjects rather than on the n of 14,876 self-reports. Tabled values represent mean z scores computed across subjects*
[b] $p < 0.001$
[c] *Since figures represent standardized z scores, all standard deviations are approximately 1.00*

Table 5.5 Subjective experience during homework by companions[a]

	Companions during homework						
	Alone $n = 296^{b}$	With a parent $n = 59^{b}$	With family $n = 159^{b}$	In class $n = 82^{b}$	With friends $n = 189^{b}$	F	$p <$
Affect[c]	−0.57	−0.25	−0.23	−0.03	0.04	14.40	0.001
Arousal	−0.47	−0.39	−0.26	−0.12	−0.08	6.11	0.001
Attention	−0.02	0.14	0.02	−0.06	−0.20	2.02	0.09
Motivation	−0.59	−0.66	−0.47	−0.68	−0.64	1.07	ns

[a] *Values represent z scores*
[b] *ns represent the number of self-reports in each category. Due to missing subjective experience data, 104 of the 889 "homework" self-reports were not included in this analysis*
[c] *Since figures represent standardized z scores, all standard deviations are approximately 1.00*

and to be significantly associated with students' academic performance (even after controlling for the influence of previous performance). However, inner subjective experience during classwork and homework (especially homework) relative to experience during other activities was similarly negative at all ages and was unrelated to academic performance. High achievers appear to spend more time on homework as they get older despite the accompanying negative affect, while the remaining students do even less in the higher grades, perhaps to avoid the negative experience.

Discussion

How well are school-related activities preparing children for adulthood? The present study examined the amount of time children and young adolescents spent engaged in schoolwork, as well as the quality of this time – their companions and inner subjective experience while doing academic tasks. The socializing influence of school was assessed by examining grade differences in these variables and their relationship to academic performance.

Present findings concur with the results of previous studies and with a recent national report: increased study time was associated with better academic performance. Time is needed to acquire the skills, knowledge, and attitudes necessary for success in our technologically sophisticated society and to compete in a world market that is increasingly technical. However, the young adolescents of our study spent only approximately 21.5 percent of their time or about 21½ hours per week engaged in classwork or homework. In contrast, Japanese and Russian children reportedly spend over 50 hours per week in school or studying (Japanese Finance Ministry, 1980; Zuzanek, 1980). Although these figures are administrative estimates and not directly comparable to the present study's measure of actual engaged time, in a more recent study of 1st- and 5th-grade American, Chinese, and Japanese students, the American children were found to spend less time in class, on task, and doing homework than did Asian students (Stevenson et al., 1986). Moreover, if school is expected to prepare the child to enter the adult world of 40-hour workweeks, the maturing child would be expected to spend gradually more time on school activities. In contrast, we found time on academic tasks decreased in the higher grades.

These results concur with findings from a similar study of high school students who spent 26 hours a week actually doing academic tasks, including both classwork and homework (Csikszentmihalyi and Larson, 1984). This is only slightly more time than our children report studying, and much less than the number of hours expected to be devoted to work as an adult. Thus it might be concluded that the socializing influence of school on development is not increasing and may actually be declining as children move toward adulthood.

In addition to the amount of time spent on schoolwork, students' subjective experience during this time presumably reflects the socializing influence of school activities. Ideally, positive learning experiences would lead to increasing intrinsic enjoyment of productive activity with age. However, our results indicate that the experience of schoolwork is not a positive one for these children, regardless of grade.

Homework was found to be especially noxious in terms of mood, as students reported feeling more unhappy, lethargic, and disinterested during homework than during other activities. Even students performing well academically reported similar negative moods during homework suggesting that they achieve despite their negative moods rather than because they enjoy the activity more. Experience during classwork was generally more neutral, similar to the experience during maintenance tasks (e.g., eating, doing chores), except that desire to be doing schoolwork was lower during school. These findings are again comparable to those reported in the comparison of American, Chinese, and Japanese elementary school students; Asian children were found to enjoy school and homework significantly more than did the American children. In addition, the study found that older American children disliked school more than did younger American students, a decline not found in the Asian children (Stevenson et al., 1986).

Although schoolwork would be expected to demand more concentration than many other activities, students' attention levels during schoolwork were similar to attention during maintenance tasks, and in fact were lower during schoolwork than during leisure activities. These findings indicate that students rarely pay close attention or concentrate hard on schoolwork. Thus, in addition to spending relatively little time on schoolwork, students do not appear to exert much effort when they do study. Overall, the experience of schoolwork does not appear intrinsically motivating or one that would facilitate an internalization of work-related values.

In contrast to these findings, students' companions during homework may reflect increasing internal motivation in the higher grades. Both boys and girls spend more time alone doing homework in the 9th relative to the 5th and 6th grades, and less time doing it in class. This developmental trend may reflect a greater capacity to engage in homework without the structure provided by adults and the time frame of school.

However, while older students report doing more homework, doing homework alone is less intrinsically rewarding (as indicated by the fact that affect is lowest when doing homework alone) and is not associated with better academic performance. Rather, homework done with a parent or the family present was associated with the highest attention levels and better academic performance. Thus, while completing homework alone may reflect increasing autonomy, it appears that young adolescents still benefit from parental structure around homework tasks. Unfortunately these data do not allow us to determine the direction of influence; overachievers may also seek out parents while doing homework more often than underachievers do. These findings speak to the importance of parental involvement in their children's education, particularly on the day-to-day basis of overseeing their academic assignments.

In addition to these age differences, several significant sex differences were also noted. Although girls did not differ from boys in achievement or in the patterns that facilitated achievement, older girls, relative to older boys, did less homework and experienced different companionship while doing academic tasks. In particular, younger girls did more homework than boys, but by 9th grade girls reported doing less homework than did boys, which has not been previously reported. While this finding may be unique to this sample, it also may reflect the sensitivity of the Experience Sampling Method. While girls have often recalled doing as much homework as boys, the actual amount may be different. Results of a study of the same data set indicate that girls spent more time socializing as they moved into the junior high and high school grades, which may account for the decreased time spent on schoolwork.

Girls were also more likely to do homework with friends and with family members (other than one parent alone) than were boys. Consistent with notions that females tend to be more interpersonal in their approach to life (e.g., Gilligan, 1982), these young adolescent girls may feel more comfortable doing homework in contexts where others are around. In addition, older girls were less likely to do homework with a parent alone than are younger girls. A different grade-related pattern described the boys' companionship: older boys, relative to younger, reported doing more homework with one parent present and alone and less with other family. By 9th grade, girls were doing more homework with family and friends, and less alone or with one parent present relative to 9th-grade boys. Although girls seemed to be doing as well academically as were the boys at this time, future research is needed to determine if the less homework time with one parent eventually leads to decreased academic achievement.

Overall, a detailed examination of the experience of school-based learning activities from the perspective of children and young adolescents reveals that these activities do not appear to be providing optimal learning experiences. The present study is consistent with several recent studies that have raised concerns about the effectiveness of the current educational system in preparing our youth to function optimally in today's society (National Commission on Excellence in Education, 1983). Results suggest a need for increased learning time, increased parental involvement in education, and education approaches that foster greater intrinsic enjoyment of learning as children get older. Toward these ends, continued research emphasizing the qualitative as well as quantitative aspects of learning time appears needed.

Notes

1 Nonacademic courses were not included mainly because they were not graded on the regular 4.00 GPA scale and thus could not be easily included in computing GPAs. Lack of inclusion is not meant to imply that these courses are not important or useful.

2 The term "overachievers" was used merely for consistency with convention and is not meant to imply that these students are achieving to excess.

3 When students were grouped based on GPA alone, *without* controlling for achievement test scores and other variables, a similar finding emerged: students in the highest GPA group were found to spend a significantly greater percentage of time doing homework than those in the middle or lowest GPA group.

4 Again, a similar finding emerged when students were grouped by GPA only, without including control variables: students in the lowest GPA group were found to do a significantly smaller percentage of homework with family members than were students in the two higher groups ($p < 0.05$), based on the standard error of the difference between proportions.

5 When controls on GPA were omitted, students in the lowest GPA group were found to do homework with a parent only significantly less often than students in either of the two higher groups.

References

Csikszentmihalyi, M., & Larson, R. (1984). *Being Adolescent*. Basic Books, New York.

Csikszentmihalyi, M., & Larson, R. (1987). The experience sampling method. *J. Nervous Mental Dis.* 175: 526–536.

Gilligan, C. (1982). *In a Different Voice*. Harvard University Press, Cambridge.

Japanese Finance Ministry. (1980). *White Paper on Adolescence*. Printing Office, Tokyo.

Karweit, N. (1984). Time on task reconsidered: Synthesis of research on time and learning. *Educat. Leader.* 41: 32–35.

Keith, T. Z., & Page, E. B. (1985). Homework works at school: National evidence for policy changes. *School Psychol. Review* 14: 351–359.

Leone, C. (1988). *Family Variables, Subjective States, and Academic Performance in Young Adolescence*. Unpublished doctoral dissertation, Loyola University of Chicago, Chicago, IL.

Loether, H., & McTavish, D. (1974). *Inferential Statistics for Sociologists*. Allyn & Bacon, Boston.

McDermott, R. P., Goldman, S. V., & Varenne, H. (1984). When school goes home: Some problems in the organization of homework. *Teachers College Rec.* 85: 391–409.

McGraw-Hill, Inc. (1982). *Comprehensive Test of Basic Skills*. McGraw-Hill, Monterey, CA.

McIntyre, D. J., Copenhaver, R. W., Byrd, D. M., & Norris, W. R. (1983). A study of engaged student behavior within classroom activities during mathematics class. *J. Educat. Res.* 77: 55–59.

National Commission on Excellence in Education. (1983). *A Nation at Risk: The Imperative for National Reform*. US Government Printing Office, Washington, DC.

Paschal, R. A., Weinstein, T., & Wahlberg, H. J. (1984). J. Educat. Res. 78: 97–104.

Patton, J. E., Stinard, T. A., & Routh, D. K. (1983). Where do children study? *J. Educat. Res.* 76: 280–286.

Sanford, J. P., & Evertson, C. M. (1983). Time use and activities in junior high classes. *J. Educat. Res.* 76: 140–147.

Science Research Associates. (1985). *SRA Survey of Basic Skills*. Science Research Associates, CA.

Stevenson, H. W., Lee, S., & Stigler, J. W. (1986). Mathematics achievement of Chinese, Japanese, and American children. *Science* 231: 693–699.

Thorndike, R. L. (1963). *The Concepts of Over- and Under-Achievement*. Columbia University Teacher's College Bureau of Publications, New York.

Timmer, S. G., Eccles, J., & Juster, O'Brien, K. (1985). How children use time. In

Juster, F. T. & Stafford, F. P. (Eds.), *Time, Goods, & Well-Being*. Institute for Social Research, University of Michigan, Ann Arbor.

Ugurolglu, M., & Wahlberg, H. (1979). Motivation and achievement: A quantitative synthesis. *Ame. Educat. Res. J.* 16: 375–389.

Wahlberg, H. J., & Frederick, W. C. (1982). Instructional time and learning. *Encyclopedia of Educational Research*, 2: 917–924.

Yule, W. (1973). Differential prognosis of reading backwardness and specific reading retardation. *British Journal of Educational Psychology*, 43: 244–248.

Zuzanek, J. (1980). *Work and Leisure in the Soviet Union: A Time-Budget Analysis*. Praeger, New York.

Longitudinal Adjustment Patterns of Boys and Girls Experiencing Early, Middle, and Late Sexual Intercourse

Introduction

Sex! The word that strikes fear into the hearts of parents of adolescents. Yet it is a natural part of being human. However, parents often worry, and rightfully so, that their adolescents might begin too early. Often parents are less afraid of their children having sexual intercourse than of their children becoming pregnant. I think that parents and teenagers alike need to worry a little about both.

With the onset of puberty come sexual desires, sex appeal, and sexual fantasies. In days when adulthood began with reproductive ability, and adolescence was a brief or even non-existent life stage, the need for early reproductive capacity was part of survival for the total population. However, with an extended adolescence, greater demands for education, and less work options and opportunities for youth, the implications for early experience of sexual intercourse become more obvious and potentially more detrimental.

The research report by Bingham and Crockett examines the adjustment patterns of both boys and girls who experience sexual intercourse at various times in their adolescent life. The sample includes a group of white adolescent teenagers in a rural setting of Pennsylvania. The study contrasts the predictive utility of two very different theories. Problem behavior theory predicts that adolescents' problems occur as a broad behavioral syndrome – where problem behaviors and sexual intercourse occur together. It assumes that this behavioral syndrome provides teenagers with an opportunity to achieve developmental objectives that are not easily attained otherwise. Further, this theory predicts that more problem behaviors and less conventional behavior are associated with transition proneness or early sexual experiences. In comparison, stage termination theory assumes that successful growth or advancement from one stage to another requires a certain minimal level of maturation. If a transition, for example from a non-coital to a coital relationship, occurs too early, then negative adjustment and consequences will occur for a teenager. This means that adolescents need to be ready to advance to the next stage if they are not to be compromised by assuming a new behavior.

I believe you will find this study to be very interesting. It investigates the use of problem behavior theory and its value in predicting poor adjustment. The investigators examine the use of a stage termination model to see if sexual experience is associated with issues of timing. And the study includes a test of the sexual double standard where negative consequences are hypothesized for early initiation by girls but not boys.

So now you can re-enter the Twilight Zone of Adolescence and read about sex. Who isn't interested in sex anyhow? When you read this study and analyze its features, look for how the issue of occasion is considered in this study. Of course, it will be easy to see that the person variable is gender. Can you find a context component to this study too? Enjoy the journey.

Suggested reading

Udry, R. J. (1990). Hormonal and social determinants of adolescent sexual initiation. In J. Bancroft, and J. Machover Reinisch (Eds.). *Adolescence and puberty* (pp. 70–87). New York: Oxford University Press.

SIX

Longitudinal Adjustment Patterns of Boys and Girls Experiencing Early, Middle, and Late Sexual Intercourse

C. Raymond Bingham and
Lisa J. Crockett

During the current century, adolescents' sexual attitudes and behaviors have changed dramatically, resulting in an increased incidence of adolescent sexual intercourse and a decreased age at first intercourse for both boys and girls (Forrest and Singh, 1990; Zelnik and Kantner, 1980). Adolescents' increased participation in sexual intercourse places them at risk for a variety of undesirable physiological outcomes, including unintended pregnancy (Jones et al., 1986; Zelnik and Kantner, 1980), sexually transmitted disease, and AIDS (Bingham, 1989; Chilman, 1980; D'Augelli and Bingham, 1993; Zelnik and Kantner, 1980). The psychosocial consequences of adolescent sexual intercourse, however, are less well understood.

Research has provided consistent evidence of an association between adolescent sexual behavior and several aspects of psychosocial development. Generally, adolescents who initiate sexual intercourse early experience greater psychosocial risk, including more problem behavior and substance use, disrupted family and parental relationships, and poor school performance (Billy et al., 1988; Crockett et al., 1996; Day, 1992; Dorius et al., 1993; R. Jessor et al., 1983; S. L. Jessor and Jessor, 1977). However, current understanding of the associations between adolescent sexual intercourse and psychosocial development is limited by the cross-sectional nature of most of the research conducted to date. In particular, it is unclear whether timing of first sexual intercourse has psychosocial consequences or simply psychosocial correlates. The present research tests these alternatives and extends the existing literature in two ways. First, it moves beyond the prediction of first sexual intercourse by using a longitudinal design to investigate the antecedent–consequent relation between timing of first intercourse and subsequent psychosocial development. Second, whereas the majority of research on adolescent sexual behavior has used urban and suburban samples, the present research examines sexual behavior among rural adolescents.

Correlates of Adolescent Sexual Behavior

Problem behavior

Research has consistently identified an association between adolescent sexual behavior and other socially proscribed behaviors. In general, adolescent involvement in deviance, alcohol use and abuse, and illicit drug use has been found to predict earlier first sexual intercourse, both cross-sectionally (Verner and Stewart, 1974) and longitudinally (Crockett et al., 1996; R. Jessor et al., 1983; S. L. Jessor and Jessor, 1977; Rosenbaum and Kandel, 1990). Longitudinal research has indicated that substance use predicts the transition to adolescent sexual involvement (R. Jessor et al., 1983; S. L. Jessor and Jessor, 1977); however, evidence regarding the temporal sequencing of problem behavior involvement and sexual intercourse is mixed, with some research suggesting that substance use precedes sexual intercourse (R. Jessor et al., 1983; S. L. Jessor and Jessor, 1977; Mott and Haurin, 1988; Rosenbaum and Kandel, 1990), other research suggesting that sexual intercourse precedes substance use (Dorius et al., 1993; Mott and Haurin, 1988), and still other evidence suggesting that the temporal ordering of substance use and sexual behavior varies by substance (Dorius et al., 1993).

Conventional behaviors

Educational attitudes and behaviors are associated with adolescent sexual behavior (Billy et al., 1988; Dorius et al., 1993). Greater investment in educational and academic pursuits is related to later initiation (Billy et al., 1988; Hayes, 1987) and lower frequency of sexual intercourse (Ohannesian and Crockett, 1993). It has also been found that girls' academic aspirations and boys' grades in school decline following first sexual intercourse (Billy et al., 1988). The association between sexual intercourse and academic performance and attitudes may result either from sexually abstinent adolescents spending more time in school activities and less time with members of the opposite sex (Chilman, 1980) or from more educationally motivated students holding less stereotyped sex role images (Cvetkovich et al., 1978).

The frequency of church attendance is inversely related to involvement in sexual intercourse (Bingham et al., 1990; Crockett et al., 1996; R. Jessor et al., 1983; S. L. Jessor and Jessor, 1977; Miller et al., 1986). Although some evidence suggests that adolescents who experience less religious commitment are more likely to be involved in sexual behavior (Crockett et al., 1996), it also appears that sexual involvement results in decreased religious commitment and less frequent church attendance (Billy et al., 1988).

Social relationships

The quality of relationships between parents and their children predicts sexual intercourse. Poorer quality family relationships are associated with more adolescent involvement in sexual behaviors, including necking, petting (Wagner, 1980), and intercourse (Crockett et al., 1996; Rob et al., 1990; Wagner, 1980). In addition, adolescent boys feel less close to their mothers, but not their fathers, following first sexual intercourse (Billy et al., 1988).

Very little is known about the association between the quality of peer relationships and the timing of first sexual intercourse. However, evidence indicates that, following first intercourse, adolescents are more likely to select friends who are also sexually active (Billy et al., 1988).

Psychological characteristics

Sexually active adolescents commonly possess a variety of psychological characteristics distinguishing them from their less sexually experienced peers. A number of studies suggest an association between self-esteem and sexual intercourse. Among adults, there is evidence that low self-esteem interferes with involvement in sexual intercourse (Long, 1976). This is congruent with research indicating that nonvirgin adolescent boys report higher self-esteem than their virgin counterparts (S. L. Jessor and Jessor, 1977; Wade, 1989), but it does not explain the negative association found between sexual intercourse and the self-esteem of adolescent girls (Day, 1992).

Although some evidence suggests that self-esteem may predict the timing of first intercourse, it is not clear whether involvement in sexual intercourse results in further changes in self-esteem. In either case, it is important to understand the relation between self-esteem and sexual intercourse, because increasing self-esteem is the target of a variety of interventions into adolescent sexual and contraceptive behaviors (Watson and Kelly, 1989). Given the small amount of research on the topic, and the assumption that higher self-esteem is important in the intervention into adolescent sexual behavior, further research is merited.

Negative affect and depression predict less participation and interest in sexual intercourse among adults (Lief, 1986). However, the association between negative affect and adolescent sexual behavior is not well understood. When knowledge regarding adult depression and sexual intercourse is generalized to adolescents, it is anticipated that (a) depressed adolescents are less interested and less involved in sexual intercourse and/or (b) adolescents who begin sexual intercourse early are more likely subsequently to suffer from depression. Further research is needed on this topic.

Gender Issues

Society has historically maintained a sexual double standard (Reiss, 1960) suggesting that premarital sexual behavior is more permissible for males than for females. Although the sexual double standard has decreased in strength (Clement, 1989; Gagnon, 1977), it still influences sexual socialization, especially among adolescents. This influence is evidenced by gender differences in adolescents' reported age at first sexual intercourse, frequency of intercourse, contraceptive use, and number of sexual partners (Bingham et al., 1990; Zelnik and Kantner, 1980), as well as their emotional responses to first coitus (Koch, 1988). Because of the differences in socialization existing for adolescent boys and girls, we included gender in the present research so that its moderating effects on the association between timing of first sexual intercourse and psychosocial development could be examined.

Models of Timing and Psychosocial Development

There are currently no comprehensive theories of adolescent sexuality (Miller and Fox, 1987). However, *problem behavior theory* (R. Jessor et al., 1983; S. L. Jessor and Jessor, 1977) and the *stage termination model* (Peskin, 1967, 1973) provide direction for the present research.

Problem behavior theory

Problem behavior theory posits that a variety of adolescent problem behaviors and sexual intercourse occur together as a behavioral syndrome. This behavioral syndrome constitutes a state of transition proneness that provides adolescents with a means of achieving otherwise unattainable developmental objectives. Transition proneness is typified by poorer psychosocial adjustment (i.e., more problem behavior and less conventional behavior) and is associated with the timing of developmental transitions (S. L. Jessor and Jessor, 1977).

Problem behavior theory categorizes psychosocial variables into three domains: the *personality system*, including the individual's perceptions and feelings about themselves; the *perceived environment system*, consisting of parental and peer influences; and the *behavior system*, encompassing problem behaviors such as delinquency and conventional behaviors such as school performance (R. Jessor et al., 1983). In the present research, we examined variables measuring these three domains so that their antecedent–consequent association with the timing of first intercourse could be tested.

The stage termination model

The stage termination model (Peskin, 1967, 1973) assumes that in each stage of development a minimum level of maturation is necessary in order for successful advancement into the next stage. This model suggests that when transitions occur too early, development is curtailed and negative individual consequences result (Erikson, 1968).

Where sexual intercourse and psychosocial development are concerned, the stage termination model suggests that earlier involvement in sexual activity increases the chances that subsequent development will be compromised. Although it is known that a variety of negative characteristics are assoiated with early first sexual intercourse (Chilman, 1980; Crockett et al., 1996; Dorius et al., 1993; R. Jessor et al., 1983; S. L. Jessor and Jessor, 1977; Mott and Haurin, 1988; Ohannesian and Crockett, 1993; Rosenbaum and Kandel, 1990), it is not known whether the timing of first sexual intercourse produces these characteristics or whether they are simply correlates of the timing of first sexual intercourse.

Hypotheses

The first hypothesis was derived from problem behavior theory, which suggests that transition proneness is associated with poorer psychosocial adjustment and earlier timing of developmental transitions. Hence, the first hypothesis was that longitudinal patterns indicative of poorer psychosocial development (i.e., more problem behavior, less conventional behavior, poorer family and peer relationships, and lower self-esteem and less positive affect [greater depression]) would be associated with earlier timing of first sexual intercourse.

The stage termination model posits that poorer outcomes result when developmental transitions are made too early and individuals are advanced beyond their developmental capability to cope positively. The second hypothesis was that earlier first sexual intercourse would be associated with negative psychosocial outcomes.

The third hypothesis was based on the sexual double standard (Reiss, 1960) and posited that the negative effects of early sexual debut would be greater for girls than for boys.

Method

Design

Using a cohort-sequential longitudinal design (Baltes, 1968; Schaie, 1965), we collected the data for the present research to measure three cohorts of adolescents: 7th, 8th, and 9th graders, initially. Each cohort was surveyed annually through 12th grade. Because only two cohorts had data collected before 9th grade, the longitudinal analyses used data collected when the students were in 9th through 12th grades; however, 7th- and 8th-grade data were used to assess psychosocial adjustment before first sexual intercourse, which was included as a covariate.

We pooled data from the three cohorts to maximize the sample size for each grade level; hence, each cohort's 9th-grade data were pooled together, as were their 10th-grade data, and so on through 12th grade. A few students repeated a grade during high school. To maintain the integrity of the design, we assigned the data to consecutive annual waves of the study as though no grade had been repeated. Tests for cohort effects in the pooled data were all nonsignificant, suggesting that the data were not biased by cohort differences.

Sample

The sample for this study consisted of Euro-American, rural adolescents from a single school district in a geographically contained, middle- to low-income (1980 median household income = $14,400; approximately 12 percent of all households were below the poverty level) rural community in the northeastern United States. At 9th grade, all participants considered together had a mean age of 14 years ($SD = 0.50$).

Data were collected during regular school hours, with trained research personnel surveying boys and girls in separate rooms. To ensure privacy and maintain confidentiality, we excluded teachers and school administrators from all aspects of the surveying process, identified surveys by a six-digit numerical code, and placed participants in noncontiguous seats while surveys were being filled out. Students who refused consent or whose parents refused consent were excluded from data collection (participation rate was about 95 percent).

The total longitudinal sample ($n = 505$; 251 girls and 254 boys) included students who participated in the first annual survey, students who completed at least three of the four annual surveys given between their 9th and 12th grades, and students for whom age at first sexual intercourse could be calculated. As a result of inconsistent reporting of sexual intercourse experience, age at first intercourse could not be calculated for 91 of the participants (35 girls and 56 boys). Because the psychosocial adjustment of these 91 adolescents did not differ from the adjustment of those who had complete and consistent sexual behavior data, the adolescents who were missing age at first intercourse data were dropped from analyses.

The remaining sample consisted of 414 participants (216 girls, 198 boys). Ninety-nine of these individuals (47 girls and 52 boys) were missing one of the four surveys given from 9th and 12th grade. Because these students were significantly less well adjusted than their peers who had complete longitudinal data, they were retained in the sample and their missing data were estimated using a method designed to estimate missing data in longitudinal data sets (Petersen, 1987; see also Galambos et al., 1990). This method imputes missing data by using two components, one nomothetic and cross-sectional, and the other idiographic and longitudinal. The nomothetic component, $\overline{X}_j$, is an arithmetic mean obtained from each of the four times of measurement and is calculated as:

$$\overline{X}_j = \frac{1}{n_j}\sum_i x_{ij} \tag{6.1}$$

where i = the ith participant at longitudinal measurement point j who is missing data at a time-point other than j; j = time-points $\{1, 2, 3, \ldots\}$; and, n_j = the number of participants at time j for which data are missing at time-points other than j.

The idiographic component, $\overline{I}_{x_i}$, is the weighted average distance between each participant's data point and the nomothetic component, calculated as

$$\overline{I}_{x_i} = \frac{1}{K}\sum_j \left(x_{ij} - \overline{X}_j\right), \tag{6.2}$$

where i = the ith participant at longitudinal time-point j who is missing data at a time-point other than j; j = time-points $\{1, 2, 3, \ldots\}$; k = the number of longitudinal time-points with non-missing data for x_i.

As an example, consider a participant who is missing the third (S3) of four surveys (S1, S2, S3, S4). The nomothetic component is calculated as the mean of variable x_{i1} measured at S1 and is based on the subsample of participants who are missing data from a time point other than S1, and so forth for x_{i2} (S2) through x_{i4} (S4). The missing data point is then estimated by adding the idiographic component to the nomothetic component. Because of the prevalence of gender (6 out of 10 measures) and timing group (9 out of 10 measures) differences in psychosocial adjustment, missing data for the present research were estimated separately for boys and girls and for the three timing groups.

To assure that data imputation had not biased the sample, we used LISREL7 (Jöreskog and Sörbom, 1989) to compare the sample covariance structure before and after imputation in a stacked two-group (the covariance structures before and after imputation) design with all parameter estimates constrained to be invariant across the two groups (Jöreskog and Sörbom, 1989). Goodness of fit exceeded 0.990, indicating that the covariance structure of the data was not altered by the estimation procedure.

Measures

Timing of first sexual intercourse. The independent variable was the relative timing of first sexual intercourse. Annual surveys asked participants if they had ever had sex.[1] The annual data from this question were used, along with chronological age, to calculate each participant's age at first intercourse.

We used age at first sexual intercourse to assign participants to one of three timing groups: early, middle, or late. Timing groups were formed separately for boys and girls, because girls in the sample became sexually active an average of 10 months later than boys. Participants were assigned to the early timing group if they had sexual intercourse before 12th grade ($n = 166$) and their age at first intercourse was below the median age at first intercourse (*Mdn* girls = 15.5 years of age; *Mdn* boys = 14.75 years of age). Participants were assigned to the middle timing group ($n = 156$) if they had sexual intercourse before 12th grade and their age at first sexual intercourse was at or above the median. Determination of the median age at first intercourse was based on the subsample of adolescents who had sexual intercourse before 12th grade. Those who remained virgins at the beginning of 12th grade were assigned to the late timing group ($n = 92$).

The adolescents in the present sample reported a lower median age at first sexual intercourse than adolescents in several notable national samples of urban adolescents, namely, the National Longitudinal Study or Youth, the National Study of Family Growth, and the national surveys of young women and men conducted by Zelnik and Kantner (1980). These three studies show a median age at first sexual intercourse ranging from 17.0 to 17.2 years. This differs markedly from the present study, in which the median age at first sexual intercourse (considering the entire sample) was 16.1 and 15.1 years for female and male adolescents, respectively. However, these three national samples represented earlier cohorts of adolescents (birth years of 1959–1963) than did the sample used in the present research (birth years ranging from approximately 1970 to 1973).

Other evidence suggests that the median age of first sexual intercourse for the present sample does not differ from other samples of adolescents from more recent cohorts, which indicate that the age at first sexual intercourse continued to decline during the 1980s (Hofferth, 1987). In addition, 71 percent of the adolescents in the present sample reported having had intercourse at least once by the beginning of 12th grade. This is comparable with national statistics indicating that approximately 80 percent of adolescents experience first sexual intercourse by the end of 12th grade (Hayes, 1987). Finally, the age at first intercourse of adolescents in the present sample is comparable with that found in other samples of rural adolescents (Alexander et al., 1989). Taken together, this evidence suggests that the age at first sexual intercourse for adolescents in the present research is similar to those in other rural samples and does not differ greatly from more recent cohorts of nonrural adolescents.

We took several precautions to ensure the validity of the timing of first sexual intercourse measure. First, no age at first intercourse was assigned to participants who reported contradictory longitudinal information regarding their virginity status (e.g., reporting that they were virgins after indicating that they had previously been nonvirgins, or retrospectively reporting an age at first intercourse[2] that disagreed with their longitudinal reports of intercourse activity), and these participants were excluded from the present analyses. As mentioned previously, the participants who were missing age at first sexual intercourse (91 participants, including those whose longitudinal data were contradictory) did not differ from the remaining sample.

Second, as a check on construct validity, we used analysis of variance to examine the association between timing of first sexual intercourse and other sexual behaviors. Results showed that earlier timing was significantly associated with more necking and petting, $F(2, 291) = 57.26$, $p < 0.0001$ and $F(2, 291) = 50.96$, $p < 0.0001$. Further examination of the data indicated that adolescents in the late timing group were more likely than their nonvirgin age-mates to have never necked or petted, whereas all but 2 of the nonvirgins had necked or petted at least once. It is unlikely that adolescents who have had sexual intercourse would not have necked or petted. In addition, it is expected that adolescents who have had sexual intercourse would be more involved than their virgin age-mates in other sexual behaviors. The observation of these expected patterns of association in the present sample provides validity for the timing measure.

Psychosocial outcomes

Problem behavior theory guided the selection of outcome measures for the present research. The measures represent the three conceptual systems of problem behavior theory (e.g., R. Jessor et al., 1983): the behavior system (conventional and problem behaviors); the perceived environment system (quality of family and peer relationships); and the personality system (self-esteem and level of affect).

Problem behaviors. Minor deviance was measured by an 11-item scale from the Primary Prevention Awareness, Attitudes and Usage Scale (PPAAUS; Swisher et al., 1985). The PPAAUS assesses behaviors such as shoplifting, truancy, cheating on exams, staying out all night without parental permission, and fighting. Responses range from 1 = *never* to 5 = *almost every day*. Scores were computed so that higher scores reflected more minor deviance. On the basis of data from the annual surveys, coefficient alphas ranged from 0.75 to 0.81.

Substance use was measured by using two single-item measures that were also taken from the PPAAUS. These two items reflected how often participants got drunk and got high on drugs, respectively. Responses to these items ranged from 1 = *never* to 5 = *almost every day*.

Conventional behaviors. Three single items measured conventional behaviors. The first item measured the frequency of church attendance. Responses ranged from 0 = *never* to 5 = *more than once per week*. The second item assessed academic expectations by asking participants how much education they planned to complete. Responses ranged from 1 = *some high school* to 6 = *beyond college*. Finally, the third item measured school performance by asking participants to report their average grades (e.g., marks) in school. Responses to this item ranged from 1 = *mostly Fs* to 8 = *mostly As*. On the basis of annual survey data, intercorrelations among these items ranged from 0.51 to 0.79.

Quality of relationships. Two multi-item subscales, taken from the Self-Image Questionnaire for Young Adolescents (SIQYA), were used to measure the quality of parent (17 items) and peer (9 items) relationships (Petersen et al., 1984). Responses to the scale items ranged from 1 = *very strongly agree* to 6 = *very strongly disagree*. A sample item from the family relationships scale is, "I can count on my parents most of the time," and a sample item from the peer relationships scale is, "I do not have a particularly difficult time making friends." Scale scores were computed so that higher scores indicated more positive relationships. On the basis of the data from the annual surveys, coefficient alphas ranged from 0.82 to 0.91 for the family relationships scale and from 0.89 to 0.93 for the peer relationships scale. Instrument validity has been demonstrated in prior studies (Petersen et al., 1984).

Psychological adjustment. Psychological adjustment was measured by two multi-item scales assessing self-esteem and positive affect. Self-esteem was measured by the Rosenberg Self-Esteem Scale (Rosenberg, 1965). Items on this scale ranged from 1 = *strongly agree* to 4 = *strongly disagree*. A sample item from this scale is, "On the whole, I am satisfied with myself." Scale scores were computed so that higher scores indicated higher self-esteem. On the basis of data from the annual surveys, coefficient alphas ranged from 0.85 to 0.91. The validity of this widely used instrument has been previously established (Rosenberg, 1965).

Positive affect was measured by the Emotional Tone subscale of the SIQYA (Petersen et al., 1984). Emotional Tone measures positive affect and correlates negatively with depression. Item responses ranged from 1 = *very strongly agree* to 6 = *very strongly disagree*. An example item from this scale is, "Most of the time I am happy." Scale scores were computed so that a higher score depicted more positive affect. On the basis of data from the annual surveys, coefficient alphas ranged from 0.82 to 0.86. Instrument validity has been demonstrated in prior studies (Petersen et al., 1984).

Results

Descriptive sample statistics for the 9th- through 12th-grade outcome variables are reported in table 6.1. Means broken down by gender and timing of first intercourse groups at each of the four grades are presented in figures 6.1, 6.2 and 6.3.

The purpose of the present research was to compare two alternative developmental models explaining the association between the timing of first sexual intercourse and psychosocial development. First, assumptions of problem behavior theory were tested by comparing the longitudinal patterns of psychosocial development of adolescents from the timing of first intercourse groups: early, middle, and late. We examined data for the presence and consistency of timing group differences in psychosocial development beginning when the participants were in 9th grade, and continuing through 10th, 11th, and 12th grades. These analyses tested whether the timing of first intercourse was associated with longitudinal patterns of poorer psychosocial adjustment.

Second, the hypotheses suggested by the stage termination model were tested by examining the partial association between the timing of first sexual intercourse and psychosocial development measured at 12th grade. That is, we tested 12th-grade psychosocial functioning for timing group differences while controlling for the level of psychosocial adjustment before first intercourse. These analyses tested the effect of the timing of first intercourse on subsequent psychosocial adjustment.

In all analyses, gender was used as an independent variable, along with timing of first sexual intercourse, so that gender differences in the association between timing of first sexual intercourse and psychosocial development could be tested.

Longitudinal patterns

Doubly multivariate analysis of variance (i.e., a repeated measures analysis of variance with multiple dependent variables; D-MANOVA) was used to test the first hypothesis. A 3 (timing group) × 2 (gender) × 4 (grade in school) design was used. Grade in school was the repeated within-subject variable. Analyses were conducted for each set of outcome variables: problem behaviors, conventional behaviors, quality

Table 6.1 Means, standard deviations, and sample sizes for psycholscial adjustment from 9th through 12th grades ($n = 414$)

Variable	Grade in school			
	9th	10th	11th	12th
Minor deviance				
M	1.68	1.68	1.70	1.68
SD	0.48	0.46	0.47	0.46
Drunkenness				
M	1.97	2.14	2.34	2.40
SD	1.04	1.06	1.06	1.05
Drug use				
M	1.21	1.25	1.39	1.44
SD	0.68	0.70	0.79	0.84
Church attendance				
M	2.77	2.51	2.26	2.05
SD	1.75	1.84	1.85	1.86
Academic plans				
M	4.26	4.14	4.16	4.03
SD	1.47	1.42	1.37	1.30
Marks in school				
M	6.16	6.03	6.11	6.18
SD	1.26	1.24	1.19	1.31
Family relationships				
M	4.55	4.57	4.50	4.53
SD	0.80	0.78	0.78	0.81
Peer relationships				
M	4.60	4.68	4.69	4.53
SD	0.72	0.73	0.71	0.73
Self-esteem				
M	3.19	3.21	3.24	3.22
SD	0.50	0.50	0.48	0.55
Positive affect				
M	4.41	4.52	4.51	4.58
SD	0.82	0.80	0.80	0.84

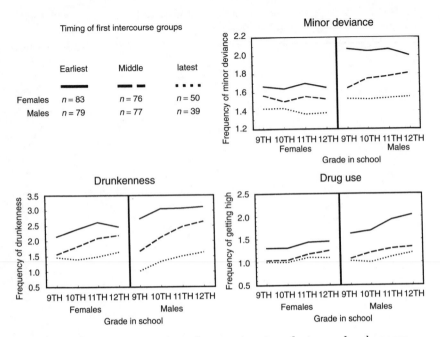

Figure 6.1 Frequency of involvement in minor deviance, drunkenness, and drug use from 9th to 12th grade by gender and timing group

of relationships, and psychological adjustment. D-MANOVA results are reported in table 6.2 and cell means are presented in figures 6.1, 6.2 and 6.3.

Problem behavior invlovement. D-MANOVA resulted in significant multivariate main effects of gender and timing group, and a significant multivariate interaction of timing and gender (see table 6.2). Univariate tests indicated that earlier timing of first sexual intercourse was associated with more minor deviance, drunkenness, and drug use (see figure 6.1). The significant multivariate interaction resulted from boys in the earlier timing group consistently reporting more problem behaviors than any other group of girls or boys.

The D-MANOVA also resulted in a significant within-subjects main effect of grade for drunkenness and drug use and a significant within-subjects interaction of grade in school and timing group for drunkenness (see table 6.2). Drunkenness and drug use increased form 9th to 12th grade for all three timing groups (see figure 6.1).

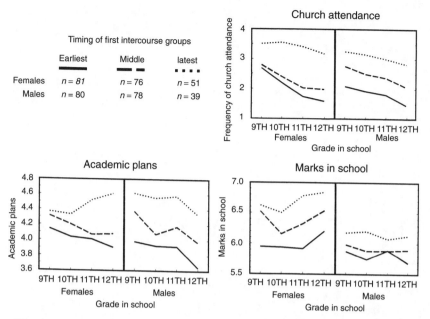

Figure 6.2 Frequency of church attendance, school aspirations, and marks in school from 9th to 12th grade by gender and timing group

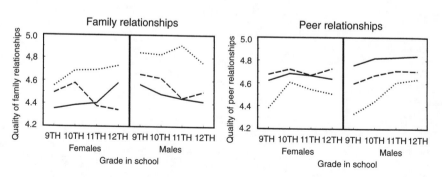

Figure 6.3 Quality of family and peer relationships from 9th to 12th grade by gender and timing group

Table 6.2 Associations between timing of first sexual intercourse and longitudinal patterns of psychosocial adjustment

Psychosocial outcome	Between-subjects effect			Within-subjects effect			
	Timing	Gender	Timing × gender	Grade	Grade × timing	Grade × gender	Grade × timing × gender
Problem behaviors							
Multivariate F	30.00***	14.48***	3.25**	13.68***	2.09**	1.00	1.56
Deviance	36.60***	43.57***	4.08*	0.44	1.34	1.00	1.56
Drunkenness	90.87***	12.06***	7.09***	36.13***	4.20***	2.55	1.13
Drug use	36.34***	11.87***	5.67**	10.78***	0.44	0.76	0.61
Conventional behaviors							
Multivariate F	7.44***	6.26***	1.18	9.37***	0.82	2.34*	0.95
Church	20.17***	0.97	0.83	23.23***	1.20	1.33	0.81
Plans	6.15**	0.10	0.28	3.94**	0.87	2.18	0.62
Marks	7.55***	14.91***	1.03	2.30	0.47	3.39*	1.36
Quality of relationships							
Multivariate F	9.06***	1.19	1.08	3.32**	1.90*	3.11**	1.11
Family	5.92**	2.39	0.25	0.89	2.85**	3.15*	1.29
Peers	4.09*	0.41	1.06	5.17**	0.92	1.78	0.60
Psychological adjustment							
Multivariate F	0.50	10.48***	0.57	5.01***	0.61	3.30**	0.34
Self-esteem	0.35	15.42***	1.10	1.79	0.38	2.95*	0.24
Positive affect	0.01	20.89***	0.70	6.93***	0.61	2.10	0.28

* $p < 0.05$. ** $p < 0.01$. *** $p < 0.001$

Conventional behavior. D-MANOVA resulted in between-subjects main effects of gender and timing (see table 6.2). Univariate effects showed one significant gender difference: girls reported higher marks in school than boys (see figure 6.2). Univariate timing group differences were found for church attendance, academic plans, and marks in school. For all three conventional behaviors, participation was greatest for the latest timing group, lower for the middle timing group, and lowest for the earliest timing group.

D-MANOVA also resulted in a significant multivariate within-subjects main effect of grade and a significant interaction of grade and gender. Academic plans increased and church attendance decreased from 9th to 12th grades for all gender and timing groups (see figure 6.2). Girls' marks in school increased from 9th to 12th grade, whereas boys' marks remained constant across all four grades, resulting in the interaction of grade and gender (see figure 6.2).

Quality of relationships. D-MANOVA resulted in a significant multivariate between-subjects main effect of timing for family relationships and peer relationships (see table 6.2). The univariate tests indicated that the quality of family relationships increased and the quality of peer relationships decreased with later first intercourse (see figure 6.3). Hence, members of the latest timing group reported the best family relationships, whereas early timing was associated with the best peer relationships.

D-MANOVA also resulted in significant multivariate within-subjects interactions between grade and gender, and between grade and timing group for quality of relationships (see table 6.2). Univariate tests indicated that family relationships increased in quality for girls and decreased for boys between 9th and 12th grades. In addition, the pattern of family relationships over time were different for the three timing groups, showing a strong cubic pattern for the middle group that was not evident for the other groups (see figure 6.3).

Psychological adjustment. D-MANOVA resulted in a multivariate between-subjects main effect of gender. Univariate analyses indicated that boys reported significantly higher self-esteem and more positive affect compared with girls from 9th to 12th grades (see table 6.2). No significant effects of timing group were found for self-esteem or positive affect.

D-MANOVA also resulted in a significant within-subjects interaction of grade and gender for self-esteem (see table 6.2). Self-esteem for girls increased steadily from 9th to 12th grade, whereas the self-esteem of boys did not change significantly. A significant main effect of grade was found for positive affect, which increased significantly between 9th and 12th grades for both girls and boys.

Summary of the longitudinal analyses. The longitudinal analyses demonstrated consistent longitudinal patterns of development associated with the timing of sexual debut. The early timing group had a longitudinal trajectory of poor psychosocial development, whereas members of the middle and late timing groups demonstrated more positive longitudinal patterns of development. These results support the problem behavior theory and suggest that first sexual intercourse is associated with a longitudinal pattern of transition proneness and poorer psychosocial adjustment.

Another question still remains: is the timing of first sexual intercourse simply part of a pattern of psychosocial development, or, consistent with the stage termination model, is having first sexual intercourse early detrimental to subsequent psychosocial adjustment? The following are analyses testing the second hypothesis.

Outcomes of first sexual intercourse

We tested assumptions of the stage termination model using a 3 (timing group) × 2 (gender) analysis of covariance (ANCOVAs). This design tested the association between the timing of first sexual intercourse and 12th-grade psychosocial adjustment when psychosocial adjustment before first intercourse was statistically controlled. This design was used to examine each of the 10 outcome measures. In each case, two covariates were used. The first was the indicator of prior adjustment, which was measured at the first survey when the participants were in 7th, 8th, and 9th grades. The time lag between the measurement of prior psychosocial adjustment and the measurement of 12th-grade adjustment varied for participants from the three grade cohorts (6, 5, and 4 years, respectively). The second covariate, grade cohort, was added to the model to control for spurious effects created by these differences in time lag.

In order for analysis of covariance to provide adequate statistical control, it is necessary that the covariate be measured before the event being examined (Neter et al., 1985). In the present case, that event was first sexual intercourse. Forty-five participants (10 girls, 35 boys) reported that they were nonvirgins when they completed the first survey. For reasons of design integrity, these participants were excluded from the 10 ANCOVAs. Some additional participants were missing at least one of the covariates, resulting in slight fluctuations in the sample size for each of the ANCOVAs.

Results of the ANCOVAs are reported in table 6.3. No negative psychosocial outcomes were associated with the timing of first sexual intercourse once prior psychosocial adjustment and grade cohort were statistically controlled. Although significant timing group differences were found for drunkenness, the adjusted means in table 6.3 indicate that this effect resulted from the late timing group having a lower level of drunkenness in comparison with the other two timing groups. These results suggest that the timing of first sexual intercourse, *per se*, is not associated with negative psychosocial outcomes. This is not to say that other factors associated with early sexual intercourse (i.e., unwanted pregnancy, sexually transmitted diseases, or AIDS) do not result in negative psychosocial outcomes.

Gender as a moderator

The third hypothesis posited that the effects of early first sexual intercourse would be more severe for girls than for boys. The moderating effect of gender was tested simultaneously with the other hypotheses by examining interactions between gender and timing of sexual intercourse in the D-MANOVAs and ANCOVAs discussed previously. In all, only three interactions of gender and timing group were observed. These interactions were found in the longitudinal association between timing and problem behavior from 9th and 12th grade, and resulted from greater timing group differences for boys than for girls (see figure 6.1). Where minor deviance and drug use were concerned, differences between the early and middle timing groups were greater for boys than for girls. For drunkenness, differences among all three timing groups were greater for boys than for girls. Despite these differences in level of problem behavior, longitudinal timing group patterns were the same for both genders; that is, earlier timing was associated with more, and later timing with less, problem behavior at all four grades and for both genders. Although it can be concluded that gender was associated with

Table 6.3 Results of analysis of covariance: unadjusted and adjusted means for timing of first intercourse

Variable/timing group	Observed M	M adjusted		
		Grade cohort	Prior adjustment	Adjustment and cohort
Minor deviance				
Early	1.79$_a$	1.82	**2.17**	1.89
Middle	1.67$_b$	1.67	**1.52**	1.56
Late	1.46$_c$	1.47	**1.37**	1.49
Drunkenness				
Early	2.70$_a$	2.79	**3.07**	**2.79**
Middle	2.43$_b$	2.41	**2.44**	**2.44**
Late	1.64$_c$	1.64	**1.35**	**1.44**
Drug use				
Early	1.71$_a$	1.80	1.66	1.72
Middle	1.30$_b$	1.28	1.38	1.32
Late	1.15$_b$	1.15	1.02	1.11
Church attendance				
Early	1.58$_a$	1.59	2.44	2.59
Middle	2.01$_b$	1.96	2.09	1.91
Late	3.00$_c$	2.99	2.05	2.04
Academic plans				
Early	3.76$_a$	3.78	3.84	3.66
Middle	4.02$_a$	4.01	4.23	3.97
Late	4.47$_b$	4.45	3.87	4.70
Marks in school				
Early	6.07$_a$	6.02	6.27	6.16
Middle	6.24$_{a,b}$	6.24	6.69	6.04
Late	6.52$_b$	6.48	5.47	6.72
Family relationships				
Early	4.57$_{a,b}$	4.55	5.17	5.17
Middle	4.44$_a$	4.43	4.26	3.86
Late	4.76$_b$	4.76	4.43	4.91
Peer relationships				
Early	4.65	4.68	**5.34**	5.34
Middle	4.72	4.71	**4.19**	4.19
Late	4.58	4.58	**4.48**	4.49
Self-esteem				
Early	3.19	3.21	**4.01**	3.50
Middle	3.24	3.24	**3.32**	3.15
Late	3.24	3.24	**2.49**	3.08
Positive affect				
Early	4.56	4.59	**5.62**	4.71
Middle	4.59	4.59	**4.56**	4.52
Late	4.58	4.59	**3.75**	4.48

Note: *Group means with the same subscripts are not significantly different. Post hoc test results are provided only for effects of timing group that were significant at alpha < 0.05. Values in boldface indicate tests in which timing group effects remained significant after the control variable was covaried* the strength of the timing effects, it cannot be concluded that the effects of early intercourse are more severe for girls than for boys. Hence, the gender moderation hypothesis was not supported.

Discussion

The present research tested hypotheses drawn from problem behavior theory, the stage termination model, and the sexual double standard regarding the association between the timing of first sexual intercourse and psychosocial development. Results indicated the following: (a) Earlier first intercourse is associated with poorer psychosocial development, thus supporting problem behavior theory (Bingham et al., 1990; R. Jessor et al., 1983: S. L. Jessor and Jessor, 1977; Ketterlinus et al., 1992); (b) contrary to hypotheses generated from the stage termination model, timing of first sexual intercourse does not result in detrimental psychosocial outcomes; and (c) contrary to hypotheses based on the sexual double standard, the effects of early intercourse are not more severe for girls than they are for boys.

Neither self-esteem nor level of affect were found to be longitudinally associated with the timing of first sexual intercourse. One of two processes may account for this lack of results. First, it may be that the timing of first intercourse is simply not related to self-esteem and level of affect. Second, perhaps other factors, such as socialization and beliefs regarding sex, act independent of timing to shape adolescents' emotional reactions to first intercourse, thus giving rise to a variety of emotional outcomes to having had intercourse that are not directly tied to its timing.

Other results from the present research demonstrated a consistent association between positive psychosocial development and the postponement of first sexual intercourse; however, the quality of peer relationships was an exception. Contrary to hypothesized expectations and other research (Hurrelmann, 1990), adolescents who initiated sexual intercourse the latest had the poorest, rather than the best, quality peer relationships. One explanation of this contradictory finding is that adolescents in the late timing group have difficulty identifying compatible peers (Billy et al., 1988). Adolescents in the late timing group reported the most positive family relationships, the most frequent church attendance, the greatest commitment to education, and the lowest involvement in problem behaviors of any of the three timing groups.

Involvement in this constellation of behaviors undoubtedly distinguished these adolescents from their earlier initiating peers. It should be recalled that the present sample consisted of a majority of the adolescents attending a single high school within a single school district, and that the late timing group was the smallest of the three groups in the sample. Because of the small size of this group of adolescents, not to mention their behavioral and interpersonal features, they may have had difficulty finding compatible peers.

A second explanation of the association between timing and peer relationships is that having positive peer relationships may catalyze involvement in problem and sexual behaviors. Having more positive peer relationships may enable adolescents to obtain beer and other substances, help them to identify peers who are willing accomplices in problem behaviors or who are available sexual partners. Having poorer quality family relationships and being less committed to social institutions such as church and school may also disinhibit adolescents, allowing them more freedom to defy the expectations of conventional society (Hirschi, 1969). Thus, positive peer relationships, especially when combined with poor family relationships and low involvement in conventional behaviors, may facilitate adolescents' involvement in problem and sexual behaviors.

One of the most important findings from the present research was the consistency of timing group differences in patterns of psychosocial development from 9th to 12th grade. Longitudinal patterns of development for the three timing groups were primarily nonintersecting between 9th and 12th grade (see figures 6.1, 6.2 and 6.3) and represent distinct developmental trajectories. Individuals who had first sexual intercourse early demonstrated the poorest psychosocial adjustment at 9th grade, and the same negative developmental trajectory persisted through 12th grade. In stark contrast, adolescents in the late timing group had the most positive 9th-grade adjustment and the most positive trajectory of development through 12th grade.

These patterns of development from 9th to 12th grade were not outcomes associated with the timing of first sexual intercourse, as results presented earlier attest. Instead, they were a continuation of enduring developmental trajectories that preceded 9th grade. Timing group differences in psychosocial development were apparent at the beginning of 9th grade, suggesting that individual trajectories of development were well established by that time (see figures 6.1, 6.2 and 6.3). Other evidence suggests that individual differences in psychosocial development were a result of childhood variation in variables such as temperament and family context (Jansen et al., 1995; Lambert and Windmiller, 1977; Patterson et al., 1989). These early individual differences are thought to set the stage for later developmental and behavioral patterns that continue into adulthood (Zucker, 1987), resulting in trajectories of development extending from childhood to adolescence, and on to adulthood.

The consistency of psychosocial development, coupled with the failure to identify any net negative outcomes connected with the timing of first sexual intercourse, implies that the association between poor psychosocial development and early sexual intercourse is not attributable to the timing of first intercourse, *per se*. Instead, these findings suggest that this association is a continuation of preexisting developmental patterns – patterns that predispose the individual to developmental risks such as unprotected intercourse, sexually transmitted disease, pregnancy, problem behaviors, and isolation from conventional social institutions such as family and school.

Results from the present research provide several implications for intervention into adolescent sexual behavior. First, the longitudinal consistency of timing group differences in psychosocial development suggests that interventions into the sexual behavior of adolescents should protect adolescents from other risks resulting from poor psychosocial development as well. Such risks include substance use and delinquency (R. Jessor et al., 1983; S. L. Jessor and Jessor, 1977), social alienation (Hirschi, 1969), and the continuation of negative patterns of development (R. Jessor et al., 1983).

Results from the present research also indicate that early intervention into poor psychosocial development might be an efficient means of simultaneously preventing numerous negative developmental outcomes. Enhancing positive psychosocial development during childhood may shift developmental trajectories and effectively prevent entire constellations of negative outcomes during adolescence, including problem behavior involvement and negative outcomes resulting from the failure of young, sexually active adolescents to use safe-sex practices.

The present research examined a sample of Euro-American adolescents attending high school in a rural area of the United States. Future research examining the association between psychosocial development and the timing of first sexual intercourse should focus on other racial and ethnic populations, as well as adolescents who have dropped out of school, or who are experiencing more severe negative adjustment generally. In addition, more research is needed to examine the formation of developmental trajectories and the continuity of these trajectories from childhood, through adolescence, and into adulthood.

In summary, the results of the present research suggest that boys and girls who initiate sexual intercourse early are involved in more problem behavior and less conventional behavior and have poorer quality family relationships. It would also appear that these patterns of negative psychosocial development are not a result of the timing of first sexual intercourse but are a continuation of long-term patterns of poor psychosocial development that were established before ninth grade. On the basis of these results, it is suggested that interventions that enhance childhood psychosocial development might effectively circumvent a host of negative development outcomes.

Notes

1 The question regarding the occurrence of sexual intercourse asked the adolescents if they "had ever been sexually active (had sex)." Because of concerns within the participating school district regarding the sexual content of survey items, no more detailed or explicit question was allowed.
2 The item added at the fourth survey was judged not to be appropriate as a sole indicator of first sexual intercourse for three reasons: (a) it was retrospective, making it inferior to the item measured longitudinally; (b) the retrospective item was asked at different grades in school for members of the three cohorts, making it impossible to use once the data were pooled (see figure 6.1); and (c) data for the retrospective item were more frequently missing than were the data for the item asked year to year.

References

Alexander, C. S., Ensminger, M. E., Kim, Y. J., Smith, J., Johnson, K. E., & Dolan, L. J. (1989). Early sexual activity among adolescents in small towns and rural areas: Race and gender patterns. *Family Planning Perspectives, 21*, 261–266.

Baltes, P. B. (1968). Longitudinal and cross-sectional sequences in the study of age and generation effects. *Human Development, 11*, 145–171.

Billy, J. O. G., Landale, N. S., Grady, W. R., & Zimmerle, D. M. (1988). Effects of sexual activity on adolescent social and psychological development. *Social Psychology Quarterly, 51,* 190–212.

Bingham, C. R. (1989). AIDS and adolescents: Threat of infection and approaches for prevention. *Journal of Early Adolescence, 9,* 50–66.

Bingham, C. R., Miller, B. C., & Adams, G. R. (1990). Correlates of age at first sexual intercourse in a national sample of young women. *Journal of Adolescent Research, 5,* 18–33.

Chilman, C. S. (1980). *Adolescent sexuality in a changing American society* (Report No. 79–1426). Bethesda, MD: US Department of Health, Education, and Welfare.

Clement, U. (1989). Profile analysis as a method of comparing intergenerational differences in sexual behavior. *Archives of Sexual Behavior, 18,* 229–237.

Crockett, L. J., Bingham, C. R., Chopak, J. S., & Vicary, J. R. (1996). Timing of first sexual intercourse: The role of social control, social learning, and problem behavior. *Journal of Youth and Adolescence, 25,* 89–111.

Cvetkovich, G., Grote, B., Lieberman, E. J., & Miller, W. (1978). Sex role development and teenage fertility-related behavior. *Adolescence, 13,* 231–236.

Day, R. D. (1992). The transition to first intercourse among racially and culturally diverse youth. *Journal of Marriage and the Family, 54,* 749–762.

D'Augelli, T. R., & Bingham, C. R. (1993). Interventions to prevent HIV infection among young adolescents. In R. M. Lerner (Ed.), *Early adolescence: Perspectives on research, policy, and intervention* (pp. 353–368). Hillsdale, NJ: Erlbaum.

Dorius, G. L., Heaton, T. B., & Steffen, P. (1993). Adolescent life events and their association with the onset of sexual intercourse. *Youth and Society, 25,* 3–23.

Erikson, E. H. (1968). *Youth, identity, and crisis.* New York: Norton.

Forrest, J. D., & Singh, S. (1990). The sexual and reproductive behavior of American Women, 1982–1988. *Family Planning Perspectives, 22,* 206–214.

Gagnon, J. (1977). *Human sexualities.* Chicago: Scott, Foresman.

Galambos, N. L., Almeida, D. M., & Petersen, A. C. (1990). Masculinity, femininity, and sex role attitudes in early adolescence: Exploring gender intensification. *Child Development, 61,* 1905–1914.

Hayes, C. D. (1987). *Risking the future: Adolescent sexuality, pregnancy, and childbearing.* Washington, DC: National Academy Press.

Hirschi, T. (1969). *Causes of delinquency.* Berkeley: University of California Press.

Hofferth, S. L. (1987). Influences on early sexual and fertility behavior. In C. D. Hayes (Ed.), *Risking the future: Adolescent sexuality, pregnancy, and childbearing: Vol. 2. Working papers* (pp. 7–35). Washington, DC: National Academy Press.

Hurrelmann, K. (1990). Parents, peers, teachers, and other significant partners in adolescence. *International Journal of Adolescence and Youth, 2,* 211–236.

Jansen, R. E., Fitzgerald, H. E., Ham, H. P., & Zucker, R. A. (1995). Difficult temperament and behavior problems in three- to five-year-old sons of alcoholics. *Alcoholism: Clinical and Experimental Research, 19,* 501–509.

Jessor, R., Costa, F., Jessor, L., & Donovan, J. E. (1983). Time of first intercourse: A prospective study. *Journal of Personality and Social Psychology, 44,* 608–626.

Jessor, S. L., & Jessor, R. (1977). Transition from virginity to nonvirginity among youth: A social psychological study over time. *Developmental Psychology, 4,* 473–484.

Jones, E. F., Forrest, J. D., Goldman, N., Henshaw, S., Lincoln, R., Rosoff, J. I., Westoff, C. F., & Wulf, D. (1986). *Teenage pregnancy in industrialized countries* (pp. 21–36). New Haven, CT: Yale University Press.

Jöreskog, K. G., & Sörbom, D. (1989). *LISREL7: A guide to the program and applications* (2nd ed.). Chicago: SPSS, Inc.

Ketterlinus, R. D., Lamb, M. E., Nitz, K., & Elster, A. B. (1992). Adolescent nonsexual and sex-related problem behaviors. *Journal of Adolescent Research, 7,* 431–456.

Koch, P. B. (1988). The relationship of first intercourse to later sexual functioning concerns of adolescents. *Journal of Adolescent Research, 3,* 345–362.

Lambert, N. M., & Windmiller, M. (1977). An exploratory study of temperament traits in a population of children at risk. *The Journal of Special Education. 11,* 37–46.

Lief, H. I. (1986). Sex and depression [Special issue: The physician's guide to sexual counseling]. *Medical Aspects of Human Sexuality, 20,* 38–53.

Long, I. (1976). Human sexuality and aging. *Social Casework, 57,* 237–244.

Miller, B. C., & Fox, G. L. (1987). Theories of adolescent heterosexual behavior. *Journal of Adolescent Research, 2,* 269–282.

Miller, B. C., McCoy, K., Olson, T. D., & Wallace, C. M. (1986). Parental discipline and control attempts in relation to adolescent sexual attitudes and behavior. *Journal of Marriage and the Family, 48,* 503–512.

Mott, F. L., & Haurin, R. J. (1988). Linkages between sexual activity and alcohol and drug use among American adolescents. *Family Planning Perspectives, 20,* 128–136.

Neter, J., Wasserman, W., & Kutner, M. (1985). *Applied linear statistical models* (2nd ed.). Homewood, IL: Irwin.

Ohannesian, C., & Crockett, L. J. (1993). A longitudinal investigation of the relationship between educational investment and adolescent sexual activity. *Journal of Adolescent Research, 8,* 167–182.

Patterson, G. R., DeBaryshe, B. D., & Ramsey, E. (1989). A developmental perspective on antisocial behavior. *American Psychologist, 44,* 329–335.

Peskin, H. (1967). Pubertal onset and ego functioning. *Journal of Abnormal Psychology, 72,* 1–15.

Peskin, H. (1973). Influence of the developmental schedule of puberty on learning and ego functioning. *Journal of Youth and Adolescence, 2*, 273–290.

Petersen, A. C. (1987, February). *Data estimation.* Paper presented to the staff of the Developmental Research Methodology Center, Pennsylvania State University, University Park.

Petersen, A. C., Schulenberg, J. E., Abramowitz, R. M., Offer, D., & Jarcho, H. D. (1984). A Self-Image Questionnaire for Young Adolescents (SIQYA): Reliability and validity studies. *Journal of Youth and Adolescence, 13*, 93–111.

Reiss, I. L. (1960). *Premarital sexual standards in America.* New York: Free Press.

Rob, M., Reynolds, I., & Finlayson, P. F. (1990). Adolescent marijuana use: Risk factors and implications. *Australian & New Zealand Journal of Psychiatry, 24*, 47–56.

Rosenbaum, E., & Kandel, D. B. (1990). Early onset of adolescent sexual behavior and drug involvement. *Journal of Marriage and the Family, 52*, 783–798.

Rosenberg, M. (1965). *Society and the adolescent self-image.* Princeton, NJ: Princeton University Press.

Schaie, K. W. (1965). A general model for the study of developmental problems. *Psychological Bulletin, 64*, 92–102.

Swisher, J. D., Shute, R. E., & Bibeau, D. (1985). Assessing drug and alcohol abuse: An instrument for planning and evaluation. *Measurement and Evaluation in Counseling and Development, 17*, 91–97.

Verner, A. M., & Stewart, C. S. (1974). Adolescent sexual behavior in middle America revisited: 1970–1973. *Journal of Marriage and the Family, 36*, 728–735.

Wade, J. T. (1989). A longitudinal analysis of sex by race differences in predictors of adolescent self-esteem. *Personality and Individual Differences, 10*, 717–729.

Wagner, C. A. (1980). Sexuality of American adolescents. *Adolescence, 15*, 567–579.

Watson, F. I., & Kelly, M. J. (1989). Targeting the at-risk male: A strategy for adolescent pregnancy prevention. *Journal of the National Medical Association, 81*, 453–456.

Zelnik, M., & Kantner, J. F. (1980). Sexual activity, contraceptive use, and pregnancy among metropolitan area teenagers: 1971–1979. *Family Planning Perspectives, 12*, 230–237.

Zucker, R. A. (1987). The four alcoholisms: A developmental account of the etiologic process. In P. C. Rivers (Ed.), *Nebraska symposium on motivation, 1986: Vol. 34. Alcohol and addictive behaviors* (pp. 27–84). Lincoln: University of Nebraska Press.

Part III

Environmental Influences

Individuals behave and develop within a context of human experience. This section focuses on research with a strong contextual flavor.

Like Father, Like Son? Predicting Male Adolescents' Adjustment From Parents' Distress and Self-Restraint
and
Adolescent Girls' Relationships with Mothers and Best Friends

Introduction

Family members – can't live with them, can't live without them. Peers – the group from which we pick our best friends. Family and peers – the two groups in a teenager's life that are most likely to connect and intermingle.

In every theory of adolescence, family and peers play a major part in understanding adolescent behavior and development. Some theories argue that family is more influential than peers. Other theories suggest peers are more influential than family. No matter what weight each social institution may have on a teenager, both are influencing adolescents each and every day, if not up close and personal, then from a distance. I believe family and friends leave deep internalized influences and they go with us wherever we go, like our shadow is always close to us.

I've selected two articles on the family and peers subject area. The first focuses on sons and fathers, the second on daughters and mothers. Anthropological research shows that the major influences and the majority of time in family socialization are divided by gender (Schlegel and Barry, 1991). So the two research reports were chosen because they focus on this division and give you an opportunity to look inside the relationships of fathers and sons, and mothers and daughters.

In the investigation by D'Angelo and colleagues the role of fathers' self-restraint on their sons' adjustment is examined. The investigators examine the effects of both mothers' and fathers' experiences and behaviors on their sons. While both parents are found to influence their sons, it appears that fathers' impact is most prominent. In the study by Gavin and Furman the role of harmonious versus non-harmonious relationships is examined for adolescent girls' relationship quality. Relationship harmony is found to be associated with having needs met, better social skills, and similar interests. The factors that contribute to harmony are found to be very similar for relationships with mothers and with friends.

Both of these reports are rich in their methodology and findings. They offer good illustrations of what can be learned about family and peer relationships by using a combination of self-report and observational methods. As you go to the Zone and read these two articles, consider how person, context, and occasion are used and what specific findings are found for each of these components. Also, consider how the two studies focused on different features of relationships. Are there implications from these studies for parenting courses or policy formulation? Let us continue on the journey together. It is time to read on!

References

Schlegel, A., and Barry, H. (1991). *Adolescence: an anthropological inquiry.* New York: Free Press.

Suggested reading

Hauser, S. T., Powers, S. I., and Noam, G. G. (1991). *Adolescents and their families: paths of ego development.* New York: Free Press.

SEVEN

Like Father, Like Son? Predicting Male Adolescents' Adjustment From Parents' Distress and Self-Restraint

Lori D'Angelo and Daniel A. Weinberger
and S. Shirley Feldman

Virtually all major theories of social development include the premise that parents' personalities and behavior patterns have a major impact on children's functioning. Constructs such as identification in psycho-analytic theory (Tyson and Tyson, 1990), modeling in social-cognitive theory (Bandura, 1986), and genetic inheritance in biological models (Loehlin, 1992) all suggest that parents affect the kind of adults their children become. In addition, parents' individual adaptations are likely to predict aspects of parenting, marital adjustment, and family functioning that have been consistently linked to children's outcomes (e.g., Elder et al., 1986; Feldman et al., 1990; Patterson and Capaldi, 1991). Nevertheless, there has been relatively little systematic focus on parents' personalities *per se* within the child development literature.

In part, the "trait debate" led to questions about the stability and cross-situational consistency of personality measures (e.g., Mischel, 1968). However, subsequent research using improved methodologies suggests that the personality styles of older children and adults are quite stable, when behaviors are aggregated across time and situations (Epstein and O'Brien, 1985; Kendrick and Funder, 1988; Patterson et al., 1992). For example, in a study assessing 460 men ranging in age from 17 to 85 years, the mean 12-year test-retest coefficient was 0.73 across 10 broad dimensions of personality (Costa et al., 1980).

Most research on the association between parent personality and child outcomes in nonclinical samples has focused on behavioral genetics and has investigated direct parent-child concordance in samples of children of high school age or older. These correlations have generally not been impressive, averaging in the 0.1 to 0.2 range (Loehlin, 1992; Rowe, 1994; Scarr et al., 1981). However, this research paradigm may reveal only part of the picture. The impact of parents' personalities is likely to be quite complex and to vary considerably depending on the nature of the particular attribute (see Scarr and McCartney, 1983). For example, whether parents are reserved or "the life of the party" may tend to have subtle but not overriding consequences for their children's developmental trajectories. In contrast, parents' long-term adjustment is likely to have important implications for a variety of central aspects of the child-rearing environment, such as parenting practices, family functioning, and external social supports.

There is persuasive evidence that parents' symptomatology and problem behaviors markedly predict negative outcomes in the next generation (e.g., McCord, 1991; Rolf et al., 1990). However, even studies of nonclinical populations in this area of research have tended to avoid using measures of adult personality and to rely on specific indicators with skewed distributions, such as depressive symptoms, drug use, and number of criminal offenses (e.g., Conger et al., 1992; Patterson and Capaldi, 1991).

One purpose of the present study was to evaluate parents' adjustment within a more general framework. There is a growing consensus that adult personality can be described in terms of a relatively few broad domains such as the "Big Five" (i.e., extraversion, neuroticism, openness to experience, agreeableness, and conscientiousness) and Tellegen's (1985) dimensions of negative emotionality, positive emotionality, and constraint (e.g., Church and Burke, 1994). Weinberger and colleagues (Weinberger, 1991; Weinberger and Schwartz, 1990) have conceptualized social-emotional adjustment in older children and adults in terms of two superordinate dimensions: distress and self-restraint. The subjective experience of distress, a composite of anxiety, depression, low self-esteem, and low well-being, refers to the tendency to feel dissatisfied with oneself and one's ability to achieve desired outcomes. It incorporates aspects of high negative affectivity and low positive affectivity (Watson and Clark, 1984). The other superordinate dimension, self-restraint, is a composite of impulse control, suppression of aggression, consideration of others, and responsibility. It refers to socialization and self-control in terms of inhibiting immediate desires that conflict with one's long-term interests or with positive relations with others. Self-restraint incorporates aspects of the Big Five dimensions of agreeableness and conscientiousness and Tellegen's dimension of constraint (e.g., Pincus and Boekman, 1993). Although the specifics differ considerably, distress and restraint (i.e., self-restraint) are generically similar to Block and Block's (1980) constructs of ego resiliency and ego control.

Patients' distress and restraint are both likely to have important implications for their children's adjustment. Parents with high distress or low restraint will tend to be relatively preoccupied with their own problems and compromised in their fulfillment of adult roles (e.g., Weinberger and Bartholomew, 1996; Weinberger and Schwartz, 1990). Of particular relevance, both distress-related problems, such as ongoing negative moods and low perceived competence and control, and restraint-related problems, such as temper outbursts and aggression, have been directly linked to poor parenting practices and family functioning (e.g., Bugental et al., 1989; Dix, 1991; Feldman et al., 1990; Patterson et al., 1992).

A predominantly clinical literature has examined the association between parents' affective states and children's functioning. Sons and daughters of depressed mothers have elevated rates of affective disorders, conduct problems, attentional problems, oppositional behavior, substance abuse, and impaired social competence (Downey and Coyne, 1990; Gelfand and Teti, 1990). Although rarely investigated, fathers' depression seems to be as much a risk factor as mothers' (Hammen, 1991; Phares and Compas, 1992).

The effects of parental depression on child outcomes are not limited to clinical depression. Studies that have used school-based samples suggest that pervasive associations can also be identified in nonclinical populations (Conger et al., 1992; Forehand et al., 1987). For example, Forehand and McCombs (1988) reported that the Beck Depression Inventory (BDI) scores of mothers of adolescents in public school predicted "more internalizing and externalizing problems and poorer prosocial and cognitive functioning" (p. 403) in their children. In this sample, mothers' BDI scores, which had a 1-year test-retest coefficient of 0.71, can be conceptualized as primarily measuring general negative affectivity (Watson and Clark, 1984), rather than the presence of a psychiatric syndrome. As a whole, the data suggest a more complex pattern than a simple family resemblance model, in which parental affective difficulties predict affective difficulties in their children. The actual consequences, though generally negative, seem multifaceted and varied.

The literature on depression in mothers, which relates to parental distress, is paralleled by one on aggressive fathers, who tend to have problems with self-restraint. Children of antisocial fathers have notably heightened rates of delinquency and conduct disorders (Farrington, 1991; Loeber, 1990; Phares and Compas, 1992). Mothers' antisocial behavior also seems to be a risk factor (e.g., Lahey et al., 1989). The intergenerational cycle of antisocial predispositions predicting from parents and grandparents to children and grandchildren is well established, especially for boys (Elder et al., 1986; Huesmann et al., 1984; McCord, 1991; Robins et al., 1975; Wahler and Dumas, 1986). Although this literature has tended to focus on the specific transmission of crime or aggression, there is evidence that children in these families are subject to an array of negative long-term outcomes, including low self-esteem, depression, alcohol problems, educational failure, unstable relationships, and irresponsible sexual behavior (e.g., Farrington, 1991; Patterson et al., 1992; Robins and Ratcliff, 1978/1979).

Hence, the degree to which mothers' and fathers' dysphoric affect versus problems with aggression and self-control differentially predict children's functioning remains unclear, especially in nonclinical populations. The present study focused on how parents' distress and self-restraint when their sons were preadolescents predicted sons' outcomes 4 years later. Boys' competence in mid-adolescence was broadly assessed, using multiple measures of school achievement, peer relations, at-risk behavior, and social-emotional adjustment, including their own distress, restraint, and depression.

Mothers' versus fathers' behaviors are likely to have notably different meanings and consequences for sons versus daughters (e.g., Beal, 1994; Rutter and Quinton, 1984). For example adolescent girls seem to be particularly sensitive to maternal depression (e.g., Hops et al., 1990). Partly because sample size limitations would not allow a full exploration of potentially complex sex differences, the present 4-year longitudinal investigation focused only on one gender. Because boys as a group manifest heightened rates of adjustment problems in general, and externalizing problems in particular (e.g., Clarizio and McCoy, 1983), they were chosen as the focus of this research.

Across the life span, tendencies to experience distress and to have problems with self-restraint are moderately correlated (Achenbach and

Edelbrock, 1983; Conger et al., 1992; Weinberger, 1991). It is well documented that negative affective states tend to be associated with lower self-control (e.g., Dix, 1991; Schwartz and Pollack, 1977; Weinberger and Gomes, 1995). In turn, impulsive behavior often has distressing consequences (e.g., Jessor, 1991). Therefore, we evaluated the degree to which independent versus shared variance in parents' levels of distress and restraint was predictive of their sons' outcomes.

The analyses of the differential role of distress versus restraint within parents' personalities were complemented by a comparable assessment across parents. Similarities in spouses' psychological functioning, attributable to spouse selection and changes during the relationship, have been documented in both clinical and nonclinical populations (Buss, 1984; Merikangas et al., 1988; Rutter and Quinton, 1984). Parents married to spouses with adjustment problems are likely to have related problems of their own (e.g., Lyon and Greenberg, 1991), which may or may not be independently related to their children's outcomes. Therefore, we explicitly addressed the possibility that one parent's personality might be associated with child outcomes because of its prediction of the other spouse's personality.

For several reasons, we hypothesized that fathers' self-restraint would be the most significant predictor of boys' outcomes across domains. The literatures on spouse abuse, substance abuse, criminal behavior, risk taking, and antisocial personality traits all suggest that fathers are more likely than mothers to have significant problems with self-control (e.g., Berkowitz, 1993; Huesmann et al., 1984). In general, parents' irresponsible or egoistic behavior, rather than subjective distress *per se*, may most broadly disrupt family functioning, including marital adjustment and parenting practices (e.g., Elder et al., 1986; Feldman et al., 1990; Patterson et al., 1992). Adolescent sons are also apt to be especially attuned to their fathers' level of maturity in performing adult roles (e.g., Bandura, 1986). Paradoxically, sons of fathers low in self-restraint may tend to have relatively negative outcomes whether they identify with their fathers or are alienated by their behavior (e.g., Brownfield, 1987; Hirschi, 1969).

It is also possible that fathers' level of self-restraint might be particularly linked to sons' outcomes for genetic reasons (see Frick and Jackson, 1993). There could simply be a passive genetic link (see Scarr and McCartney, 1983) between parents' personalities and sons' temperaments that mediates the associations. A genetic explanation is unlikely to be the complete one, in that restraint-related problem behaviors, such as delinquency, and distress-related problems, such as mood disorders, are actually two of the few areas of psychological functioning in which both notable shared-family environment effects and genetic effects have been identified (e.g., DiLalla and Gottesman, 1989; Mednick et al., 1987; Rowe, 1994; Tsuang and Faraone, 1990).

The present design could not directly address the degree to which observed correlations were due to genetic similarity. We did have the ability to address whether associations between parents' and sons' personalities on the identical measures at the initial assessment could account for observed correlations between parents' functioning and sons' subsequent outcomes. If, as hypothesized, parents' personalities function as an ongoing influence on adolescents' development, one would expect parents' measures to be predictive beyond what could be accounted for by their association with sons' initial personality scores.

Method

Participants

The participants in the present study were initially recruited from a sample of 685 sixth graders (336 boys and 349 girls) enrolled in 33 public schools in two noncontiguous, broadly middle-class, public school districts as part of a multistage investigation of sixth-grade boys and their families (see Weinberger et al., 1990). Self-report measures, peer nominations, and teacher ratings were obtained for this sample, which consisted of the 82 percent of children in these classrooms whose parents agreed both to their participation and to the family being contacted about subsequent studies of family interaction. The boys participating in the present longitudinal study were recruited for an intensive multimethod study of family functioning, including videotaped home observations. An initial sample size of 108 was targeted, and families were contacted until this number was achieved. A total of 62 percent (108/174) of the families contacted agreed to participate and were paid $35 for their assistance.

As documented in Weinberger et al. (1990), families with boys who were high in distress but not high in self-restraint in this sample had differentially high refusal rates. To mitigate sampling bias due to selective attrition, we monitored emerging cell sizes to ensure that the participating boys adequately represented each of the six groups within Weinberger and Schwartz's (1990) typology of adjustment styles (high–moderate–low restraint × high–low distress). This procedure resulted in a final sample that was more representative of the distribution of adjustment scores within the original sample than would have otherwise been the case.

Boys who participated initially ranged in age from 11 to 12.6 years ($M = 11.4$). Four years later, 88 of the original 108 boys were located, and 82 agreed to participate in the follow-up. Family members completed questionnaires in their homes, and each participant received $15 on receipt of the completed questionnaires. Boys ranged in age from 15 to 17.1 years ($M = 15.8$). Sixty-one percent of the boys lived in two-parent families (including 12 percent stepparent families), and 39 percent lived with a single parent. Seventy-five mothers and 60 fathers participated in the follow-up study.

There were 55 married couples who participated fully. This subsample included 14 stepparents whom boys identified as one of their two primary parental figures at both assessments. Within analyses of the two-parent families, patterns were comparable but more variable when nonbiological parents were excluded. Therefore, the analyses presented are based on the combined sample.

The participants were 79 percent White, 10 percent Asian American, 9 percent Hispanic, 1 percent African American, and 1 percent other. They were predominantly middle-class with an average score of 3.65 on the 7-point Hollingshead index of socioeconomic status. Sixty-nine percent of fathers and 64 percent of mothers reported some postsecondary education, including technical training courses.

To determine whether families that participated in the follow-up study differed systematically from the nonparticipants, we compared them on over 40 Time 1 measures, including sociodemographics, family and peer relationships, parents' and sons' individual characteristics, and sons' school functioning. Because only one significant difference between groups emerged, we concluded that the samples were generally comparable.

Procedure

At Time 1, boys completed the Weinberger Adjustment Inventory (WAI; Weinberger, 1991; Weinberger and Schwartz, 1990) as part of a battery of questionnaires that they filled out in two 1-hr sessions in their regular classroom setting. Three to 6 months later, their parents also provided self-reports on the WAI as part of a packet of questionnaires mailed to their homes before the scheduling of videotaped home observations (see Feldman et al., 1990; Weinberger et al., 1990).

Four years later, parents and their sons again completed the WAI as part of the packet of questionnaires that they filled out in their homes. Sons also completed a number of measures related to their functioning as mid-adolescents, and parents provided numerous parallel reports to corroborate their sons' assessments. Parents also completed a measure of their own depression at follow-up.

Parents' personal adjustment

Parents' reports of their own distress and self-restraint on the WAI during the Time 1 assessment served as the primary independent variables in this study. As a supplemental measure, sons' self-restraint at Time 1 was also included in the final set of analyses (see later). The WAI has been validated using multimethod confirmatory factor analysis for use with clinical and nonclinical populations from ages 10 to 70 years (Weinberger, 1991). The scales are predictive of a variety of aspects of adults' functioning, including personal adjustment (e.g., Weinberger and Schwartz, 1990), problem drinking (Weinberger and Bartholomew, 1996), and quality of family relationships (Feldman et al., 1990).

Subjective distress. Distress is a 29-item composite of four reliable subscales assessing general predispositions related to experiencing anxiety (e.g., "I worry too much about things that aren't important"), depression (e.g., "I often feel sad or unhappy"), low self-esteem (e.g., "I'm not very sure of myself"), and low well-being (e.g., "I'm the kind of person who has a lot of fun" [reverse scored]). Items are scored on 5-point Likert scales. In the original validation sample, distress scores in adults correlated 0.71 with the Taylor Manifest Anxiety Scale and − 0.65 with the Rosenberg Self-Esteem Scale (Weinberger, 1991). Distress had an internal consistency of 0.92 in the Time 1 sample of parents ($n = 171$). Among the couples participating in the present study, mothers had higher levels of subjective distress ($M = 66.4$, $SD = 17.8$) than fathers ($M = 60.3$, $SD = 13.7$), $t(54) = 2.30$, $p < 0.05$. This pattern is consistent with sex differences found in other samples (Weinberger, 1991). Mothers' ($M = 65.3$, $SD = 17.3$) and fathers' ($M = 58.9$, $SD = 15.1$) mean distress scores at Time 2 did not significantly differ from those at Time 1.

Self-restraint.   Self-restraint refers to a broad assessment of the control of egoistic desires in the interest of promoting long-term goals and positive relations with others. The scale is a 30-item composite measuring suppression of aggression (e.g., "I lose my temper and let people have it when I am angry" [reverse scored]), consideration of others (e.g., "Before I do anything, I think about how it will affect the people around me"), impulse control (e.g., "I become wild and crazy and do things people might not like" [reverse scored]), and responsibility (e.g., "I will cheat on something if I know no one will find out" [reverse scored]). The restraint items had an internal consistency alpha of 0.85 for the parents. In the original validation sample, restraint scores in adults correlated -0.57 with the assaultive aggression subscale of the Buss-Durkee Aggression Inventory and 0.46 with the Responsibility subscale of the Jackson Personality Inventory.

Among the couples participating in the present study, fathers at Time 1 ($M = 121.8$, $SD = 11.0$) had significantly lower self-restraint than did mothers ($M = 126.6$, $SD = 10.7$), $t(54) = 2.59$, $p < 0.01$. Fathers at Time 2 ($M = 127.6$, $SD = 10.9$) also reported lower self-restraint than did mothers ($M = 132.0$, $SD = 8.9$), $t(50) = 2.43$, $p < 0.05$, even though both fathers and mothers reported a significant increase in their restraint over the 4-year period, $t(50) = 4.70$, $p < 0.001$ and $t(51) = 4.61$, $p < 0.001$, respectively.

Depression.   Mothers and fathers also completed the 13-item short form of the BDI (Beck and Beck, 1972) at the Time 2 follow-up. The short form has been well validated and correlates above 0.9 with the long form (e.g., Reynolds and Gould, 1981). The BDI is currently the most widely used measure in studies of parents' adjustment in non-clinical populations (e.g., Forehand et al., 1987). The mothers' depression scores ranged from 0 to 18 ($M = 3.40$, $SD = 3.74$), with 24 percent scoring above the cutoff suggesting at least mild depression (5 or above; Beck and Beck, 1972) and 12 percent above the cutoff for moderate depression (8 or above). The fathers' scores ranged from 0 to 7 ($M = 1.92$, $SD = 1.95$) with only 7 percent having a score of 5 or above.

Measures of sons' outcomes

At the time of the 4-year follow-up, sons and their parents completed parallel assessments of the boys' psychological, social, and academic functioning. They also completed measures of parents' behavior and family functioning that are discussed elsewhere (e.g., Feldman and Weinberger, 1994). To control for potential biases due to overlapping informants, we used parents' reports of their own personalities at the initial assessment as the primary independent variables in this investigation, and sons' subsequent self-reports of their own functioning served as the primary dependent variables. When appropriate, parents' perceptions of their sons were used to establish convergent validity for the individual measures, which are presented later.

Fourteen measures of son's functioning were assessed within four domains: school achievement, positive peer relations, at-risk behavior, and social-emotional adjustment. The measures of achievement were the following.

Grades. Boys described their grades in high school on a 1–8 scale ranging from 1 = *mostly below D* to 8 = *mostly As*. These self-reports correlated highly with mothers' reports ($r = 0.83$, $p < 0.001$) and with fathers' reports ($r = 0.84$, $p < 0.001$). For the sample as a whole, the mean was 5.41 ($SD = 1.60$). Approximately one third of the boys reported grades of mostly Cs or lower, one third reported half Bs and Cs, and one third reported mostly Bs or higher. Self-reported grades correlate about 0.8 with actual grades (e.g., Dornbusch et al., 1990).

Effort in class. Boys were asked on 5-point Likert scales "How hard do you really try?" and "How often do you really pay attention?" in each of four classes: mathematics, English, social studies, and science (see Dornbusch et al., 1990). The alpha coefficient for the eight-item effort score was 0.84. The mean score averaged across the two items was 3.14 ($SD = 0.65$). Boys' self-reports of effort in school were significantly correlated with mothers' reports ($r = 0.70$, $p < 0.001$) and with fathers' reports ($r = 0.55$, $p < 0.05$).

Regular attendance. Following the procedure of Dornbusch et al. (1990), boys were also asked how often they "cut" (had an unexcused absence) in each of the four classes (0 = *never*, 4 = *almost every day*). This score was reverse coded as a measure of regular attendance. The alpha coefficient for the four-item scale was 0.99. The mean reversecoded score averaged across the four classes was 3.70 ($SD = 0.64$). Twenty-six percent of the boys reported being truant an average of a few times a month or more. Mothers confirmed boys' reports of cutting class ($r = 0.64$, $p < 0.001$); however, fathers were generally unaware of their sons' behavior ($r = 0.16$, *ns*).

Peer relations are another domain that has been linked to family factors (Parke and Ladd, 1992). The three following measures were selected to represent this area of functioning.

Emotional support. The Emotional Support and Intimacy subscale of the Adolescent Friendship Inventory (Rubenstein and Rubin, 1986) was used to assess the boys' establishment of peer relations that serve as a source of social support. the six-item subscale had an alpha coefficient of 0.78 in this sample and had a test-retest reliability of 0.78 in the original validation sample of high school students. The scale has been validated in relation to reciprocal sociometric choices, referral to the school psychologist for adjustment problems, and the prediction of depressive affect (e.g., Rubenstein and Rubin, 1986; Rubin et al., 1992). Items such as "I feel free to talk with my good friend about almost anything" are scored on 5-point Likert scales. The average item mean was 4.01 ($SD = 0.79$).

Close friendships. This measure developed for this study was a composite of ratings on a 1 (*never*) to 5 (*daily*) scale of how often adolescents and their friends engaged in positive activities together such as "hang out and talk" and "support each other through problems." The four-item scale had an alpha coefficient of 0.70. The average item mean was 3.14 ($SD = 0.74$).

Nondeviant peers. A parallel measure of peer deviance was reverse coded so that all outcomes in this domain were scored in the same direction. Six items rated on a 1 (*never*) to 5 (*daily*) scale asked how often participants' friends engaged in six antisocial behaviors, including cutting school and fighting with other groups. The alpha coefficient for the scale was 0.74. The average item mean for the reverse coded scale was 3.68 ($SD = 0.48$).

The following are several measures of at-risk behavior that were included in the study.

Antisocial acts. Antisocial behavior during the previous 6 months was assessed using a scale adapted from Feldman, Rosenthal, Mont-Reynaud, Leung, and Lau (1991). The scale consisted of nine items measuring school deviance, such as cheating, acting up in class, and school suspension, and seven items measuring more serious delinquent behavior, such as getting into trouble with the law and purposely damaging school property. The composite scale had an alpha coefficient of 0.89. Mothers' ratings were significantly correlated with boys' ratings ($r = 0.60$, $p < 0.001$), as were fathers' ratings ($r = 0.56$, $p < 0.001$). The mean score on the scale was 3.52 ($SD = 6.06$). To provide information about the level of antisocial behavior within the sample, we analyzed frequencies on specific items. Among these primarily 15- to 16-year-old boys in public schools, 55 percent admitted cheating on an in-class test, 22 percent had been "in trouble with the police," and 16 percent had "carried a weapon to school." These percentages are comparable with those found in other samples (e.g., Farrington, 1991).

Drug and alcohol use. The eight items of the misconduct scale adapted by Feldman et al. (1991) that dealt with involvement with drugs and alcohol were analyzed separately. Sons' reports were validated by mothers ($r = 0.65$, $p < 0.001$) and by fathers ($r = 0.64$, $p < 0.001$). The alpha coefficient for the scale was 0.88. Items included "drank enough alcohol to become drunk," "smoked marijuana," and "used other drugs (e.g., crack, cocaine, speed)." The mean score on the scale was 2.15 ($SD = 4.00$).

Multiple sexual partners. Participants were asked to identify the number of partners with whom they had had sexual intercourse. Among the 23 adolescents who reported having intercourse by the age of 16, 3 had one partner, 6 had two partners, 6 had three to five partners, and 7 reported six or more partners. The measure is described more fully in Feldman and Brown (1993).

Early emancipation. Early emancipation was measured by a reverse coding of the Teen Timetable, a 22-item questionnaire assessing adolescents' expectations of autonomy from parental control across a variety of everyday behaviors (Feldman and Wood, 1994). Participants rated each item on a 5-point scale indicating the age at which they engaged or expected to engage in the behavior described (e.g., "come home at night as late as you want"). The full scale alpha was 0.77. The mean score per item was 2.21 ($SD = 0.39$).

Poor conflict resolution. The subscale of the conflict resolution measure developed by Rubenstein and Feldman (1993) that was most predictive of negative outcomes in adolescence was used. Adolescents were asked on 5-point Likert scales how often they engaged in a variety of specific behaviors "when you disagree with a parent about something that is important to you." The nine-item subscale that measures angry, attacking responses had an alpha coefficient of 0.78. Sample items include "get sarcastic," "get mad and throw something at them," and "say or do something to hurt their feelings." The average item mean for the sample was 1.41 (*SD* = 0.65).

The final three outcome measures assessed the boys' social-emotional adjustment in terms of distress, self-restraint, and depression.

Subjective distress. Boys' distress and self-restraint were assessed using the same items on the WAI that their parents completed. In a larger sample of sixth-grade children (*n* = 381), distress scores had an alpha coefficient of 0.91, indicating that older children's reports on this scale tend to be as reliable as those of adults. Preadolescents' test-retest reliability is 0.84 for a 2-week period (*n* = 49) and 0.73 across a 7-month period (*n* = 337; Weinberger, 1991). For the boys participating in the present study, the 4-year test-retest correlation for distress was 0.54. The distress scale has been validated in a variety of studies of children in this age range (e.g., Feldman et al., 1990; Weinberger et al., 1990). In terms of concurrent validity among early adolescents, distress scores correlated 0.71 with the Anxiety scale of the Spielberger State-Trait Anxiety Inventory for Children and −0.60 with the global self-worth subscale of Harter's Perceived Competence Scale for Children.

Self-restraint. The restraint scale of the WAI also had a coefficient alpha of 0.91 in a large sample of preadolescents (*n* = 381). Preadolescents' test-retest reliability was 0.89 for a 2-week period (*n* = 49) and 0.76 across a 7-month period (*n* = 337). In a preadolescent sample, restraint correlated −0.71 with Youth Self-Report Aggression and −0.63 with Youth Self-Report Delinquency (Weinberger, 1991).

As described later, sons' initial restraint scores were also included in supplemental analyses as the only measure from the Time 1 data collection other than parents' distress and restraint that served as an independent variable. The correlation over 4 years for the boys in the present sample was 0.55. Their mean reports of self-restraint in preadolescence (*M* = 111.5, *SD* = 20.5) did not differ significantly from their reports in mid-adolescence (*M* = 107.9, *SD* = 18.6).

Depression. Sons' cognitive, somatic, and affective symptoms depression were assessed by using the Children's Depression Inventory (CDI; Kovacs, 1980/1981). The CDI is a widely used 27-item questionnaire that generally parallels the Beck Depression Inventory. The scale is reported to have an internal consistency of 0.86 and test-retest reliability of 0.84 (Kovacs, 1980/1981). The boys' scores on the CDI for this sample ranged from 0 to 28, with a mean score of 7.8 (*SD* = 6.2).

Approximately 20 percent of the boys scored in the depressed range, with a score of 13 or above.

Results

The focus of this study is on associations between parents' distress and restraint when their sons were 12 years of age and sons' outcomes 4 years later. Because the measures of parents' functioning were intercorrelated, part correlations as well as zero-order correlations were evaluated to allow a direct comparison of the overall versus independent association between predictors and the various outcome measures. The magnitudes of part (or semipartial) correlations are ordinarily very similar to those of the corresponding beta weights within non-hierarchical multiple regression analyses, when predictors are entered simultaneously; the significance levels of the part correlations and corresponding beta weights are identical (Cohen and Cohen, 1975).

Fathers' distress and restraint and sons' subsequent functioning

Table 7.1 presents the zero-order and part correlations between fathers' self-reported self-restraint and subjective distress at Time 1 and sons' outcomes 4 years later. The pattern of results was consistent across the domains of school achievement, positive peer relations, at-risk behavior, and social–emotional adjustment. Fathers' general levels of self-restraint were significantly correlated with all 14 measures of their sons' functioning as adolescents. Most of these correlations, uncorrected for attenuation, represent moderate affect sizes, according to Cohen's (1988) designations. Two were especially large. Fathers' reports of high self-restraint at Time 1 correlated 0.48 with sons' reports of regular school attendance and −0.52 with sons' reports of antisocial behaviors, such as stealing and carrying a weapon 4 years later.

Fathers' distress was generally a more modest predictor, significantly correlating with about half of the measures. There was at least one significant correlation within each of the four domains of functioning, suggesting that fathers' distress was not simply a predictor of sons' affective states. For example, fathers' distress correlated as strongly with sons' poor school attendance and antisocial behavior as with sons' distress.

Table 7.1   Associations between sons' functioning at age 16 and their fathers' personality 4 years earlier

| | Fathers' personality | | | |
| | Restraint | | Distress | |
Sons' functioning	r	Part r^a	r	Part r^b
School achievement				
1. Grades	0.33**	0.48***	−0.01	0.21
2. Effort	0.31**	0.29*	−0.20	−0.01
3. Attendance	0.48***	0.38**	−0.30**	−0.05
Positive peer relations				
4. Emotional support	0.26*	0.17	−0.18	−0.07
5. Close friendships	0.30**	0.24*	−0.23*	−0.08
6. Nondeviant peers	0.30**	0.32**	0.06	−0.12
At-risk behavior				
7. Antisocial acts	−0.52***	−0.41***	0.22*	−0.05
8. Drug/alcohol abuse	−0.31**	−0.34**	0.04	−0.16
9. Sexual partners	−0.25*	−0.25*	0.08	−0.07
10. Early emancipation	−0.30**	−0.18	0.28*	0.14
11. Poor conflict resolution	−0.36**	−0.27*	0.31**	0.14
Social–emotional adjustment				
12. Restraint	0.27*	0.27*	−0.14	−0.01
13. Distress	−0.25*	−0.14	0.23*	0.12
14. Depression	−0.34**	−0.27*	0.19	0.02

Note: *Sample sizes ranged from 56 to 60*
^{a} *Part r for fathers' restraint scores independent of fathers' distress scores.* ^{b} *Part r for fathers' distress scores independent of fathers' restraint scores*
*p < 0.05. **p < 0.01. ***p < 0.001*

Because fathers' levels of distress and self-restraint correlated −0.54 ($p < 0.001$, $n = 60$), part correlations were used to reveal the independent contributions of these two interrelated aspects of personality. The results clearly indicated that fathers' restraint emerged as having unique predictive power. For 11 of the 14 measures, fathers' restraint remained a significant predictor independent of variance that overlapped with their distress. In contrast, none of the correlations between fathers' distress (i.e., anxiety, depression, low self-esteem, and low well-being) and sons' outcomes remained significant once their associations with fathers' restraint scores were accounted for. In several instances, distress functioned to some degree as a suppressor variable, in which the part correlation for restraint was actually larger than the zero-order correlation. This pattern was most notable for high school grades, in which the zero-order correlation with father's restraint was 0.33 and the part correlation was 0.48.

In summary, fathers who were high in self-restraint (impulse control, suppression of aggression, consideration of others, and responsibility) tended to have sons who were doing relatively well across domains 4 years later, in terms of school achievement, supportive relations with peers, avoidance of at-risk behavior, and positive social–emotional adjustment. There also was consistent evidence that the correlations between fathers' distress and sons' outcomes could be accounted for by the tendency of unhappy fathers to have problems maintaining adequate self-restraint.

Mothers' distress and restraint and sons' subsequent functioning

Table 7.2 presents a parallel set of analyses predicting sons' outcomes from their mothers' personalities 4 years earlier. In contrast to the pattern for fathers, mothers' restraint only correlated with 2 of the 14 outcomes (regular school attendance and antisocial acts). Mothers' distress, like fathers', correlated with about half of the measures, although not with sons' distress or depression.

Mothers' initial distress and restraint scores correlated −0.25, ($p < 0.05$, $n = 76$). Calculations of part correlations indicated that mothers' levels of restraint, independent of their distress, continued to predict sons' having poorer school attendance and more antisocial behavior. In addition, mothers' distress, independent of their self-restraint, predicted sons' expending less effort at school, associating with a more deviant peer group, using more drugs and alcohol, having a larger number of sexual partners, and using more aggressive conflict resolution strategies. Hence, there was some evidence that the part correlations between mothers' distress and sons' outcomes were more robust than those for fathers' distress.

Table 7.2 Associations between sons' functioning at age 16 and their mothers' personality 4 years earlier

	Mothers' personality			
	Restraint		Distress	
Sons' functioning	*r*	Part *r*[a]	*r*	Part *r*[b]
School achievement				
1. Grades	0.19	0.14	−0.21*	0.16
2. Effort	0.12	0.05	−0.23*	−0.26*
3. Attendance	0.30*	0.26*	−0.19*	−0.12
Positive peer relations				
4. Emotional support	0.13	0.11	−0.09	−0.06
5. Close friendships	0.12	0.12	−0.03	−0.01
6. Nondeviant peers	0.14	0.08	−0.24*	−0.22*
At-risk behavior				
7. Antisocial acts	−0.25*	−0.23*	0.12	0.06
8. Drug/alcohol abuse	−0.18	−0.13	0.24*	0.20*
9. Sexual partners	−0.12	−0.06	0.26*	0.24*
10. Early emancipation	−0.16	−0.13	0.13	0.09
11. Poor conflict resolution	−0.06	−0.01	0.21*	0.20*
Social–emotional adjustment				
12. Restraint	0.01	−0.03	−0.16	−0.16
13. Distress	−0.03	−0.02	0.05	0.05
14. Depression	−0.11	−0.08	0.15	0.13

Note: *Sample sizes ranged from 71 to 75*
[a] *Part r for mothers' restraint scores independent of mothers' distress scores.* [b] *Part r for mothers' distress scores independent of mothers' restraint scores*
*p < 0.05. **p < 0.01. ***p < 0.001*

Spouses' distress and restraint and sons' subsequent functioning

Among the two-parent families in our sample, fathers' and mothers' reports of their own restraint at Time 1 correlated 0.53 ($p < 0.001$, $n = 55$), and their distress scores correlated 0.23 ($p < 0.05$, $n = 55$). In addition, although fathers' distress was unrelated to mothers' restraint, mothers who reported relatively high distress were likely to be married to fathers with relatively low self-restraint ($r = -0.27$, $p < 0.05$). Hence, the ability of one parent's personality to predict the son's outcomes might actually be mediated by its prediction of his or her spouse's personality.

As illustrated in tables 7.1 and 7.2, fathers' restraint and mothers' distress were the most important predictors of sons' outcomes. Therefore, zero-order and part correlations evaluating the independent contributions of fathers' restraint and mothers' distress were assessed within the subsample of two-parent families. The results are presented in table 7.3. Fathers' restraint continued to predict 12 of the 14 outcomes, independent of mothers' distress. More striking was that mothers' distress no longer predicted any of their sons' outcomes, once their husbands' restraint was partialed out.

When only two predictors are involved, part correlations such as those presented in table 7.3 can be interpreted in pathanalytic terms (Asher, 1983). Hence, in this sample, the tendency for distressed mothers to have relatively troubled adolescent sons was primarily an indirect relation, as a result of their tendency to be married to husbands who had problems with self-control. Of particular note, it was the presence of an undercontrolled father, rather than a distressed mother, that independently correlated with sons having higher levels of distress and depression.

As shown in tables 7.1 and 7.2, there were two measures (i.e., regular school attendance and antisocial acts) for which the best individual predictors were mothers' and fathers' restraint. When the part correlations for these predictors were calculated, fathers' restraint but not mothers' restraint remained an independent predictor of sons' class attendance (part $r = 0.39$, $p < 0.01$) and antisocial behavior (part $r = -0.36$, $p < 0.01$). Hence, all of the significant correlations in table 7.2 between mothers' personality and sons' outcomes could be accounted for by their covariance with fathers' levels of restraint.

Parents' distress and restraint as a predictor of parents' subsequent adjustment

The extensive association between parents' distress and restraint when sons were 12 and sons' functioning at age 16 suggests that parents' characteristics are likely to be fairly stable over time. As evidenced in table 7.4, this was clearly the case. The 4-year test-retest correlations

Table 7.3 Associations between sons' functioning at age 16 and fathers' restraint and mothers' distress 4 years earlier

	Parents' personality			
	Fathers' restraint		Mothers' distress	
Sons' functioning	r	Part r^a	r	Part r^b
School achievement				
1. Grades	0.33**	0.30*	−0.21*	−0.12
2. Effort	0.35**	0.30*	−0.28*	−0.19
3. Attendance	0.48***	0.45**	−0.19	−0.06
Positive peer relations				
4. Emotional support	0.26*	0.20	−0.09	−0.03
5. Close friendships	0.30**	0.30*	−0.03	0.06
6. Nondeviant peers	0.30**	0.26*	−0.24*	−0.17
At-risk behavior				
7. Antisocial acts	−0.45***	−0.45***	0.13	−0.01
8. Drug/alcohol abuse	−0.31**	−0.26*	0.24*	0.16
9. Sexual partners	−0.25*	−0.19	0.26*	0.20
10. Early emancipation	−0.30**	−0.28*	0.13	0.05
11. Poor conflict resolution	−0.36**	−0.32*	0.21*	0.11
Social–emotional adjustment				
12. Restraint	0.27*	0.24*	−0.15	−0.09
13. Distress	−0.25*	−0.24*	0.06	−0.01
14. Depression	−0.34**	−0.31*	0.15	0.06

Note: *These analyses are based on the subsample of 55 two-parent families*
[a] Part r for fathers' restraint scores independent of mothers' distress scores. [b] Part r for mothers' distress scores independent of fathers' restraint scores
*$p < 0.05$. **$p < 0.01$. ***$p < 0.001$

were 0.58 for fathers' restraint, 0.69 for fathers' distress, 0.71 for mothers' restraint, and 0.77 for mothers' distress.

Mothers' initial distress (but not restraint) predicted both parents' distress and depression 4 years later. In contrast, it was fathers' initial lack of restraint (but not heightened distress) that predicted both parents' subsequent distress and depression (see table 7.4) as well as their sons' (see table 7.3).

Table 7.4 Correlations of parents' social–emotional adjustment over 4 years

Parents' functioning 4 years later	Parents' personality			
	Restraint		Distress	
	Fathers'	Mothers'	Fathers'	Mothers'
Restraint				
Fathers'	0.58***	0.31**	−0.34**	−0.02
Mothers'	0.36**	0.71***	−0.35**	−0.11
Distress				
Fathers'	−0.42**	−0.07	0.69***	0.32**
Mothers'	−0.26*	−0.16	0.21	0.77***
Depression				
Fathers'	−0.29*	0.10	0.39**	0.22*
Mothers'	−0.26*	0.02	0.16	0.45***

Note: *Sample sizes ranged from 51 to 57 for fathers and from 72 to 74 for mothers.*
*$p < 0.05$. **$p < 0.01$. ***$p < 0.001$

Parents' depressive symptoms and sons' concurrent functioning

Because parents' initial distress and restraint scores correlated with parents' depression 4 years later, it was of interest to compare these measures as relative predictors of sons' functioning at the follow-up assessment. Neither mothers' nor fathers' reports of depressive symptoms when their sons were 16 years old had extensive associations with their sons' concurrent functioning. Of the 14 measures of boys' outcomes in table 7.1, mothers' concurrent depression scores only correlated modestly with 2 measures: an aggressive style of conflict resolution ($r = 0.20$, $p < 0.05$, $n = 73$) and depression ($r = 0.23$, $p < 0.05$, $n = 73$). These associations were not simply due to short-term fluctuations in behavior. Part correlations based on mothers' current depression and general distress 4 years earlier indicated that the prediction of sons' outcomes was due to overlapping variance. Moreover, when fathers' restraint from 4 years earlier was added to these multiple regression models, it remained the sole significant predictor of sons' conflict resolution style (part $r = -0.35$, $p < 0.05$) and depression (part $r = -0.26$, $p < 0.05$), independent of both mothers' initial distress and subsequent depression.

Fathers' ratings of their own depression significantly correlated with only one of the concurrent measures of sons' functioning. There was a 0.30 ($p = 0.01$, $n = 56$) correlation with sons' aggressive conflict resolution style. Once again, when fathers' restraint from 4 years earlier was added as a predictor, it remained the only significant predictor of sons' scores on this measure (part $r = -0.24$, p < 0.05).

Fathers' and sons' initial restraint and sons' subsequent functioning

Because fathers' initial restraint scores were such a robust predictor of sons' later functioning, supplemental analyses were undertaken to evaluate if these associations could be explained by the initial correlations between fathers' and sons' restraint scores. Parents and their preadolescent sons had completed the identical set of 30 restraint items at the Time 1 assessment as well as at Time 2. Sons' Time 1 restraint correlated significantly with their fathers' restraint ($r = 0.25$, $p < 0.05$, $n = 60$) but not with their mothers' ($r = -0.02$, ns, $n = 75$).

If the influences of fathers' restraint were limited to sons' inheritance of similar temperamental characteristics, one would expect fathers' restraint to have little predictive power independent of sons' initial restraint. However, if fathers' restraint had a more multifaceted and dynamic impact on their children's development, one would expect fathers' restraint to continue to be predictive independent of sons' initial restraint.

Given that restraint was designed as a superordinate measure of socialization and self-control (e.g., Feldman and Weinberger, 1994; Weinberger and Schwartz, 1990), it is not surprising that sons' Time 1 restraint scores significantly correlated with 11 of the 14 outcome measures 4 years later (see table 7.5). However, for 10 of the 14 measures, fathers' restraint, independent of sons' restraint, continued to significantly predict sons' subsequent outcomes. For 7 of these 10 measures (grades, class attendance, nondeviant peers, drug/alcohol use, early emancipation expectations, conflict resolution skills, and depression), fathers' restraint, rather than sons' restraint, significantly predicted independent variance in the outcome measures. For the other 3

Table 7.5 Associations between sons' functioning at age 16 and fathers' and sons' restraint 4 years earlier

Sons' functioning	Fathers' restraint		Sons' restraint	
	r	Part r^a	r	Part r^b
School achievement				
1. Grades	0.30**	0.29*	0.19	0.12
2. Effort	0.35**	0.28*	0.34**	0.27*
3. Attendance	0.48***	0.42***	0.29*	0.18
Positive peer relations				
4. Emotional support	0.26*	0.14	0.34*	0.29*
5. Close friendships	0.30*	0.22*	0.35*	0.29*
6. Nondeviant peers	0.30*	0.24*	0.28*	0.21
At-risk behavior				
7. Antisocial acts	−0.48***	−0.40***	−0.41***	−0.31**
8. Drug/alcohol abuse	−0.31*	−0.28*	−0.15	−0.08
9. Sexual partners	−0.25*	−0.19	−0.31**	−0.25*
10. Early emancipation	−0.30**	−0.25*	−0.24*	−0.17
11. Poor conflict resolution	−0.36**	−0.31*	−0.25*	−0.17
Social–emotional adjustment				
12. Restraint	0.27*	0.14	0.55***	0.50***
13. Distress	−0.25*	−0.18	−0.31**	−0.23
14. Depression	−0.34*	−0.31*	−0.17	−0.09

The table is headed by a spanning label "Parents' personality" over the "Fathers' restraint" and "Sons' restraint" columns.

Note: *Sample sizes ranged from 56 to 60 for families with a father or stepfather in the home*
[a] *Part r for fathers' restraints scores independent of sons' restraint scores.* [b] *Part r for sons' restraint scores independent of fathers' restraint scores*
*p < 0.05. **p < 0.01. ***p < 0.001

measures (effort in school, close friendships, and antisocial acts), both fathers' restraint and sons' restraint were significant independent predictors of sons' later behavior.

The tendency for fathers' Time 1 restraint to be a more consistent independent predictor of sons' outcomes than sons' own restraint is especially notable given that sons' initial self-reports, unlike fathers', had overlapping method variance with the self-report measures of sons' outcomes. In only three cases (emotional support from peers, number of sexual partners, and restraint) did sons' restraint, rather than fathers' restraint, remain a unique predictor. Sons' distress was the only 1 of the 14 measures in which neither fathers' nor sons' initial restraint had an independent association with the outcome.

These results suggest that both fathers' and preadolescent sons' self-restraint scores are important predictors of sons' functioning in mid-adolescence. More specifically, they indicate that fathers' restraint scores when their sons were 12 years old provided considerable information about sons' future outcomes beyond direct resemblance between fathers and sons at the initial assessment.

Discussion

In this longitudinal study, parents' personalities significantly predicted sons' psychological, academic, and social functioning 4 years later. Given the largely independent and primarily clinical literatures on maternal depression and paternal antisocial behavior, it was of particular interest to evaluate the unique associations of mothers' and fathers' distress versus self-restraint with subsequent adjustment among adolescents attending public schools.

The most striking finding in the present study was the pervasive and robust association between fathers' restraint when their sons were 12 years old and their adolescents' self-assessments at age 16. Sons of fathers low in self-restraint fared relatively poorly on all 14 outcome measures and collectively provided a portrait of a markedly at-risk adolescence. As a group, they did relatively poorly at school, had problematic peer relations, engaged in a variety of impulsive and antisocial behaviors, and were prone to general subjective distress and symptoms of depression.

Fathers' initial subjective distress, which correlated negatively with fathers' self-restraint, predicted about half of the measures of sons' outcomes. However, it was consistently the variance unique to self-restraint, rather than distress (or subsequent depression), that was predictive. In addition, once fathers' initial restraint scores were included in the multiple regression models, none of the associations between mothers' distress and restraint (or subsequent depression) and sons' functioning remained significant. These data indicate that mothers' own personal adjustment generally did not significantly alter the negative consequences of fathers' low self-restraint. That is, partialing out whether mothers were high or low in distress, restraint, or depression did not notably diminish the association between fathers' and sons' functioning.

Within this nonclinical sample, it may have been that the adjustment difficulties manifested by the mothers were generally not of the same magnitude as those of the fathers with relatively antisocial tendencies. As expected, mothers self-reported significantly fewer problems with self-restraint in comparison with fathers. Almost by definition, it may be especially difficult for individuals with problems of impulse control, a lack of consideration of others, aggression, and irresponsibility (i.e., the four subdimensions of restraint) to keep their problems from disrupting their social interactions, including the emotional and instrumental functioning of their families. Mothers did report higher levels of subjective distress than did fathers. However, it may be that only relatively severe dysphoria, as manifested in the literature on clinically depressed mothers, has comparably disruptive effects on children's lives (e.g., Downey and Coyne, 1990).

The present results found linear relations between problems of undercontrol and negative child outcomes. However, several authors, including Block and Block (1980) and Weinberger and colleagues (Weinberger, 1990; Weinberger and Davidson, 1994; Weinberger and Schwartz, 1990), have also highlighted potential problems associated with excessive self-restraint. Although fathers' lack of restraint predicted boys' internalizing symptoms in terms of subjective distress and depression, a different pattern of results may have emerged if measures of inhibition, such as shyness and a lack of assertiveness, had been included.

The strength of the association between fathers' restraint and sons' outcomes was quite robust, given that there was no correction for attenuation of the measures, as is typically done in structural equation models of longitudinal data. Moreover, studies of selective attrition suggest that the results may underestimate the strength of the actual associations because of a restriction of range. Individuals who are aggressive and low in self-restraint are less likely to volunteer to participate in research and are more likely to drop out as the study proceeds (e.g., Huesmann et al., 1984; Weinberger et al., 1990). Procedures used

in initial recruitment for this study were designed to minim¹
tial attrition, and no overall differences between participar
participants in the follow-up study were identified. Non¹
finding that parents who remained in the study reported sɪgnᴴᴵᴄ
higher restraint at Time 2 than at Time 1 may reflect some selective attrition of low-restraint parents in addition to a normative increase
in restraint in midlife that has been identified in other samples
(Weinberger, 1991).

The association between fathers' restraint and sons' outcomes is
undoubtedly multidetermined. Part of the relation is likely to be genetic,
including possibly the sex-linked inheritance of temperaments. For
example, genetic components of relevant dimensions such as anger and
impulsivity have been identified (e.g., Achenbach, 1993; DiLalla and
Gottesman, 1989; Rowe, 1986). However, there is now ample evidence
from studies of twins that children's social competence, and particularly
adolescent delinquent behavior, is significantly influenced by shared
family environments in addition to genetic similarity (Achenbach,
1993; DiLalla and Gottesman, 1989; Edelbrock et al., 1995; Rowe,
1994).

The environmental influences of parents' individual characteristics
on their children can be conceptualized in terms of several distinguish-
able but interrelated facets. First, it is almost tautological to highlight
that parents serve as primary attachment figures and adult role models.
However, there has been relatively little research on how general individual differences in parents' personalities relate to these processes.
Current evidence suggests that the resemblances that emerge between
low-restraint fathers and their sons are often not simply the result of
intentional modeling (see Bandura, 1986). On a variety of measures,
delinquency-prone adolescents are more likely to reject their parents as
role models than to express a desire to be like them (Brook et al., 1986;
Brownfield, 1987; Hirschi, 1969).

More research is needed to explain how the pattern of "like father like
son" emerges in cases in which sons repudiate their fathers' behavior
in contrast to those who idealize it. Psychodynamic theories related
to attachment, object relations, and self-psychology all emphasize that
having parental figures with whom one can identify and internalize is
critical to most individuals' development of self-regulatory controls
(Bowlby, 1988; Greenberg and Mitchell, 1983; Kohut, 1977). Given this
perspective, it may be that some children of dysfunctional parents follow

in their parents' footsteps because they fail to develop the skills necessary to do otherwise, whatever their intentions (see Rutter and Quinton, 1984).

To date, there has been little evaluation of the degree to which the impact of parents' individual differences are mediated by the more didactic aspects of parenting practices and family socialization versus the more affective processes involved in children's attachment to and identification with parental figures (see Darling and Steinberg, 1993). There is now broad recognition that undercontrolled adults tend to create the kinds of harsh, inconsistent, and conflictual family environments that predict antisocial behavior in the next generation (e.g., Elder et al., 1986; Huesmann et al., 1984; Wahler and Dumas, 1986). Although many researchers in this area have highlighted the potential role of genetics in this cycle (e.g., Frick and Jackson, 1993; McCord, 1991), individual differences in one generation can also serve as an environmental influence on the development of stable individual differences in the next. For example, Feldman and Weinberger (1994) illustrated how parenting and family functioning during childhood may influence boys' subsequent delinquency through the boys' development of self-restraint. Almost by definition, effective socialization entails creating predispositions in individuals that they maintain in settings outside their families of origin. Hence, future longitudinal research will be necessary to determine the independent contributions of genetics, family practices, and identification with parental figures in the intergenerational associations between parents' personalities and children's development.

The finding that fathers' restraint continued to be a predictor of 10 of the 14 measures of sons' outcomes, independent of overlapping variance with sons' initial restraint, adds considerable important information. First, it helps to rule out the possibility that the fathers' behavior was epiphenomenal, in the sense of being a reaction to or otherwise determined by the sons' behavior. In addition, it suggests that there is more to the story than the passive inheritance of temperament (see Scarr and McCartney, 1983). It may be that there is an additional genetic component involved that has an interacting or changing influence during development (Plomin and Dunn, 1986). It is also highly plausible that disruptive effects of fathers' low-restraint behaviors on the family environment continue to accumulate during their sons' adolescence. Finally, sons' reactions to their fathers' adult antisocial behaviors may have new meanings as the sons themselves become more actively engaged in developing their own adult identities.

References

Achenbach, T. M. (1993). Taxonomy and comorbidity of conduct problems: Evidence from empirically based approaches. *Development and Psychopathology*, 5, 51–64.

Achenbach, T. M., & Edelbrock, C. (1983). *Manual for the child behavior checklist and revised child behavior profile*. Burlington: University of Vermont, Department of Psychiatry.

Asher, H. B. (1983). *Causal modeling*. Newbury Park, CA: Sage.

Bandura, A. (1986). *The social foundations of thought and action*. Englewood Cliffs, NJ: Prentice Hall.

Beal, C. R. (1994). *Boys and girls: The development of gender roles*. New York: McGraw-Hill.

Beck, A. T., & Beck, R. W. (1972). Screening depressed patients in family practice. *Postgraduate Medicine*, 52, 81–85.

Berkowitz, L. (1993). *Aggression: Its causes, consequences, and control*. Philadelphia: Temple University Press.

Block, J. H., & Block, J. (1980). The role of ego-control and ego-resiliency in the organization of behavior. In E. A. Collins (Ed.), *Minnesota symposium on motivation* (Vol. 13, pp. 39–101). Hillsdale, NJ: Erlbaum.

Bowlby, J. (1988). *A secure base*. New York: Basic Books.

Brook, J. S., Whiteman, M., Gordon, A. S., & Brook, D. W. (1986). Father–daughter identification and its impact on her personality and drug use. *Developmental Psychology*, 22, 743–748.

Brownfield, D. (1987). Father–son relationships and violent behavior. *Deviant Behavior*, 8, 65–78.

Bugental, D. B., Blue, J., & Cruzcosa, M. (1989). Perceived control over caregiving outcomes: Implications for child abuse. *Developmental Psychology*, 25, 532–539.

Buss, D. M. (1984). Toward a psychology of person–environment (PE) correlation: The role of spouse selection. *Journal of Personality and Social Psychology*, 47, 361–377.

Church, A. T., & Burke, P. J. (1994). Exploratory and confirmatory tests of the Big Five and Tellegen's three and four-dimensional models. *Journal of Personality and Social Psychology*, 66, 93–114.

Clarizio, H. F., & McCoy, G. F. (1983). *Behavior disorders in children*. New York: Harper & Row.

Cohen, J. (1988). *Statistical power analysis for the behavioral sciences* (2nd ed.). Hillsdale, NJ: Erlbaum.

Cohen, J., & Cohen, P. (1975). *Applied multiple regression/correlations analysis for the behavioral sciences.* New York: Wiley.

Conger, R. D., Conger, K. J., Elder, G. H., Lorenz, F. O., Simons, R. L., & Whitbeck, L. B. (1992). A family process model of economic hardship and adjustment of early adolescent boys. *Child Development, 63,* 526–541.

Costa, P. T., McCrae, R. R., & Arenberg, D. (1980). Enduring dispositions in adult males. *Journal of Personality and Social Psychology, 38,* 793–800.

Darling, N., & Steinberg, L. (1993). Parenting style as context: An integrative model. *Psychological Bulletin, 113,* 487–496.

DiLalla, L. F., & Gottesman, I. I. (1989). Heterogeneity of causes of delinquency and criminality: Life-span perspectives. *Development and Psychopathology, 1,* 339–349.

Dix, T. (1991). The affective organization of parenting: Adaptive and maladaptive processes. *Psychological Bulletin, 110,* 3–25.

Dornbusch, S. M., Ritter, P. L., Mont-Reynaud, R., & Chen, Z. (1990). Family decision making and academic performance in a diverse high school population. *Journal of Adolescent Research, 5,* 143–160.

Downey, G., & Coyne, J. C. (1990). Children of depressed parents: An integrative review. *Psychological Bulletin, 108,* 50–76.

Edelbrock, C., Rende, R., Plomin, R., & Thompson, L. A. (1995). Genetic and environmental effects on competence and problem behavior in childhood and early adolescence. *Journal of Child Psychology and Psychiatry 36*(5), 775–785.

Elder, G. H., Caspi, A., & Downey, G. (1986). Problem behavior and family relationships: A multi-generational analysis. In A. Sorenson, F. Weinert, & L. Sherrod (Eds.), *Human development in the life course: A multidisciplinary perspective* (pp. 293–340). Hillsdale, NJ: Erlbaum.

Epstein, S., & O'Brien, E. J. (1985). The person–situation debate in historical and current perspective. *Psychological Bulletin, 98,* 513–537.

Farrington, D. P. (1991). Childhood aggression and adult violence: Early precursors and later life outcomes. In D. J. Pepler, & K. H. Rubin (Eds.), *The development and treatment of childhood aggression* (pp. 5–29). Hillsdale, NJ: Erlbaum.

Feldman, S. S., & Brown, N. (1993). Family influences on adolescent male sexuality: The mediational role of self-restraint. *Social Development, 2,* 16–35.

Feldman, S. S., Rosenthal, D. A., Mont-Reynaud, R., Leung, K., & Lau, S. (1991). Ain't misbehavin': Adolescent values and family environments as correlates of misconduct in Australia, Hong Kong, and the United States. *Journal of Research on Adolescence, 1,* 109–134.

Feldman, S. S., & Weinberger, D. A. (1994). Self-restraint as a mediator of family influences on boys' delinquent behavior: A longitudinal study. *Child Development, 65,* 195–211.

Feldman, S. S., Wentzel, K. R., Weinberger, D. A., & Munson, J. A. (1990).

Marital satisfaction of parents of preadolescent boys and its relationship to family and child functioning. *Journal of Family Psychology, 4,* 213–234.

Feldman, S. S., & Wood, D. N. (1994). Parents' expectations for preadolescent sons' behavioral autonomy: A longitudinal study of correlates and outcomes. *Journal of Research on Adolescence, 4,* 45–70.

Forehand, R., & McCombs, A. (1988). Unraveling the antecedent-consequence conditions in maternal depression and adolescent functioning. *Behaviour Research and Therapy, 26,* 399–405.

Forehand, R., McCombs, A., & Brody, G. H. (1987). The relationship between parental depressive mood states and child functioning. *Advances in Behaviour Research and Therapy, 9,* 1–20.

Frick, P. J., & Jackson, Y. K. (1993). Family functioning and childhood antisocial behavior: Yet another reinterpretation. *Journal of Clinical Child Psychology, 4,* 410–419.

Gelfand, D. M., & Teti, D. M. (1990). The effects of maternal depression on children. *Clinical Psychology Review, 10,* 329–353.

Greenberg, J. R., & Mitchell, S. A. (1983). *Object relations in psycho-analytic theory.* Cambridge, MA: Harvard University Press.

Hammen, C. (1991). *Depression runs in families: The social context of risk and resilience in children of depressed mothers.* New York: Springer-Verlag.

Hirschi, T. (1969). *Causes of delinquency.* Berkeley: University of California Press.

Hops, H., Sherman, L., & Biglan, A. (1990). Maternal depression, marital discord, and children's behavior: A developmental perspective. In G. Patterson (Ed.), *Depression and aggression in family interaction* (pp. 185–208). Hillsdale, NJ: Erlbaum.

Huesmann, L. R., Eron, L. D., Lefkowitz, M. M., & Walder, L. O. (1984). The stability of aggression over time and generations. *Developmental Psychology, 20,* 1120–1134.

Jessor, R. (1991). Risk behavior in adolescence: A psychosocial framework for understanding and action. *Journal of Adolescent Health, 12,* 597–605.

Kendrick, D. T., & Funder, D. C. (1988). Profiting from controversy: Lessons from the person–situation debate. *American Psychologist, 43,* 23–34.

Kohut, H. (1977). *The restoration of the self.* New York: International Universities Press.

Kovacs, M. (1980/1981). Rating scales to assess depression in school-aged children. *Acta Paedopsychiatrica, 46,* 305–315.

Lahey, B. B., Russo, M. F., Walker, J. L., & Piacentini, J. C. (1989). Personality characteristics of the mothers of children with disruptive behavior disorders. *Journal of Consulting and Clinical Psychology, 57,* 512–515.

Loeber, R. (1990). Development and risk factors of juvenile antisocial behavior and delinquency. *Clinical Psychology Review, 10,* 1–41.

Loehlin, J. C. (1992). *Genes and environment in personality development.* Newbury Park, CA: Sage.

Lyon, D., & Greenberg, J. (1991). Evidence of codependency in women with an alcoholic parent: Helping out Mr. Wrong. *Journal of Personality and Social Psychology, 61*, 435–439.

McCord, J. (1991). The cycle of crime and socialization practices. *Journal of Criminal Law and Criminology, 82*, 211–228.

Mednick, S. A., Gabrielli, W. F., & Hutchings, B. (1987). Genetic factors in the etiology of criminal behavior. In S. A. Mednick, T. E. Moffitt, & S. A. Stack (Eds.), *The causes of crime: New biological approaches* (pp. 74–91). Cambridge, England: Cambridge University Press.

Merikangas, K. R., Prusoff, B. A., & Weissman, M. M. (1988). Parental concordance for affective disorder: Psychopathology in offspring. *Journal of Affective Disorder, 15*, 279–290.

Mischel, W. (1968). *Personality and assessment.* New York: Wiley.

Parke, R. D., & Ladd, G. W. (1992). *Family–peer relationships: Models of linkages.* Hillsdale, NJ: Erlbaum.

Patterson, G. R., & Capaldi, D. M. (1991). Antisocial parents: Unskilled and vulnerable. In P. A. Cowan, & E. M. Hetherington (Eds.), *Advances in family research: II. Family transitions* (pp. 195–218). Hillsdale, NJ: Erlbaum.

Patterson, G. R., Reid, J. B., & Dishion, T. J. (1992). *Antisocial boys.* Eugene, OR: Castalia.

Phares, V., & Compas, B. E. (1992). The role of fathers in child and adolescent psychopathology: Make room for daddy. *Psychological Bulletin, 111*, 387–412.

Pincus, A. L., & Boekman, L. F. (1993, August). *Social–emotional adjustment and the five-factor model of personality.* Paper presented at the annual meeting of the American Psychological Association, Toronto, Ontario, Canada.

Plomin, R., & Dunn, J. (Eds.). (1986). *The study of temperament: Changes, continuities and challenges.* Hillsdale, NJ: Erlbaum.

Reynolds, W. M., & Gould, J. W. (1981). A psychometric investigation of the standard and short form of the Beck Depression Inventory. *Journal of Consulting and Clinical Psychology, 49*, 306–307.

Robins, L. N., & Ratcliff, K. S. (1978/1979). Risk factors in the continuation of childhood antisocial behavior into adulthood. *International Journal of Mental Health, 7*, 96–116.

Robins, L. N., West, P. A., & Herjanic, B. L. (1975). Arrests and delinquency in two generations: A study of Black urban families and their children. *Journal of Child Psychology and Psychiatry, 16*, 125–140.

Rolf, J., Masten, A. S., Cicchetti, D., Neuchterlein, K. H., & Weintraub, S. (Eds.). (1990). *Risk and protective factors in the development of psychopathology.* New York: Cambridge University Press.

Rowe, D. C. (1986). Genetic and environmental components of antisocial behavior: A study of 265 twin pairs. *Criminology, 24,* 513–532.

Rowe, D. C. (1994). *The limits of family influence: Genes, experience, and behavior.* New York: Guilford.

Rubenstein, J. L., & Feldman, S. S. (1993). Conflict resolution in adolescent boys. Antecedents and adaptational correlates. *Journal of Research on Adolescence, 3,* 41–66.

Rubenstein, J. L., & Rubin, C. (1986). *The Adolescent Friendship Inventory.* Unpublished manuscript.

Rubin, C., Rubenstein, J. L., Stechler, G., Heeren, T., Halton, A., Houseman, D., & Kasten, L. (1992). Depressive affect in "normal" adolescents: Relationship to life stress, family and friends. *American Journal of Orthopsychiatry, 62,* 430–441.

Rutter, M., & Quinton, D. (1984). Parental psychiatric disorder: Effects on children. *Psychological Medicine, 14,* 853–880.

Scarr, S., & McCartney, K. (1983). How people make their own environments: A theory of genotype–environment interaction. *Child Development, 54,* 424–435.

Scarr, S., Webber, P. L., Weinberg, R. A., & Wittig, M. A. (1981). Personality resemblance among adolescents and their parents in biologically related and adoptive families. *Journal of Personality and Social Psychology, 40,* 885–898.

Schwartz, J. C., & Pollack, P. R. (1977). Affect and delay of gratification. *Journal of Research in Personality, 11,* 147–164.

Tellegen, A. (1985). Structures of mood and personality and their relevance to assessing anxiety with an emphasis on self-report. In A. H. Tuma, and J. D. Maser (Eds.), *Anxiety and the anxiety disorders* (pp. 681–706). Hillsdale, NJ: Erlbaum.

Tsuang, M. T., & Faraone, S. V. (1990). *The genetics of mood disorders.* Baltimore: Johns Hopkins University Press.

Tyson, P., & Tyson, R. L. (1990). *Psychoanalytic theories of development: An integration.* New Haven, CT: Yale University Press.

Wahler, R. G., & Dumas, J. E. (1986). "A chip off the old block": Some interpersonal characteristics of coercive children across generations. In P. S. Strain, M. J. Guralnick, & H. M. Walker (Eds.), *Children's social behavior* (pp. 49–91). New York: Academic Press.

Watson, D., & Clark, L. A. (1984). Negative affectivity: The disposition to experience aversive emotional states. *Psychological Bulletin, 55,* 465–490.

Weinberger, D. A. (1990). The construct validity of the repressive coping style. In J. L. Singer (Ed.), *Repression and dissociation: Implications for personality theory, psychopathology, and health* (pp. 337–386). Chicago: University of Chicago Press.

Weinberger, D. A. (1991). *Social–emotional adjustment in older children and adults: Psychometric properties of the Weinberger Adjustment Inventory.* Unpublished manuscript, Case Western Reserve University.

Weinberger, D. A., & Bartholomew, K. (1996). Social–emotional adjustment and patterns of alcohol use among young adults. *Journal of Personality.*

Weinberger, D. A., & Davidson, M. N. (1994). Styles of inhibiting emotional expression: Distinguishing repressive coping from impression management. *Journal of Personality, 62,* 587–613.

Weinberger, D. A., & Gomes, M. E. (1995). Changes in daily mood and self-restraint among undercontrolled preadolescents: A time-series analysis of "acting out." *Journal of the American Academy of Child and Adolescent Psychiatry, 34,* 1473–1482.

Weinberger, D. A., & Schwartz, G. E. (1990). Distress and restraint as superordinate dimensions of adjustment: A typological perspective. *Journal of Personality, 58,* 381–417.

Weinberger, D. A., Tublin, S. K., Ford, M. E., & Feldman, S. S. (1990). Preadolescents' social–emotional adjustment and selective attrition in family research. *Child Development, 61,* 1374–1386.

EIGHT

Adolescent Girls' Relationships with Mothers and Best Friends

Leslie A. Gavin and Wyndol Furman

Researchers have devoted considerable attention to both parent-adolescent relationships and adolescent friendships (see Savin-Williams and Berndt, 1990; Steinberg, 1990). However, with some notable exceptions (Furman and Buhrmester, 1985; Gold and Yanof, 1985), most investigators have focused on only one relationship at a time. Moreover, investigators often employ different constructs to explore characteristics of these two kinds of relationships. For example, family researchers have extensively examined conflict between parents and adolescents, but we know relatively little about conflict between friends. Conversely, more is known about the role of similarity in friendships than in parent-adolescent relationships. As a consequence, research on these two relationships has remained relatively isolated from one another. Often we do not know if results pertaining to one relationship are specific to that relationship or may be applied to adolescents' relationships in general.

The purpose of the present study was to use a common theoretical framework to identify factors associated with adolescents' perceptions of harmony in relationships with mothers and best friends. By harmony, we mean frequent supportive interactions and infrequent conflictual interactions. The construct of harmony was of interest because it incorporates a wide range of supportive and conflictual relationship features, can be used to examine both family and peer relationships, and is associated with perceptions of adjustment in adolescence (Furman, 1987).

Relationship Harmony

What factors may be associated with harmonious relationships? We expected such variables to fall into two categories (Furman, 1984). First, having certain individual characteristics, such as social skill, may be associated with being a good relationship partner. Second, harmony may stem from similarity between partners' individual characteristics, such as interests or perceived socioemotional needs. In the present study, we considered both individual characteristics of each partner and similarity of characteristics between partners in our examination of harmony in adolescents' relationships with peers and parents.

Individual characteristics. Although few studies have specifically examined interpersonal harmony, many variables have been related to interpersonal attraction. For example, social skill has received considerable attention as an important variable in friendship formation and maintenance. Buhrmester (1990) found that social competence in peer relationships was associated with greater intimacy in friendships. To date, social skills have not been examined as extensively in parent-adolescent relationships, although clinical investigators have taught parents and adolescents communication skills as a way of improving their relationships (Robin and Foster, 1989). Other potentially important individual characteristics include emotional attunement, display of positive affect, high self-esteem, psychological mindedness, and ability to manage power and jealousy within the relationship.

Similarity of partners' characteristics. Similarity of interests and similarity of attitudes are also major predictors of interpersonal attraction (see Hinde, 1979; Huston and Levinger, 1978). Children emphasize the importance of shared activities in their conceptions of friendship (Bigelow, 1977; Furman and Bierman, 1984), and in their reasons for liking friends (Rubin, 1980). Attitudes are more similar among adolescent friends than among those who are not friends, and friends' attitudes become more similar to one another over time (Kandel, 1978). Although similarity has been shown to be important in friendships, it has not been examined empirically in parent-adolescent relationships. Relationship harmony may also be related to the degree to which the two partners have similar socioemotional needs and the degree to which each partner perceives that their needs are being met in the relationship.

We believe that a common framework may be used to understand harmony or disharmony in relationships with both parents and friends. We generally expected the same factors to be associated with harmony in the two kinds of relationships, but some differences may occur. For example, similarity of interests may be more important in peer relationships than in relationships with parents. Furthermore, it is important not to equate these relationships. For example, we expected relationship harmony to be related to how well the adolescents perceived their needs were met by each partner, although the specific needs could vary across parent and peer relationships.

The Present Study

In the present study, adolescent girls' relationships with their mothers and best friends were investigated. For both parent-adolescent and friendship pairs, relationship harmony was hypothesized to be related to (1) certain individual characteristics of each partner that lend themselves to maintaining harmonious relationships (i.e., positive social skills and prosocial interpersonal characteristics, ability to meet partners' needs) and (2) similarity of certain characteristics of the two people (i.e., similarity of interests and socioemotional needs).

Method

Subjects

The participants were 60 adolescent girls, their mothers, and best female friends. The age range for the focal adolescents was 15–18 years (mean = 16.5), for friends was 12–18 (mean = 16.2), and for mothers was 34–58 (mean = 43.5). The sample comprised 57 Caucasian, one African-American, and two Hispanic females. The participants were primarily from middle-class urban and suburban families, with the mean family income being $30,000–$40,000 per year. Fifty-eight percent of the target adolescents' parents were married, 3 percent were separated, 37 percent were divorced, and 2 percent of the mothers were widowed.

Procedure

Questionnaires were administered to a large pool of subjects to identify adolescents with particularly harmonious or disharmonious relationships. The questionnaires were distributed through local school systems and through televised public service announcements. Approximately 450 interested adolescents completed a 16-item short version of the Network of Relationship Inventory (NRI; Furman and Buhrmester, 1985), which assessed supportive and negative interactions with their mothers and their best female friends. The adolescent's perception of harmony was defined as the degree of perceived support minus the degree of perceived negative interaction in that relationship. Harmonious relationships were considered to be those with scores at least one-half of a standard deviation above the mean, whereas disharmonious were those at least one-half of a standard deviation below the mean. Although the terms *harmonious* and *disharmonious* are used to describe these relationships, it should be noted that they are defined in terms of their relative degree of harmony and not in any absolute sense of harmony or disharmony.

Using these criteria, we identified equal numbers of adolescents who had relatively harmonious relationships with both partners, relatively disharmonious relationships with both, relatively harmonious relationships with mothers and relatively disharmonious relationships with friends, and vice versa. Thus, our screening procedure yielded a group of adolescents with diverse relational experiences with mothers and friends.

At the time of the actual study, the recruited adolescents again rated their relationships using the full version of the NRI, and final assignment to the four groups was done by median splits on these full harmony scale scores. In particular, the 60 adolescents were assigned to the following groups: (1) those with relatively harmonious relationships with both mothers and friends ($n = 17$), (2) those with relatively disharmonious relationships with both ($n = 16$), (3) those with relatively harmonious relationships with mothers and relatively disharmonious relationships with friends ($n = 14$), and (4) vice versa ($n = 13$).

During their visit to the laboratory, adolescents, parents, and friends all completed sets of questionnaires, and adolescent-mother and adolescent-friend dyads were observed interacting. Adolescents and their friends were each paid $15.00. Mothers participated voluntarily.

Questionnaire measures

Network of Relationships Inventory (NRI). The NRI (Furman and Buhrmester, 1985) was used to assess the adolescent's perceptions of supportive and negative interactions with mother and best friend. For example, subjects were asked, "How much does this person help you when you need to get something done?" Ratings were done on standard five-point Likert scales, and anchor points ranged from 1 (little or none) to 5 (the most). The NRI includes 10 three-item scales that load on two factors: (1) Support (affection, admiration, reliable alliance, intimacy, companionship, instrumental help, and nurturance of the other) and (2) Negative Interactions (conflict, punishment, and irritation). Cronbach's alphas of the factors exceeded 0.90.

The NRI was used because it is one of the few validated measures available that poses parallel questions across relationships, thus providing comparable data. Additionally, the NRI also taps a total of 10 different supportive or negative features of relationships, permitting us to examine a relatively broad construct. The harmony scores used for assigning subjects to groups were calculated by subtracting standardized negative interaction scores from the standardized support scores.

The focal adolescents' and their partners' reports of harmony were highly related (adolescent-friend $r = 0.55$; adolescent-mother $r = 0.61$). We chose to use only the one rater, the focal adolescent, so that the rater was consistent across relationships.

Activities and Interests Inventory. This questionnaire was used to assess the similarity of each set of partners' activities and interests. Each of the three participants was asked how much they enjoyed a range of 66 activities, including various sports, artistic hobbies, and recreational and daily activities. The format for each item was a five-point Likert scale ranging from 1 (not at all) to 5 (*extremely* much). The similarity between the adolescent's and partner's interests was determined by correlating the adolescent's ratings with those of each of her partners.

Emotional Needs Inventory. The Emotional Needs Inventory comprised a list of 16 social and emotional needs derived from the work of Maslow (1954), Murray (1938), Sullivan (1953), and Weiss (1974). Initially, participants were asked to rate how important each need was within a particular relationship. Mothers rated the items in terms of their parent-adolescent relationship, best friends rated items in terms of their best friend relationship, and focal adolescents did both. Ratings for each item

were done on a five-point Likert scale, ranging from 1 (not at all important) to 5 (*extremely* important). Having rated all the items, participants
were asked to choose their three most important needs in a particular
relationship and rate how well the partner met those needs. These latter
ratings were used to assess need fulfillment, whereas an index of needs
similarity was derived by correlating the two full sets of needs ratings.

Social skills. All participants were asked to rate how well their partners performed a series of 11 social skills. Some items were derived from
the Perceived Interpersonal Competencies Inventory (PICI; Buhrmester
et al., 1988), and others were created specifically for this study. Mothers
and friends rated their perceptions of the focal adolescent. The focal adolescent rated both the mother and the best friend. A five-point Likert
scale (1 = poor to 5 = extremely good) was employed. The Cronbach's
alpha for the mother, friend, and adolescent ratings ranged from 0.83
to 0.88.

Observational measures

Tasks. Adolescent-mother and adolescent-friend dyads were videotaped
while participating in three 8-min interactions. Order of dyad was coun-
terbalanced across subjects. In the first segment, the pair was asked to
plan a week-long vacation. This task, developed by Grotevant and
Cooper (1983), was used to elicit cooperation and fun in the relationship. In the second segment, each partner identified three problems in
their relationship. They were then asked to agree upon and discuss the
most severe problem, including why it was a problem, feelings about the
problem, and possible solutions. This task is similar to conflict tasks used
in previous studies of adolescents' family interactions (Hauser et al.,
1984). The third segment was designed to examine parent and friend
supportiveness. Specifically, dyads were asked to discuss a problem the
adolescent was experiencing outside of the present relationship.

Observational ratings. Each individual in each dyad was coded using
the Interactional Q-sort. The Q-sort consisted of 58 items which focused
on (a) characteristics of the individual during the interaction (e.g., affect
and mood) and (b) how the individual manages the relationship with
the partner (e.g., social skills, ability to manage conflict, attunement).
Raters sorted the items using a fixed seven-point distribution, with each
pole representing items that are most characteristic of the individual
being coded.

There were three raters, each with extensive clinical and coding experience. To avoid carry-over effects, a rater observed only one of the two sets of dyadic interactions for a particular focal adolescent. A subset of 24 sorts per pair of coders (48 total) was used to calculate interrater reliability. The interrater reliability was 0.75 (mean correlation with Spearman-Brown correction for proportion with composite ratings).

A principal components analysis with an oblique rotation was performed on the 240 sorts. A nine-factor solution accounting for 51.2 percent of the variance was selected because it provided the most theoretically coherent results (see table 8.1 for Q-sort items and factor loadings).

Factors are labeled as follows: Cooperative relationship characteristics (15 items, Cronbach's alpha = 0.92); Psychological mindedness (five items, Cronbach's alpha = 0.78); Affect (seven items, Cronbach's alpha = 0.86); Self-esteem (five items, Cronbach's alpha = 0.66); Self-centeredness (four items, Cronbach's alpha = 0.60); Problem-solving (three items, Cronbach's alpha = 0.73); Power (three items, Cronbach's alpha = 0.66); Attunement (seven items, Cronbach's alpha = 0.86); and Jealousy (three items, Cronbach's alpha = 0.52).

Results

Preliminary analyses

Measures of similarity of interests and needs were determined by calculating the correlations between the adolescent's and each partner's scores. Next, preliminary analyses were performed to investigate questions of discriminant validity among the self-report measures. These analyses revealed that the internal consistency of the different self-report measures (harmony, need fulfillment, and social skills) were higher than their intercorrelations with one exception. Reports of social skills were highly related to reports of need fulfillment (mean $r = 0.71$). Other than this, the measures had satisfactory discriminant validity.

Next, 2 × 2 MANOVAs (harmonious/disharmonious relationship with mother × harmonious/disharmonious best friend relationship) were conducted on the set of scores for the mother-adolescent relationship and those for the adolescent-friend relationship. The MANOVA of the variables concerning the mother-adolescent relationship revealed a

Table 8.1   Q-sort factors and loadings

Cooperation:		**Self-esteem:**	
Interacts smoothly	0.78	High self-esteem	0.72
Exits negative cycles	0.73	Relaxed	0.48
Validates	0.73	Reflective	0.46
Not angry	0.71	Mature	0.42
Sees other point of view	0.66	Offers help	0.41
Supportive	0.64	**Self-centeredness:**	
Not aggressive	0.62	Appropriate attention to self	0.66
Cooperative	0.58	Not center of attention	0.47
Trusts partner	0.54	Not over-dramatic	0.40
Not guilt inducing	0.53	**Problem-solving:**	
Responds to criticism	0.49	Negotiates	0.70
Expresses negative affect	−0.49	Problem solves	0.68
Takes turns	0.35	Talks about problems	0.48
Expresses specialness of dyad	0.34	**Power:**	
Acknowledges role	0.32	Self-assertive	−0.78
Psychological mindedness:		Act as equal	−0.59
Self-observing	0.71	Has equal power	−0.45
Self-disclosing	0.69	**Attunement:**	
Deep, introspective	0.68	Nurturant	−0.73
Responds clearly	0.44	Acts interested	−0.59
Manages negative affect	0.38	Warm	−0.46
Affect:		In tune with partner	−0.46
Animated	0.81	Interested, not bored	−0.44
Fun	0.68	Not sarcastic	−0.40
Humorous	0.67	Checks in with partner	−0.39
Happy	0.61	**Jealousy:**	
Open body language	0.51	Not rivalrous	−0.52
Escalates positively	0.46	Not jealous	−0.50
		Not possessive	−0.32

significant effect for harmony in the mother-adolescent relationship, Wilks's lambda $= 0.23$, $p < 0.01$, whereas the effects of harmony in the friendship and the interaction of harmony in the two relationships were not significant. Conversely, the MANOVA of the friendship variables yielded a significant effect for harmony in the friendship relationship, Wilks's lambda $= 0.36$, $p < 0.05$, whereas the effects of harmony in the mother-adolescent relationship and the interaction term were not significant. Two by two ANOVAs (harmonious/disharmonious relationship with mother × harmonious/disharmonious best friend relationship) were then performed to determine the specific nature of the significant multivariate effects. The results of these analyses are presented in the following sections.

Interests and activities

Table 8.2 depicts the mean scores of the four groups. As predicted, harmonious mother-daughter pairs displayed more similarity in interests than disharmonious ones, $F(1, 59) = 6.34$, $p < 0.05$. Not surprisingly, similarity between mother and adolescent in interests was not related to friendship harmony or the interaction between harmony in the two relationships.

Next, 2×2 ANOVAs of the friend-adolescent similarity scores were conducted. Contrary to expectations, these analyses did not reveal any significant effects for the degree of harmony in friendships.

Emotional needs

As expected, adolescents who had harmonious relationships with mothers reported that their most important needs were met better by their mothers than did those with disharmonious relationships, $F(1, 58) = 29.55$, $p < 0.01$. The mothers of these same adolescents also reported that their needs were fulfilled better, $F(1, 59) = 19.48$, $p < 0.01$. Similarly, adolescents who had harmonious friendships reported that their most important needs were better fulfilled by their friends than those with disharmonious friendships, $F(1, 59) = 21.38$, $p < 0.01$. Interestingly, for friends' reports of need fulfillment, the main effect of the adolescents' harmony with their friendships was not significant, but the main effect of harmony with relationships with their mothers was, $F(1, 59) = 5.01$, $p < 0.05$. Specifically, friends reported greater need fulfillment in relationships with adolescents who had harmonious relationships with their mothers. This latter finding should be interpreted cautiously as the corresponding effect was not significant in the initial MANOVA.

It was also hypothesized that partners in harmonious relationships would have more similar relationship needs than those in disharmonious relationships. As expected, adolescents and mothers with harmonious relationships had more similar needs than those in disharmonious

Table 8.2 Mean scores (and standard deviations) on interests, values, needs, and social skills self-report measures

Variables	Group 1 Harmony mother Harmony friend	Group 2 Harmony mother Disharmony friend	Group 3 Disharmony mother Disharmony friend	Group 4 Disharmony mother Harmony friend	Significant effects
Correlation of interests:					
Mother and teen	0.33 (0.17)	0.39 (0.20)	0.21 (0.15)	0.20 (0.14)	Harmony with mother*
Friend and teen	0.49 (0.12)	0.48 (0.10)	0.44 (0.14)	0.47 (0.14)	ns.
Need fulfillment within relationship:					
Teen with mother	4.29 (0.53)	4.19 (0.61)	2.90 (1.08)	3.06 (1.19)	Harmony with mother*
Teen with friend	4.47 (0.44)	3.60 (0.81)	3.42 (0.90)	4.26 (0.64)	Harmony with friend**
Mother with teen	3.94 (0.67)	3.83 (0.86)	2.98 (0.75)	2.97 (0.92)	Harmony with mother*
Correlation of needs					
Mother and teen	0.54 (0.21)	0.47 (0.21)	0.58 (0.19)	0.39 (0.28)	Harmony with mother*
Friend and teen	0.50 (0.25)	0.19 (0.35)	0.52 (0.36)	0.44 (0.24)	Harmony with friend**
Reported social skill:					
Mother of teen	3.83 (0.49)	3.44 (0.51)	3.58 (0.72)	3.06 (0.60)	Harmony with mother**
Friend of teen	4.16 (0.44)	3.92 (0.63)	3.86 (0.68)	3.76 (0.44)	ns.
Teen of mother	3.92 (0.46)	3.88 (0.52)	2.77 (0.77)	3.08 (0.72)	Harmony with mother**
Teen of friend	4.03 (0.45)	3.46 (0.62)	3.40 (0.59)	3.93 (0.35)	Harmony with friend**

Note: The natures of the significant interactions are described in the text

* $p < 0.05$

** $p < 0.01$

relationships, $F(1, 57) = 8.05$, $p < 0.01$, and adolescents and friends with harmonious relationships had more similar needs than those in disharmonious friendships, $F(1, 59) = 7.05$, $p < 0.01$.

Reported social skills

As reported in table 8.2, adolescents who reported harmonious relationships with their mothers were rated as more socially skilled by their mothers and in turn rated their mothers as more socially skilled, $F(1, 59) = 9.02$, $p < 0.01$, $F(1, 59) = 35.99$, $p < 0.01$. Similarly, adolescents who had harmonious friendships rated their friends as more socially skillful, $F(1, 59) = 17.18$, $p < 0.01$. Friends' ratings of the adolescents' social skill did not differ as a function of the harmony ratings.

Observational ratings of interpersonal characteristics

As described in the "Method" section, the 58 Q-sort items were subjected to a principal components analysis. Using the nine factors that emerged from this analysis, 2×2 ANOVAs were carried out for each factor to determine whether certain interpersonal characteristics differed as a function of the adolescent's reports of relationship harmony with mother and friend (see table 8.3). Analyses of the ratings of interactions with mothers revealed that adolescents with more harmonious relationships with mothers displayed more cooperative relationship skills, $F(1, 59) = 17.37$, $p < 0.01$, more positive affect, $F(1, 59) = 7.81$, $p < 0.01$, more attunement to mother, $F(1, 59) = 9.58$, $p < 0.01$, and better ability to negotiate power, $F(1, 59) = 4.04$, $p < 0.05$.

Similarly, mothers who had harmonious relationships with their adolescents received higher ratings on the following variables: cooperative relationship skills, $F(1, 59) = 7.61$, $p < 0.01$, display of positive affect, $F(1, 59) = 4.10$, $p < 0.05$, ability to problem solve, $F(1, 59) = 4.95$, $p < 0.05$, ability to negotiate power with daughter, $F(1, 59) = 4.88$, $p < 0.05$, and attunement with daughter, $F(1, 59) = 7.43$, $p < 0.01$. Analyses of the interactions with friends revealed that adolescents with harmonious friendships displayed more positive affect, $F(1, 59) = 7.37$, $p < 0.01$, better ability to share power in the relationship, $F(1, 59) = 7.37$, $p < 0.01$, and less jealousy, $F(1, 59) = 7.25$, $p < 0.01$. The main effect for the adolescent's display of positive affect, however, was moderated by a

Table 8.3 Mean scores and standard deviations of four groups on observational Q-sort variables

Variables	Group 1 Harmony mother Harmony friend	Group 2 Harmony mother Disharmony friend	Group 3 Disharmony mother Disharmony friend	Group 4 Disharmony mother Harmony friend	Significant effects
Teen with mother:					
Cooperation	4.16 (1.18)	4.39 (1.10)	3.50 (0.81)	2.84 (0.94)	Harmony with mother**
Psychological mindedness	3.68 (1.33)	4.27 (1.55)	3.68 (1.36)	3.73 (1.02)	
Affect	4.07 (1.09)	3.88 (1.16)	3.16 (0.88)	3.32 (0.89)	Harmony with mother**
Self-esteem	3.62 (1.12)	4.08 (1.14)	3.39 (0.75)	3.44 (0.88)	
Self-centeredness	5.04 (1.02)	4.82 (1.38)	4.64 (0.90)	4.78 (1.07)	
Problem solving	3.23 (1.13)	4.09 (1.24)	3.47 (1.34)	3.24 (0.78)	
Power	4.77 (1.11)	4.80 (1.02)	4.36 (1.03)	4.09 (1.14)	Harmony with mother*
Attunement	4.42 (1.18)	4.33 (1.03)	3.69 (1.0)	3.41 (0.79)	Harmony with mother**
Jealousy	4.50 (0.39)	4.19 (0.60)	4.28 (0.39)	4.18 (0.75)	
Mother with teen:					
Cooperation	4.19 (1.15)	4.43 (0.99)	3.40 (0.83)	3.69 (1.25)	Harmony with mother*
Psychological mindedness	3.83 (1.27)	3.85 (1.00)	3.34 (0.81)	3.37 (1.13)	
Affect	4.14 (1.07)	4.24 (1.10)	3.41 (1.15)	3.83 (1.04)	Harmony with mother*
Self-esteem	4.83 (0.69)	4.44 (0.92)	4.36 (0.88)	4.50 (0.99)	
Self-centeredness	4.83 (0.96)	4.64 (1.06)	4.23 (1.23)	4.52 (1.11)	
Problem solving	3.97 (1.02)	4.55 (1.30)	3.64 (1.20)	3.53 (1.18)	Harmony with mother*
Power	4.62 (1.09)	4.55 (1.13)	4.17 (1.24)	3.69 (1.05)	Harmony with mother*
Attunement	4.79 (1.12)	4.48 (1.52)	3.53 (1.32)	3.97 (0.98)	Harmony with mother**
Jealousy	3.93 (0.65)	3.98 (0.97)	4.01 (0.66)	3.91 (0.91)	

Teen with friend:					
Cooperation	4.77 (0.86)	4.15 (1.12)	4.04 (1.09)	4.36 (0.71)	
Psychological mindedness	3.94 (1.29)	3.93 (1.58)	4.03 (1.33)	3.94 (1.40)	
Affect	4.90 (0.90)	3.60 (0.90)	4.20 (1.09)	4.27 (1.13)	Friendship harmony,** interaction*
Self-esteem	4.05 (0.91)	3.32 (0.89)	3.40 (1.07)	3.37 (1.15)	
Self-centeredness	4.89 (1.25)	4.73 (1.12)	4.49 (1.10)	4.60 (0.92)	
Problem solving	3.37 (1.00)	3.72 (1.34)	4.03 (0.95)	3.43 (1.47)	Friendship harmony**
Power	4.77 (1.16)	4.24 (0.67)	4.35 (1.12)	5.35 (0.69)	
Attunement	4.42 (1.04)	3.86 (0.84)	4.25 (0.99)	4.04 (1.29)	Friendship harmony,** interaction
Jealousy	4.26 (0.71)	3.18 (1.10)	3.69 (0.90)	3.73 (0.53)	
Friend with teen:					
Cooperation	4.51 (0.97)	3.74 (0.77)	4.05 (0.79)	4.48 (0.87)	Friendship harmony**
Psychological mindedness	3.48 (1.20)	3.39 (1.23)	3.15 (0.92)	3.34 (0.92)	
Affect	4.84 (1.09)	3.94 (0.97)	4.44 (1.16)	4.64 (0.98)	Friendship harmony*
Self-esteem	4.01 (0.82)	3.88 (0.72)	3.60 (0.89)	3.83 (0.88)	
Self-centeredness	4.71 (1.21)	4.42 (1.19)	3.93 (1.20)	3.89 (0.77)	Friendship harmony*
Problem solving	3.39 (0.79)	3.84 (1.35)	3.69 (1.14)	3.70 (1.45)	
Power	4.60 (1.12)	3.87 (1.02)	4.54 (1.01)	5.09 (0.61)	Friendship harmony**
Attunement	4.39 (1.22)	3.50 (1.03)	3.69 (1.08)	4.26 (1.22)	Friendship harmony*
Jealousy	4.33 (1.07)	3.32 (0.67)	3.90 (0.93)	3.87 (0.80)	Friendship harmony,* interaction*

Note: *The natures of the significant interactions are described in the text*

$* p < 0.05$

$** p < 0.01$

significant interaction between harmony with friend and harmony with mother, $F(1, 59) = 5.62$, $p < 0.05$. Newman-Keuls tests indicated that adolescents perceiving harmony in both relationships displayed more positive affect than adolescents with harmonious relationships with mothers and disharmonious friendships; scores for the other two cells fell in between. The main effect for jealousy was also moderated by a similar interaction effect, $F(1, 59) = 5.75$, $p < 0.05$. Again, adolescents who were satisfied with both relationships displayed less jealousy with their friends than girls with harmonious relationships with mothers and disharmonious relationships with friends.

Analyses of friends' interpersonal characteristics as displayed with the focal adolescents revealed the following. Compared to those in disharmonious friendships, friends in harmonious relationships had higher ratings on cooperative social skills, $F(1, 59) = 7.29$, $p < 0.01$, display of positive affect, $F(1, 59) = 4.18$, $p < 0.05$, ability to not be self-centered, $F(1, 59) = 7.25$, $p < 0.01$, ability to negotiate power in the relationship, $F(1, 59) = 6.53$, $p < 0.01$, attunement, $F(1, 59) = 6.22$, $p < 0.05$, and lack of jealousy, $F(1, 59) = 5.04$, $p < 0.05$. The main effect for lack of jealousy was moderated, however, by an interaction effect, $F(1, 59) = 5.28$, $p < 0.05$. Follow-up tests indicated that girls with harmonious relationships with mothers and friends had friends who were significantly less jealous than girls with harmonious relationships with mothers and disharmonious ones with friends; scores for the other two cells fell in between. Once again, this interaction and those described in the preceding paragraph should be interpreted cautiously as the interaction effect was not significant in the MANOVA.

Discussion

Much of the literature on adolescent relationships has focused on understanding normative developmental changes in adolescents' relationships with parents and friends. In contrast, the present study examined individual differences in these relationships. In particular, we tried to determine whether a common framework of variables could be used to understand variations in the degree of harmony in adolescents' relationships with mothers and best friends. We found that both individual characteristics and the match of individual characteristics were important correlates of relationship harmony. Our findings are strengthened by our reliance on multiple methods and multiple agents, as the inclusion of observational techniques helps rule out the possibility of shared method variance accounting for all associations. Moreover, many of the significant questionnaire results were based on correlations of the adolescent's and her partners' responses, and thus were multimethod in themselves.

The common framework helped identify similarities and differences in predictors of harmony across mother-adolescent and friendship relationships. Harmony in both relationships was predicted by partner's perceptions that the other person was meeting their socioemotional needs, and by the degree of similarity of their needs. Regarding observed interactional characteristics, harmony in both relationships was related to partners displaying positive affect and attunement, and being able to share power appropriately. Due to the cross-sectional nature of the present study, the causal directions of these and other relations remain unclear. For example, need fulfillment may facilitate harmony and/or vice versa.

Although much of the literature on adolescence emphasizes differences between parent and peer relationships, the present results offer a contribution to the literature by demonstrating that many of the findings are not specific to one particular relationship. In fact, we suggest that explanations of these findings should not be based on the special properties of one particular kind of relationship but, instead, should be based on the common processes underlying friendships, mother-adolescent relationships, and perhaps other close relationships. For example, one could argue that positive affect is associated with friendship harmony because positive affective exchanges foster close ties between equals. However, the fact that positive affect was also related to harmony in mother-adolescent relationships indicates that such positive affective exchanges play a critical role in asymmetrical (parental) as well as egalitarian (friendship) relationships. In fact, expression of positive affect may be a fundamental correlate of harmony across many different kinds of relationships.

Although some of the processes within these two relationships are similar, the variables may not be operationalized in the same way in asymmetrical versus egalitarian relationships. For example, although power management is important in both, one would expect friends to treat each other as equals, whereas equality of power between parent and adolescent is probably not expected by either partner. Instead, it may be the parent's ability to negotiate with the adolescent and remain in authority while giving the adolescent an increasing amount of autonomy and control that is most important. Differentiating the exact nature of these distinctions requires further exploration.

Moreover, it is also important to emphasize that some results were different for the two relationships. Unlike harmonious mother-daughter relationships, harmonious friendships did not have higher levels of common interests and activities. These results may reflect the fact that all best friends have common interests by virtue of being adolescents and having chosen each other as friends (Ball, 1981; Kandel, 1978). In fact, the degree of similarity in interests in all four groups of adolescents tended to be rather high (adolescent-friend interests, mean $r = 0.47$) and are higher than the reports of similarity in interests of mother and daughter (mean $r = 0.26$).

Differences also occurred in the links between harmony and social skills in the two relationships. Both the mother's and daughter's ability to use cooperative social skills with one another were related to perceived relationship harmony. This result was a robust one, being found in both the self-report and the observational data. The social skills data within the friendship relationship were less consistent. In the self-report data, the adolescent's report of the friend's social skills differentiated harmonious and disharmonious dyads, but the friend's report of the adolescent's skills did not. In the observational data, ratings of the friends' cooperative social skills differentiated harmonious and disharmonious dyads, but ratings of the focal adolescents did not. Although this inconsistency could indicate that social skills are less important within the friendship domain, this explanation is implausible in light of other research (Asher and Renshaw, 1981; Buhrmester, 1990). It may be that social skill and friendship harmony are not related in a linear fashion; instead, it may only be important to have some minimal level of social skill in order to have relatively harmonious friendships.

Alternatively, the social skills important in an adolescent friendship may not be readily perceived by an outside observer or may not have been tapped in the structured interactions employed in this study. Informal observations made during the study suggested that adolescent girls' overt behaviors and how they behaved socially were not always concordant with their reports of harmony in the friendship. There appeared to be some pressures within the friendship interactions to "be nice" and not confront conflict directly, whereas in the mother-daughter interactions, conflict was discussed openly. Whether or not the adolescents were consciously aware of any difficulties in their friendships, or whether they intentionally disguised difficulties is an interesting question for interactional researchers that deserves further investigation.

Finally, several observational variables were only associated with reports of harmony in one of the two relationships. For example, problem-solving ability was related to relationship harmony with mother, but not friends. Compared to peer dyads, mothers and daughters are likely to have more experience and spend more energy discussing problems and working out day-to-day hassles, perhaps making it a more important skill within this domain. In contrast, the management of jealousy was not related to harmony within the mother-daughter relationship, but it was in the adolescent friendship. Girls who saw both relationships as harmonious were significantly less jealous and had friends who displayed less jealousy than girls who only saw their relationships with their mothers to be harmonious. These latter girls may be less secure socially, perhaps because they are more identified with adults than with peers. The fact that this group of girls was also the least able to display positive affect and have fun with friends may reflect a pseudo-adult quality that may be less attractive to peers.

More generally, fewer variables were significantly related to perceptions of friendship harmony than to perceptions of mother-daughter harmony. This difference was particularly true for the measures completed by the friend and mother. Perhaps mothers are more accurate or insightful reporters because they have known their daughters longer and more intimately. In addition, friends may show a positivity bias. Girls may be less likely to talk about the negative aspects of their relationships, due to discomfort about conflict or a desire to avoid awkwardness.

References

Asher, S. R., & Renshaw, P. D. (1981). Children without friends: Social knowledge and social skill training. In S. R. Asher & J. M. Gottman (Eds.), *The development of children's friendships* (pp. 273–296). New York: Cambridge University Press.

Ball, S. J. (1981). *Beachside comprehensive.* Cambridge: Cambridge University Press.

Bigelow, B. J. (1977). Children's friendship expectations: A cognitive developmental study. *Child Development,* **48**, 246–253.

Buhrmester, D. (1990). Intimacy of friendship, interpersonal competence, and adjustment during preadolescence and adolescence. *Child Development,* **61**, 1101–1111.

Buhrmester, D., Furman, W., Wittenberg, M., & Reis, H. (1988). Five domains of interpersonal competence in peer relations. *Journal of Personality and Social Psychology,* **55**, 991–1008.

Furman, W. (1984). Issues in the assessment of social skills of normal and handicapped children. In T. Field, M. Siegal, & J. Roopnarine (Eds.), *Friendships of normal and handicapped children* (pp. 3–30). New York: Ablex.

Furman, W. (1987). *Social support, stress, and adjustment in adolescence.* Paper presented at the Meeting of the Society for Research in Child Development, Baltimore.

Furman, W., & Bierman, K. L. (1984). Children's conceptions of friendship: A multimethod study of developmental changes. *Developmental Psychology,* **20**, 925–933.

Furman, W., & Buhrmester, D. (1985). Children's perceptions of the personal relationship in their social networks. *Developmental Psychology,* **21**, 1016–1024.

Gold, M., & Yanof, D. S. (1985). Mothers, daughters, and girlfriends. *Journal of Personality and Social Psychology,* **49**, 654–659.

Grotevant, H. D., & Cooper, C. R. (1983). *New directions for child development: Adolescent development in the family.* San Francisco: Jossey-Bass.

Hauser, S. T., Powers, S. I., Noam, F. F., Jacobson, A., Weiss, B., & Follansbee, D. J. (1984). Familial context of adolescent ego development. *Child Development,* **55**, 195–213.

Hinde, R. A. (1979). *Towards understanding relationships.* New York: Academic.

Huston, T. L., & Levinger, G. (1978). Interpersonal attraction and relationships. *Annual Review of Psychology,* **29**, 115–156.

Kandel, D. (1978). Similarity in real-life adolescent friendship pairs. *Journal of Personality and Social Psychology,* **36**, 306–312.

Maslow, A. (1954). *Motivation and personality.* New York: Harper.

Murray, H. A. (1938). *Explorations in personality.* New York: Oxford.

Robin, A. L., & Foster, S. L. (1989). *Negotiating parent-adolescent conflict.* New York: Guilford.

Rubin, Z. (1980). *Children's friendships.* Cambridge, MA: Harvard University Press.

Savin-Williams, R. C., & Berndt, T. J. (1990). Friendship and relationships. In S. S. Feldman & G. R. Elliott (Eds.), *At the threshold: The developing adolescent* (pp. 277–307). Cambridge, MA: Harvard University Press.

Steinberg, L. (1990). Autonomy, conflict and harmony in the family relationship. In S. S. Feldman & G. R. Elliott (Eds.), *At the threshold: The developing adolescent* (pp. 255–276). Cambridge, MA: Harvard University Press.

Sullivan, H. S. (1953). *The interpersonal theory of psychiatry.* New York: Norton.

Weiss, R. (1974). The provisions of social relationships. In Z. Rubin (Ed.), *Doing unto others.* Englewood Cliffs, NJ: Prentice Hall.

Work Experience, Mental Health, and Behavioral Adjustment in Adolescence

Introduction

Erik Erikson (1968), as he wrote about adolescent identity formation, often stated that occupational choice is at the heart of identity. The jobs we take and commit our energy to are also at the heart of who we are as a person. Just as school provides the "ecology of achievement", work provides the foundation for "learning the applications of technology of a society." Work not only provides a youth with experiences at labor and industry but also provides for other lesser and more tangible things. Work contributes to feelings and emotions, to our adjustment with peers, and facilitates buying power. It also can compete for energy and time that could be spent on homework or extracurricular activities.

I worked as an adolescent and I worked hard. I had, at any time, a couple of part-time jobs. While I worked I met a lot of interesting and sometimes scary people. Some of my jobs were at gas stations, truck stops, packing plants or what were called slaughter houses, and on farms, at garbage dumps, and worse. I found work makes you strong, tests your ability to succeed and sometimes to simply endure. It provides you with money that can be used to buy things you otherwise might not have a chance to purchase. My own daughters, as they grew up, were expected to work. I think it helped to teach them responsibility and reliability. They were fortunate. They didn't have to work to be certain of necessities like I did. But they worked anyhow and I believe they profited from a variety of work experiences.

I suspect it is once again my mother's German heritage and the focus on the work ethic that shaped my beliefs about the usefulness, even the essential necessity, of work. So if I am trying to be authentic to my true self (a goal worthy of considering), I must include a reading on work.

The selection is by a sociologist who is doing some very interesting work out of the Life Course Center at the University of Minnesota. Mortimer and colleagues have been examining work experience contributions to mental health and adjustment among adolescents. True to my own beliefs, adolescents appear to profit from work. But the picture is not all sunny and rosy. Likewise, the connections between school and work may have certain psychological ramifications, especially for girls.

Here we go again, into the Twilight Zone of Adolescence, where we read and think about the adolescent experience. The Zone is a comfortable and informative place to be. It is a place where we can read and think about what adolescents experience and what they benefit from during this life stage. In this report the context is examined in an interesting way. See if you can see what is interesting about context in this study.

Reference

Erikson, E. H. (1968). *Identity: youth and crisis.* New York: Norton.

Suggested reading

Steinberg, L. D., Greenberger, E., Garduque, L., Ruggiero, M., and Vaux, A. (1982). Effects of working on adolescent development. *Developmental Psychology*, 18, pp. 385–395.

NINE

Work Experience, Mental Health, and Behavioral Adjustment in Adolescence

Jeylan T. Mortimer, Michael Finch, Michael Shanahan, and Seongryeol Ryu

Adolescence is a critical life stage for the development of occupational values and for the formation of an occupational identity (Erikson, 1963). It is also the beginning of a life-long process of socioeconomic achievement (Featherman, 1980). Given the crucial importance of adolescent achievement for future socioeconomic attainments, much research on the effects of adolescent work experience has focused on its implications for grade point average (with mixed results, see Bachman et al., 1986; D'Amico, 1984; Finch and Mortimer, 1985; Greenberger and Steinberg, 1986; Hotchkiss, 1982; Lewin-Epstein, 1981; Schill et al., 1985; Steinberg and Dornbusch, 1991; Steinberg et al., 1982; Steinberg et al., 1982), time spent on homework (Bachman et al., 1986; Greenberger and Steinberg, 1986), and educational and occupational aspirations (Finch and Mortimer, 1985; Mortimer and Finch, 1986). However, early work experience may also significantly influence adolescent well-being. In view of the crucial developmental tasks and choices surrounding work in adolescence, initial encounters with the workplace may be highly salient experiences. This article explores the relationships between work experiences and important indicators of mental health and behavioral adjustment.

Part-time employment among adolescents attending school has become an increasingly prevalent phenomenon in the US. In the three decades between 1953 and 1983, the percentage of 16- and 17-year-old boys who were in the labor force while attending school increased from 29 to 36; for girls of the same age, the rate of labor force participation doubled to reach the identical figure to boys (from 18 percent to 36 percent; US Department of Labor, 1985). By 1987, 41 percent of high school students were in the labor force, and there was no gender difference (US Department of Labor, 1987). Employment rates are even higher when measured by self-report. About 60 percent of high school sophomores and 75 percent of seniors report that they are employed, currently or very recently (Bachman, 1987; Bachman et al., 1987), and most young people work sometime while attending high school (D'Amico, 1984). In 1986, only 7 percent of a national sample of high school seniors said that they had never worked for pay (Bachman et al., 1987).

Furthermore, adolescents commit substantial amounts of time to work. A 1987 study of close to 4,000 students in California and Wisconsin high schools found that 14 percent of employed sophomores, 30 percent of juniors, and 56 percent of seniors worked more than 20 hr per week (Steinberg and Dornbusch, 1991). Whereas boys and girls have virtually identical levels of labor force participation (US Department of Labor, 1987) and employment (Bachman et al., 1987; Manning, 1990), adolescent boys have been found to devote more time to work (Lewin-Epstein, 1981). There is also evidence that middle-class employed youth work fewer hours than their counterparts from lower social strata (Schill et al., 1985).

Given the increasing prevalence of work among in-school youth, the merits of adolescent employment have been vigorously debated. One popular rhetoric extolls the virtues of employment for character development. Employment is said to promote self-confidence, responsibility, a feeling of usefulness, positive work values, appreciation of the value of both money and education, and high occupational aspirations. Support for this sanguine view is found in Elder's (1974) monumental study of *Children of the Great Depression*. Children in economically depressed families were found to contribute to the family economy, either by paid work (more common among boys) or through labor in the home (prevalent among girls). These children exhibited a wide range of positive outcomes in adulthood. The more positive mental health and achievement of this cohort, in comparison to younger children whose families suffered the same economic decline, were attributed largely to the self-confidence gained from being able to help the family at this time of crisis (Elder and Rockwell, 1979). The experience of caring for others, and having others dependent on one's actions, is widely recognized as developmentally beneficial (Garmezy, 1988; Panel on Youth, 1974). But most youth are no longer working to help their families; instead, income is typically used for immediate personal consumption (Bachman et al., 1986; Bachman et al., 1987).

On the negative side of this controversy are those who point out that young workers may prematurely take on adult-like responsibilities at a time when they should be attending to other psychosocial tasks (Cole, 1980; Greenberger, 1983; Greenberger and Steinberg, 1986). According to these critics, paid employment takes up inordinate amounts of time that could be spent more constructively – at homework, in extracurricular activities, with the family, developing friendships, exploring personal interests and identities, and serving the community (Greenberger and Steinberg, 1986).

Empirical evidence for this view derives from many of the achievement-related studies, as well as from research that examines indicators of behavioral adjustment. Employment is found to be associated with the use of cigarettes and marijuana (Greenberger and Steinberg, 1986; Steinberg and Dornbusch, 1991; Steinberg et al., 1982). Long work hours have been linked to cigarette, alcohol, and drug use (Bachman et al., 1986; Steinberg and Dornbusch, 1991); and stressful work, to alcohol and marijuana use for both sexes (Greenberger et al., 1981). Adolescents who work have reported that they have less close relationships with their peers (Greenberger et al., 1980; Steinberg et al., 1982). Long hours of work are found to be associated with greater adolescent freedom from parental control (Steinberg and Dornbusch, 1991; see also Manning, 1990) and more disagreement with parents (Bachman et al., 1986; Manning, 1990). There is also evidence that adolescent workers, especially those who work long hours, engage in more school-related and money-related deviance (Greenberger, 1988; Ruggiero, 1984; Ruggiero et al., 1982; Steinberg and Dornbusch, 1991), as well as aggressiveness and truancy (Bachman et al., 1986).

Though few studies have examined psychological dimensions directly, there is reason to believe that adolescent work may also be linked to mental health. In this phase of life, adolescents are grappling with major issues surrounding the development of vocational identity and career decision making (Crites, 1965; Vondracek et al., 1986). Early jobs provide initial contact with a critically important adult role. The ability to function in the work world – to get a job, to develop skills that may be important later in life, to successfully deal with the tasks and problems at work, and to effectively manage one's diverse commitments with respect to work, family, school, and peers – may signal to the adolescent an immediate capacity to control important outcomes as well as to "make it" in the future. Successful functioning in this new environment could likewise heighten well-being and self-esteem. Success in the workplace is an indicator of competence, which Clausen (1991) showed to be intimately related to mental health outcomes.

By the same token, the experience of problems and stressors in the work environment, overloads, and difficulties in managing diverse responsibilities may translate into a general sense of ineffectuality, and increase strain, depressive affect, and self-derogation. Adolescence is a period of life in which numerous stressors are introduced (Simmons et al., 1987), including those encountered at work. If younger employed adolescents are encouraged to "grow up faster," given a new reference group of somewhat older working peers, this too may be a stressful experience (Simmons and Blyth, 1987).

It is also important to consider the extent to which the various contexts of adolescent development – family, school, and workplace – support or interfere with one another. Bronfenbrenner (1979), in setting forth a theory of the ecology of human development, argued convincingly that the effects of a given context on the person depend not only on what occurs in that context but also on experiences in other settings (see also Hamilton and Crouter, 1980; Mortimer and Yamoor, 1987; Vondracek et al., 1986; Young, 1983). Participation in multiple settings makes it imperative to study ecological contexts in tandem, as they relate to one another in the "mesosystem."

Finally, it is plausible that the experiences associated with employment, as well as their impacts, are conditional on gender. Vondracek et al.'s (1986) life-span developmental approach emphasizes the importance of considering both the features of the individual and the attributes of the context, in interaction, to fully understand developmental processes. Boys and girls tend to have different kinds of jobs (Mortimer et al., 1990); for example, girls are more likely to be employed in informal work contexts (i.e., in the private household) and boys report more stressors at work. Given the general expectation that boys will work in adulthood, and the many conflicts that often surround career decision making among girls, it is probable that the psychological consequences of employment in adolescence differ by gender. Gilligan's (1982) work suggests that work experiences relevant to achievement may be more salient for males; for females, variables pertaining to the character of relationships on the job may be more important. Employment has been found to increase girls', but not boys', self-reliance (Greenberger, 1984, 1988), and there could be gender-specific implications for other indicators of mental health as well.

In this article, using information about ninth graders' current jobs, we examine a wide range of work conditions in relation to key dimensions of mental health and behavioral adjustment. We also examine the hypothesis that experience at work affects problems in school and substance use indirectly, through its impacts on adolescent psychological states.

Data Source

The sample was chosen randomly from a list of enrolled ninth-grade students in the St. Paul Public School District. Although it cannot be claimed that St. Paul, MN is typical of the US (nor would any other single city be), it should be noted that socioeconomic indicators describing St. Paul are comparable to the US population at large. The 1980 Census (US Bureau of the Census, 1982, 1983a, 1983b) showed somewhat higher socioeconomic well-being for the St. Paul population. For example, per capita income in St. Paul was $7,694; it was $7,298 in the US at large. St. Paul had lower unemployment rates (4.7 percent vs. 6.5 percent) and fewer families in poverty (8.0 percent vs. 9.6 percent). The St. Paul population was also more highly educated (of persons 25 years old or older, 19.8 percent were college graduates vs. 16.2 percent in the country as a whole), and had a greater proportion of women 16 or older in the labor force (55.0 percent vs. 49.9 percent). The city of St. Paul had a smaller minority population (9.9 percent) than the US (16.6 percent). However, although the classification used by the Census and the St. Paul schools is not exactly comparable, it is pertinent to note that the school minority population was 30 percent in 1985. Though a national study would be necessary to ascertain whether there are significant regional variations in youth employment and its psychological correlates, the rather small discrepancies between these and other indicators support the supposition that the findings obtained in this study are not unique to this particular community.

Consent to participate was obtained from 1,139 parents and children who represented 64 percent of all eligible invitees. (Eligibility was defined by enrollment in the district at the time of the data collection and by the absence of physical disabilities, e.g., blindness, that would prevent the child from filling out a questionnaire.) The total sample ($n = 1,105$) from whom data were obtained appears to be quite representative.

Data were also obtained from 1,575 general sample parents (925 mothers and 650 fathers) who were living with the child at the time of the data collection. Child "coverage" is quite complete, as data from either one or both parents of 96 percent of the children were obtained. The analyses presented here rely almost exclusively on the child questionnaire data; however, information regarding family SES (family income and parental education) was obtained from the parents.[1]

Measurement

The mental health variables included depressive affect and well-being (from the "General Well-Being Scale" of the Current Health Insurance Study Mental Health Battery, Ware et al., 1979), self-esteem and self-derogation (from the Rosenberg Self-Esteem Scale, Rosenberg, 1965), and external and internal control orientation (from the Pearlin Mastery Scale, Pearlin et al., 1981).

Behavioral adjustment was measured by problem behavior in school (Simmons and Blyth, 1987) and by alcohol and cigarette use. The measures of each variable are given in the Appendix. The correlations of the mental health and behavioral adjustment constructs are given in table 9.1.

The occupational data were coded using the 9-digit *Dictionary of Occupational Titles* (US Department of Labor, 1977, 1986) code. Measures of adolescent work complexity are based on the *Dictionary of Occupational Titles* ratings. The ninth-grade work experience measures were obtained from several prior studies of adolescents and adults, including Bachman's Youth in Transition Study (Bachman et al., 1978), Quinn and Staines's (1979) Quality of Employment Survey, the Michigan Panel Study (Mortimer et al., 1986), and Kohn and Schooler's (1983) national longitudinal study of American workers. Items representing similar work experience dimensions were subject to exploratory and confirmatory factor analyses.

Table 9.1 Correlation matrix of the mental health and adjustment variables

Variables	School problems	Alcohol use	Smoking	Self-esteem	Self-derogation	Depressive affect	Well-being	External control	Internal control
School problems	1.000	0.393	0.427	-0.101**	0.124	0.170	-0.151	0.156	-0.081*
Alcohol use		1.000	0.533	-0.156	0.097**	0.143	-0.180	0.126	-0.105
Smoking			1.000	-0.186	0.188	0.181	-0.157	0.186	-0.103**
Self-esteem				1.000	-0.515	-0.399	0.471	-0.370	0.430
Self-derogation					1.000	0.527	-0.377	0.654	-0.269
Depressive affect						1.000	-0.371	0.490	-0.170
Well-being							1.000	-0.349	0.335
External control								1.000	-0.248
Internal control									1.000

Note: *All coefficients are significant at the 0.001 level except those indicated*
* $p < 0.05$. ** $p < 0.01$

In the analyses that follow, we first examine the differences between adolescent workers and nonworkers in mental health and behavioral adjustment. Second, we assess the implications of work hours. Third, in a departure from previous studies, we investigate whether the features of adolescent work experiences are related to the criteria. Finally, we consider the possibility that work may have indirect effects on adolescent behaviors through its impacts on the psychological dimensions. To reveal any differences between boys and girls in the consequences of employment, all analyses are conducted separately by gender.

Findings

Differences between workers and nonworkers

Among the ninth graders in this study, 52 percent were working for pay (i.e., employed outside their own homes) regularly, at least once a week. On the basis of a multiple regression analysis incorporating dummy variable predictors, we found that girls who are employed in the ninth grade (coded 1) have higher self-esteem ($\beta = 0.106$, $p < 0.05$) and internal control ($\beta = 0.101$, $p < 0.05$) than those who are not (coded 0), with controls for parental socioeconomic status (see note 1), race (coded 1 if White), family composition (coded 1 if two-parent), and the child's nativity (coded 1 if born in the US).[2] But boys who are working express a weaker sense of internal control ($\beta = -0.099$, $p < 0.05$) than ninth-grade boys who are not employed. There were no significant differences between workers and nonworkers in self-derogation, external control, well-being, depressive affect, alcohol and cigarette use, or school problem behavior. All of this suggests that working *per se* in the ninth grade does not have uniformly deleterious mental health and adjustment correlates. What should be taken into account to understand the psychosocial implications of work is first, the amount of time spent working, and second, the features of adolescent work.

Work hours, mental health, and behavioral adjustment

In our analyses of the adolescent work history (Mortimer et al., 1992), we found that a relatively long duration of work, measured over the entire work history, had at least one salutary consequence for boys (it diminished their problem behavior in school). However, work intensity (the average number of hours worked per month over the course of the work career) had adverse behavioral correlates for each gender. We therefore consider the possibility that in comparison to students who are not employed, working a small number of hours may be beneficial. Two dummy variables were constructed: the first was coded 1 if the student was working the mean number of hours (11.44) or more; the second was coded 1 if the student was working fewer hours. When both of these variables are included in regression analyses, the reference category consists of those working no hours, or not employed. Constructing the variables in this way allows one to discern whether working a moderate number of hours has a different effect than working a larger number of hours.

Students of higher socioeconomic background obtained their first jobs at younger ages (Mortimer et al., 1992). However, adolescents of lower social class background, when they do work, are employed longer hours. The correlation of current job hours (for employed adolescents) with parental SES is -0.23 ($p < 0.001$); with family composition, -0.14 ($p < 0.01$); and with race, -0.10 ($p < 0.05$). Given these associations, it is especially important to control socioeconomic background when assessing the effects of current investment in work, as indicated by job hours.

Therefore, with controls for these background variables (and the child's nativity), we regressed each of the mental health and behavioral adjustment indicators on the two dummy hours measures. Table 9.2 shows that when hours of employment are moderate (less than the mean) there are no significant negative effects.[3] In fact, there is some indication that low-intensity employment may be beneficial for girls and boys. In comparison with those girls who are not employed, girls working relatively few hours express a more internal control orientation ($\beta = 0.114$, $p < 0.05$), and boys express a higher level of well-being ($\beta = 0.101$, $p < 0.05$).[4] Girls working such a small number of hours also engage in less alcohol use ($\beta = -0.159$, $p < 0.01$) and smoking ($\beta = -0.173$, $p < 0.001$). They also report less school problem behavior ($\beta = -0.166$, $p < 0.001$) than girls who are not working. Boys and girls working more hours were not found to be significantly different on the criteria from those who work no hours.[5]

We conclude that adolescent work in itself does not have deleterious consequences for mental health. To the contrary, the significant

Table 9.2 Regressions of internal control, well-being[a], and the behavioral indicators on current work hours (beta coefficients)

Predictors	Internal control		Well-being[a]	School problems		Alcohol use		Smoking	
	Girls	Boys	Boys	Girls	Boys	Girls	Boys	Girls	Boys
High hours	0.021	-0.062	0.057	-0.001	-0.070	0.038	-0.022	0.092†	0.041
Low hours	0.114*	-0.064	0.101*	-0.166***	-0.095*	-0.159**	-0.075	-0.173***	-0.099†
SES	0.022	0.071	0.090†	-0.141**	-0.230***	0.100*	-0.039	0.022	-0.065
Child nativity	0.118*	0.079	-0.023	0.134***	0.137***	0.092†	0.064	0.107*	0.047
Race	-0.115*	-0.164**	-0.119*	-0.027	0.037	0.084†	0.160**	0.133**	0.118*
Family composition	0.048	-0.063	-0.27	-0.035	0.004	-0.052	-0.026	-0.126**	-0.040
r^2	0.035	0.039	0.032	0.075	0.087	0.053	0.040	0.095	0.039
p^b	0.013	0.010	0.034	0.000	0.000	0.000	0.010	0.000	0.013
n	462	428	425	473	430	457	418	455	412

* $p < 0.05$. ** $p < 0.01$. *** $p < 0.001$. † $p < 0.10$

[a] The well-being equation for girls is not presented because it was not statistically significant. [b] Designates significance level of the equation

coefficients associated with current job hours are positive – for girls and boys whose work hours are limited. It is especially important to note that there were no significant differences on the criteria between students who work at higher levels of intensity and those who were not currently employed.

Features of work in relation to mental health and behavioral adjustment

We next examined the features of the current job in relation to the mental health outcomes, considering a large number of characteristics of work. These included job hours, intrinsic features (autonomy and self-direction, the amount of innovative thinking required by the job, and the complexity of work with data, people, and things); the extrinsic characteristics of the job (pay, job security, advancement opportunity, the extent to which the job is perceived as conferring status among one's peers); problems on the job (work stress, role strain, predictability of work, being held responsible for things that one cannot control), and the social context of work (closeness to work friends). Finally, we assessed the context of work, whether informal (in a private household) or formal (in a business or other organizational setting).

We also examined students' perceptions of the job in relation to their present and future circumstances. As discussed earlier, the impact of a given context on development may importantly depend on its integration with, and the degree of support obtained from, other life contexts (Bronfenbrenner, 1979). Consistent with this proposition, we expected that adolescents who view their work experience as complementary to their school work should exhibit more positive correlates of employment. Similarly, those who see their jobs as contributing to longer range, future goals may gain more psychological benefits from working.

In assessing the effects of current work experiences it is necessary to take into account the fact that many students are not employed in the ninth grade. If the 52 percent who are employed are systematically different from those who are not, regression coefficients could be biased. To investigate the possibility of selection-to-work bias, we did a probit analysis (with LIMDEP), predicting the likelihood of ninth-grade employment with the following variables: SES, race, gender, family composition, child age, and an indicator of the length of time prior to starting the first job (this variable is measured by the student's age for the

17.5 percent of students who never worked). The equation is statistically significant, $\chi^2(6, n = 905) = 126, p < 0.001$. It showed that boys were less likely to be employed than girls and those who had started to work at an earlier age were more likely to report current employment. To control for any bias that the selection pattern may entail, we included hazard rates indicating the probability of employment, based on the entire set of predictors, in our equations (Heckman, 1976, 1979).

In preliminary analyses, a relatively small number of the work experience indicators were found to have significant independent effects on the mental health and adjustment criteria when background variables and other work dimensions (found, in prior analyses, to be significantly correlated with any of the psychological criteria) were controlled. Only these variables were retained in the equations shown in tables 9.3 and 9.4. The findings are very different for boys and girls. Table 9.3 shows that boys who report more stress at work (overload; time pressure; the need to work very hard; being drained of energy after working; and exposure to excessive heat, noise, and cold) express more depressive affect ($\beta = 0.230$, $p < 0.01$), self-derogation ($\beta = 0.294$, $p < 0.001$), greater externality ($\beta = 0.407$, $p < 0.001$), and a lesser degree of internal control ($\beta = -0.212$, $p < 0.01$).

A second significant predictor for boys is the extent to which work imparts skills that are perceived to be beneficial in later life (i.e., the ability to follow directions, to get along with people, to be on time, to take responsibility, and to manage money). This construct had substantial positive effects on boys' sense of internal control ($\beta = 0.310$, $p < 0.001$), well-being ($\beta = 0.290$, $p < 0.001$), and self-esteem ($\beta = 0.244$, $p < 0.01$). Complexity of work with things in the ninth grade also predicted a sense of well-being ($\beta = 0.226$, $p < 0.01$).

The remaining statistically significant coefficient in the upper panel of table 9.3 is difficult to interpret. Boys who think that their jobs are more secure exhibit weaker internality ($\beta = -0.208$, $p < 0.01$; the correlation between these variables is also negative: $r = -0.221$, $p < 0.01$).

It is interesting to observe that the selection to work hazard rate has a significant positive effect on boys' self-derogation and a negative effect on boys' well-being, indicating that those factors that increase the likelihood of ninth-grade employment are associated with poorer self-concepts and lower levels of well-being. But even with these effects and those of the other background variables controlled, work experiences significantly predict boys' mental health.[6]

Table 9.3 Regressions of the psychological constructs on ninth-grade work dimensions, boys (significant beta coefficients)

	Depressive affect	Self-derogation	External control	Internal control	Well-being	Self-esteem
Work dimensions						
Work stress	0.230**	0.294***	0.407***	−0.212**	–	–
Job skill	–	–	–	0.310***	0.290***	0.244**
Complexity – things	–	–	–	0.144†	0.226**	–
Job security	–	–	–	−0.208**	–	–
Background variables						
SES	–	–	–	–	–	0.205*
Race	–	–	–	−0.162*	–	−0.211*
Child nativity	–	–	–	0.160*	–	–
Selection-to-work hazard	–	0.186*	–	–	−0.216**	–
r^2	0.087	0.121	0.194	0.231	0.189	0.147
p^a	0.116	0.019	0.000	0.000	0.000	0.004
n	147	147	147	149	148	149

[a] *Designates significance level for the equation*
* $p < 0.05$. ** $p < 0.01$. *** $p < 0.001$. † $p < 0.10$

Table 9.4 Regressions of the psychological constructs on ninth-grade work dimensions, girls (significant beta coefficients)

	Depressive affect	Self-derogation	External control	Internal control	Well-being	Self-esteem
Work dimensions						
Negative work–school	0.305***	0.217**	0.260***	−0.136*	−0.280***	−0.255***
Positive work–school	−0.185**	−0.116†	–	–	0.204**	0.299***
Role strain	–	0.140*	–	–	–	–
Job security	–	–	–	–	0.105†	–
Predictability	–	–	–	0.191**	–	0.126*
Job skill	–	–	–	0.215**	0.112†	0.153*
Self-direction	–	–	–	–	–	0.120†
Complexity – people	–	−0.118†	−0.118*	–	–	–
Complexity – things	−0.122†	–	−0.150*	–	–	–
Background variables						
SES	–	–	–	–	–	–
Race	–	–	–	−0.133*	–	−0.164**
Child nativity	–	0.127†	–	–	–	–
Selection-to-work hazard	–	–	–	–	−0.129*	–
r^2	0.122	0.148	0.167	0.135	0.160	0.231
p^a	0.002	0.000	0.000	0.001	0.000	0.000
n	259	255	258	259	260	257

[a] Designates significance level for equation
* $p < 0.05$. ** $p < 0.01$. *** $p < 0.001$. † $p < 0.10$

For girls, there is a very different and a more complex pattern (see table 9.4). The dominant issue for girls appears to be whether work experiences interfere with, or are supportive of, schoolwork. (The measures are reported in the Appendix.) When girls perceive such interference, all of the mental health indicators are adversely affected. There is more depressive affect ($\beta = 0.305$, $p < 0.001$), greater self-derogation ($\beta = 0.217$, $p < 0.01$), and a stronger external control orientation ($\beta = 0.260$, $p < 0.001$). Girls who perceive these negative connections between work and school also have lower self-esteem ($\beta = -0.255$, $p < 0.001$), lesser feelings of well-being ($\beta = -0.280$, $p < 0.001$), and a weaker sense of internal control ($\beta = -0.136$, $p < 0.05$). Girls who perceive positive connections between work and school manifest higher self-esteem ($\beta = 0.229$, $p < 0.001$), greater well-being ($\beta = 0.204$, $p < 0.01$), and less depressive affect ($\beta = -0.185$, $p < 0.01$). Interestingly, the correlation between the negative and positive school connection constructs among girls is a positive 0.259 ($p < 0.001$), indicating that those who recognize positive interrelations of work and school are also more sensitive to a lack of integration.

Whereas the degree of incompatibility between school and work was found to be associated most pervasively with the psychological outcomes for girls, other work variables were likewise consequential (see table 9.4). Role strain predicted heightened self-derogation ($\beta = 0.140$, $p < 0.05$); predictable work was associated with a sense of internal control ($\beta = 0.191$, $p < 0.01$) and high self-esteem ($\beta = 0.126$, $p < 0.05$). Turning to the intrinsic job features, girls who believed that their jobs helped them to develop skills that would be useful to them in the future, like boys, manifested stronger internal control ($\beta = 0.215$, $p < 0.01$) and higher self-esteem ($\beta = 0.153$, $p < 0.05$). Finally, complex work had a negative effect on external control orientation ($\beta = -0.118$, $p < 0.05$ for complex work with people; $\beta = -0.150$, $p < 0.05$ for complex work with things). It is noteworthy that the selection hazard coefficient is negatively related to girls' well-being, as it was for boys.

It should be acknowledged that the particular value of a regression coefficient will depend on the other variables that are entered in an equation, and that multicollinearity among the variables could produce unstable findings. We investigated this potential problem in two ways. First, examination of the correlations among the work variables indicated few problems (see table 9.5).[7] Secondly, we estimated a set of "reduced models" including only those variables whose coefficients were

Table 9.5 Correlations of current job attributes

Boys

	Work stress	Job security	Job skill	Complexity things
Work stress	1.0			
Job security	-0.05	1.0		
Job skill	0.15†	0.05	1.0	
Complexity – things	0.14†	-0.11	0.18*	1.0

Girls

	Negative school	Positive school	Role strain	Job security	Predict- ability	Job skill	Self- direction	Complexity – people	Complexity – things
Negative school	1.0								
Positive school	0.26***	1.0							
Role strain	0.27***	0.12*	1.0						
Job security	0.02	0.05	0.03	1.0					
Predictability	-0.15**	-0.12*	-0.01	0.06	1.0				
Job skill	-0.05	0.32***	0.04	0.10†	-0.13*	1.0			
Self-direction	-0.21***	0.00	-0.07	0.11†	0.07	0.06	1.0		
Complexity – people	-0.03	0.13*	-0.10ᵃ	0.09	-0.04	0.05	0.01	1.0	
Complexity – things	0.02	-0.03	0.04	0.06	0.07	0.02	-0.35***	-0.03	1.0

*p < 0.05. **p < 0.01. ***p < 0.001. †p < 0.10

found to be statistically significant in tables 9.3 and 9.4, thus eliminating much potential collinearity.[8] From these analyses we conclude that multicollinearity is not a serious problem and that the general pattern of findings remains robust under different model specifications.

Indirect linkages of work and behavioral adjustment

Preliminary regression analyses (not shown, including the four background variables shown in table 9.2, the selection hazard rate, and selected work variables) suggested that several work attributes are implicated in boys' and girls' behavioral adjustment. But in our final analyses we investigated the plausible hypothesis that the mental health constructs may also influence behavioral problems. This expectation is consistent with the work of some investigators who have examined adolescent drug use as a function of depression (see, e.g., Paton and Kandel, 1978; Stein, Newcomb, and Bentler, 1987). We recognized that behavioral adjustment could also influence mental health, but cannot adequately address possible two-way causation within the context of this particular data set. A series of regression equations, predicting school problem behavior, smoking, and alcohol use, included those work attributes that were found to be related to the criteria, the background variables, and only one mental health construct. Given the rather high correlation of the mental health variables with one another (see table 9.1), instead of "pitting" each such construct against the others, each was examined separately.

Certain work experiences are found to be related to the behavioral adjustment indicators in all the equations, irrespective of which psychological variables are included (not shown). Boys who thought they were gaining skills on the job that would be useful in later life reported less alcohol use ($\beta = -0.245$, $p < 0.01$). (For comparability this coefficient, and those that follow, are from the equations including external control orientation; however, the absolute magnitude of the coefficients for the work constructs varied little across equations.) However, boys' smoking was unrelated to the work attributes. Boys who described their work days as more predictable consistently reported less school problem behavior ($\beta = -0.199$, $p < 0.05$).

Girls who worked longer hours reported more drinking ($\beta = 0.208$, $p < 0.001$) and smoking ($\beta = 0.295$, $p < 0.001$).[9] For girls, the need to think innovatively at work was associated with fewer problems in school ($\beta = -0.127$, $p < 0.05$). For girls, however, the feeling that one is responsible for things that happen at work that are beyond one's control ($\beta = 0.169$, $p < 0.01$) and complex work with things ($\beta = 0.230$, $p < 0.01$) consistently increased school problem behavior.

It is intriguing to find that complex work with things is linked to girls', but not boys', problem behavior in school. This pattern may be attributable to the different work features that are associated with complex work with things in ninth-grade boys' and girls' jobs. Specifically, for ninth-grade boys, complex work with things has some quite positive correlates which are not evident among girls. It is positively related to boys' reports of obtaining valuable skills on the job ($r = 0.18$, $p < 0.05$; $r = 0.022$, ns, for girls) and to positive connections between work and school ($r = 0.30$, $p < 0.001$; $r = -0.027$, ns for girls). (Both of these pairs of correlations are significantly different, $p < 0.001$ for each pair: for job skills, $z = 17.24$; for positive work–school connections, $z = 3.49$.) Moreover, for both genders, complex work with things also has some rather oppressive concomitants. For example, complex work with things was related to low levels of self-direction ($r = -0.35$, $p < 0.001$ for girls; $r = -0.23$, $p < 0.01$ for boys), little opportunity for innovative thinking on the job ($r = -0.319$, $p < 0.001$ for girls; $r = -0.161$, $p < 0.05$ for boys), and work stress ($r = 0.306$, $p < 0.001$ for girls; $r = 0.136$, $p < 0.10$ for boys). (Although these latter correlations are stronger in absolute magnitude among girls, none are significantly different.)

Further investigation showed that jobs of low complexity with things (i.e., given the lowest score of 1 in the *Dictionary of Occupational Titles*), for both boys and girls, are informal in character (e.g., babysitting and yardwork). Newspaper delivery is another typical boys' job rated as having low complexity. Boys and girls who held more complex jobs were likely to be employed in restaurants (mainly in the fast-food industry); girls whose jobs were given more complex ratings were also more frequently found in saleswork.

In addition to these relations, there appear to be significant linkages between the mental health constructs and the behavioral outcomes (see table 9.6). That is, girls with more positive self-esteem ($\beta = -0.203$, $p < 0.001$), a greater sense of well-being ($\beta = -0.233$, $p < 0.001$), and internal control ($\beta = -0.123$, $p < 0.05$) use alcohol less frequently. Girls' external control orientation ($\beta = 0.152$, $p < 0.01$), depressive affect ($\beta = 0.170$, $p < 0.001$), and self-derogation ($\beta = 0.151$, $p < 0.01$) had

Table 9.6 Regressions of substance use and school problem behavior on the psychological constructs (significant beta coefficients)

	Alcohol use		Smoking		School problems	
	Girls[a]	Boys[b]	Girls[c]	Boys[d]	Girls[e]	Boys[f]
Well-being	−0.233***	−0.183*	−0.155**	−0.146**	—	—
Self-esteem	−0.203***	−0.155†	−0.158**	−0.136**	—	—
Internal control	−0.123*	−0.157†	—	−0.136**	—	−0.185*
Depressive affect	0.170***	—	0.181**	0.092†	0.113†	—
Self-derogation	0.151**	—	0.240***	—	—	0.170*
External control	0.152**	—	0.270***	0.134**	—	0.128†

a All equations controlled five background variables (SES, race, family composition, child nativity, and the selection-to-work hazard) and current job hours. *b* All equations controlled five background variables and job skill. *c* All equations controlled five background variables, current job hours, complexity of work with data, and innovative thinking. *d* All equations controlled five background variables. *e* All equations controlled the five background variables, formal work, complex work with things, innovative thinking, work stress, and responsibility for things that are beyond one's control. *f* All equations controlled five background variables and the predictability of work
* p < 0.05. ** p < 0.01. *** p < 0.001. † p < 0.10

positive effects on alcohol use. Girls' smoking was related to the psychological variables in a similar fashion (excepting internal control which had no significant effect on girls' smoking behavior; see table 9.6). Boys with a stronger sense of well-being ($\beta = -0.183$, $p < 0.05$) were less likely to use alcohol. Boys' smoking behavior was negatively associated with well-being ($\beta = -0.146$, $p < 0.01$), self-esteem ($\beta = -0.136$, $p < 0.01$), and internal control ($\beta = -0.136$, $p < 0.01$), and positively related to external control orientation ($\beta = 0.134$, $p < 0.01$). Boys' school problem behavior decreased with internal control ($\beta = -0.185$, $p < 0.05$) and increased with self-derogation ($\beta = 0.170$, $p < 0.05$).

We realize that these estimates are based on cross-sectional data, and that there are other plausible model specifications. For example, direct effects of work on behavioral adjustment may indirectly influence mental health. However, these findings are consistent with the supposition that those work experiences that are related to the mental health outcomes could assume greater significance because of their indirect effects, through the mental health variables, on behavioral adjustment.

Summary and Conclusion

This article has examined the relationships between adolescent work experience and mental health and behavioral adjustment, using the first wave of data from an ongoing longitudinal study. The analyses of current job experiences indicated some positive correlates of employment when work hours are restricted. Girls who worked less than the mean number of hours in the ninth grade expressed a more internal control orientation than did girls who were not employed. Boys whose hours of work were similarly limited expressed higher levels of well-being. Under conditions of restricted work intensity, there is also less substance use and school problem behavior for girls. However, students who worked at higher levels of intensity were not found to be significantly different on the psychological and behavioral criteria from students who were not employed.

We find substantial evidence that the actual character of adolescent jobs, and their perceived connection to present and future life circumstances, are related to mental health. Moreover, there are major differences by gender. Boys who reported more stress at work also manifested more depressive affect, more self-derogation, less internality, and a more external control orientation. Boys' internal control, well-being, self-esteem, and alcohol use were also related to their perceptions of the extent to which their jobs provide skills that will be useful to them in the future. Complex work with things was found to be positively linked to boys' well-being.

For girls, the positive and negative integration of school and work had pervasive associations with the psychological outcomes. When school and work were perceived as mutually supportive of one another, girls reported higher self-esteem and well-being, and less depressive affect. However, when they perceived negative connections or conflicts between school and their jobs, they expressed more depressive affect, greater self-derogation, and a stronger external control orientation. They also had lower self-esteem, a weaker sense of internality, and lesser well-being.

It has been suggested that adolescent girls' values and peer groups are more supportive of academic achievement than those of boys. Girls have also been found to be more conscientious, conforming, and docile in class (Simmons and Blyth, 1987). Some investigators of sex role socialization believe that girls do well in school because they are taught to be dutiful, decorous, and compliant. In contrast, the male sex role ideal, especially among working-class White boys, requires some resistance to authority figures and devaluation of school work because it is "feminine" (Mickelson, 1989; Willis, 1977). In the early years girls get higher grades than boys, and there is evidence that girls are more interested in academic achievement and acquiring school-related skills (Maccoby and Jacklin, 1974). Simmons and Blyth (1987) reported that 10th-grade girls care more about their school work than boys, and that girls have significantly higher grades than boys (in Grades 6, 7, 9, and 10).

In our ninth-grade data, we found that girls have higher grades ($p < 0.05$), educational aspirations ($p < 0.001$), and educational plans ($p < 0.05$) than boys. If school is indeed a more salient, important domain of achievement for girls of this age, it would follow that perceived interference of work with school would be more distressing for girls than boys, and perceived positive interrelations would have more salutary consequences for them. This is precisely what we found. The pattern is also interesting in view of our analysis of time spent at work which indicated that working a moderate number of hours may be beneficial for girls (see table 9.2). Working a moderate number of hours would likely be more compatible with the demands of schoolwork. In contrast, perceived negative and positive connections of work and school bore no significant independent relationships to the mental health and adjustment outcomes for boys. There were indications that work that enhances skills for the future may also be psychologically beneficial for girls.

With respect to the behavioral variables, boys who thought their jobs fostered the development of useful skills reported less alcohol use. Work hours were consistently related to girls' smoking and alcohol use. Boys who described their work as more predictable, and girls whose jobs required them to think innovatively, exhibited fewer problems in school. Girls' problem behavior in school was also positively related to the complexity of work with things and to the perception that one has responsibility for things that one cannot control.

The fact that satisfying and even growth-inducing aspects of jobs (e.g., the opportunity to acquire skills and to think innovatively at work) are negatively related to behavioral problems, whereas stressful work (being responsible for things outside of one's control) appears to increase their prevalence, is not surprising. What is somewhat perplexing is the positive relationship between girls' (but not boys') complex work with things and school problem behavior, given the generally positive relationships between work complexity and manifold adult outcomes. The answer may be found in the various features and types of work, for boys and girls, that are associated with more and less complex jobs along this dimension of work with things. For example, we found that complex work with things is more likely to be related to the perception that one is developing skills on the job and to positive connections between school and work for boys.

However, this pattern is also intriguing given that complex work with things and the more formal work with which it is associated among girls (restaurant and sales work) suggests a departure from personal caregiving that is typical of teenage girls' (as well as much of adult females') work. There is substantial evidence that caring for others yields positive developmental outcomes (Garmezy, 1988; Panel on Youth, 1974). Werner's (1984) review of the literature on child care noted that sibling caregiving leads to earlier and greater social maturity and a heightened sense of social responsibility in adolescence, especially among girls. Hetherington (1989) also noted developmental benefits related to girls' caring for younger sisters in divorced families. In view of this research, it may be that less complex work with things, as would be the case in babysitting and other more person-oriented occupational endeavors, is more developmentally beneficial.

Finally, although we recognize that other causal specifications are plausible, the pervasive linkages between the mental health dimensions and the behavioral variables suggest that work experiences may be important not only because they affect mental health but also because they have indirect consequences, through the psychological variables, for school problem behavior and substance use. Whereas most prior studies of adolescence have focused on experiences and relationships in the family, school and peer group, this research indicates that the work setting should also be considered as a potentially important contextual determinant of adolescent development (Greenberger and Steinberg, 1986; Vondracek et al., 1986).

Notes

1 The SES construct was formed by summing standardized values of parent education (the average of the mother's and father's education; when one parent's education is missing, the measure consists of the other parent's value) and family income.

2 In the general sample, 75 children (7.5 percent) were born outside the US, the largest number from Cambodia (11) and Vietnam (9). Although there were 8 from Germany and 4 from the Philippines, the rest were from a wide range of countries. In view of the small size of this group, it is interesting to find that nativity does have some significant effects on mental health and behavioral adjustment. We include this variable as a control, but investigating the reasons for its effects is beyond the scope of this article.

3 In table 9.2, the total sample size ranges from 867 to 903, depending on the dependent variable. Given the controversy surrounding imputation procedures for missing cases, we chose to use listwise deletion in these and other reported analyses. Comparison of cases with no missing data and those with at least one variable missing (among the variables analyzed in this article) revealed no significant differences on eight of the nine dependent variables. These were no significant differences on any of the mental health variables, school problem behavior, or smoking. However, the group with missing data reported more alcohol use. Although the two groups did not differ in SES, individuals with at least one variable missing were less likely to be White, born in the US, or to have two-parent families. Examination of the correlations between the work and "outcome" variables indicated a generally similar pattern; moreover, discrepancies between the two groups were not

of uniform direction (e.g., consistently stronger in one group than another). We conclude that the problem of missing data is not serious.

4   White boys and girls report a less internal control orientation than Blacks do. This somewhat anomalous pattern parallels the often-reported finding that Black students have higher self-esteem than Whites (Simmons and Blyth, 1987). Native-born girls are more internally oriented than foreign-born girls.

5   Using the same strategy of analysis of data from the National Survey of Children (aged 11 to 16), Yamoor and Mortimer (1990) only found deficits associated with relatively high hours of work among older girls, aged 15 to 16.

6   Family composition was also controlled in an earlier set of analyses but was found to have no significant effects on the psychological variables.

7   For boys, the highest correlation among the four work dimensions is 0.18. For girls, of 36 unique entries in the matrix of 9 work variables (not counting the diagonals), 23 are less than 0.10, 8 are between 0.10 and 0.19, and 5 are greater than 0.19. The highest correlations are between job skill and positive school connections ($r = 0.32$) and between self-direction and complexity of work with things ($r = -0.35$).

8   Comparison of "full" and reduced models suggests no change in our conclusions regarding the effects of boys' work. For girls, only two coefficients, significant in the full models, become insignificant with the reduced set of predictors – probability values associated with the effect of predictability of work on internal control and the complexity of work with things on external control are reduced from 0.05 to 0.10. However, the coefficients representing several work variables increase in magnitude in the girls' reduced models.

9   Positive relationships between girls' work hours and substance use, among students who are employed, arise from the fact that low intensity employment is associated with a reduction in use, in comparison to girls who are not employed (see table 9.2).

References

Bachman, J. G. (1987, July). Adolescence: An eye on the future. *Psychology Today*, 6, 8.

Bachman, J. G., Bare, D. E., & Frankie, E. I. (1986). *Correlates of employment among high school seniors* (Monitoring the Future Occasional Paper 20). Ann Arbor, MI: Institute for Social Research.

Bachman, J. G., Johnston, L. D., & O'Malley, P. M. (1987). *Monitoring the future: Questionnaire responses from the nation's high school seniors, 1986*. Ann Arbor MI: Survey Research Center, Institute for Social Research.

Bachman, J. G., O'Malley, P. M., & Johnston, J. (1978). *Youth in transition: Vol. VI. Adolescence to adulthood – Change and stability in the lives of young men*. Ann Arbor, MI: Survey Research Center, Institute for Social Research.

Bronfenbrenner, U. (1979). *The ecology of human development.* Cambridge, MA: Harvard University Press.

Cole, S. (1980). *Working kids on working.* New York: Morrow.

Crites, J. O. (1965). Measurement of vocational maturity in adolescence. I. Attitude test of the vocational development inventory. *Psychological Monographs, 79,* 1–36.

D'Amico, R. (1984). Does employment during high school impair academic progress? *Sociology of Education, 57,* 152–164.

Elder, G. H., Jr. (1974). *Children of the great depression.* Chicago: University of Chicago Press.

Elder, G. H., Jr., & Rockwell, R. C. (1979). Economic depression and postwar opportunity in men's lives: A study of life patterns and health. In R. G. Simmons (Ed.), *Research in community and mental health: Vol. 1* (pp. 249–303). Greenwich, CT: JAI Press.

Erikson, E. H. (1963). *Childhood and society* (2nd ed.). New York: Norton.

Featherman, D. (1980). Schooling and occupational careers: Constancy and change in worldly success. In O. G. Brim, Jr., & J. Kagan (Eds.), *Constancy and change in human development* (pp. 675–738). Cambridge, MA: Harvard University Press.

Finch, M. D., & Mortimer, J. T. (1985). Adolescent work hours and the process of achievement. In A. C. Kerckhoff (Ed.), *Research in sociology of education and socialization: Vol. 5* (pp 171–196). Greenwich, CT: JAI Press.

Garmezy, N. (1988). Longitudinal strategies, causal reasoning and risk research: A commentary. In M. Rutter (Ed.), *Studies of psychosocial risk: The power of longitudinal data* (pp. 29–44). Cambridge, England: Cambridge University Press.

Gilligan, C. (1982). *In a different voice: Psychological theory and women's development.* Cambridge, MA: Harvard University Press.

Greenberger, E. (1983). A researcher in the policy arena: The case of child labor. *American Psychologist, 38,* 104–111.

Greenberger, E. (1984). Children, families, and work. In N. D. Reppucci, L. A. Weithorn, E. P. Mulvey, & J. Monahan (Eds.), *Children, mental health, and the law* (pp. 103–122). Beverly Hills, CA: Sage.

Greenberger, E. (1988). Working in teenage America. In J. T. Mortimer, & K. M. Borman (Eds.), *Work experience and psychological development through the life span* (pp. 21–50). Boulder, CO: Westview.

Greenberger, E., & Steinberg, L. (1986). *When teenagers work.* New York: Basic Books.

Greenberger, E., Steinberg, L. D., & Vaux, A. (1981). Adolescents who work: Health and behavioral consequences of job stress. *Developmental Psychology, 17,* 691–703.

Greenberger, E., Steinberg, L. D., Vaux, A., & McAuliffe, S. (1980). Adolescents who work: Effects of part-time employment on family and peer relations. *Journal of Youth and Adolescence, 9,* 189–202.

Hamilton, S. F., & Crouter, A. C. (1980). Work and growth: A review of research on the impact of work experience on adolescent development. *Journal of Youth and Adolescence, 9,* 323–338.

Heckman, J. J. (1976). The common structure of statistical models of truncation, sample selection and limited dependent variables and a simple estimator for such models. *Annals of Economic and Social Measurement, 5,* 475–492.

Heckman, J. J. (1979). Sample selection as a specification error. *Econometrica, 45,* 153–161.

Hetherington, E. M. (1989). Coping with family transitions: Winners, losers, and survivors. *Child Development, 60,* 1–14.

Hotchkiss, L. (1982). *Effects of work time on school activities and career expectations.* Columbus, OH: National Center for Research in Vocational Education.

Kohn, M. L., & Schooler, C. (1983). *Work and personality: An inquiry into the impact of social stratification.* Norwood, NJ: Ablex.

Lewin-Epstein, N. (1981). *Youth employment during high school.* Washington, DC: National Center for Educational Statistics.

Maccoby, E. E., & Jacklin, C. N. (1974). *The psychology of sex differences.* Stanford, CA: Stanford University Press.

Manning, W. D. (1990). Parenting employed teenagers. *Youth and Society, 22,* 184–200.

Mickelson, R. A. (1989). Why does Jane read and write so well? The anomaly of women's achievement. *Sociology of Education, 62,* 47–63.

Mortimer, J. T., & Finch, M. D. (1986). The effects of part-time work on self-concept and achievement. In K. Borman, & J. Reisman (Eds.), *Becoming a worker* (pp. 66–89). Norwood, NJ: Ablex.

Mortimer, J. T., Finch, M. D., Owens, T., & Shanahan, M. (1990). Gender and work in adolescence. *Youth and Society, 22,* 201–224.

Mortimer, J. T., Finch, M., Shanahan, M., & Ryu, S. (1992). Adolescent work history and behavioral adjustment. *Journal of Research on Adolescence, 2,* 59–80.

Mortimer, J. T., Lorence, J., & Kumka, D. (1986). *Work, family and personality: Transition to adulthood.* Norwood, NJ: Ablex.

Mortimer, J. T., & Yamoor, C. (1987). Interrelations and parallels of school and work as sources of psychological development. In R. G. Corwin (Ed.), *Research in sociology of education and socialization* (Vol. 7, pp. 221–246). Greenwich, CT: JAI Press.

Panel on Youth of the President's Science Advisory Committee (James S. Coleman, Chair). (1974). *Youth: Transition to adulthood.* Chicage: University of Chicago Press.

Paton, S., & Kandel, D. B. (1978). Psychological factors and adolescent illicit drug use: Ethnicity and sex differences. *Adolescence, 13*, 187–198.

Pearlin, L. I., Menaghan, E. G., Lieberman, M. A., & Mullan, J. T. (1981). The stress process. *Journal of Health and Social Behavior, 22*, 337–356.

Quinn, R. P., Staines, G. L. (1979). *The 1977 Quality of Employment Survey*. Ann Arbor, MI: Survey Research Center, University of Michigan.

Rosenberg, M. (1965). *Society and the adolescent self-image*. Princeton, NJ: Princeton University Press.

Ruggiero, M., Greenberger, E., & Steinberg, L. (1982). Occupational deviance among first-time workers. *Youth and Society, 13*, 423–448.

Schill, W. J., McCartin, R., & Meyer, K. (1985). Youth employment: Its relationship to academic and family variables. *Journal of Vocational Behavior, 26*, 155–163.

Simmons, R. G., & Blyth, D. A. (1987). *Moving into adolescence: The impact of pubertal change and school context*. New York: Aldine.

Simmons, R. G., Burgeson, R., Carlton-Ford, S., & Blyth, D. A. (1987). The impact of cumulative change in early adolescence. *Child Development, 58*, 1220–1234.

Stein, J. A., Newcomb, M. D., & Bentler, P. M. (1987). An 8-year study of multiple influences on drug use and drug consequences. *Journal of Personality and Social Psychology, 53*, 1094–1105.

Steinberg, L., & Dornbusch, S. M. (1991). Negative correlates of part-time employment during adolescence: Replication and elaboration. *Developmental Psychology, 27*, 304–313.

Steinberg, L. D., Greenberger, E., Garduque, L., & McAuliffe, S. (1982). High school students in the labor force: Some costs and benefits to schooling and learning. *Education Evaluation and Policy Analysis, 4*, 363–372.

Steinberg, L. D., Greenberger, E., Garduque, L., Ruggiero, M., & Vaux, A. (1982). Effects of working on adolescent development. *Developmental Psychology, 18*, 385–395.

US Bureau of the Census. (1982). *State and metropolitan area data book*. Washington, DC: US Government Printing Office.

US Bureau of the Census. (1983a). *1980 Census of population. General social and economic characteristics: Minnesota*. Washington, DC: US Government Printing Office.

US Bureau of the Census. (1983b). *1980 Census of population. General social and economic characteristics* (PC 80-1-C1). Washington, DC: US Government Printing Office.

US Department of Labor. (1977). *Dictionary of occupational titles* (4th ed.). Washington, DC: US Government Printing Office.

US Department of Labor. (1985). *Handbook of labor statistics* (Bureau of Labor Statistics Bulletin 2217). Washington, DC: US Government Printing Office.

US Department of Labor. (1986). *Dictionary of occupational titles* (4th ed., Suppl.). Washington, DC: US Government Printing Office.

US Department of Labor. (1987). *Employment and earnings,* 34(10). Washington, DC: US Government Printing Office.

Vondracek, F. W., Lerner, R. M., & Schulenberg, J. E. (1986). *Career development: A life-span developmental approach.* Hillsdale, NJ: Lawrence Erlbaum Associates, Inc.

Ware, J. E., Johnston, S. A., Davies-Avery, A., & Brook, R. H. (1979). Current HIS mental health battery (R-19897/3-Hew). In *Conceptualization and measurement of health for adults in the health insurance study: Vol. III, mental health* (pp. 94–105). Santa Monica, CA: Rand.

Werner, E. E. (1984). *Child card: Kith, kin and hired hands.* Baltimore: University Park Press.

Willis, P. (1977). *Learning to labor: How working class kids get working class jobs.* New York: Columbia University Press.

Yamoor, C., & Mortimer, J. T. (1990). An investigation of age and gender differences in the effects of employment on adolescent achievement and well-being. *Youth and Society, 22,* 225–240.

Young, R. A. (1983). Career development of adolescents: An ecological perspective. *Journal of Youth and Adolescence, 12,* 401–417.

Appendix

Measures

Mental Health and Behavioral Adjustment
  Depression
  During the past month, how much of the time:
    Have you been under any strain, stress, or pressure? (0.507)
    Have you felt downhearted and blue? (0.760)
    Have you been moody or brooded about things? (0.670)
    Have you felt depressed? (0.828)
    Have you been in low or very low spirits? (0.798)
  Self-derogation
    I certainly feel useless at times. (0.669)
    I feel I do not have much to be proud of. (0.589)
    I wish I could have more respect for myself. (0.614)
    At times I think I am no good at all. (0.742)
  External control
    There is really no way I can solve some of the problems I have.
      (0.630)
    Sometimes I feel that I'm being pushed around in life. (0.442)
    I have little control over the things that happen to me. (0.497)
    I often feel helpless in dealing with the problems of life. (0.725)
    There is little I can do to change many of the important things in my
      life. (0.485)
  Internal control
    I can do just about anything I really set my mind to do.
    What happens to me in the future mostly depends on me.
  Well-being
    Have you felt that the future looks hopeful and promising? (0.425)
    Have you generally enjoyed the things you do? (0.656)
    Have you felt calm and peaceful? (0.628)
    Have you felt cheerful, lighthearted? (0.606)
  Positive self-esteem
    I feel I have a number of good qualities. (0.447)
    I take a positive attitude toward myself. (0.788)
    On the whole, I am satisfied with myself. (0.702)
  School problem behavior
  Since the beginning of school this year, how often have you:
    Gotten into trouble for misbehaving or breaking school rules?
    Been sent to the principal's office or to detention because of something
      you have done?

Substance use

How many times have you had alcoholic beverages to drink during the past 30 days?

How often have you smoked cigarettes during the past 30 days?

Work Experience Constructs

Work stress

How often is there time pressure on your job? (0.607)

How often are you exposed to excessive heat, cold or noise at work? (0.479)

I have too much work to do everything well. (0.508)

My job requires that I work very hard. (0.487)

I feel drained of my energy when I get off work. (0.528)

Job skill

How much has your job helped you to develop the following abilities?

To follow directions. (0.601)

To get along with people. (0.721)

To be on time. (0.667)

To take responsibility for your work. (0.699)

Do you think that the things you are learning in your job will be useful to you in your later life? (0.514)

Negative school connections

Because of my job, I have less time to do my homework. (0.551)

Because of my job, I come to school tired. (0.669)

Because of my job, it's difficult to get to school on time. (0.806)

Because of my job, I come to class unprepared. (0.721)

Positive school connections

What I have learned in school helps me do better on my job. (0.595)

My job provides information about things I am studying in school. (0.688)

I contribute more to class discussions because of what I learn at work. (0.693)

My job has taught me the importance of getting a good education. (0.505)

My job has made me recognize the subjects I really like and don't like. (0.637)

My job has influenced my career choice. (0.558)

Self-direction

How much control do you have over the way you spend your time at work (over the order and the amount of time you work on the various parts of your job)?

Overall, how much freedom do you have to make important decisions about what you do at work and how you do it?

Job security

Do you think you can stay on your present job as long as you like?

Role strain

To satisfy some people on my job, I have to upset others.

Sometimes I am unclear about what I have to do on my job.

Predictability

When you arrive at work, how well can you predict what kinds of things are going to happen that day?

Innovative thinking

Do you have to think of new ways of doing things or solving problems on your job?

Responsibility for things beyond control

How often are you held responsible for things that are really outside your control?

Complexity Ratings

Data	People	Things
7 Synthesizing	9 Mentoring	8 Setting-Up
6 Coordinating	8 Negotiating	7 Precision Working
5 Analyzing	7 Instruction	6 Operating – Controlling
4 Compiling	6 Supervising	5 Driving – Operating
3 Computing	5 Diverting	4 Manipulating
2 Copying	4 Persuading	3 Tending
1 Comparing	3 Speaking – Signaling	2 Feeding – Offbearing
	2 Serving	1 Handling
	1 Taking Instructions – Helping	

Note: *The data are from US Department of Labor (1977), p. 1369. The modal ninth grade job category for girls is babysitter, assigned ratings of 1, for complexity of work with data; 2 for work with people; and 2 for work with things. Frequent boys' jobs are yard worker (respective scores are 1, 1, 1), newspaper carrier (3, 4, 1) and fast food worker (3, 2, 6).*

The High School "Junior Theme" as an Adolescent Rite of Passage

Introduction

People often have very strong opinions about their high school experience. Some view it as a time to simply grow, develop, mature. Others talk about high school as some form of a prison where their individuality was stifled and creativity smothered. Seems to me that high schools offer a little of both for most students.

I had mixed experiences in high school. My own sentiment of that experience doesn't compel me to go back for reunions, but I do have some good as well as bad memories. I was an OK student, but not great. I got mostly Bs with an occasional A–. I was an athlete and played basketball – after all if you are 6'6" tall the coaches almost demand that you play. I wasn't very good at sports either – just middling. So I was an average guy, who liked some of his classes, had a girlfriend, played on the basketball team, and held down a couple of jobs. Teachers didn't like me or dislike me. None of them was very friendly, but then they didn't pick on me either. I wasn't in the popular group or in the unfavored group either. I was just a "middler" and was mostly left alone to find my own way in life.

But I was in a hurry to grow up. I didn't want to be an adolescent. I wanted to be an adult. But I couldn't find how to move this process along. I didn't think that age mattered, just what you could do, endure, or complete. I knew at work I could do what any man was doing beside or around me. But at school I didn't really know how to move the process of growing up along.

I suspect other youth find themselves in a similar place. Fortunately, I found a research report that actually addresses this kind of issue. Larson reports on a small study that examines how writing a particular "junior theme" paper can help students experience a form of rite of passage. I think you will find this paper unusual because it addresses some issues that people don't talk much about in regards to school. It deals with an emotional experience that involves a personal search, an exploration, even a form of an identity quest.

Go to the Zone and see if you can identify with the experiences reported by students in writing their junior theme paper.

Suggested reading

Csikszentmihalyi, M., and Larson, R. (1984). *Being adolescent: conflict and growth in the teenage years.* New York: Basic Books.

TEN

The High School "Junior Theme": as an Adolescent Rite of Passage

Reed Larson

Introduction

A person's capacity to influence the world and exercise control over his or her life is limited by the ability to mobilize deep and sustained attention in the service of personal goals. Without the ability to exert cumulative thought and action toward a self-defined end, a person is a helpless pawn of his or her environment. While children can experience deep absorption (Tellegen and Atkinson, 1974), their attention is impulsive; it is at the mercy of custom and instinct. Dewey (1913) and Ribot (1890) before him referred to this childhood engrossment as "spontaneous attention." With age, the developing individual must attain what Dewey calls "voluntary attention," an ability to direct his or her energies to objects or tasks with more remote ends. In Western culture, with its emphasis on individualism and productivity, the capacity to use this sustained voluntary attention to be generative, to create a product that is uniquely one's own, is a hallmark of mature adulthood.

It is fitting, therefore, that some of the most significant adolescent milestones in our society involve tests that demand this capacity in the extreme, tasks of solitary labor in the production of a personal product, such as a senior paper, a master's thesis, or a Ph.D. dissertation. The young initiate who can endure the notorious personal trials of these projects, who can control his or her attention and come up with a final product, has made a significant step toward the autonomous status of adulthood in our society.

It is commonly lamented that our society lacks an adolescent rite of passage (e.g., Benedict, 1939; Myerhoff, 1982), and clearly we do not have a singular public rite enacting a transition in status with regard to all the spheres of an adolescent's life (family, school, religion, society). Yet our romantic image of a serene ceremony that would gently transform the child into an adult is far afield from what adolescent rites of passage are typically like in cultures that have them. Adolescent rites, more commonly termed "initiation rites," quite often involve tests of courage, physical pain, and prolonged liminal periods of uncertainty (Muus, 1970; Young, 1965). Ndembu boys, for example, must endure not only repeated beatings and the physical pain of circumcision, they must spend several months of confinement under difficult and fearful conditions. And the outcome is by no means certain: even a chief's son whose courage fails him is marked for life as one who did not live up to the test (Turner, 1967). If we are looking for an equivalent of an adolescent rite of passage in our society we might look for situations that present this kind of strenuous challenge, rites that call for a demonstration of what is deemed critical to prestigious adult roles in our society – probably not physical mettle, as much as personal independence and a capacity to think and work on one's own. Academic projects such as dissertations, theses, and major themes most closely approximate this description.

The Junior Theme

Large writing projects involving more than a month of work are assigned in a great number of American high schools (Applebee, 1981). In the high school studied here the "Junior Theme," required in either the sophomore or junior year, typically takes two to three months and is considered by students to be an enormous undertaking (even though the final paper is rarely more than 12 pages long). Within the school it is referred to as a rite of passage and carries some of the fearful anticipation of such rites (one student wrote, "The Junior Theme is a monster that lurks in dark passages to devour innocent students"), as well as demarking an unofficial transition to a more advanced academic status.

The task of doing a Junior Theme, and the ritual it entails, can be understood in terms of a sequence of stages that the teachers require students to follow. In the first three weeks of the project students are to choose a topic and develop a bibliography. In the following weeks they are to research their topic, usually in a library, although sometimes students will conduct interviews with appropriate people. Notes from this work are put onto 3 by 5 notecards that are checked by the teacher at a specific deadline. Next students have about a week to turn in an outline, another week to write a rough draft, and another week or two to write and type up the final paper. The final product is expected to conform to fixed conventions of format and style.

On the surface the assignment can be seen as an information processing task. In the early research stages it involves identifying and collating information from pertinent sources. In the later writing stages it involves cognitive processes of planning, partitioning the problem, "treeing ideas," and editing that have been described by numerous researchers interested in the writing process (e.g., Flower and Hayes, 1977, 1980; Gregg and Steinberg, 1980). From the students' experience, however, the most salient part of the task is its size. In middle adolescence they have a limited capacity to control and sustain their attention (Hamilton, 1983a, b). The biggest challenge for them is the motivational and emotional one of sticking to their work, maintaining a cumulative train of thought despite the obstacles that arise and the numerous distractions that occur in their lives.

For many students the Junior Theme also becomes a personal inquiry into a topic that is meaningful to them. They view it as a unique chance to have a say, to formulate what they really think. In this respect it resembles the tapa rugs woven by Samoan girls (Mead, 1929) and the quest for a vision of Native American youth (Erikson, 1950) in yielding a product that represents the self. In some cases, students become invested to the extent that the process of putting their ideas into words takes on characteristics of the adolescent search for identity: they become preoccupied with the authenticity of what they write as a personal statement. The experiences students go through, therefore, provide a chance to observe, in a controlled setting, processes that may resemble those of the identity quest.

Because of the high expectations, the size of the project, and the tendency for students to make it into a personal quest, the Junior Theme becomes much more than just another school assignment. A pilot study indicated that students encounter extremes of boredom, tension, and anxiety, as well as occasions of deep enthrallment (Larson, 1985; Larson et al., 1985). Anthropological studies of rites of passage suggest that the impact of such transitional episodes needs to be understood in terms of the progression of subjective experiences; it is the phenomenological sequence from beginning to middle to end that creates their unique meaning (Herdt, 1982; Van Gennep, 1909). In this paper, therefore, I describe the stages of experience students go through in carrying out the Junior Theme in an attempt to understand the personal significance of this episode in adolescents' movement toward adulthood.

Method

The study was carried out in a large and diverse middle-class high school in a suburb bordering the city of Chicago. In this school the Junior Theme, also known as the "Research Project," is assigned in advanced sophomore and regular junior English classes during the latter half of the year. The 154 students in the study were the members of three sophomore classes and three junior classes. In four of these six classes the topic of the Junior Theme was unrestricted; while teachers did occasionally encourage or discourage students' specific ideas, topics ranged from Scott Joplin to Woodstock to "Why all Women Are Not for the ERA." In one sophomore class the project was restricted to literary topics (examples of topics selected by students were "America as Seen through the Eyes of Carl Sandburg," "Prophesy and Prediction in Science Fiction," and "Human Frailty as the Basis of James Thurber's Humor") and in a junior class the teacher restricted students to papers about the 1950s ("The Korean War," "Elvis Presley," "The Beat Poets").

In the study, students reported on their experiences at eight different points before, during, and after their work on the Junior Theme (table 10.1). Data were obtained from questionnaires administered by the investigator. The first questionnaire was given about one week before the Junior Theme was first presented to the class. The last was administered about six weeks after the project was completed when all students had received their final grades.

The content of the questionnaires varied according to stage. At all eight stages students completed a set of 7-point semantic differential ratings dealing with their attitude toward the project, themselves in relation to the project, and their final paper "as they expect it." Three of these items comprise a scale of personal involvement (alpha = 0.76). The four questionnaires filled out during the students' work included twenty

Table 10.1　The sequence of questionnaires

Questionnaire	Timing	Content
1. Pre-project	1 week before the Junior Theme is presented in class	Attitude toward project Plans for doing it Prior experience with projects Lifestyle data
2. Bibliography stage	2–3 days before getting bibliography checked by teacher	Attitude toward project Inventory of experiences Topic choice Progress report
3. Reading stage	2–3 days before getting notecards checked	Same as above
4. Outline stage	2–3 days before getting outline checked	Same as above
5. Writing stage	2–3 days before turning in final paper	Same as above
6. Final paper	The day papers are turned in	Attitude toward project Checklist of strategies Did project become personal?
7. Post No. 1	1 week later	Attitude toward project What they learned Inventory of help from others
8. Post No. 2	After receiving final grade (about 5 weeks later)	Attitude toward project Feelings about a typical week of homework

5-point items, which obtained an inventory of experiences at that point in their work on the project. Seven of these items asked about various cognitive, motivational, and affective dimensions of enjoyment, based upon Csikszentmihalyi's (1975) research. These form a scale assessing the experience of enjoyment (alpha = 0.82). The remaining items deal with negative experiences. Factor analyses suggested three nonorthogonal, overlapping scales: an 8-item scale of aversion (alpha = 0.79), a 7-item scale of obsession/anxiety (alpha = 0.70), and a weak 5-item scale of boredom (alpha = 0.10). On the final questionnaire, in addition to questions about the Junior Theme, they were asked to respond to the same set of questions with regard to their homework for that week.

In addition to the self-report information obtained from students, the teachers provided grades and other evaluative ratings of the students. Copies were obtained of the students' final papers, which were rated for overall quality by a graduate student in English at the University of Illinois (these ratings correlated $r = 0.51$ with the grades assigned by teachers). The students' high school GPAs and achievement test scores were obtained from school records. Lastly, the author conducted informal interviews with a number of students at various stages in the process to obtain more in-depth descriptions of their experiences.

Results and Discussion

As a transitional episode, the Junior Theme's significance lies in the unfolding sequence of expectation, worry, enthrallment, catharsis, and ultimately, recollection. Figure 10.1 shows that the overall progression of students' experience is one of increasing personal involvement in the work, peaking on the day the final paper is handed in. Even after the paper is turned in the level of personal involvement is sustained at a high level for weeks after that. The findings are presented and discussed below with the objective of understanding this sequence, and how it relates to emotional and thought processes within each student.

Anticipating the project

The students' feelings before beginning the project include a mixture of dread and hopefulness. In the pilot study, 80 percent of the students reported anticipating the project with some degree of negative affect (Larson et al., 1985). At least part of the explanation can be seen in table 10.2. On the first questionnaire, filled out before the project has been assigned, the students report the Junior Theme to be much more difficult and to involve a higher degree of organization than their usual homework (which was rated on Questionnaire 8). Students also report

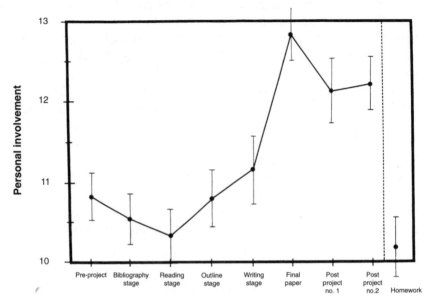

Figure 10.1 Average levels of personal involvement reported at each stage of the project (graph showing means and standard errors of the means at each stage)

feeling less skilled in relation to this task. For 73 percent this is the largest project they have ever done and only 37 percent indicate that they "have an idea of how they will do the project"; for many their idea of how to do it amounts to nothing more than "willpower" or "doing my best." The Junior Theme is anticipated as a large ominous undertaking that they do not understand well.

While feeling wary and insecure, the students also see the project as personally important. On the first questionnaire 84 percent of the students indicate that there is something besides the grade that they want to get out of it. In comparison to homework they consider the project to be "worthwhile" and the product to be "meaningful" (table 10.2). They already rate themselves as more involved than with their typical homework. Although they have not yet started work and the teacher has not yet presented the assignment, the Junior Theme already stands out from their other schoolwork as a unique and different experience, one that is more difficult and onerous, but also more personally significant.

Table 10.2 Attitudes toward the project in comparison to attitudes toward homework

| | | The project[a] | |
How you feel about (1–7)	Homework	Before starting (Questionnaire 1)	In process (Questionnaires 2–5)
The project/your homework			
Worthwhile (vs. a waste of time)[b]	3.75	4.25**	4.19**
Difficult (vs. easy)	2.97	4.35***	4.22***
Important for myself (vs. for grade)	2.79	2.50	2.57
Yourself in relation to the project/your homework			
Happy (vs. unhappy)[b]	4.29	4.06	4.19
Involved (vs. detached)[b]	4.04	4.78***	4.44*
Skilled (vs. incompetent)	4.24	4.01	3.88**
Your final paper as you expect it/the quality of what you turn in			
Imaginative (vs. dull)	4.91	5.09	5.19*
Organized (vs. disorganized)	3.98	4.39**	4.52***
Says something meaningful (vs. does not)	3.69	4.29***	4.55***

[a] Asterisks indicate significance of difference from homework: * $p < 0.05$. ** $p < 0.01$. *** $p < 0.001$

[b] These items compose the scale of personal involvement used in figure 10.1

Selecting a topic area

The majority of students look for a Junior Theme topic that relates to some activity or interest in their lives: a potential career, a hobby, or some positive aspect of their experience. In total, 79 percent of the students in the study explain why they chose their topic in terms of a personal interest, experience, or goal. Sometimes the idea comes from the inspiration or model of a parent or some other important person in their lives. One girl, who plays the flute, had had a chance that summer to see Haydn's flute, and now she wants to learn everything she can about the historic evolution of the instrument. A boy who is adopted and believes he is part Indian chooses as his topic the "American Indian, his culture, and the effects of European expansionism on the Indian's life."

Perhaps because of the desire to find a personally meaningful topic, for many students the initial stage of choosing a topic area is experienced as a very difficult, seemingly insurmountable task. It requires finding a domain worthy of being made a part of one's life. It may also require exclusion of numerous intriguing and personally significant alternatives. Many students pass through three or four topics before their teacher or a parent intervenes and forces them to settle on something. Even then some students may still feel an uncertainty or ambivalence toward their selection and never feel fully committed. A student's degree of uncertainty about his or her topic at Stage 2 is related to never experiencing the project as "inside and personal" ($r = 0.22, p = 0.02$). Students who were unsure of their topics at this stage also report more aversive affect in the following stages of their work ($r = 0.36, p < 0.001$) and less enjoyment ($r = -0.31, p < 0.001$).

The degree of difficulty experienced in selecting a topic area and the degree of continuing difficulty in working with that topic, may be a litmus test for a student's state of identity resolution. Waterman and Archer (1979) have documented a relationship between adolescents' disposition to write and their identity status. In addition, the turmoil students experience might be examined as a limited, "laboratory version" of what a full-blown identity crisis is like. Some of these students, like Arthur Miller's portrait of Biff in *Death of a Salesman*, "can't take hold"; they are unable to make a commitment to a topic area and as a result become trapped in a cycle of negative feelings (for an example of this pattern in a college student, see Larson, 1985).

Increasing engagement

Selection of a topic area is only a first stage toward arriving at a central issue or "problem" for the paper. In contemporary theories of artistic creation, final resolution of the topic is not a single step but an ongoing process, involving exploration, experimentation, and progressive discovery and focusing. In a study of artists at work, the best drawings were created by those who kept the problem open as long as possible, who engaged in a process of "problem finding" in which they progressively defined the personal and visual issues that their sketches addressed (Getzels and Csikszentmihalyi, 1976). Often this process took the form of an internal dialogue between their own experiences and emotions and the content of the ongoing work. This set of relationships was replicated in a study of the creativity of essays written by middle school students (Moore, 1985).

Many of the students working on the Junior Theme went through a similar internal dialogue and sometimes a "struggle" whereby their topics progressively focused, developed, and took on life. While less than ideal, as a loose index of this process I rated the degree to which each student's response to the question, "What is your research project about?" gained specificity from Questionnaire 2 to Questionnaire 5. Lateral topic changes (e.g., from "The Beatles" to "Antique Cars") did not count – only those that showed increased specificity (e.g., from "Film in the Depression" to "The Portrayal of Blacks in Film" to "The Misportrayal of Blacks in Film Through Stereotypes and Such"). Students who showed this progressive focusing from stage to stage obtained higher grades from their teachers ($t = 2.05$, $p = 0.04$) and higher ratings from the independent rater ($t = 2.27$, $p = 0.03$).

Likewise, students who drew on their own feelings to guide their work appeared to do better. In total 52 percent of the students reported that there was a "point at which the project ceased to be something 'out there' and neutral and became inside and personal" (on Questionnaire 6). These students turned in papers that were judged superior both by their teachers ($t = 1.55$, $p = 0.12$) and by the independent rater ($t = 2.67$, $p = 0.009$). Creative success appeared facilitated by an openness to allowing one's topic to focus slowly, on the one hand, and a willingness to become personally involved on the other.

A good example of problem finding and personal involvement is provided by a student doing his paper on Thoreau, who started out motivated by a general desire to apply Thoreau's ideas to his own life. In his readings he came upon a critic who described Thoreau as a tragic character, like King Lear, whose life was a shambles because he was unable to resolve his very idealistic dreams with reality. Upset by this characterization, the student turned his focus first to evaluating and then to disproving this critic's claim. The discovered problem for him became finding out whether Thoreau's spirit had been broken by his failures and then showing that Thoreau's ideals, even though they may not be realizable, have a pertinence both to life then and to life now, including implicitly the student's own life. In the critic's claim he had discovered a personal and intellectual problem, an articulate challenge to his own beliefs, that focused his thinking, resulting in what was ultimately a very compelling paper.

Marshaling resources

Whether engaged by their topic or merely responding to the approaching deadline, the project imposed increasing time demands upon students. How adolescents responded to an extraordinary activity like this provides valuable insight into their capacity for mobilizing internal resources. They had to start saying "no" to friends, staying up later at night in order to work, and missing out on other activities. The time required began to conflict with other things in their lives and to create stress. Students complained of losing sleep. Those with greater time commitments to other activities – sports, music, jobs – ultimately did less adequate papers ($r = -0.29$, $p = 0.01$), presumably because they did not have the flexibility to become as involved.

Students reported a wide range of methods for structuring their work on the project. On a checklist of strategies filled out in Questionnaire 6, 58 percent said they set up a schedule and 23 percent said they thought of it like an athletic challenge. They also reported using extrinsic motivation devices; 75 percent said there were times when they forced themselves to work, 30 percent said they promised themselves rewards for getting some part of it done, 14 percent said they used coffee or other drugs to help them work, and 51 percent said they would wait until the last minute until they knew they had to do it. In one case, a boy said his father threatened to ground him for a month if the project was not done on time.

While the Junior Theme resembles a rite of autonomy, a remarkable 60 percent of the students reported getting help from their parents at some point in the process. While symbolizing their transition toward adulthood, paradoxically, it also threw them back upon family dependencies.

Emotional climax

Along with the increased involvement of time comes an increasing range of emotional experiences, from intense psychological pain to deep enjoyment. At all four stages the students report emotional states that are far outside what is typically experienced when doing homework (table 10.3). Peak values for the scale of aversive affect were recorded at the reading and notecard stage – at this stage the dominant negative affect involves personal uncertainty and avoidance of the task. In subsequent stages, this aversive affect is replaced by extremes on the scales of obsession/anxiety and boredom. On the one hand, many students experience the agitation of "being too anxious to work," not being able to "get it out of my head," and "losing sleep and getting physically run down." On the other hand, many students also find it "too easy to be challenging" and report feeling "bored with the whole thing." Boredom, but not obsession/anxiety are correlated negatively with the quality of the final papers (Larson, 1997).

At the same time that negative states are occurring more frequently, positive states are also experienced more often. Elements of enjoyment are reported with greater frequency from stage to stage, peaking while the students are writing their final drafts (table 10.2). They report more

Table 10.3   The experience of different psychological states: the five stages of work on the project

Types of experiential/state	Homework	Stage				
		Bibliography[a]	Reading[a]	Outline[a]	Writing[a]	F value[b]
Aversion	9.5	11.7***	13.1*	12.2	12.0	3.12*
Enjoyment	10.0	12.4***	13.9**	14.5	15.4	7.83***
Obsession/anxiety	5.4	8.2***	9.4**	9.3	10.5**	8.36***
Boredom	14.3	10.1***	11.1***	12.2***	12.8*	25.74***

[a] *Asterisks indicate a significant difference from the prior column*
[b] *Based on an analysis of variance with person and class treated as repeated measures. The p value for stage is reported here*

absorption, challenge, and "flow" in their work; they are more likely to feel the project "has an energy of its own." Elsewhere I have reported that this experience of enjoyment is positively correlated with the quality of the final product (Larson et al., 1985). Being able to enjoy one's work appears one of the keys to achieving the kind of cumulative attention that the project demands (Larson, 1985).

The culmination of work on the Junior Theme, then, is a fugue of extreme emotional states: anxiety and a sense of flow, boredom and enjoyment, often occurring within the same person. Such emotional extremes bring to mind the analogy with the identity crisis: the extreme anguish Erikson describes in Martin Luther and the oceanic "acute identity experiences" noted by Waterman (1984). The experience can also be compared to the climactic state of liminality associated with rites of passage by Van Gennep (1909) and Turner (1969). During this final week students have a feeling of being detached and cut off from their ordinary lives to the extent that some question their own health and sanity. One boy writes, it "feels like I've been fighting cancer"; another describes himself as "emotionally disturbed." Many are unsure that they will actually finish; indeed, most come down to the absolute deadline, staying up well past midnight that last night.

Turning it in

The scene in class on the day papers are turned in is like what one might imagine at the finishing line of the Paris to Dakar Road Rally. The students come in, often blurry-eyed and punchy, with their papers in neatly bound covers. Everyone has a story to tell about his or her last hours, and there is a general state of euphoria, evident in the upward leap of figure 10.1. One student wrote, "I don't believe I'm done! I survived! It's a miracle!" Another student said later, "Walking out of class I just felt incredible, like I could run 100 miles." Asked how they felt, the nearly unanimous (78 percent) word in people's minds was "relieved."

There were also casualties – people who are not there, people for whom something went wrong and put them on the absentee list for that day. In total 16 percent of the people did not bring in a paper that day, and 5 percent withdrew from the class or had not turned in a paper by the end of the year. For a few this was the final straw for dropping out of school. A few of the people who were there were quite angry and bitter. At an open space for comments at the bottom of the questionnaire, students wrote: "The paper was a boring, senseless waste of time." "It's a pain in the ass, and ought to be against the law." "I would rather have all my teeth pulled without novocaine than do that again!" It is part of the task of rites of passage to separate "adults" from "children." Through the strain of the experience and the grading process that follows it, students are sorted out into those who survived and those who did not.

Afterwards

Whether successful or not, the Junior Theme leaves its mark on each student; never again are they quite the same person. As seen in figure 10.1, for the majority of students there remains a pride in and attachment to the product even many weeks later. While ambivalent about the task at the beginning, now that they are through, they endorse it. At Stage 7 a remarkable 85 percent say that they think the Junior Theme is a good thing to be assigned.

How were they changed? 81 percent said they learned something about doing projects; 82 percent said they learned something about themselves. One girl wrote, "I am now positive that I can handle any challenge that comes my way." She has become more autonomous. Another girl, in what sounds like a caricature of a psychologist, wrote, "The research paper helped me learn a lot about myself and how I can help myself so I don't try and go out and get pregnant. I have accomplished that goal."

For a great majority, what they have learned is something about their capacity to work, to extend themselves toward a distant objective. They have learned that "I have a lot of will power," that "I must like the topic," that starting earlier and putting in regular hours is critical, that they work better late at night. The most common thing volunteered, mentioned by 42 percent of the students, was simply that they can do it, that they can take on a project of this size and complete it.

Conclusion

Whereas tests of courage are important in many societies in which warfare, famine, and other threats to basic survival are common, in our society an important mark of adulthood is the ability to act and think on one's own, to stick with and carry out one's ideas over an extended period of time. For students in the school studied the Junior Theme is a milestone in the development of this capacity for sustained generative effort. For many students, work on the Junior Theme also becomes an enactment of an identity quest and, in some cases, an identity crisis. Students struggle to define a topic and give it words that are an expression of themselves and their own integrity. They draw on personal interests and feelings in trying to create a final paper that is a representation of the adult they are striving to become.

The process of working on the Junior Theme, we have found, is fraught with emotional and motivational extremes that gain intensity as the deadline approaches. Students swing between excitement and boredom, grandiose feelings of power and anxiety-ridden self-doubt. Often the negative extremes interfere with their work and some students become trapped in a cycle of negative feelings (Larson, 1985). It is in the challenge of dealing with and controlling these extremes, I believe, that the Junior Theme is most meaningful. Poignantly, Erikson defines identity as "a subjective sense of an invigorating sameness and continuity" (1968, p. 19). Work on the Junior Theme demands this sense of continuity and sameness; it requires that the student overcome internal blocks and divergent impulses; it requires that a student become personally involved, yet remain open and flexible in order to build a meaningful train of thought through a complex body of facts and ideas. In mastering the Junior Theme, therefore, one is also mastering one's emotions and oneself.

The jubilation on the day papers are turned in comes not only from having completed the project, but also from having a new capability that sets them apart from what they were before. They can do it. They can control their attention. They can create something large and meaningful that is their own. We might expect similar kinds of transitional experiences in more advanced writing projects, such as college senior papers and Ph.D. dissertations. It would also be useful to examine and compare the sequences of personal transformation associated with other deep adolescent involvements such as participation in plays, sports experiences, and musical involvements.

References

Applebee, A. (1981). *Writing in the Secondary School*. National Council of Teachers of English, Urbana, IL.

Benedict, R. (1939). Continuities and discontinuities in cultural conditioning. *Psychiatry* 1: 161–167.

Csikszentmihalyi, M. (1975). *Beyond Boredom and Anxiety.* Jossey-Bass, San Francisco.

Dewey, J. (1913). *Interest and Effort in Education.* Southern Illinois Press, Carbondale, IL.

Erikson, E. (1950). *Childhood and Society.* Norton, New York.

Erikson, E. (1968). *Identity: Youth and Crisis.* Norton, New York.

Flower, L., & Hayes, J. (1977). Problem solving strategies and the writing process. *College English* 39: 449–461.

Flower, L., & Hayes, J. (1980). The cognition of discovery: Defining a rhetorical problem. *College Comp. Commun.* 31: 21–32.

Getzels, J., & Csikszentmihalyi, M. (1976). *The Creative Vision.* Wiley – Interscience, New York.

Gregg, L., & Steinberg, E. (1980). *Cognitive Processes in Writing.* Lawrence Erlbaum, Hillsdale, NJ.

Hamilton, J. (1983a). Development of interest and enjoyment in adolescence. Part I. Attentional capacities. *Journal of Youth and Adolescence,* 12: 355–362.

Hamilton, J. (1983b). Development of interest and enjoyment in adolescence. Part II. Boredom and psychopathology. *J. Youth Adoles.* 12: 363–372.

Herdt, G. (1982). *Rituals of Manhood.* University of California Press, Berkeley.

Larson, R. (1985). Emotional scenarios in the writing process: An examination of young writers' affective experiences. In M. Rose (ed.), *When a Writer Can't Write.* Guilford Press, New York.

Larson, R. W. (1997). The emergence of solitude as a constructive domain of experience in early adolescence. *Child Development,* 68(1): 80–93.

Larson, R., Hecker, B., and Norem, J. (1985). Students' experience with research projects: Pains, enjoyment and success. *The High School Journal,* 68: 61–69.

Mead, M. (1929). *Coming of Age in Samoa.* Mentor Books, New York.

Moore, M. (1985). The relationship between the originality of essays and variables in the problem-discovery process: A study of creative and noncreative middle school students. *Research on Teaching English,* 19: 84–95.

Muuss, R. (1970). Puberty rites in primitive and modern societies. *Adolescence* 5: 109–128.

Myerhoff, B. (1982). Rites of passage: Process and paradox. In V. Turner (ed.), *Celebration: Studies in Festivity and Ritual.* Smithsonian Institution Press, Washington, DC.

Ribot, T. (1890). *The Psychology of Attention.* Open Court, Chicago.

Tellegen, A., & Atkinson, G. (1974). Openness to absorbing and self-altering experiences ("absorption"), a trait related to hypnotic susceptibility. *Journal of Abnormal Psychology,* 83: 268–277.

Turner, V. (1969). *The Ritual Process*. Aldine Publishing Co., Chicago.

Turner, V. (1967). *The Forest of Symbols*. Cornell Press, Ithaca, NY.

Van Gennep, A. (1909). *The Rites of Passage*. University of Chicago Press, Chicago.

Waterman, A. (1984). Identity formation: Discovery or creation? *Journal of Early Adolescence*, 4: 329–341.

Waterman, A., & Archer, S. (1979). Ego identity status and expressive writing among high school and college students. *Journal of Youth and Adolescence*, 8: 327–341.

Young, F. (1965). *Initiation Ceremonies: A Cross Cultural Study of Status Dramatization*. Bobbs-Merrill, Indianapolis, IN.

Social Context and the Subjective Experience
of Different Types of Rock Music

Introduction

I was born in 1946 and I have seen marvelous new technologies emerge ever since. The expansion of the phone system, television, radio and stereo, microwave technology, airplane travel, elaborations on X-rays to include MRI and CAT scans, new drugs, and much more. In fact, I am one of the first in the original baby boom generation, having been born on June 2. So I have profited from, and contributed to, the expanded use of all of this technology. I am, indeed, a fortunate person to be born in a wonderful historical era. You probably take all of this for granted if you are in your late teens or early twenties. But one day you will go to movie theaters and marvel at the sight, the sound, the smells, you will experience. Or you will find phone systems replaced by some new sound technology. One day you will get genetic treatment for diseases and you'll never catch a cold, due to a vaccine. You may travel in space like we now travel around the earth in airplanes. You too will marvel at how much things have changed. This experience is waiting for you in the not too distant future.

I was also blessed with being part of the generation that invented their own musical tastes, known today as rock music. I was able to see the King (Elvis Presley) and grow up watching him mature as a musician. I experienced the Beatles and their musical empire. I saw rock music move from a form of lower-class barstool sound to become part of the Top 40. Other forms of music have moved rock to new heights, but the classics of the early 1960s and beyond are still played today. In fact, new generations continue to find rock music, over and over again. Of course, it helps to have 50 year-old rock stars, like the Rolling Stones, still traveling around and performing. Although, I have always wondered why anyone would want to see a 50 plus year-old Rolling Stone or Beach Boy sing, mostly off key now, to an audience filled with aging hippies from the 1960s.

Music experience is part of the culture of any society. In North America and Europe youth culture imbeds itself within music subcultures. Because there is so much money put into music by contemporary youth, it is one of the biggest features of pop culture today. We can actually understand much about contemporary youth by simply study-ing their music, the sounds, lyrics, and artists. It is likely each genera-tion has its own music themes, but we can question whether music themes are always consistent with parental values or desires for their children.

In my day had I come home with a studded necklace, a couple of ear rings (in my ears or elsewhere), and a tattoo, playing loud hard rock sounds, I would have been taken to the woodshed for a little lesson on normalcy. Things have changed since my youth. Many of the changes have been for the good, I believe. But I still wonder, from time to time, whether pop culture music doesn't have a dark side.

There are a multitude of studies available regarding rock music and its implications for teenagers. I've selected the reading by Thompson and Larson because it uses the methodology that is part of today's teenagers lives – the pager. I also included it because the investigation includes social context and reported subjective experience that is associated with different kinds of rock music. This report shows us the many places where music is listened to, the feelings and emotions that accompany a listening experience, and the psychological power of music for youth.

Maybe as you enter the Zone this time, you should put a little rock music on the old phonograph – oops, you are not likely to have a phono-graph, but you could try the new technology called the CD, I guess! If you don't have either, then just hum some kind of song as you read . . . but not zippity do-da.

Suggested reading

Larson, R., Kubey, R., and Colletti, J. (1989). Changing channels: early adoles-cent media choices and shifting investments in family and friends. *Journal of Youth and Adolescence*, 18, 583–600.

ELEVEN

Social Context and the Subjective Experience of Different Types of Rock Music

Robert L. Thompson and Reed Larson

Introduction

Rock music is generally considered to be an important mechanism through which adolescents negotiate age-specific developmental tasks (Smothers, 1961; Kaplan, 1984). One of the ways this is most evident is in the emphasis adolescents place on choosing a context appropriate for music listening. Research has found that adolescents almost always listen to music alone or with friends (Kubey and Larson, 1990; Larson and Kubey, 1983), that adolescents' frequency of music listening is related negatively to the amount of time he/she spends with family and positively to the amount of time he/she spends with friends (Larson and Kubey, 1983; Larson et al., 1989) and that music is listened to most frequently in the bedroom (Larson and Kubey, 1983), a location where adolescents gain privacy from others and are able to explore issues and concerns that are important to them (Larson 1990; Parke and Sawin, 1979).

Unfortunately, while this research is noteworthy because it identifies the importance of context in the uses adolescents have for rock music, it is limited because it fails to differentiate among different types of rock and does not consider the possibility that how adolescents experience this music could be a function of not just whom it is listened to with and where it is listened to, but how these different types of music are mediated by the context in which listening takes place. Research conducted by Murdock and Phelps (1973) and Frith (1978) indicates that rock consists of distinct types and suggests that how rock is experienced is related not just to whom it is listened to with and where it is listened to but what the type of rock is and how its properties are mediated by the social context. Using radically different methodologies – factor analysis of semantic differential ratings of rock songs (Murdock and Phelps, 1973) and interpretive insight based on experience as a rock music critic and sociologist (Frith, 1983) – these researchers found that adolescent response to it varies, (1) in terms of whether it has a collective or private orientation, and (2) whether it is conventional or unconventional in its approach to various themes and issues. That such disparate approaches to categorizing rock arrive at basically the same types of classifications is, in and of itself, testament to their validity.

Collectively oriented music, as described by Murdock and Phelps (1973) and Frith (1978), tends to emphasize the musical properties of a song and, in doing so, allows for public expression of various values and concerns. Top 40 and hard rock/heavy metal each exemplify this type of music: Top 40 because its strong beat makes it ideal for demonstrating physical and sexual abilities through dancing, and hard rock/heavy metal, even though they are distinct types of music, because the loud amplification and rebellious spirit both share and stress the importance of power and being in control. Privately oriented music, in contrast, is lyrically dominant. Represented mostly by ballads characteristic of soft rock performers and individual singer/songwriters, this music is written to be listened to and reflected upon. Soft rock, in particular, is contemplative in nature with its tales of loneliness and frustration, of being let down and stood up (Frith, 1978).

The second distinction, between conventional and unconventional music, is exemplified by the contrast between "teen" and "youth" music (Murdock and Phelps, 1973; Frith, 1978). Teen music, best represented by Top 40 and soft rock, is that which is most available for consumption. Concerned with naive expressions of love and romance, this music is notable for its attempt to be acceptable to the widest possible audience. Youth music, on the other hand, is more oppositional than teen music and articulates this through aggressive displays (hard rock/heavy metal) or specific criticisms of existing social conventions (singer/songwriter).

Consistent with past research, this investigation contends that adolescents will have their most positive experience with rock when listening alone or with friends and their most negative states when listening with family members. Unlike previous research, however, it argues that the four different types of music identified by Murdock and Phelps (1973) and Frith (1978) will interact with social companionship contexts (alone, friends, family) to determine adolescents' mood states. Collectively oriented music such as Top 40 and hard rock/heavy metal, for example, should be associated with higher levels of psychological involvement and more positive mood states when adolescents listen to music alone than privately oriented music like soft rock. This is because this music focuses more on public mastery of the environment and thus may make solitude easier to handle than does privately oriented music whose sad themes and accompanying melody often center around loneliness and, hence, may be painful to listen to when alone. Teen music, on the other hand, should be more associated with positive mood states when it is listened to with family members than youth music whose controversial themes and issues are less suited to a family context and may be at odds with parental values.

In addition to whom music is listened to with, subjective experiences of rock should also be a function of the interaction between type of music and the location in which it is listened to. The importance of the bedroom to adolescents as a place of contemplation and reflection suggest that privately oriented music might be more engaging when listened to in this context whereas collectively oriented music might be engaging regardless of context. This is because soft rock and singer/songwriter are written mostly to be listened to and thought about and not acted upon like Top 40 and hard rock/heavy metal.

The following hypotheses are based on the preceding discussion. Although the data used to test them come from a small sample and involve only those adolescents who reported the full extent of their music listening behavior, they do contain some useful insights into the importance of addressing adolescent responses to rock as a joint function of the type of music and the social context in which it is listened to. As such, the research should not be seen as definitive but merely suggestive of further lines of inquiry into this area.

H1:   Mood and subjective involvement will be greater when rock music is listened to with friends than alone (H1a) or with family (H1b). These differences will be more pronounced for soft rock and singer/songwriter than they will be for Top 40 and hard rock/heavy metal.

H2: Hard rock/heavy metal and singer/songwriter will be associated with lower levels of mood and subjective involvement than Top 40 and soft rock when these types of music are listened to with family members.

H3: Mood and subjective involvement will be greater when rock music is listened to in the bedroom than in other settings. This difference will be more pronounced for soft rock and singer/songwriter than it will be for Top 40 and hard rock/heavy metal.

Method

Sample

Participants in the study were 483 fifth to ninth graders (ages 9–15). The sample was selected randomly from a working-class, blue-collar community on the edge of Chicago and an outlying middle-class suburb. Given the nature of the communities, all the participants were White. A stratification procedure was used to ensure equal representation by grade, sex, social class, and time of year (spring, summer, fall, winter). The final sample of 483 represents 70 percent of the students initially invited to participate. An anonymous survey of all students in the target populations indicated that sample nonparticipation was not related to age, sex, social class, or self-esteem, but was more common among students in families with remarried parents (Larson, 1989a). The data were collected between 1985 and 1987.

Procedures

Participants carried electronic pagers for approximately one week and, following the procedures of the Experience Sampling Method (Larson and Csikszentmihalyi, 1983; Csikszentmihalyi and Larson, 1987), provided reports on their experience at random times when signaled by the pagers. One signal occurred at a random time within every two-hour block of time between 7.30 a.m. and 9.30 p.m. for seven days. When signaling occurred, participants were instructed to stop what they were doing and fill out a self-report form. The self-report form asked about their activity, companionship, location, and psychological state immediately prior to receipt of the signal.

In total, the students responded to 18,022 signals by filling out a self-report form. This represents a response rate of 86 percent to the signals students received. Analysis of the signals they missed suggest that non-response occurred across a wide range of situations and activities, and that the final sample of self-reports provides a relatively unbiased representation of the students' experience during the hours covered by the study (Larson, 1989a).

Measures

Music listening

Two items on the self-report form were used to identify music listening. One item asked simply, "Just before you were signaled. . . . What were you doing?" The only data pertaining to music analyzed are instances where the respondent identified listening to music as the *primary* activity engaged in. A substantial number of cases where listening to music was reported as the secondary activity were not considered because of the difficulty in separating out the effect of the primary activity upon the experience of the situation. In total 248 students reported listening to music 628 of the times they were signaled with 164 reporting music listening as their primary activity 275 times.

A second item asked the students to identify the song, record, or tape they were listening to when they were listening to music. Responses to this item were categorized as either Top 40, hard rock/heavy metal, soft rock, or singer/songwriter by three trained coders. Each of the coders was instructed to classify the music according to the following definitions:

- Top 40: musically dominant and can be danced to. Lyrics deal primarily with simple romantic desires.
- Hard rock/heavy metal: musically dominant and cannot be danced to. Lyrics, when understandable, deal mostly with the expression of power and physical conquest.
- Soft rock: lyrically dominant; emphasis of the song is to explore private feelings about loves won, lost, and desired. Melody is slow but can be danced to.
- Singer/songwriter: lyrically dominant; emphasis of the song is to criticize and/or provide insight into various social phenomena. Melody is slow and cannot be danced to.

Of the 164 students who reported listening to music as their primary activity, 95 provided information pertaining to the types of music they were listening to 138 times. The overwhelming majority of the identified music (91 students reporting 132 instances of listening to music) was considered to be rock (as opposed to country and western, classical, opera, etc.) and coded into one of the four music categories.

Participants reported music in terms of the song, the performer, or in a few cases, the name of the radio station being listened to. The coders were instructed to accommodate the differences in how the music listened to was reported by coding the songs and, if the song was not available, the types of songs most associated with the performer or radio station recorded. The reliability of coding was computed using Krippendorf's alpha (Krippendorf, 1980). The value for this figure is 0.901, which indicates that the coding is reliable 90.1 percent above that which would be expected by chance.

Companionship

An item on the self-report form asked students who they were with at the time signaling took place. Fifteen fixed-response choices could be checked. For the purpose of this investigation, responses have been grouped into three mutually exclusive categories: family, friends, alone. A fourth main category, in class, is not used here because music listening never occurred in class.

Location

Response to an open-ended question – "Where were you?" – was coded into 68 categories (interrater agreement = 99 percent). For the purposes of this paper, the categories are collapsed into two categories: bedroom and not bedroom.

Affect and arousal

Students rated their mood state at the time of each signal on five 7-point semantic differential items. Factor analysis of these items suggested the formation of two scales (Larson, 1989b). A scale of affect (alpha = 0.75) was composed of responses to the items happy–unhappy, cheerful–irritable, friendly–angry. A scale of arousal (alpha = 0.60) was composed of items strong–weak and alert–drowsy. The values for each of the scales was transformed into z scores so that they could be compared across a wide variety of activities, including type of music being listened to. The construct validity of the affect scale was indicated by statistically significant correlations ($p \leq 0.05$) between individual's mean scores for this scale and teachers' ratings of adolescents' general mood level, motivation, and mental health (Larson, 1989b).

Psychological investment

Students also rated their subjective involvement at the time of each signal on three 10-point unipolar items that asked the following: "How much choice did you have about doing this activity?" "Do you wish you had been doing something else?" "How well were you paying attention?" These items are correlated moderately with each other (alpha = 0.60) and have been considered as a scale (Larson, 1989b). The values of this scale were also transformed into z-scores and the scale itself was construct validated in the same way the affect scale was.

Social class

Social class was measured by taking father's occupation and categorizing it into a working-class–middle-class dichotomy. To be classified as middle class, occupations had to reflect some degree of ownership of and/or control over the employing organization and decisions made within it such as being an owner, manager, supervisor, or professional. Working-class occupations exhibited neither ownership nor organizational control. With the exception of not including a measure of education in the classification, these categories are consistent with Wright's (1985) work on social class.

Data analysis

To test the hypotheses, the music listening data were aggregated to obtain average values of affect, arousal, and psychological investment for each respondent who reported listening to one of the four types of rock music at least once in a specific context. The effect social context and type of music listened to had on mood states was determined using a regression equation employing weighted least squares.

Results

Hypothesis 1a states that affect, arousal, and psychological investment should be greater for listening done with friends compared to listening alone and that this difference should be more pronounced for soft rock. This hypothesis is supported partially for arousal and totally for psychological investment. Only limited support is evident for affect.

For arousal, there is a significant main effect for the contrast between being alone and being with friends. The conditional mean (CM) for listening alone is −0.747, which differs significantly from that of listening with friends (CM = 1.213) at the 0.05 level. However, only one of the two predicted interaction effects is significant. The conditional means in table 11.1 reveal a significant difference between hard rock/heavy metal and soft rock in the degree of arousal adolescents experience listening to these types of music alone as opposed to with friends. Contrary to what was hypothesized, however, there is no difference in the magnitude of arousal adolescents experience listening to Top 40 and soft rock in these two contexts.

Psychological investment is also greater for music listening with friends compared to alone. The conditional mean for listening with

Table 11.1 Conditional means pertaining to interaction effects between who music is listened to with and type of music listened to[a]

Type of music		Alone	Family	Friends
		Who music is listened to with		

Type of music		Alone	Family	Friends
Top 40	Arouse	0.223	0.278	0.992
	Invest	−0.271[b]	−0.430	−0.009
Hard rock/ heavy metal	Arouse	0.480[b]	−2.180	0.706
	Invest	−0.527[b]	−0.503	−0.300
Soft rock	Arouse	−0.747	−0.086	1.213
	Invest	−1.867	−0.764	0.392

[a] *Data pertaining to affect are not presented because interactions are not statistically significant*
[b] $p \leq 0.05$

friends is 0.392 compared to −1.083 for listening alone ($p \leq 0.01$). Also, as expected, there is a significant difference between Top 40 and soft rock and hard rock/heavy metal and soft rock in the magnitude of this increase. The conditional means in table 11.1 reveal that this greater psychological involvement is more pronounced for soft rock than it is for Top 40 and hard rock/heavy metal.

For affect, there is a significant main effect for the contract between listening to rock alone vs. with friends. Consistent with Hypothesis 1a, affect is more positive when listening occurs with friends (friends CM = 1.840, alone CM = 0.762; $p \leq 0.01$). No significant interactions, however, are evident.

Hypothesis 1b, predicting more positive mood and involvement when listening occurs with friends vs. family members, receives only limited support from the data. There is a significant positive change in psychological investment for the contrast between being with family members vs. being with friends (family CM = −0.764, friends CM = 0.392; $p \leq 0.01$). This finding is also evident for affect (family CM = 1.059, friends CM = 1.840; $p \leq 0.01$) but not for arousal. The predicted interaction effects are not supported despite large differences in the conditional means (table 11.1). This is attributable to the small cell sizes for hard rock/heavy metal ($n = 2$ for family; $n = 5$ for friends) and soft rock ($n = 5$ for family; $n = 3$ for friends).

Hypothesis 2, which contends that affect, arousal, and psychological investment will be lower when adolescents listen to hard rock/heavy metal with family members than when they listen to Top 40 and soft rock, receives only limited support from the data. The data indicate that adolescents do differ in the level of affect they report when listening to hard rock/heavy metal with family members than when they listen to Top 40 and soft rock. The conditional means show clearly that these differences are the result of hard rock/heavy metal (CM = −3.664) being associated with substantially lower levels of affect when it is listened to in this context than Top 40 (CM = −1.294) and soft rock (CM = −1.194). This difference is significant at the 0.05 level. There is no significant difference in the levels of psychological investment and arousal adolescents experience when listening to the three types of music with family members.

Hypothesis 3 contends that affect, arousal, and psychological investment will be greater when music is listened to in the bedroom than elsewhere and that this difference should be most pronounced for soft

Table 11.2 Conditional means pertaining to interaction effects between where music is listened to and type of music listened to[a]

Type of music		Where music is listened to	
		Bedroom	Elsewhere
Top 40	Arouse	0.452^b	0.992
	Invest	0.108^c	−0.009
Hard rock/ heavy metal	Arouse	$−0.187^b$	0.706
	Invest	0.103^b	−0.300
Soft rock	Arouse	1.844	1.213
	Invest	1.378	0.392

[a] *Data pertaining to affect are not presented because interactions are not statistically significant*
[b] $p \leq 0.05$
[c] $p \leq 0.01$

rock. This hypotheses is not supported for affect, but receives partial support for the other two variables.

For arousal, a significant main effect is not evident, although interaction effects are apparent. Consistent with the hypotheses, Top 40 and hard rock/heavy metal each differ from soft rock in the degree of arousal experienced by location. The conditional means in table 11.2 indicate that the level of arousal is greater for Top 40 and hard rock/heavy metal when listened to elsewhere, while it is greatest for soft rock when listened to in the bedroom.

Hypothesis 3 is supported fully for psychological investment. Table 11.2 reveals a significant main effect for location (bedroom CM = 1.378, elsewhere (CM = 0.392; $p \leq 0.01$), attributable to greater investment when music is listened to in the bedroom. Further, the magnitude of the change differs significantly when Top 40 and hard rock/heavy metal are each compared to soft rock. The conditional means in table 11.2 reveal that the lower psychological investment outside the bedroom is more pronounced for soft rock than it is for Top 40 and hard rock/heavy metal.

Discussion

This investigation demonstrates that adolescent responses to rock music are not simply a function of the listening context *per se* as prior studies have reported but, rather, the interaction between the context and the type of music listened to. Although the data are limited by a small sample size and involve only those adolescents who reported the full extent of their music listening, they do suggest that who rock music is listened to with and where it is listened to play key roles in mediating how adolescents experience Top 40, hard rock/heavy metal, and soft rock. In terms of the former, the data reveal that while adolescents experience lower mood states when they listen to rock alone as opposed to with friends, this finding is more true of soft rock than it is Top 40 and hard rock/heavy metal. That adolescents experience extremely low levels of arousal when they listen to soft rock alone rather than with friends is probably due to the private and downbeat nature of this music reinforcing the negative state adolescents typically experience when alone (Larson, 1990) but being perceived as a more positive and binding experience when listened to with friends. On the other hand, the finding that adolescents' experiences of Top 40 and hard rock/heavy metal do not differ significantly when listened to alone or with friends is likely the result of the music being able to provide adolescents with a sense of power and mastery over their lives in both these instances.

Variation in the way social companionship mediates adolescent experiences of different types of rock music occurs not only when listening takes place alone or with friends but when family members are present as well. This is particularly true of hard rock/heavy metal, which is associated with very low levels of affect when listened to with family members but, interestingly, not Top 40, which adolescents experience similarly regardless of whether the listening occurs with friends or family members. That hard rock/heavy metal is associated with less positive levels of affect should not be surprising considering the inconsistency between the music's unconventional and rebellious nature and the familial pecking order that emphasizes the authority and dominance of parents. In fact, this is undoubtedly why hard rock/heavy metal is listened to rarely with family members. However, the finding that adolescents experience Top 40 similarly with friends or family members is surprising considering that rock is generally considered to be a medium that adolescents use to negotiate social and sexual autonomy from parents (Brittain, 1963; Kandel and Lesser, 1969; Kaplan, 1984). That this finding is true is likely due to the music's mostly upbeat and simplistic message being so innocuous that the presence of family members does not threaten its enjoyment.

In addition to who rock music is listened to with, the data also reveal that where adolescents listen to music has the ability to enhance or diminish the degree to which Top 40, hard rock/heavy metal, and soft rock are emotionally and psychologically engaging. The association of Top 40 and hard rock/heavy metal with higher levels of arousal outside the bedroom, for example, suggests that the energizing qualities of these two types of music may be used to provide mastery over environments that, unlike the bedroom, are not subject to ongoing adolescent control. This is, of course, controlling for the effect that being alone, with friends, or with family have on this experience. The decline in arousal and psychological investment experienced when the context for listening changes from the bedroom to elsewhere, on the other hand, indicates that this music's concern with private issues and concerns such as love and romance is best suited to a familiar domain.

References

Brittain, C. V. (1963). Adolescent choices and parent-peer cross pressures. *American Sociological Review*, 28: 385–391.

Csikszentmihalyi, M. & Larson, R. (1987). Validity and reliability of the experience-sampling method. *Journal of Nervous and Mental Disorders*, 175: 526–536.

Frith, S. (1978). Youth culture/youth cults: A decade of rock music consumption. In Gillette, C., & Frith, S. (Eds.), *Rock File 5*. Panther, London.

Frith, S. (1983). *Sound Effects: Youth, Leisure, and Rock and Roll*. Constable, London.

Kandel, D., & Lesser, G. S. (1969). Parent-adolescent relationships and adolescent independence in the United States and Denmark. *Journal of Marriage and the Family*, 31: 348–358.

Kaplan, L. J. (1984). *Adolescence: The Farewell to Childhood*. Simon & Schuster, New York.

Krippendorf, K. (1980). *Content Analysis: An Introduction to Its Methodology*. Sage, Beverly Hills, CA.

Kubey, R., & Larson, R. (1990). The use and experience of the new video media among children and young adolescents. *Communication Research*, 17: 107–130.

Larson, R. (1989a). Beeping children and adolescents: A method for studying time use and daily experience. *Journal of Youth and Adolescence*, 18: 511–530.

Larson, R. (1989b). The factor structure of moods and emotions in a sample of young adolescents. Unpublished manuscript, University of Illinois at Urbana – Champaign.

Larson, R. (1990). The solitary side of life: An examination of the time people spend alone from childhood to old age. *Developmental Review*, 10: 155–185.

Larson, R., and Csikszentmihalyi, M. (1983). The experience sampling method. In H. T. Reis (Ed.), *Naturalistic Approaches to Studying Social Interaction: New Directions for Methodology of Social and Behavioral Science, No. 15.* Jossey-Bass, San Francisco.

Larson, R., & Kubey, R. (1983). Television and music: Contrasting media in adolescent life. *Youth Society*, 15: 13–31.

Larson, R., Kubey, R., & Colletti, J. (1989). Changing channels: Early adolescent media choices and shifting investments in family and friends. *Journal of Youth and Adolescence*, 18: 583–600.

Murdock, G., & Phelps, G. (1973). *Mass Media and the Secondary School.* MacMillan, London.

Parke, R. D., & Sawin, D. B. (1979). Children's privacy in the home: Developmental, ecological, and child rearing determinants. *Environment and Behaviour*, 11: 87–104.

Smothers, J. (1961). The public and private meanings and uses of popular music for American Adolescents. Unpublished Ph.D. dissertation, University of Chicago.

Wright, E. O. (1985). *Classes.* Verso, London.

Part IV

Social Problems

Adolescence is associated with a wide array of social problems. In this section two readings address some of the social problems associated with adolescence.

Alcohol Use, Suicidal Behavior, and Risky Activities Among Adolescents
and
Internalizing Problems and Their Relation to the Development of Disruptive Behaviors in Adolescence

Introduction

For many people the thought most closely associated with adolescence is risk-taking and disruptive behaviors. There is no doubt that adolescents take many risks. There is no doubt that they can become loud, obnoxious, and disruptive. Anytime, though, where one has youthful energy, and reduced or unavailable adult supervision, there will be potential social problems.

I go to the movies often. I like all kinds of movies. I am particularly entertained by high adventure or science fiction. These movies draw in a lot of teenage boys. And they often come in a group. Very consistently when young boys, or young men for that matter, see a lot of violence they shout in support of the victor over the victorless. Sometimes they get so aroused that they either forget about courtesy and start talking and shouting and yelling at the screen and each other. I often notice how the girls or women with these boys or men simply sink down in their seats, embarrassed by the male bravado. You put unsupervised or undisciplined young boys together and create an environment of extreme excitement or observed violence and you get disruptive behavior.

There are many features that reduce disruptive behavior and risk-taking among teenagers. We know that conventional church attendance reduces these forms of behaviors. We know parental monitoring and supervision and social bonding with the family diminishes such behaviors. Even community norms and social expectations reduce problem behaviors. However, social problems will remain an issue for the adolescence experience for the near future and probably well beyond it.

Some contemporary social critics suggest the conditions are worsening for teenagers. In one report by the United States National Research Council (1993), which is titled *Losing Generations*, the argument is advanced that social problems abound and that the conditions supporting adolescent well-being and productive behavior are rapidly declining. This form of doom-prophesying may be extreme, but it is suggestive that social problems may expand in the years to come.

I have selected two studies for you to read that focus on risky activities or on disruptive behaviors. There are a multitude of social problem behaviors that could be included. However, I believe the two readings offer you an excellent examination of how person, context, and occasion factors are included in the study of adolescent social problems.

Time to go Zoning again. This time shut the rock music off, go to a quiet room, and read about such things as alcohol consumption, suicidal behavior, risk taking, depression, and disruptive behavior. When you come back from the Zone, take a walk or have a cup of coffee. Be glad you aren't where some of the kids in these studies were at the time of these investigations. For some, the place wasn't so happy and it was in the hard part of the Twilight Zone of Adolescence.

Suggested reading

National Research Council (1993). *Losing generations: adolescents in high-risk settings*. Washington DC: National Academy Press.

TWELVE

Alcohol Use, Suicidal Behavior, and Risky Activities Among Adolescents

Michael Windle, Carol Miller-Tutzauer, and Donna Domenico

Suicide was the fifth-leading cause of death among teenagers and young adults in 1960; in 1985 it was the second-leading cause of death among teenagers (Centers for Disease Control, 1985). Research regarding suicidal behavior has indicated that the peak age of attempted suicide, or parasuicide, is during the 15 to 19 age range (Hawton and Goldacre, 1982; Rutter, 1986). Furthermore, whereas completed suicides are more frequent among males, suicide attempts are more frequent among females. In addition to sex differences in attempted and completed suicides, numerous studies have been conducted to identify factors that distinguish adolescents with suicidal ideation from adolescent attempters and completers (see reviews of Hawton, 1986; Spirito et al., 1989). That is, rather than conceptualizing these suicidal behaviors along a continuum with a common etiology, different factors are posed to contribute to the specified behaviors. For example, Kosky et al., (1990) used an outpatient sample of children/adolescents and reported that those who had attempted suicide (relative to those who had had suicidal thoughts but no attempt) had higher levels of chronic family discord and substance abuse. Rutter (1986) reported that overt depressive disorders were more highly associated with suicide attempts than with suicidal ideation among adolescents. Shaffer (1986) studied differences between adolescent suicide attempters and completers and indicated that the groups did not differ with regard to depression; however, suicide attempters and completers manifested higher levels of antisocial behavior and inter-personal aggression than nonsuicidal depressives.

Whereas most studies of adolescent suicide have been conducted with clinical samples, several studies of suicidal behaviors have been conducted with nonclinical adolescent samples. The rates of suicidal ideation and attempts have been markedly high for those nonclinical sample studies that have been reported (e.g., Albert and Beck, 1975; Garrison, 1989; Smith and Crawford, 1986). For example, Smith and Crawford (1986) reported that 63 percent of a high school sample indicated prior suicidal ideation and 11 percent had attempted suicide on one or more occasions. Research reviewed by Hawton (1986) and Spirito et al. (1989) has suggested that alcohol or substance abuse is often associated with adolescent suicide attempts, though the magnitude of the association varies across studies. Garfinkel et al. (1982) reported that the rate of substance abuse at the time of the suicide attempt for a sample of children and adolescents seen in an emergency room was 11.3 percent.

The generalizability of relations between adolescent suicidal behaviors and alcohol use among clinical and emergency room samples to national adolescent samples is largely unknown. As such, using data from a nationally representative adolescent sample, the first objective of this study was to investigate the interrelations between adolescent alcohol use and suicidal ideation and attempts. The second objective was to study interrelations between alcohol use and nonsuicidal, but risky, activities that may result in accidental serious injury or death (e.g., unsupervised swimming, taking someone else's prescribed medicine). Suicidal behavior and risky activities are viewed as distinct conceptual domains that are associated with risk for adolescent health and mortality. Alcohol use during adolescence is proposed as a correlate of both suicidal behaviors and risky activities, though the function(s) served by alcohol (e.g., self-medication vs. enhancement) may differ. Associations have been reported between adolescent suicidal behavior and substance use (e.g., Hawton, 1986; Shaffer, 1986). In addition, Zuckerman (1972) reported that higher sensation seeking is associated with higher levels of substance use among adolescents. Although the measure of risk-taking behavior used in this study has not been compared with standardized measures of sensation seeking, we view it as containing ratings of items that yield scores consistent with the domain of risk-taking behaviors.

The third objective was to investigate the combined associations of alcohol use and risky activities on suicidal behaviors. That is, for instance, was the combination of lowered inhibitions, influenced by alcohol use and a risk-taking propensity, associated with a higher probability of suicidal behavior among adolescents? Clark et al. (1990) suggested that at least a portion of adolescent high risk takers had a history of suicide attempts. In addition, R. Jessor and S. L. Jessor's (1977) research has suggested that problematic behaviors tend to covary during adolescence.

The data used in this study are from the National Adolescent Student Health Survey (NASHS; 1989), which was administered to more than 11,000 8th- and 10th-grade students nationwide in the fall of 1987. The large, nationally representative sample of early and mid-adolescents provided a unique data source for investigating the three primary objectives stated previously, and for studying possible sex differences in interrelations between alcohol use, suicidal behavior, and risky activities.

Method

The NASHS was initiated in 1985 by the American Health Association, the Association for the Advancement of Health Education, and the Society for Public Health Education. All three organizations worked in conjunction with the American Alliance for Health, Physical Education, Recreation, and Dance. Other Federal agencies that participated in the planning and development of the survey were the National Institute on Drug Abuse, the Center for Disease Control, and the US Department of Education.

The NASHS is the first major national study of adolescent health issues in more than 20 years. The goal of the survey was to assess adolescents' knowledge of health issues and to use this information to plan new health objectives in the future. Eight health areas were addressed in this survey including drug and alcohol use, suicide, violence, acquired immune deficiency syndrome, sexually transmitted diseases, nutrition, consumer skills, and injury prevention. These eight health areas were selected through committees created by governmental agencies and co-sponsoring health organizations. Survey questions for each health area were developed by a panel of nationally known experts from that area.

Subjects

The NASHS data were drawn from a representative sample of 224 public and private schools in 20 states randomly selected by Macro Systems, Inc. of Silver Springs, MD. Of the 224 schools, 190 were public and 34 were private. Three mandatory classes (e.g., English) were randomly selected for 8th and 10th graders from each school. Standard informed-consent forms describing the purpose of the study and the content areas to be surveyed were distributed by teachers to students to take home. Those parents who preferred that their child not participate in the study were requested to sign and return the form to the teacher and their child would then be excluded from participation in the study. Approximately 89 percent of eligible 8th graders and 86 percent of eligible 10th graders participated in the study; 7 percent of 8th graders and 11 percent of 10th graders were absent on the day of the survey assessment; and 3 percent of 8th graders and 3 percent of 10th graders were excluded due to lack of parental or adolescent consent. There was no make-up day to survey those students who were absent on the regularly scheduled survey day. The participation rate of adolescents in the NASHS is equivalent to or exceeds the rate of participation among adolescents in other large-scale high school surveys.

The sample consisted of approximately 11,400 8th- and 10th-grade students ranging from 11 to 17 years of age ($M = 13.44$, $SD = 0.76$, for 8th graders; $M = 15.33$, $SD = 0.72$, for 10th graders). Eighth-grade students were selected as representative of the junior high school population because the 8th grade represents the middle level of junior high/middle school; 10th-grade students were chosen as representative of the high school population based on the higher dropout rate of 11th- and 12th-grade students.

The students' racial and ethnic backgrounds were as follows: White = 72.7 percent, Black = 12.6 percent, Hispanic = 8.6 percent, Asian = 2.6 percent, Native American = 1.1 percent, other = 2.4 percent. The number of females nearly equaled the number of males for each grade level: females comprised 50.2 percent of the 8th graders and 50.7 percent of the 10th graders; males comprised 49.8 percent of the 8th graders and 49.3 percent of the 10th graders. Data were pooled across racial and ethnic groups because comparisons for the three most highly represented groups (Whites, Blacks, and Hispanics) indicated minor differences in suicidal ideation and attempts. Specifically, the percentages of affirmative responses to suicidal ideation for Whites, Blacks, and Hispanics were 33.5 percent, 28.5 percent, and 36.1 percent, respectively. The percentages of affirmative responses to suicidal attempts for Whites, Blacks, and Hispanics were 13.3 percent, 12.7 percent, and 16.8 percent, respectively.

Measures

In order to sample a wide range of issues relating to adolescent health, three separate survey forms were developed. All three forms contained a "seed" set of 11 questions pertaining to demographics (age, sex, ethnicity) and substance use (alcohol, cigarettes, and drugs). In addition to the identical set items across the three forms, each form included a specialized set of items related to various aspects of adolescent health. The data from the survey form used in this study included questions about suicide, alcohol use, and adolescents' risky behaviors.

Our assessment of adolescents' suicidal behaviors involved two questions – one related to suicidal ideation and the other related to suicide attempts. The suicidal ideation item asked, "Have you ever seriously thought about trying to hurt yourself in a way that might result in your death?" Suicide attempts were evaluated through the question, "Have you ever actually tried to hurt yourself in a way that might have resulted in your death?" Both questions utilized a dichotomous (yes–no) response format.

The alcohol consumption measure involved asking students "On how many occasions, if any, have you had alcoholic beverages to drink such as wine, wine coolers, beer, mixed drinks, or hard liquor during the last 30 days?" Response options included 0 occasions, 1 to 2 occasions, 3 to 5 occasions, 6 to 9 occasions, 10 to 19 occasions, 20 to 39 occasions, and 40 or more occasions. We formed three drinking groups on the basis of responses to this question – abstainers (0 occasions), light drinkers (1 to 5 occasions), and moderate/heavy drinkers (6 or more occasions). We recognize the limitations inherent in assessing alcohol involvement solely on the basis of number of occasions of drinking due to the absence of information on the amount (quantity) consumed per occasion. Unfortunately, data on the amount consumed per occasion were not available as part of the NASHS. Nevertheless, correlation of the frequency of alcohol use with an index of number of occasions of heavy drinking (i.e., number of occasions of drinking five or more drinks) resulted in a Pearson correlation coefficient of 0.70 ($p < 0.001$), thus lending some support to our use of frequency of drinking as an indicator of level of alcohol involvement.

Our assessment of risk-taking behaviors centered around nine specific risky activities adolescents may or may not have engaged in: taking another person's medication; swimming alone; diving in water of unknown depth; taking alcohol/drugs while playing sports; driving an all terrain vehicle; using a gun for any reason; riding with a driver who is under the influence of alcohol/drugs; skating in an unsupervised area; and surfing or swimming in an unsupervised area. By risk taking, we are referring to an individual difference variable in which some individuals selectively engage in activities that increase the probability of serious injury or death, whereas other individuals either engage in these activities at a much lower rate or not at all. Each of the nine items was phrased "During the past year how many times have you participated in each of these behaviors?" A 6-point scale response format was utilized: *0 times* (1), *1 to 3 times* (2), *4 to 6 times* (3), *7 to 10 times* (4), *11 to 20 times* (5), and *more than 20 times* (6). We constructed a measure of adolescent risk taking by recoding responses for the nine risky behaviors to the midpoints of the response categories. The items were then summed to form a single index of risky behavior. The internal consistency estimates for the risk measure were 0.67 for 8th graders and 0.71 for 10th graders. We then formed three risk groups on the basis of the summed risk index: low risk takers (4 or fewer instances of engaging in risky behaviors), moderate risk takers (greater than 4 risky incidences up to 30 incidences), and high risk takers (more than 30 incidences). Each of the three risk groups contained approximately one third of the total sample.

Results

Examination of the frequency distribution of adolescents' suicidal behaviors across the three alcohol consumption categories confirmed our expectations. As shown in table 12.1, the incidence of both suicidal ideation and attempts increased with increasing levels of alcohol use. Furthermore, this pattern remained consistent with boys and girls

Table 12.1 Percentage of adolescents reporting various suicidal behaviors

Grade	Sex	Alcohol group	Thought about committing suicide	Attempted suicide	Knew someone who attempted suicide	n
8	Female	Abstain	29.8	11.0	49.0	588
		Light	52.7	22.6	70.5	259
		Heavy	59.6	37.0	76.6	47
	Male	Abstain	17.4	6.2	32.3	599
		Light	36.2	15.2	51.9	243
		Heavy	51.1	27.7	74.5	47
10	Female	Abstain	33.5	12.3	60.0	441
		Light	52.0	21.4	70.7	352
		Heavy	63.1	38.8	83.5	103
	Male	Abstain	22.7	5.9	43.4	389
		Light	28.1	10.9	51.7	331
		Heavy	38.4	21.9	84.8	139

as well as across grade levels. Of particular interest are the extremely high levels of suicidal ideation among girls in the heavy alcohol-consumption group. Among 8th-grade girls, 60 percent of the heavy drinkers thought about committing suicide and 37 percent reported attempting suicide, while among 10th-grade girls 63 percent of those in the heavy drinking category contemplated suicide with 39 percent reporting carrying through with an attempt. There was also a linear trend between level of alcohol involvement and the percentage of respondents who answered affirmatively to knowing someone who had attempted suicide. To the extent that the person known to have attempted suicide serves as a role model, suicidal risk among adolescents may be increased.

Although attempted suicides constitute direct lethal threats, other nonsuicidal behaviors contribute to accidental deaths and, thus, increase adolescent mortality. However, rather than contemplating immediately lethal actions, adolescents may place themselves at increased risk for fatal or serious injury accidents by engaging in a variety of reckless or otherwise imprudent behaviors. We performed two-way analyses of variance (ANOVAs; Sex × Alcohol group) separately for 8th and 10th graders on a continuous, composite risk score (summed across all nine risk behavior items) as the dependent variable.[1] The ANOVA models were statistically significant for both 8th, $F(2, 1,773) = 9.03$, $p < 0.001$, and 10th graders, $F(2, 1,745) = 15.13$, $p < 0.001$. The Sex × Alcohol group interaction was statistically significant across grade levels, and a graphical plot of the interactions is illustrated in figure 12.1. It appears that a slightly steeper slope for boys than girls at each grade level may account for the significant interaction effects. However, these interaction effects do not appear to be salient with regard to the substantive findings which indicate that sex and alcohol group are both predictive of higher levels of risk-taking behaviors.

In order to investigate the combined influence of alcohol use and risk taking by adolescents, we specified four logistic-regression models. The dependent variables for the models were suicidal ideation and attempts for each grade level, and the predictor variables were sex, alcohol use, and number of risky activities. Second-order interaction terms (e.g., Sex × Alcohol use) were also entered in the logistic-regression models and were typically nonsignificant or trivial with respect to their association with the dependent variables.[2] The most parsimonious and significantly consistent model across grade levels and across the two dependent variables was the "main effects" model. The results of the main effects logistic-regression models are presented in table 12.2. The logistic-regression models indicate that all three predictors were statistically significant ($p < 0.001$) across grade levels and dependent variables; the magnitude of effects was generally in the low-to-moderate range.

So as to provide clarity regarding the expected probabilities of having had suicidal thoughts or having attempted suicide, we used a categorical logit model predicting suicidal ideation and attempts by: sex, drinking group (abstain, light, heavy), and risk category (low, moderate, or high).[3] As shown in table 12.3, both suicidal ideation and attempts are more probable among individuals in the heavy alcohol groups and among high risk takers than among the other groups. The highest likelihood of suicidal behaviors was among heavy drinkers who also engaged in high levels of risky behaviors. Abstainers engaging in low levels of risk taking were least likely to think about or attempt suicide. Again, this pattern emerged for both boys and girls across both grade levels.

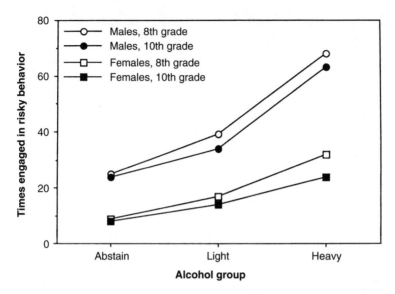

Figure 12.1 Graphical plot of statistically significant interactions (Alcohol group × risky behaviors) for 8th- and 10th-grade adolescent males and females

Discussion

The alcohol use and suicidal behavior findings of this study with a nationally representative sample of early and mid-adolescents are similar in several ways to prior research conducted with nonrepresentative community and clinical samples (e.g., Brent et al., 1988; Garrison, 1989; Smith and Crawford, 1986). First, the prevalence of suicidal ideation and attempts was soberingly high for both early and mid-adolescents. These rates of suicidal ideation and attempts are consistent not only with prior adolescent suicide studies (e.g., Garrison, 1989), but also with findings regarding the prevalence of dysphoria and depression among children and adolescents (e.g., Kendall et al., 1989). Both the childhood/adolescent suicide and depression literatures suggest that there are a number of children and adolescents who are experiencing disturbed affective states (e.g., helplessness, hopelessness, rejection, hostility, guilt) and engaging in self-destructive thought processes and behaviors. Second, the prevalence of suicidal ideation and attempts for both adolescent groups (i.e., 8th and 10th graders) increased with the

Table 12.2 Logistic-regression models predicting suicidal behaviors by sex, alcohol use, and risky activities

Models/Predictors	Coefficient	SE	Significance	R	Exp(B)
Model 1: Suicidal ideation (8th graders)					
Intercept	−2.24	0.14	0.000		
Sex (0 = M, 1 = F)	0.87	0.12	0.000	0.15	2.39
Alcohol use	0.46	0.06	0.000	0.17	1.58
Risky activities	0.22	0.05	0.000	0.08	1.24
Model 2: Suicidal attempts (8th graders)					
Intercept	−3.65	0.20	0.000		
Sex (0 = M, 1 = F)	0.94	0.17	0.000	0.15	2.55
Alcohol use	0.41	0.06	0.000	0.17	1.50
Risky activities	0.39	0.07	0.000	0.14	1.48
Model 3: Suicidal ideation (10th graders)					
Intercept	−1.81	0.14	0.000		
Sex (0 = M, 1 = F)	1.03	0.12	0.000	0.18	2.80
Alcohol use	0.19	0.04	0.000	0.09	1.21
Risky activities	0.24	0.05	0.000	0.09	1.27
Model 4: Suicidal attempts (10th graders)					
Intercept	−3.28	0.20	0.000		
Sex (0 = M, 1 = F)	1.03	0.16	0.000	0.16	2.81
Alcohol use	0.31	0.05	0.000	0.15	1.36
Risky activities	0.21	0.07	0.000	0.07	1.23

Note: *The R statistic corresponds to a partial correlation between the dependent variable and each of the independent variables. The Exp(B) reflects the odds of change for the dependent variable when the independent variable increases by one unit. Sample size for the 8th graders was 1,772 and for the 10th graders it was 1,746. M = male; F = female*

level of alcohol use. Over 20 percent of heavy drinkers (regardless of sex or grade level) reported having attempted suicide. Third, the relation between suicidal behaviors and alcohol use paralleled the relation between exposure to suicide and level of alcohol use. That is, higher levels of alcohol use were associated with a higher probability of knowing someone who had attempted suicide. Brent et al. (1988) reported that the social networks of suicide attempters are more likely to contain individuals who have engaged in suicidal behaviors than individuals in social networks of nonsuicide attempters. Fourth, sex differences were found across grade levels for both suicidal ideation and attempts, with a larger percentage of girls reporting having engaged in suicidal thoughts and attempts. This finding is consistent with prior research on adolescent suicidal behaviors (e.g., Bettes and Walker,

Table 12.3 Expected probabilities of engaging in suicidal behaviors as a function of alcohol use and risk taking

Grade	Sex	Alcohol group	Probability of suicidal ideation			Probability of attempted suicide		
			Low risk taking	Moderate risk taking	High risk taking	Low risk taking	Moderate risk taking	High risk taking
8	Female	Abstain	0.26	0.33	0.41	0.08	0.13	0.23
		Light	0.46	0.54	0.62	0.14	0.23	0.37
		Heavy	0.55	0.63	0.70	0.24	0.35	0.52
	Male	Abstain	0.13	0.17	0.22	0.03	0.05	0.10
		Light	0.26	0.33	0.40	0.06	0.10	0.19
		Heavy	0.33	0.41	0.49	0.11	0.17	0.30
10	Female	Abstain	0.33	0.39	0.50	0.12	0.13	0.20
		Light	0.44	0.51	0.62	0.19	0.21	0.30
		Heavy	0.51	0.58	0.68	0.33	0.35	0.47
	Male	Abstain	0.15	0.19	0.26	0.04	0.05	0.08
		Light	0.22	0.27	0.37	0.08	0.09	0.13
		Heavy	0.27	0.33	0.43	0.15	0.16	0.24

Note: *Table entries are based on the results of categorical logistic-regression analysis*

1986), but must be tempered by findings indicating that boys complete more suicides than girls (e.g., Hawton and Goldacre, 1982).

In addition to the significant associations between alcohol use and suicidal behaviors, significant associations were found between alcohol use and risky behaviors. A high sensation-seeking predisposition has been found to be associated with alcohol use, illicit drug use, and driving while intoxicated arrests with adolescents and young adults (Johnson and White, 1989; Windle and Barnes, 1988; Zuckerman, 1972). The findings of this study are of importance because they generalize the range of risk-taking behaviors beyond strictly substance-related and delinquent or deviant activities discussed by R. Jessor and S. L. Jessor (1977) to include recreational activities. The association of these activities with alcohol use thus broadens the scope of problem behavior theory to include leisure, or recreational, activities that may increase the threat of injury, serious injury, or accidental death among adolescents. The alcohol–recreational activity association is important because it is possible that moderate to heavy alcohol use during some of these activities may impair motor performance, reduce judgmental capacities, and limit self-monitoring skills.

The logistic-regression analyses indicated that sex, alcohol use, and risky activities were significant predictors of suicidal ideation and attempts. Sex was the most potent of the three predictors, as the odds of suicidal ideation and attempts were between two and one half and three times greater for girls than boys for samples in both grade levels. Higher levels of alcohol use and risky activities also significantly increased the odds of suicidal ideation and attempts. Subgroup comparisons using the categorical logit model indicated that the associated estimated probability of attempted suicide among heavy alcohol-using girls who were high risk takers was relatively high. For the 8th graders, the probability of having attempted suicide for this subgroup was 0.52, and for the 10th grade subgroup was 0.47. Therefore approximately one half of heavy alcohol-using, high risk-taking female adolescents had attempted suicide. Subsequent research should be pursued to investigate the factors and processes involved in these interrelations between alcohol use, high risk-taking activities, and suicidal behaviors.

Notes

1 Analyses were conducted for each of the 9 risky behaviors and were consistent with the risk composite score findings in showing that a large proportion of adolescents in the high alcohol use group engaged more frequently in high-risk behaviors than those who consume little or no alcohol. A table summarizing these analyses is available upon request from the authors.
2 Only one of six interaction terms was significant for 10th graders (Drinking group × risk category on suicidal ideation). The partial r for this association was −0.05.
3 Consistent with the findings of the logistic-regression models, all parameters in the categorical logit models were statistically significant ($p < 0.001$) and overall model fit was indicated for each of the four specified models.

References

Albert, N., & Beck, A. T. (1975). Incidence of depression in early adolescence: A preliminary study. *Journal of Youth and Adolescence, 4,* 302–307.

Bettes, B. A., & Walker, E. (1986). Symptoms associated with suicidal behavior in childhood and adolescence. *Journal of Abnormal Child Psychology, 14,* 591–604.

Brent, D. A., Perper, J. A., Goldstein, C. E., Kolko, D. J., Allan, M. J., Allman, C. J., & Zelenak, J. P. (1988). Risk factors for adolescent suicide. *Archives of General Psychiatry, 45*, 581–588.

Centers for Disease Control. (1985). *Youth suicide surveillance 1985.* Atlanta, GA: Author.

Clark, D. C., Sommerfeldt, L., Schwarz, M., Hedeker, D., & Watel, L. (1990). Physical recklessness in adolescence: Trait or byproduct of depressive/suicidal states? *Journal of Nervous and Mental Disease, 178*, 423–433.

Garfinkel, B. D., Froese, A., & Hood, J. (1982). Suicide attempts in children and adolescents. *American Journal of Psychiatry, 139*, 1257–1261.

Garrison, C. Z. (1989). The study of suicidal behavior in the schools. *Suicide and Life-Threatening Behavior, 19*, 120–130.

Hawton, K. (1986). *Suicide and attempted suicide among children and adolescents.* Newbury Park, CA: Sage.

Hawton, K., & Goldacre, M. (1982). Hospital admissions for adverse effects of medicinal agents (mainly self-poisoning) among adolescents in the Oxford region. *British Journal of Psychiatry, 141*, 106–170.

Jessor, R., & Jessor, S. L. (1977). *Problem behavior and psychosocial development: A longitudinal study of youth.* New York: Academic.

Johnson, V., & White, H. R. (1989). An investigation of factors related to intoxicated driving behaviors among youth. *Journal Studies on Alcohol, 50*, 320–330.

Kendall, P. C., Cantwell, D. P., & Kazdin, A. E. (1989). Depression in children and adolescents: Assessment issues and recommendations. *Cognitive Therapy and Research, 13*, 109–146.

Kosky, R., Silburn, S., & Zubrick, S. R. (1990). Are children and adolescents who have suicidal thoughts different from those who attempt suicide? *Journal of Nervous and Mental Disease, 178*, 38–43.

National Adolescent Student Health Survey. (1989). *A report on the health of America's youth.* Oakland, CA: Third Party.

Rutter, M. (1986). The developmental psychopathology of depression: Issues and perspectives. In M. Rutter, C. E. Izard, & P. B. Read (Eds.), *Depression in young people* (pp. 3–30). New York: Guilford.

Shaffer, D. (1986). Developmental factors in child and adolescent suicide. In M. Rutter, C. E. Izard, & P. B. Read (Eds.), *Depression in young people* (pp. 383–396). New York: Guilford.

Smith, K., & Crawford, S. (1986). Suicidal behavior among "normal" high school students. *Suicide and Life-Threatening Behavior, 16*, 313–325.

Spirito, A., Brown, L., Overholser, J., & Fritz, G. (1989). Attempted suicide in adolescence: A review and critique of the literature. *Clinical Psychology Review, 9*, 335–363.

Windle, M., & Barnes, G. M. (1988). Similarities and differences in correlates of alcohol consumption and problem behaviors among male and female adolescents. *International Journal of the Addictions, 23,* 707–728.

Zuckerman, M. (1972). Drug usage as one manifestation of a "sensation seeking" trait. In W. Keup (Ed.), *Drug abuse: Current concepts and research* (pp. 154–163). Springfield, IL: Thomas.

THIRTEEN

Internalizing Problems and Their Relation to the Development of Disruptive Behaviors in Adolescence

Rolf Loeber, Mary F. Russo, and
Magda Stouthamer-Loeber, and
Benjamin B. Lahey

It has become increasingly clear that earlier studies on child psychopathology, which often focused on single disorders, were too narrow in predicting later adjustment and impairment. Very often, children have multiple disorders. In recent years, attention has focused on the course of comorbid conditions as they unfold over time (Caron and Rutter, 1991; Zoccolillo, 1992). In the area of externalizing or disruptive problems, the most commonly studied comorbidity has been between Conduct Disorder (CD) and Attention Deficit-Hyperactivity Disorder (ADHD). Another form of comorbidity is between childhood and adolescent externalizing problem behaviors, such as CD or ADHD, and internalizing problems, such as depression, anxiety, or withdrawn behavior (Achenbach, 1993; Feehan et al., 1993; Russo and Beidel, 1994). There is increasing evidence of the importance of the interaction between externalizing (especially conduct symptoms) and the internalizing problems of anxiety and depression (Kovacs et al., 1988; McBurnett et al., 1991; Puig-Antich, 1982; Russo and Beidel, 1994; Rutter et al., 1970; Walker et al., 1991; Woolston et al., 1989). This is of particular importance because conduct-disordered youth appear at an increased risk for suicidal ideation (Capaldi, 1992).

Several issues present themselves for further investigation. To what extent is the diagnosis of ADHD related to internalizing problems? Researchers have found that the diagnoses of ADHD and CD are associated with depressive symptoms (Biederman et al., 1987; Kovacs et al., 1988), but it remains unclear to what extent such a link applies equally well to each disorder and to different manifestations of internalizing problems, such as depression, anxiety, and withdrawal. Moreover, it is also possible that the diagnosis of ADHD constitutes a precursor to depression (Jensen et al., 1988).

It also remains to be established to what extent there are age-related shifts in the relationship between internalizing and externalizing problems. Past research has shown that the prevalence of hyperactivity tends to decrease between childhood and adolescence (Szatmari et al., 1989), whereas internalizing behaviors, such as depression, tend to increase with age (Kashani et al., 1989; Quay and LaGreca, 1986). Therefore, we would expect that ADHD is more related to depressed mood in middle than in late adolescence, especially when such mood is stable – that is, persisting over a year or more – rather than being transitory.

Gray (1982, 1987) and others (Quay, 1986; Walker et al., 1991) have made a distinction between the neurological strata of a behavioral excitation and a behavioral inhibition system. According to this conceptualization, anxiety is seen as antithetical to overactivity. Therefore, we expect that a diagnosis of ADHD is not associated with stable anxiety.

Research findings over the past decades have made it clear that conduct problems are not a homogeneous phenomenon and manifest themselves differently at various stages of deviant development. Studies indicate that conduct problems can be distinguished between overt or confrontive problem behaviors and covert or concealing problems (Achenbach, 1993; Loeber and Schmaling, 1985; Loeber et al., 1993). In addition, persistent disobedience has been considered pivotal to the emergence of conduct problems (Loeber et al., 1993; Patterson, 1982).

A developmental model (Loeber et al., 1993) that postulates three developmental pathways toward disruptive behavior has been tested among an all-male sample (see figure 13.1). The sample used in the latter study, as well as in the current study, consisted of all male subjects in light of the predominance of conduct problems among male youths. Youth reach different stages of a pathway, with few advancing to the most serious levels; some youth occupy positions on more than one

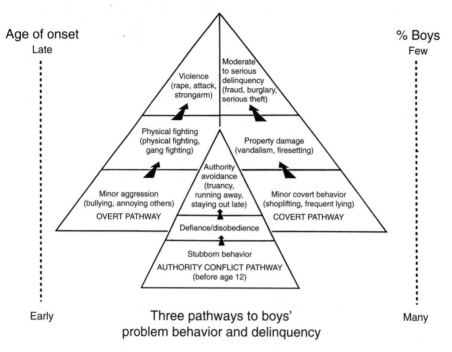

Age of onset — Late ... Early

% Boys — Few ... Many

Three pathways to boys' problem behavior and delinquency

Figure 13.1 Summary of three developmental pathways in disruptive child behavior (Loeber et al. 1993)

pathway. A first pathway, called the authority conflict pathway, has stubborn behavior as a first step, defiance as the next step, and authority avoidance as a third step. Age of onset before age 12 was applied to this pathway as an additional criterion so that more normative adolescent conflict would not be included. A second pathway, called the covert pathway, has minor covert acts as a first step (e.g., frequent lying, shoplifting), property damage as a next step (e.g., firesetting, vandalism), and moderate to serious delinquency as a last step (e.g., car theft, fraud). The final pathway, called the overt pathway, has minor aggression as a first step (e.g., annoying others, bullying), physical fighting as a second step, and violence as a third step (e.g., strongarming, rape).

A review of the literature indicates that the relationship between developmental pathways in disruptive behavior and internalizing problems has not been investigated. Our impression is that the worse the covert behavior of youngsters, the worse the presence of internalizing problems, such as depression. Also, aggressive youths are known to be prone to depression (Bettes and Walker, 1986; Kashani et al., 1989). But does this mean that the higher the seriousness of aggression, the higher the risk of depression? And does the same apply to the nonaggressive covert and authority conflict pathways? And are youth in multiple pathways of disruptive behavior (i.e., any combination of the three pathways) more prone to be depressed than those whose development is characterized by a single form of problem behavior? The same types of questions can be asked for the relationships between conduct problems and stable anxiety and between conduct problems and stable withdrawal. The issue of whether particular combinations of multiple pathways are associated with a high degree of internalizing problems is of considerable clinical and theoretical importance.

Much of the past research is hampered by the fact that the measurement of internalizing behaviors is often far from perfect. Usually, the test–retest reliability for adults' ratings of internalizing child behaviors is substantially lower than those for externalizing child behaviors (Pierce and Klein, 1982; Rutter et al., 1976). This may indicate that one would need to aggregate measures of internalizing behaviors to obtain more stable indices of the behaviors. One way of resolving this problem, used in this study, is to focus on those youth who repeatedly receive high ratings on measures of internalizing difficulties over time. Thus, for youth with the most stable internalizing problems, this procedure allows examination of developmental changes in disruptive behavior as they unfold during adolescence.

Another measurement issue is the fact that adult caretakers may have a different perception of the youth's internalizing problems than the youth is able or willing to admit. Therefore, under the best of circumstances, one would like to have measures of, for example depression, that are based on either repeated caretakers' reports or on repeated youths' self-reports.

Briefly, this article addresses the following questions: (a) Are diagnoses of CD and ADHD equally related to stable internalizing problems in boys? (b) Are diagnoses of CD and ADHD equally related to boys' pathways in disruptive behavior? (c) Are boys' stable internalizing problems associated with their degree of advancement into a disruptive pathway? (d) Are stable internalizing problems more prevalent among boys with multiple pathway escalation, and are certain combinations of disruptive pathways particularly associated with stable internalizing problems?

Method

Subjects

Subjects were drawn from the Pittsburgh Youth Study, a longitudinal survey of boys and their primary caretakers. The study involved only male subjects, among whom the prevalence of conduct problems is more common, so that the development of delinquent and disruptive behavior might be explored among a large community sample. Three samples of boys in Grades 1, 4, and 7 participated in the study, of which the elder two samples were of sufficient age levels to be included in the current research (mean age at initial assessment 10.2 and 13.4 years for the middle and oldest samples, respectively). Subjects were randomly selected from lists of all boys in the target grades in the Pittsburgh Public School System. An 84.7 percent participation rate was obtained for families among the middle and oldest samples selected in this manner.

Upon initial assessment, procedures described elsewhere (Loeber et al., 1991) were utilized to screen a sample of boys for which antisocial behavior was overrepresented. Thus, the top 30 percent of the most antisocial boys ($n = 250$) and an equal number of the remaining boys were randomly selected from each grade, resulting in final samples of 508 and 506 boys in the middle and oldest samples, respectively. Subjects and their caretakers were interviewed twice yearly over a period of 3 years. Attrition rates for the two samples were low, with 93.9 percent of the families in the middle sample and 89.5 percent of the families in the oldest sample participating in the six assessments. However, only those subjects with complete interview data over six phases of assessment were included in this study (90.6 percent of middle sample, $n = 460$; 85.0 percent of oldest sample, $n = 430$).

The two samples were comparable with respect to racial composition; African-American and White boys composed 53.7 percent and 43.3 percent of the middle sample, respectively, and 56.2 percent and 41.2 percent of the oldest sample, respectively (the remaining boys were of Asian or Native American descent). The socioeconomic status of subject's families were also similar, at Hollingshead (1975) levels 36.2 for the middle sample and 37.2 for the oldest sample. For further description of the demographic characteristics of the boys in the Pittsburgh Youth Study, see Van Kammen et al., (1991).

Measures

At each of the six assessment phases, boys' primary caretakers (usually the mother) and boys' teachers completed respective versions of the Child Behavior Checklist (CBCL; Achenbach and Edelbrock, 1983; Loeber et al., 1991). At the second assessment phase, caretakers were administered the Diagnostic Interview Schedule for Children (DISC; Costello et al., 1984), in which assessment of lifetime and past 6 month manifestation of *Diagnostic and Statistical Manual of Mental Disorders* (DSM-III-R) conduct and ADHD symptoms are included.

Subjects themselves completed a variety of measures, including the youth self-report version of the CBCL at each assessment and the mood and Feelings Questionnaire (MFQ; Costello and Angold, 1988) at the second, fourth, and sixth assessments. The MFQ is a self-report measure of depressed mood (past 2 weeks' assessment), which contains 13 items in a Likert-type format (0 = *not true*, 1 = *sometimes true*, 2 = *true*); sample items include "You didn't enjoy anything at all" and "You hated yourself." Complete psychometric data on the MFQ can be found in the report by Costello and Angold (1988).

Subjects also completed self-report measures of delinquency at each assessment – the Self-Reported Antisocial Behavior scale for the middle sample (SRA, 33 items; Loeber et al., 1989) and the Self-Reported Delinquency instrument for the oldest sample (SRD, 36 items; Loeber et al., 1989). The SRA and SRD assess delinquent behavior over the past 6 months in an interview format, with questions such as "Have you taken something from a store without paying for it?" The SRA assesses the child's understanding of and familiarity with each behavior prior to each question. The SRD assesses further detail, such as where the behavior occurred and who else was present. Additional psychometric data on the SRA and the SRD are reported by Loeber et al., 1989.

Procedures

Subject diagnoses were determined using DSM-III-R criteria for ADHD and CD. Information as to ADHD symptom presence or absence was taken from caretaker DISC interviews, for which a diagnostic threshold of eight or more symptoms was utilized. As such, 12.5 percent of the middle sample ($n = 63$) and 9.4 percent of the oldest sample ($n = 47$)

received a diagnosis of ADHD. (Note: nine subjects did not complete the DISC interview.) The diagnosis of CD was made if either the caretaker (DISC) or the subject (SRD and SRA at second assessment) confirmed the presence of three or more DSM–III–R symptoms. Under DSM-III-R classification, 37 (3.6 percent) and 57 (5.6 percent) of the middle and oldest samples, respectively, were diagnosed with CD. The utilization of both parent and child reports for the diagnosis of CD is described in detail by Russo et al., (1994).

Subjects were classified according to developmental pathways in disruptive behavior (Loeber et al., 1993), which consisted of an overt pathway, a covert pathway, authority conflict pathway (figure 13.1), and the four possible combinations of pathways. Disruptive behavior pathway classification was based on the age of onset of different behaviors as reported by the caretaker (DISC, CBCL) and the subject (SRD, SRA, CBCL) at each of the six assessment phases, thus sharing considerable overlap with the diagnosis of CD (for details, see Loeber et al., 1993).

As a measure of stable self-reported depressed mood, boys' MFQ scores (range, 0 to 13) were aggregated over the three yearly administrations of the questionnaire. Specifically, those who scored above the 75th percentile on any administration of the MFQ were considered to exhibit elevated self-reported depressed mood. To define stability, scores were then dichotomized to distinguish between boys who scored among the upper 25 percent for at least two of the three MFQ administrations and boys who scored lower.

Utilizing CBCL reports from parent, teacher, and child – aggregated over the six assessments – similar internalizing constructs were developed for stable anxiety, stable withdrawal, and stable depressed mood. For the oldest sample, parent and teacher reports of internalizing problems were supplemented with youth self-reports, because parents and teachers experience decreasing levels of knowledge regarding children's internal thoughts and feelings as children mature. Thus, in reference to the oldest sample, internalizing constructs are termed *joint reports*. For the middle sample, only parent and teacher reports were used, and, therefore, the constructs are termed *adult reports*.

Boys' internalizing scores were dichotomized at the 75th percentile at each of the six assessment phases. Each subject then received a score that represented the total number of phases during which he scored among the upper 25 percent for each internalizing construct. To aggregate the data in the definition of stability over the 3-year period, the latter distribution was dichotomized also at the 75th percentile, thus yielding the upper 25 percent of those who scored above the 75th percentile over the six data phases. The CBCL items that were included in the anxiety construct included phobic, nervous, and anxious behaviors (Cronbach's α = 0.65 and 0.69 for the middle and oldest samples, respectively). For the depressed mood construct, CBCL items included sadness, mood changes, and suicidal ideation/attempts (Cronbach's α = 0.76 and 0.75 for the middle and oldest samples, respectively). The withdrawal construct included items such as self-consciousness, shyness, and preference for being alone (Cronbach's α = 0.61 and 0.57 for the middle and oldest samples, respectively).

Results

Preliminary analyses

Before addressing the questions raised in the introduction, we briefly describe the prevalence and the intercorrelation between the internalizing constructs. The prevalence of aggregated internalizing problems among the middle and oldest samples, respectively, was as follows: stable self-reported depressed mood, 17.7 percent and 17.2 percent; stable adult-reported and stable joint-reported depressed mood, 23.3 percent and 26.2 percent; stable anxiety, 21.9 percent and 21.2 percent, and stable withdrawal, 22.9 percent and 28.5 percent. Eight separate analyses, one for each internalizing construct by ethnicity and subsample, showed, with one exception, nonsignificant findings. The exception was joint-reported stable anxiety among the oldest sample, with a prevalence of 27.1 percent for the White boys and 16.7 percent for the African-American boys, χ^2 (1, n = 473) = 7.56, p = 0.006. Because only one of the eight analyses reached significance, and the magnitude of the difference was small in absolute terms (10 subjects), subsequent analyses are reported for the combined White and African-American boys. (To conduct separate analyses by ethnicity for each sample, as well as for each internalizing construct and pathway, would unduly inflate the experimentwise error rate.) Intercorrelations between the constructs ranged from 0.12 to 0.42 for the middle sample and 0.30 to 0.56 for the oldest sample (e.g., the correlation between self-reported depressed mood and adult-reported anxiety among the middle sample was 0.12, and the correlation between joint-reported depressed mood and joint-reported withdrawal was 0.56 among the oldest sample).

To determine the comparability of the two types of depressed mood ratings, Pearson's product–moment correlation was computed. Among boys in the middle sample, the correlation between adult and self-reported depressed mood was $r(497) = 0.16$, $p < 0.01$. Similarly, among the oldest sample the correlation between joint-reported depressed mood and self-reported depressed mood was $r(485) = 0.30$, $p < 0.01$. Due to the low agreement between the two ratings, cross-tabulations were utilized to determine the nature of the disagreement. For both samples, the source of disagreements was primarily in ratings that included adult reports that were positive for the presence of depressed mood when self-reports denied the presence of depressed mood: $\chi^2(1, n = 497) = 13.38$; $\chi^2(1, n = 485) = 42.50$, both $ps < 0.001$. Although relatively few boys ($n = 6$) received diagnoses of major depression or dysthymia according to parent DISC interviews, the agreements between these diagnoses and adult- and self-reported ratings were also computed. As expected, for parent-reported data, all six boys were correctly placed, whereas with respect to self-reports, parent ratings that were positive for the presence of major depression again outnumbered those of self-reports, although not significantly: $\chi^2(1, n = 1012) = 3.14$, $p = 0.08$. In summary, the preliminary analyses indicate that close to one in five of the boys had stable forms of internalizing problems, with no major differences between the grade samples. The intercorrelations between adult report and self report of depressed mood were low, and the correlations between the internalizing constructs were sufficiently low to consider them separately.

Substantive analyses

The first question raised was whether the diagnoses of CD and ADHD were equally related to different forms of stable internalizing problems. For this purpose, chi-squares were computed for each diagnosis cross-tabulated with each internalizing construct. These analyses are summarized in table 13.1, in which greater comorbidity is evident between ADHD and each of the internalizing problems than between CD and such problems. For example, about half of the boys with a diagnosis of ADHD also showed adult- or joint-reported stable depressed mood (57.4 percent and 42.2 percent in the middle and oldest samples,

Table 13.1 Overlap of DSM–III–R conduct disorder and attention deficit-hyperactivity disorder with internalizing constructs

		% Boys with diagnoses				
		Middle sample[a]			Oldest sample[b]	
Internalizing construct		CD[c]	ADHD[d]		CD[e]	ADHD[f]
Stable depressed mood	(SR)	11.2	27.9*	(SR)	23.0**	31.1*
Stable depressed mood	(AR)	14.7**	57.4**	(JR)	22.0**	42.2**
Stable anxiety	(AR)	11.9*	41.0**	(JR)	21.4**	42.4**
Stable withdrawal	(AR)	11.4*	32.8†	(JR)	20.3**	48.9**

Note: *AR = Adult report. JR = Joint report. SR = Self-report. DSM–III–R = Diagnostic and Statistical Manual of Mental Disorders. ADHD = Attention Deficit-Hyperactivity Disorder. CD = Conduct Disorder*
[a] $n = 497 – 496$. [b] $n = 485 – 479$. [c] $n = 36$. [d] $n = 61$. [e] $n = 53$. [f] $n = 45$
† $p = 0.05$. * $p < 0.05$. ** $p < 0.001$ *(Chi-square significance)*

respectively), compared with only about one in five of the boys with a diagnosis of CD (14.7 percent and 22.0 percent in the two respective samples). Of the four measures of internalizing problems, adult reports of stable depressed mood were slightly more common in ADHD boys than either stable anxiety or stable withdrawal, but this applied to the middle sample only. However, the prevalence of self-reported stable depressed mood was lower in the ADHD boys than the prevalence of the other internalizing problems in both samples. In summary, ADHD was more associated with stable internalizing problems than was CD and ADHD in the younger boys was slightly more often accompanied by stable, adult-reported depressed mood than by either stable anxiety or withdrawal.

Next, we examined the extent to which diagnoses of CD and ADHD are related to boys' escalation (i.e., at least two steps into a pathway) within the three disruptive pathways. An answer to this question is needed before we inquire as to what extent internalizing problems are associated with differences in boys' advancement (i.e., from Step 1 to Step 2 to Step 3) within each pathway. Table 13.2 summarizes the results first for escalation within the single pathways (covert pathway, overt pathway, and authority conflict pathway), next for escalation

Table 13.2   Percent of boys with DSM–III–R conduct disorder and attention deficit-hyperactivity disorder across single and multiple pathways

	Sample			
	Middle[a]		Oldest[b]	
Pathway	CD[c]	ADHD[d]	CD[e]	ADHD[f]
Single pathways				
C	0.0	1.7	5.1	9.8
O	0.0	0.0	0.0	4.9
A	1.9	15.3	0.0	2.4
Dual pathways				
CA	4.9	10.2	24.1	22.0
CO	9.1	3.4	17.5	26.8
OA	2.6	13.6	18.2	4.9
Triple pathways				
COA	29.2	50.8	30.0	26.8
One or no behaviors in any pathway	0.0	5.1	0.0	2.4

Note: *Pathways include subjects two or more steps into progression. C = Covert Behavior Pathway. O = Overt Behavior Pathway. A = Authority Conflict Pathway.* DSM–III–R = Diagnostic and Statistical Manual of Mental Disorders. *ADHD = Attention Deficit-Hyperactivity Disorder. CD = Conduct Disorder. For all chi-square equations, p = 0.001*
[a] $n = 460$. [b] $n = 425$. [c] $n = 36$. [d] $n = 59$. [e] $n = 53$. [f] $n = 41$

within the dual combinations of pathways (e.g., covert and overt pathways), and finally for escalation within the triple pathways (covert, overt, and authority conflict pathways). It should be noted that the diagnosis of CD is not fully independent of the formulation of the pathways, because some of the symptoms of CD were also used in the computation of the pathways. With this caveat in mind, the results showed that the percentage of boys with CD is lowest for those who had escalated within a single pathway, higher for those who had escalated within dual pathways, and highest among those who had escalated within the triple pathways. (Statistical analyses were not executed because of the confound.) These results are more distinct for the oldest than for the middle sample.

To what extent is ADHD related to single or multiple pathways? Table 13.2 shows that half (50.8 percent) of the ADHD boys in the middle sample had escalated within triple pathways (COA), with lower percentages showing escalation within the dual and single pathways (highest, 13.6 percent and 15.3 percent, and lowest 3.4 percent and 0.0 percent, respectively). The results for the oldest sample are less distinct: About a quarter (26.8 percent) of the ADHD boys had escalated within triple pathways, compared to a quarter who had escalated within either the dual covert–authority conflict pathways (22.0 percent) or in the dual covert–overt pathways (26.8 percent). The lowest percentage of ADHD boys in that sample had escalated within a single pathway only. In conclusion, the relation between ADHD and boys' escalation within multiple pathways was more distinct for the younger than for the older boys.

The association of disruptive pathway advancement with ADHD was more independent than that with CD, because different criteria were used for the diagnosis of ADHD and for advancement into pathways. Thus, to answer the question as to whether ADHD is related to increased advancement within the pathways, chi-square analyses were conducted using cross-tabulations of the prevalence of ADHD with Step 1, Step 2, and Step 3 in each pathway. The prevalence of ADHD reached significance for the middle sample for advancement into the overt pathway, χ^2 $(2, n = 163) = 7.87$, $p = 0.02$, covert pathway χ^2 $(2, n = 159) = 6.43$; $p = 0.04$, and into the authority conflict pathway, χ^2 $(2, n = 110) = 11.75$, $p = 0.003$. For the oldest sample, the prevalence of ADHD reached significance for advancement into the authority conflict pathway only, χ^2 $(2, n = 109) = 6.34$, $p = 0.04$.

The next question addresses the extent to which boys' stable internalizing problems were associated with their further advancement into a disruptive pathway. For this purpose, the four internalizing constructs were cross-tabulated with the first, second, and third step into each pathway. The results (figure 13.2) showed that stable self-reported depressed mood was associated with boys' advancement into the covert pathway in the middle sample only, χ^2 $(2, n = 158) = 11.92$, $p < 0.01$. Both self-reported and adult-reported stable depressed mood were associated with boys' advancement into the overt pathway (figure 13.2), but again for the boys in the middle sample only, self report χ^2 $(2, n = 162)$ $= 7.40$; adult report χ^2 $(2, n = 162) = 8.04$, both $ps < 0.05$. For instance, in the overt pathway, 25.0 percent of the boys in the first step of that pathway (consisting of minor aggression only) showed adult-reported

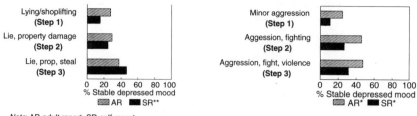

Note: AR-adult report; SR-self-report;
**$p < 0.01$; *$p < 0.05$

Figure 13.2 Left is boys' stable depressed mood and their advancement into the covert pathway (middle sample); right is boys' stable depressed mood and their advancement into the overt pathway (middle sample)

depressed mood, compared with 46.0 percent and 47.4 percent in the second and third steps of that pathway (the second step consists of minor aggression, physical fighting; the third step consists of minor aggression, physical fighting, and violence). No significant relationship was observed for internalizing problems and boys' advancement in the authority conflict pathway in the middle sample.

In contrast, for boys in the older sample, joint reports of both stable anxiety and stable withdrawal, but not joint-reported stable depressed mood, were related to advancement into the authority conflict pathway, stable anxiety χ^2 (2, $n = 106$) = 15.87, $p < 0.001$; stable withdrawal χ^2 (2, $n = 106$) = 6.79, $p < 0.05$. These associations are depicted in figure 13.3. For example, of the boys who had advanced to the first step in this pathway, (stubborn behavior) only 19.1 percent had stable anxious problems, compared to 34.6 percent of those who had advanced into the second step (stubborn and defiant behavior) and 75.0 percent of those who had advanced into the third step in the pathway (stubborn, defiant behavior and truancy). Thus, in several of the observed significant findings, boys' advancement into a disruptive pathway was associated with a higher likelihood of the presence of stable internalizing problems. The results suggest an age effect, with the association between depressed mood and overt and covert problem behavior being distinct for the younger boys only, whereas the association between stable anxiety and stable withdrawal and the authority conflict pathway was pronounced for the older boys only.

The final set of analyses addressed the extent to which boys' stable internalizing problems were related to their escalation (two or more

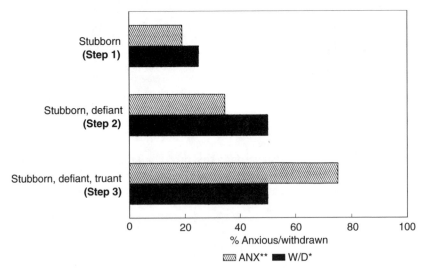

Note: **p < 0.01; *p < 0.05;
ANX = stable anxiety;
W/D = stable withdrawal

Figure 13.3 Boys' stable anxiety and withdrawal and their advancement
into the authority conflict pathway (oldest sample)

steps) within multiple, compared to single, pathways. The top part of
figure 13.4 illustrates the results of the analyses of self-reported stable
depressed mood across single and multiple pathways. Chi-square analysis reached significance for the middle sample only, χ^2 (7, n = 460) =
35.5, $p < 0.001$. The results, however, do not clearly show a linear relation. *Post hoc* comparisons (by means of chi-squares) indicated that
escalation within the dual covert–overt pathways was associated with
the highest prevalence of self-reported stable depressed mood, followed
by escalation within the triple pathway, and within the covert, the overt,
and the dual overt–authority conflict pathways.

Chi-square analyses were repeated to examine the relationships
between adult reports and joint reports of stable depressed mood and
escalation within multiple versus single disruptive behavior pathways.
A statistically significant relationship between stable depressed mood
and the number of pathways subjects had escalated in was evident for
the middle sample, χ^2 (7, n = 460) = 40.30, and for the oldest sample,
χ^2 (7, n = 430) = 33.50, both $ps < 0.001$. The results are shown in the

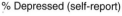

% Depressed (self-report)

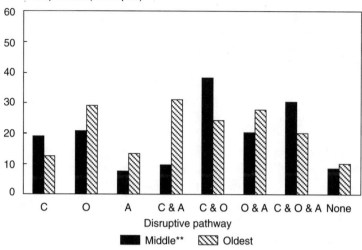

% Depressed (adult or joint reports)

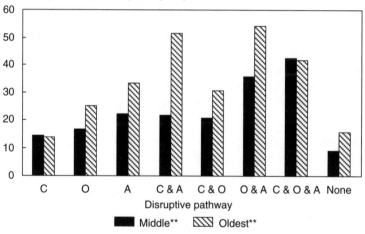

Note: **Chi-square *p* < 0.001
C = Covert; O = Overt; A = Authority Conflict

Figure 13.4 Top is boys' stable depressed mood (self-reported) and escalation within single and multiple disruptive pathways; bottom is boys' stable depressed mood (adult- or joint-reported) and escalation within single and multiple disruptive pathways

bottom part of figure 13.4, indicating that, especially for the middle sample, the lowest percentage of stable depressed mood was evident among the boys who had not escalated within a pathway, followed by those who had escalated within a single pathway, slightly higher among those who had escalated within dual pathways, and highest among those who had escalated within the triple pathways. Post hoc analyses revealed significantly higher prevalence of adult-reported stable depressed mood among boys from the middle sample who had escalated within the triple pathway, followed by those in the dual overt–authority conflict pathways, the single authority conflict pathway, the dual covert–authority conflict pathways, and the dual covert–overt pathways. Among the oldest sample, boys who had escalated within the triple pathway, the dual covert–authority conflict pathways, and the dual overt–authority conflict pathways exhibited significantly higher prevalence rates of joint-reported stable depressed mood than boys who had escalated within the remaining pathways.

Figure 13.5 depicts parallel findings for stable anxiety and stable withdrawal. For the middle sample, no significant relationship between stable anxiety or stable withdrawal and escalation within multiple disruptive pathways was found. However, for the oldest sample, stable anxiety was significantly associated with escalation within multiple pathways, $\chi^2 (7, n = 430) = 26.36, p < 0.001$. The same applied to stable withdrawal, $\chi^2 (7, n = 430) = 26.98, p < 0.001$. Post hoc comparisons indicated that escalation within the triple pathway, the dual covert–authority conflict pathways, and the dual overt–authority conflict pathways, was associated with the highest prevalence of boys with stable anxiety and stable withdrawal. In summary, with one exception, internalizing problems were not linearly related to the number of disruptive pathways boys had escalated within (the exception being adult-reported depressed mood in the middle sample). Stable internalizing problems were least common among boys who had escalated within single pathways, and they were more common among boys who had escalated within two or more pathways, but not more common among those in triple pathways compared to those in dual pathways. Internalizing problems, however, were not equally distributed among all combinations of pathways. Stable anxiety and stable withdrawal were less common for boys who had escalated within the dual covert–overt pathways (oldest sample), whereas stable self-reported depressed mood was less common for boys who had escalated within the dual covert–authority conflict pathways (middle sample).

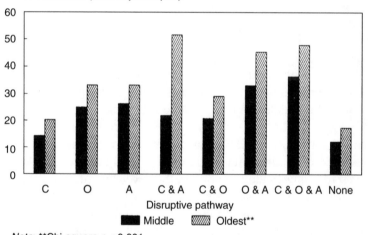

Note: **Chi-square $p < 0.001$
C = Covert; O = Overt; A = Authority Conflict

Figure 13.5 Top is boys' stable anxiety (adult- or joint-reported) and escalation within single and multiple disruptive pathways; bottom is boys' stable withdrawal (adult- or joint-reported) and escalation within single and multiple disruptive pathways

Discussion

The results of the study can be summarized as follows. A diagnosis of ADHD was more strongly associated with internalizing problems than was a diagnosis of CD. This finding agrees with results reported by Bird, Gould, and Staghezza (1993), who found an association between Attention Deficit Disorder and depression, but especially for 9- to 12-year-olds compared to 13- to 16-year-olds. Furthermore, Russo and Beidel (1994), concluded from their review of the literature that anxiety problems are more commonly related to the diagnosis of ADHD among preadolescent children than among adolescents. It is possible that depressed mood or anxiety may be the result of the comorbid ADHD, or that apparent ADHD symptoms result from depressed mood or anxiety. Our data do not allow us to make this distinction.

This study demonstrated that, in early adolescence, stable depressed mood, but not stable anxiety or stable withdrawal, was associated with boys' advancement in the covert and overt pathways. However, in mid-adolescence, stable anxiety and stable withdrawal, but not stable depressed mood, were associated with boys' early advancement into the authority conflict pathway (and not into the covert or overt pathways). It is not clear whether the latter finding is an artefact of measurement (we had self-reports available on anxiety and withdrawal in the oldest but not in the middle sample). Leaving this possible artefact aside, the study showed a shift in the manifestation of internalizing problems associated with disruptive child behavior, that is, from depression in early adolescence to anxiety and withdrawal in mid-adolescence. Whereas the present analyses did not address the developmental order between internalizing problems and boys' advancement in disruptive behavior, other analyses on the two samples have shown that depressed mood was one of the predictors of the onset of delinquency in the middle, but not in the oldest sample (Loeber et al., 1991). This previous finding also agrees with the results of this study in that early adolescent boys' stable self-reported depressed mood was more common in association with multiple pathway escalation (covert and overt) than with escalation within a single pathway.

What is rather perplexing is that internalizing problems in early adolescence are more related to boys' advancement in the covert and overt pathways, whereas in mid-adolescence they are more related to their advancement in the authority conflict pathway. Obviously, these and the preceding findings are in need of replication. It should be pointed out, however, that once we consider boys' escalation in multiple pathways, the current findings for both samples indicate that in early and late adolescence, adult and joint reports of boys' depressed mood were more common in multiple pathways (including the authority conflict pathway) than in most single pathways. Also, the findings indicate that, in late adolescence, joint reports of boys' stable anxiety and stable withdrawal were more common in multiple pathways, particularly those that included the authority conflict pathway, than in any single pathway. Thus, boys with authority conflict problems may be especially prone to developing internalizing problems.

Another issue concerns the temporal and functional relationships between internalizing problems and escalation within disruptive behavior pathways. During early adolescence, many boys who had escalated to Step 2 or beyond within the disruptive pathways, whether overt or covert, also experienced depressed mood. Those who had escalated within multiple disruptive pathways seemed to experience depressed mood more commonly than those involved with a single type of disruptive behavior. Perhaps depressed mood is a result of escalation in disruptive behavior, or perhaps disruptive behavior results from the experience of depressed mood. However, the temporal direction of influences could not be directly inferred from the available data.

In reviewing our findings on the relation between internalizing and externalizing problems, we want to stress that boys who displayed both types of problems may have experienced more serious difficulties in emotional self-regulation than boys without serious disruptive behavior. Boys who escalated in multiple pathways appeared particularly prone to poor emotional self-regulation in that they experienced either depression, anxiety, or withdrawal, or a combination of these problems. This was especially true for the older boys in our study. Unfortunately, we could not establish more directly how impaired the boys were in their self-regulation. Russo and Beidel (1994), in their literature review of comorbid anxiety and externalizing problems, found that high anxiety may be indicative of severe disturbances in conduct during adolescence, but not during preadolescence. Perhaps the persistence of multiple behavioral problems in adolescence results in an increase in emotional difficulties, ranging from depression to anxiety and withdrawal, all reflecting poor self-regulation of emotions.

The results of this study should be accepted with some caution. The prevalence of clinical diagnoses of depression in the two samples was too low to allow analyses; moreover, a diagnosis of anxiety disorders was not available. It is important to establish the temporal order between escalation in disruptive behavior and escalation in internalizing problems. It is also important to answer the question: how often do internalizing problems precipitate the onset of disruptive behaviors, and how often does the reverse take place? These issues were not examined in this study, partly because only continuous measures of internalizing problems were available and because data on the onset of internalizing problems had not been collected. Future work should focus on the extent that increased difficulties experienced by boys with internalizing problems may affect the onset and course of disruptive behavior. Also, we need to know more about the factors that cause boys' escalation in seriousness in each domain, and whether such factors are similar for disruptive behavior and for internalizing problems. Despite these limitations, however, the study showed how disruptive behaviors are interwoven with internalizing problems, and that the pattern of relationship may change with age. Future work is planned to examine relations between stability of disruptive behavior and single versus multiple internalizing problems.

References

Achenbach, T. M. (1993). Taxonomy and comorbidity of conduct problems: Evidence of empirically based approaches. *Development and Psychopathology, 5*, 51–64.

Achenbach, T. M., & Edelbrock, C. S. (1983). *Manual for the Child Behavior Checklist and Revised Child Behavior Profile.* Burlington: University of Vermont Press.

Biederman, J., Munir, K., Knee, D., Armentano, M., Autor, S., Waternaux, C., & Tsuang, M. (1987). High rate of affective disorders in probands with attention deficit disorder and in their relatives: A controlled family study. *American Journal of Psychiatry, 144,* 330–333.

Bettes, B. A., & Walker, E. (1986). Symptoms associated with suicidal behavior in childhood and adolescence. *Journal of Abnormal Child Psychology, 14,* 591–604.

Bird, H. R., Gould, M. S., & Staghezza, B. M. (1993). Patterns of diagnostic comorbidity in a community sample of children aged 9 through 16 years. *Journal of the American Academy of Child and Adolescent Psychiatry, 32,* 61–68.

Capaldi, D. M. (1992). Co-occurrence of conduct problems and depressive symptoms in early adolescent boys: II. A 2-year follow-up at grade 8. *Development and Psychopathology, 4,* 125–144.

Caron, C., & Rutter, M. (1991). Comorbidity in child psychopathology: Concepts, issues, and research strategies. *Journal of Child Psychology and Psychiatry, 32,* 1063–1080.

Costello, A. J., Edelbrock, C. S., Dulcan, M. K., Kalas, R., & Klaric, S. H. (1984). *Report on the NIMH Diagnostic Interview Schedule for Children (DISC).* Unpublished manuscript, Western Psychiatric Institute and Clinic, Pittsburgh, PA.

Costello, E. J., & Angold, A. (1988), Scales to assess child and adolescent depression: Checklists, screens, and nets. *Journal of the American Academy for Child and Adolescent Psychiatry, 27,* 726–737.

Feehan, M., McGee, R., Raja, S. N., & Williams, S. M. (1993). DSM–III–R disorders in New Zealand 18-year-olds. *Australian and New Zealand Journal of Psychiatry, 28*(1), 87–99.

Gray, J. A. (1982). *The neuropsychology of anxiety: An enquiry into the functions of the septohippocampal system.* Oxford, England: Oxford University Press.

Gray, J. A. (1987). *The psychology of fear and stress* (2nd ed.). Cambridge, England: Cambridge University Press.

Hollingshead, A. B. (1975). *Four factor index of social status.* Unpublished manuscript, Department of Sociology, Yale University, New Haven, CT.

Jensen, J. B., Burke, N., & Garfinkel, B. D. (1988). Depression and symptoms of attention deficit disorder with hyperactivity. *Journal of the American Academy of Child and Adolescent Psychiatry, 27,* 742–747.

Kashani, J. H., Goddard, P., & Reid, J. C. (1989). Correlates of suicidal ideation in a community sample of children and adolescents. *Journal of the American Academy of Child and Adolescent Psychiatry, 28,* 912–917.

Kashani, J. H., Orvaschel, H., Rosenberg, T. K., & Reid, J. C. (1989). Psychopathology in a community sample of children and adolescents: A developmental perspective. *Journal of the American Academy of Child and Adolescent Psychiatry, 28,* 701–706.

Kovacs, M., Paulauskas, S., Gatsonis, C., & Richards, C. (1988). Depressive disorders in childhood: III. A longitudinal study of comorbidity with and risk for conduct disorders. *Journal of Affective Disorders, 15,* 205–217.

Loeber, R., & Schmaling, K. B. (1985). Empirical evidence for overt and covert patterns of antisocial conduct problems: A meta-analysis. *Journal of Abnormal Child Psychology, 13,* 337–352.

Loeber, R., Stouthamer-Loeber, M., Van Kammen, W. B., & Farrington, D. P. (1989). Development of a new measure of self-reported antisocial behavior for young children: Prevalence and reliability. In M. Klein (Ed.), *Self-report methodology in criminological research* (pp. 203–225). Boston: Kluwer-Nijhoff.

Loeber, R., Stouthamer-Loeber, M., Van Kammen, W. B., & Farrington, D. P.

(1991). Initiation, escalation, and desistance in juvenile offending and their correlates. *The Journal of Criminal Law and Criminology, 82*, 36–82.

Loeber, R., Wung, P., Keenan, K., Giroux, B., Stouthamer-Loeber, M., Van Kammen, W. B., & Maughan, B. (1993). Developmental pathways in disruptive behavior. *Development and Psychopathology, 5*, 101–132.

McBurnett, K., Lahey, B. B., Frick, P. J., Risch, C., Loeber, R., Hart, E. L., Christ, M. A. G., & Hanson, K. S. (1991). Anxiety, inhibition, and conduct disorder in children: II. Relation to salivary cortisol. *Journal of the American Academy of Child and Adolescent Psychiatry, 30*, 197–201.

Patterson, G. R. (1982). *A social learning approach: Vol. 3. Coercive family process.* Eugene, OR: Castalia.

Pierce, L., & Klein, H. (1982). A comparison of parent and child perception of the child's behavior. *Behavioral Disorder, 7*, 69–74.

Puig-Antich, J. (1982). Major depression and conduct disorder in prepuberty. *Journal of the American Academy of Child Psychiatry, 21*, 118–128.

Quay, H. C. (1986). The behavioral reward and inhibition systems in childhood behavior disorder. In L. M. Bloomingdale (Ed.), *Attention deficit disorder: Vol. 3. Child psychology and psychiatry, supplement* (pp. 176–186). Elmsford, NY: Pergamon.

Quay, H. C., & LaGreca, A. M. (1986). Disorders of anxiety, withdrawal, and dysphoria. In H. C. Quay & J. S. Werry (Eds.), *Psychopathological disorders of childhood* (pp. 73–110) New York: Wiley.

Russo, M. F., & Beidel, D. C. (1994). Comorbidity of childhood anxiety and externalizing disorders: Prevalence, associated characteristics, and validation issues. *Clinical Psychology Review, 14*(3), 199–221.

Russo, M. F., Loeber, R., Lahey, B. B., & Keenan, K. (1994). Oppositional defiant and conduct disorders: Validation of the DSM–III–R and an alternative diagnostic option. *Journal of Clinical Child Psychology, 23*, 56–68.

Rutter, M., Graham, P., Chadwick, D. F. D., & Youle, W. (1976). Adolescent turmoil: Fact or fiction? *Journal of Child Psychology and Psychiatry, 17*, 35–56.

Rutter, M., Tizard, J., & Whitmore, K. (1970). *Education, health and behavior.* New York: Wiley.

Szatmari, P., Offord, D. R., & Boyle, M. H. (1989). Ontario child health study: Prevalence of attention deficit disorder with hyperactivity. *Journal of Child Psychology and Psychiatry, 30*, 219–230.

Van Kammen, W. B., Loeber, R., & Stouthamer-Loeber, M. (1991). Substance use and its relationship to antisocial and delinquent behavior in young boys. *Journal of Youth and Adolescence, 20*, 399–414.

Walker, J. L., Lahey, B. B., Russo, M. F., Frick, P. J., Christ, M. A. G., McBurnett, K., Loeber, R., Stouthamer-Loeber, M., & Green, S. M. (1991). Anxiety, inhibition, and conduct disorder in children: I. Relations to social impairment. *Journal of the American Academy of Child Psychiatry, 30*, 187–191.

Woolston, J. L., Rosenthal, S. L., Riddle, M. A., Sparrow, S. S., Cicchetti, D., & Zimmerman, L. D. (1989). Childhood comorbidity of anxiety/affective disorders and behavior disorders. *Journal of the American Academy of Child Psychiatry, 28,* 707–713.

Zoccolillo, M. (1992). Co-occurrence of conduct disorder and its adult outcomes with depressive and anxiety disorders: A review. *Journal of the American Academy of Child Psychiatry, 31,* 973–981.

Part V

A Controversy about Coming of Age in Samoa

Controversy abounds around issues of adolescent behavior and development. Often the issues are created by media frenzy around a recent event involving adolescents. Sometimes it emerges around some issue within scholarship about adolescence. Controversy pushes a field to think and rethink its position. This final section focuses on one such controversy.

Was Mead Wrong About Coming of Age in Samoa? An Analysis of the Mead/Freeman Controversy for Scholars of Adolescence and Human Development

Introduction

The scholarship about adolescence is not void of controversy. There are many differences of opinion. One recent controversy involved a confrontation about the accuracy of Margaret Mead in her work on *Coming of Age in Samoa*. To many scholars this is a classic work that should never be challenged. However, Derek Freeman in his book *Margaret Mead and Samoa* challenged the quality of her work, the findings, and its credibility. You can imagine how much this stirred the blood of many an anthropologist loyal to the late Margaret Mead.

I have included as the last report an analysis of the Mead/Freeman controversy. Côté examines the nature of the two separate pieces of scholarship and attempts to unfold the truth in the midst of controversy within the academic community.

In your last trip into the Zone you might want to sit down in a soft chair, take along a drink to quench your thirst because it is warm in Samoa, and turn on some soft South Pacific music, to put you into the mood. Now as you read the article by Côté, remember he has no reason to either confirm or deny Mead or Freeman. He's simply working, like a detective, to see who is most likely to be correct.

Have fun. And thank you for letting me be your guide in our journey together.

Suggested reading

Freeman, D. (1983). *Margaret Mead and Samoa: The Making and Unmaking of an Anthropological Myth*. Cambridge, Massachusetts: Harvard University Press.

Berliner, D. C., and Biddle, B. J. (1995). *The Manufactured Crisis: Myths, Fraud, and the Attack on America's Public Schools*. Reading, Massachusetts: Addison-Wesley.

FOURTEEN

Was Mead Wrong About Coming of Age in Samoa? An Analysis of the Mead/Freeman Controversy for Scholars of Adolescence and Human Development

James E. Côté

Introduction

The publication of Derek Freeman's *Margaret Mead and Samoa: The Making and Unmaking of an Anthropological Myth* in 1983 sparked what has been called "the biggest debate in the social sciences for years" (Crocombe, 1989, p. 38). At the heart of this debate is Freeman's claim to have refuted a cornerstone of the "nurture" side of the perennial "nature–nurture debate," the *great* debate of twentieth century social science. According to Freeman, early proponents of the nurture side of the debate needed crucial evidence in support of their position, and Mead provided it with her conclusion in *Coming of Age in Samoa*; namely, that biology alone cannot account for the "storm and stress" believed at the time to characterize adolescence (Freeman, 1983).

The Mead/Freeman controversy, as it is now called, has been a lively one, but it has also been a difficult one to follow because of the large and steady stream of commentary about it. Moreover, it is virtually impossible for those unfamiliar with Samoa to adjudicate the controversy. This is partly because of the diametrically opposing claims that have been made about Samoan culture, and partly because Samoan culture differs from other cultures in a number of important respects.

This paper has been written to help scholars of adolescence and human development to understand the controversy itself, as well as help them judge whether or not Freeman has in fact refuted Mead's findings. The analysis will be limited here to those issues raised by Freeman that are directly related to the study of adolescence; elsewhere, a more detailed analysis of the controversy and related issues is presented (Côté, 1994).

The Context of the Controversy

In 1925–1926 Margaret Mead conducted a study of the experiences of 50 Samoan females, who ranged in age from nine to 20 years (Mead, 1928, p. 260). She was in Samoa for nine months: the first two she devoted to learning the language, and the remainder were spent collecting ethnographic-type data, mainly on the island of Ta'u. Her principal conclusion was that, in Samoa, the transition from childhood, through adolescence, and into adulthood was one of relative ease. She based this conclusion on the observation that none of the young females she studied appeared to exhibit symptoms of adolescent "storm and stress" – the psychological "affliction" ostensibly affecting American youth and believed at the time to be biological in origin. Mead herself noted that the answer to the question of why there was such a difference between the two cultures in the way adolescents behaved "has enormous implications and any *attempt* to answer it will be subject to many *possibilities of error*." But she thought that it was "possible to *try* to answer it" by identifying those "aspects of Samoan life which irremediably affect the life of the adolescent girl" but which are different from the forces affecting the development of American female adolescents (p. 198, emphases added).

Mead's *attempt* to answer the crucial question regarding the absence of storm and stress in her sample of adolescents is presented in the second to last chapter of *Coming of Age* entitled "Our Educational Problems in the Light of Samoan Contrasts." In that meandering, 40-page chapter she speculates that the absence of adolescent difficulties was attributable to two general factors: (1) that Samoan culture was a homogeneous one where choices were few but well defined, and beliefs and roles were unambiguous and uniform throughout the community; and (2) the apparent casual nature of Samoan culture itself. It is upon her second conclusion that the controversy has focused, primarily because this became the focus of Freeman's critique. It should be noted that throughout the controversy very little detailed attention has been paid to her thesis and the substance of her book – namely, the psychological processes and social structures associated with maturing into adulthood in 1920s Ta'u.

It is crucial in evaluating the controversy to note that the island of Ta'u is not only the most remote island in the Samoan archipelago, but that it is a small rugged island on which the old volcanic cones reach one kilometer in elevation. As Hunt and Kirch (1988) describe,

> The Manu'a Islands of Ofu, Olesega, and Ta'u form a separate cluster at the eastern end of the Samoan archipelago. Mutually intervisible, they are separated from Tutuila to the west by 100 km of often turbulent ocean which *reduced the frequency of voyaging contacts with the larger islands.* . . . Ofu, Olesega, and Ta'u are remarkable in their dramatic topography; steep-sided, majestic volcanic cones thrust out of the turbulent waters, with summits often shrouded in clouds. . . . The smallest of the principal Samoan islands, *their steep topography offers little area suitable for settlements* and gardens. . . . Coastlines are rock-bound, with narrow fringing reefs only in places, restricting the possibilities of marine subsistence. (p. 155, emphases added)

In addition to this rugged topography, Ta'u island is only 28.5 square kilometers in area (Hunt and Kirch, 1988, p. 156). Freeman, however, conducted most of his research on the island of 'Upolu, which is 1115 square kilometers in area. Thus, 'Upolu is at least 30 times larger than Ta'u. With respect to population, 'Upolu in the 1960s (Freeman's reference point) had a population of 90,000 living in over 200 villages, compared with Ta'u in the 1920s comprising four villages with a population of about 1200. Thus, the population of Freeman's reference point is some 75 times that of Mead's reference point. Of the four villages on Ta'u, three are crowded into the flat areas on its northwestern corner. Together, these three villages occupied less than one square mile of territory and at the time of Mead's research were inhabited by some 600 people (Mead, 1928, p. 260). The fourth village, Fiti'uta, was on the flat section on the northeast extreme of the island, travel to which required an arduous trip that many residents of Ta'u had apparently never made (p. 266).

These geographical features, which continue to restrict population growth and movement on Ta'u, are important to bear in mind in evaluating Freeman's contention that life on that small, remote island was no different than life on the larger Samoan islands. This is especially the case because, on the basis of data and observations primarily from 'Upolu, Freeman makes the strong claim to have refuted virtually *all* of Mead's findings and conclusions.

Had Freeman left the matter as an academic critique, it is doubtful that the controversy would have become as heated and convoluted. In fact, an academic critique of Mead's work was published in the same year but has received virtually no attention (Goodman, 1983). But, in his work, Freeman has attempted to discredit those associated with the early nature–nurture debate, to embarrass the American cultural anthropology "establishment," and to call into serious question Mead's character and competence. Moreover, his attack on Mead's competence has continued with vigor in the many rejoinders he has written in response to criticisms of his work (e.g., Freeman, 1984, 1985a, 1985b, 1986). Commenting on statements made in his book, one reviewer remarked that it would be "an understatement to say that Freeman's attack on Mead and her work defies the normal conventions of scientific discourse, not to mention courtesies" (Yans-McLaughlin, 1984, p. 410). The result was predictable: outrage, a taking of sides, accusations and counteraccusations. These are all recorded for posterity in dozens of journal articles, reviews, rejoinders and letters, a few books, and even talk shows and a documentary film (Caton, 1990; Heimans, 1988; Kuper, 1989).

The controversy itself is of sociological interest and is discussed elsewhere (Côté, 1994; Feinberg, 1988; Leacock, 1987; Mageo, 1988; Rappaport, 1986). Those interested in reading the various commentaries, can consult sources that

1 support Freeman (e.g., Appell, 1984; Appell and Madan, 1988; Caton, 1984; Caton, 1990; Leach, 1983; Tribe, 1984);
2 criticize him (e.g., Baker, 1984; Brady, 1983; Ember, 1985; Goodale, 1984; Handler, 1984; Kuklick, 1984; Laing, 1987; Leacock, 1987; Murray, 1990; Nardi, 1984; Patience and Smith, 1986; Paxman, 1988; Rappaport, 1986; Reyman, 1985; Scheper-Hughes, 1984; Schoeffel and Meleisea, 1983; Shore, 1983; Turnbull, 1983);

3   both support and criticize him (e.g., Badock, 1983; Buchholz, 1984; Hooper, 1984; Muensterberger, 1985); and

4   both support and criticize Mead (Feinberg, 1988; Leacock, 1988; Levy, 1984; Mageo, 1988; Nardi, 1984; Rappaport, 1986; Scheper-Hughes, 1984; Schoeffel and Meleisea, 1983; Shore, 1983; Young and Juan, 1985).

Partly as a result of Freeman's efforts, a mythology now seems to surround Mead's involvement in Samoa, among both academics and contemporary Samoans. Consequently, not only has her reputation been seriously impugned, but misconceptions abound regarding what she actually wrote in *Coming of Age*. However, Freeman is very persuasive in his writing style, and from an office in a distant university or clinical setting, someone with no knowledge of Samoa might find his arguments compelling. For example, after reviewing Freeman's arguments in the most recent edition of his *Theories of Adolescence*, Muuss states that "Freeman's critique of Mead's work is effectively documented and well reasoned" (1988, p. 142). Muuss then goes on to severely criticize Freeman, but Freeman's work still seems to have swayed Muuss's views on the matter, and therefore the views of many of Muuss's readers.

Initially, I too found some of Freeman's arguments to be plausible, but I was concerned about the vast disparity between his and Mead's accounts, as well as about the tone of his critique. Because it was difficult to arrive at a satisfactory conclusion of my own regarding the various claims involved in the controversy, I decided that visits to the islands of American Samoa and Western Samoa were necessary. These visits were of a fact-finding nature, but they facilitated the analysis of the controversy presented below and helped me arrive at a satisfactory conclusion. Thus, it should be noted that the present paper focuses *mainly* on the literature related to the controversy, and not on my own field research.

Understanding Mead

In order to gain a good sense of the controversy, and why it came about, it is useful to first examine Mead's role in it. While she died five years before the publication of Freeman's book, she did comment on earlier criticisms of her work in Samoa. In addition, it is interesting to note how her own behavior appears to have contributed to both the current bad press about her book and the loss of reputation she has suffered personally. For example, as we see below, the extent to which she wrote *Coming of Age* as a popular book appears to have contributed to this controversy, as has the way she handled criticisms of that book since it was published.

Mead's own defense

As mentioned above, criticisms of Mead's work had been circulating for some time before Freeman's book was published. Although she expressed her feelings about the book itself and reactions to the book on several occasions, she never provided a full defense of her position. However, the two most complete responses to criticisms of her work are in the introduction and conclusion to the 1969 edition of *Social Organization* and in the preface of the 1973 printing of *Coming of Age*.

In the latter source, Mead commented on encounters she apparently had with Samoan university students who were embarrassed by her frank and sometimes uncomplimentary portrayal of their grandparents (compare F. Wendt's, 1984, criticisms of the book). She lamented that they and other readers tended to disregard the fact that the study was carried out in the 1920s and describes life at that time. In her own defense, she stated,

> It seems more than ever necessary to stress, as loud as I can, this is about the Samoa . . . of 1925–26. When you read it remember this. Do not confuse yourselves and the Samoan people by expecting to find life in the Manu'an islands of American Samoa as I found it.

She continued in that preface to note that she did not want to alter the contents of the book (despite its many reprintings) because it was a historical document and she did not want to change its style of writing. In her words,

> I can emphasize that this was the first piece of anthropological fieldwork that was written without the paraphernalia of scholarship designed to mystify the lay reader and confound one's colleagues. . . . I did not write it as a popular book, but only with the hope that it would be intelligible to those who might make the best use of its theme. . . .

In spite of her protestations, however, Mead was not being entirely forthright. The book has been widely read by the general public; in fact, it is "the most widely read anthropological book ever published [with] sixteen translations and millions of copies sold" (Muuss, 1988; p. 139). Moreover, it would appear that she wrote in a way to make it marketable, particularly with the inclusion of the academically controversial chapter entitled "A Day in Samoa." This is the second chapter of the book and was likely placed near the beginning in order to grab readers' interest before they encountered the more mundane details of her ethnography. In this chapter, she employed the now familiar popularizing technique of providing a composite sketch of daily life. Unfortunately, to imply that all of those events could happen in one day is inaccurate and not acceptable academically. In any event, Mead instructed that "[f]or the scholarly reader, there is a new edition (1969) of *The Social Organization of Manu'a* . . . revised in the light of contemporary ethnographic theory" (preface, 1973 printing of *Coming of Age*).

Yet, contrary to these declarations, it seems that Mead was occasionally embarrassed about *Coming of Age* because of its nonacademic style. For example, in the introduction to the 1969 edition of *Social Organization* she noted that "I incorporated in [*Coming of Age*] a section originally intended for this monograph, called "A Day in Samoa", which I had decided was too literary in character for the style of a Bishop Museum monograph!" (p. xvii). And when it was subjected to academic scrutiny by the American anthropologist, Lowell Holmes, Mead equivocated regarding how authoritative she saw that book to be:

> Holmes' quotations are from reprints of paperbacks which make the whole dating system into pulp. I wrote *Social Organization of Manu'a* (1930) after I wrote *Coming of Age in Samoa* (1928), and the former should therefore be regarded as the more complete and definitive. (p. 224)

In the 1969 edition of *Social Organization*, Mead went on to comment on what was then mounting criticism of her characterization of Samoan "character" as one of "mildness and low affect" (p. 226). She raised two possibilities regarding the discrepancy between her own analyses and those of others. The first possibility was that the Ta'u that she witnessed in the 1920s was a historical anomaly in which there was a "temporary felicitous relaxation of the quarrels and rivalries, the sensitivity to slights and insults, and the use of girls as pawns in male rivalries" (p. 228). The second was that she saw the culture through the eyes of her informants – young females. In her words,

> The other possibility is that to the young girl, herself either a virgin but not a *taupou*, or experimenting quietly with lovers of her own choosing, uninvolved in the rivalries that were related to rank and prestige, moving gently, unhurriedly into adulthood, the preoccupations of the whole society may have seemed more remote than they would have appeared from any other vantage point. *And this is the vantage point from which I saw it.* I was alone, very slight and smaller than the Samoan adolescent girls. My subject of research called for my spending the largest proportion of my time with them. . . . My primary task was to get to know and understand adolescent girls; the ethnography of this monograph was a by-product, an extra dividend. (1969, p. 228, emphasis added)

Those who now stand in judgment of Mead's work have a responsibility to acknowledge her admission regarding the above-noted discrepancies regarding Samoan character and to appraise her explanation for them. Her admission also requires, though, that the generalizability of some of her findings beyond Ta'u of the 1920s and beyond the experiences of those "coming of age" be carefully examined. On the other hand, problems of generalizability (external validity) do not necessarily mean that there are problems in the accuracy of her records (internal validity).

Mead's accountability in the controversy

As an academic, Mead could have handled matters much better, beginning with the initial publication of her book in 1928. This is the wisdom of hindsight, however, and for the young academic the prospect of publishing can make other concerns seem unimportant. At the time, she was new to the scene and this book was to lead to immediate recognition and acclaim. To make the book marketable, her publisher apparently urged her to write three additional chapters in a popular style, and it is primarily the content of these chapters that has been the object of criticism. Indeed, those added chapters contain several generalizations that are difficult to defend academically.

It is also possible that Mead did not understand Samoan culture as well as she thought. While she did spend nine months intensively and directly studying the culture, even after years of study, elements of any culture may not be fully appreciated by an outsider. In particular, she may not have fully understood the "casualness" of Samoans, but she would not be the only one to have had this problem (Swaney, 1990). Clearly, many Westerners accustomed to a time-managed, hurried, compartmentalized existence have a difficult time understanding the "laid back" nature of many non-Western cultures. It is common that "relaxed" behaviors and attitudes are mistaken by Westerners for laziness or dullness, or in Mead's case, emotional shallowness. From the accounts of Samoans commenting on the controversy, however, Freeman may not be any closer to understanding "true" Samoan character, if any such thing exists (compare Ala'ailima, 1984; Schoeffel and Meleisea, 1983; Wendt, 1983; F. Wendt, 1984).

In this context, it is important to note that Samoan culture is complex, and is based on a long history of intricate and subtle customs and oral traditions. In fact, it is known as the most conservative of the Polynesian cultures (Hanson, 1973; Holmes, 1980), and Samoans proudly refer to their way of life as "*fa'a Samoa*" ("the Samoan way"). Moreover, Samoans are still careful to protect it from outside influence, and appear to have been successful in employing a strategy, noted by Mead and others, of incorporating an influence as much as possible before the influence incorporates them (Baldauf and Ayabe, 1977). Such appears to be the case regarding Christianity, for example; a number of observers have remarked that it is difficult to say whether Samoa was Christianized, or whether Christianity there was "Samoanized" (e.g., Hanson, 1973; Meleisea, 1987; Stanner, 1953).

As indicated above, Mead eventually entertained the notion that her informants provided her with a skewed view of Samoan culture. Unfortunately, she should have considered this problem much sooner, and she should have at least warned readers in a preface. After all, much of her information came from these young women who were "coming of age" and by Mead's own account were experiencing the best years of their lives. Her informants were temporarily free from many responsibilities and obligations, and were able to experiment in a playful fashion (particularly those *not* under the pastor's supervision, the main informants who described sexual intrigues; Mead, 1928, pp. 264–265). One's culture can look very benign from this point of view; indeed, such a "moratorium period" (Mageo, 1988; compare Erikson, 1968) is by definition one where the individual is largely free from responsibilities and from irreversible commitments, so the "stakes" are often not "high" for those involved and they are free to casually move from one interest to the next.

The possibility that Mead's perspective was somewhat askew, however, does not mean that Freeman's is any more accurate. For instance, Freeman was given a Samoan chiefly title in 1943 (Freeman, 1983, p. xv) and it is evident from his writings that his perspective of Samoan culture is that of the *matai* (chief) in contemporary Samoan culture, a culture that has been described as "macho" and patriarchal (compare Wendt, 1983). The *matai* is a "guardian of order" (Levy, 1984) who must police the family and village, and who therefore deals with the "worst" of the culture. To the extent that Freeman has identified with the *matai* role, he may also have adopted that perspective concerning order and transgressions of that order. Hence, his overall portrayal of Samoan culture as ridden with crime, violence, and discord may be a byproduct of viewing Samoans through the eyes of the authority structure (compare Schoeffel and Meleisea, 1983, for an analysis of the "dualism" of Samoan culture, wherein *actual* behavior can be totally at odds with culture *ideals* of conduct, particularly in sexual matters).

Finally, while it is possible to give Mead the benefit of the doubt in most instances, she was clearly in error in stating that:

> . . . because one girl's life was so much like another's, in an uncomplex uniform culture like Samoa, *I feel justified in generalizing* although I studied only fifty girls in three small neighboring villages (Mead, 1926, p. 11, emphasis added)

Not only is it unclear about whom she is generalizing, it is also unclear as to where and when. She wrote that she went to Ta'u "as a corrective for the degree of culture contact" elsewhere in American Samoa (Mead, 1969, p. xv), so there is an obvious flaw in her logic if she selected the island of Ta'u because of its remoteness, but still felt justified in generalizing to the rest of Samoa. Why bother going to Ta'u when by the logic of the above quotation she could have found the same thing anywhere in Samoa? Logically, she cannot have it both ways. Moreover, she was also aware that what she observed on Ta'u was no longer completely traditional either, and that the culture there was undergoing changes when she conducted her study. The reader is directed to Appendix III of *Coming of Age* (1928) in which Mead identifies the historical uniqueness of the "Samoa" she witnessed.

It is worth stressing, therefore, that there were several things about Ta'u that make it unique in comparison with the rest of Samoa, both during Mead's visit and now. These unique circumstances, all of which weaken Freeman's critique, include the following geographical, historical, political, and chance factors:

1   *Geographical differences.* As mentioned above, the island of Ta'u has particular geographical characteristics that restrict the size and density of population, and that therefore should have produced a high level of community control over behavior.

2   *Historical and political differences.* American Samoa had not experienced any wars for several decades, and it had been annexed by the United States two decades earlier. Manu'a, of which Ta'u is a part, had recently seen its long-reigning line of royalty come to an end, so an authority void would have existed. In addition, Mead noted repeatedly how Christianization, still in progress at the time, had tempered many of the cruel practices found in the precontact culture and had ameliorated intervillage and inter-island hostility. Thus, the period prior to and during her visit seems to have been one of peace, optimism, and accord (Mead, 1928, Appendix III; compare Schoeffel and Meleisea, 1983).

3   *Chance differences.* Shortly after Mead arrived, a severe hurricane hit, devastating the island. During most of her stay the villagers were busy rebuilding their dwellings, an undertaking that is often a highly cooperative effort. As is well known from social psychological research, disasters and other external "threats" tend to unite a population and mitigate internal social conflicts and psychological disturbances (Sherif et al., 1961).

Given these particular features of Ta'u, then, there is sufficient reason to doubt both Mead's generalizations to the rest of Samoa, and Freeman's contention that Ta'u in 1925 would have been no different from Western Samoa in the 1960s.

As for the "real" Samoa, I do not think that anyone, even Samoans themselves, can lay claim to having a complete understanding of Samoan culture in all of its forms in all places and times. If anything, Freeman may have simplified it as much as Mead is thought to have simplified it (Ala'ailima, 1984; Bock, 1983; Feinberg, 1988; Hooper, 1984; Levy, 1984; Wendt, 1983; F. Wendt, 1984). Moreover, the answer to the controversy is not to be found "somewhere in between" the two versions as some have suggested (e.g., Swaney, 1990); rather it lies with a complex and flexible culture, which survives and maintains its integrity by appropriating the forces that seek to change it, and by defying easy definition and understanding (compare Laing, 1987). Sometimes change can overwhelm these conservative mechanisms, however, and conditions within even one village can apparently change rapidly if something goes awry with the powerful village council (*fono*), as noted by Schoeffel and Meleisea (1983):

> the Samoan village which Schoeffel studied between 1976 and 1982 was the subject of a short socio-economic survey by Lockwood (1971) a decade earlier. She was amazed at the difference between her own observations and those of Lockwood; apparently in the space of ten years a progressive, prosperous, well-governed and peaceful community had become a strife-torn, faction-ridden, economically stagnant village in which leadership was virtually absent. (p. 64)

In the context of Schoeffel and Meleisea's experiences, then, an observer might find "Freeman's Samoa" in one village, while another observer might find "Mead's Samoa" in the next village; neither observer would be wrong, and both would have seen different facets of the "same Samoa."

To conclude this analysis of Mead's accountability in the controversy, had she initially titled the book something like "Coming of Age on Ta'u," and not engaged in inappropriate generalization to other Samoan islands and to other historical periods, there would be little basis for a critique.

Freeman's Critique of Mead's *Coming of Age* Thesis

This examination of Freeman's critique of Mead's thesis begins with the acknowledgment that some of Mead's generalizations to other parts of Samoa are questionable. To the extent that Freeman has brought this to our attention, we are indebted to him. However, as part of his harsh treatment of Mead, Freeman has denied the validity of *most* of her observations, even as they apply to the island of Ta'u. Accordingly, we will examine Freeman's critique of Mead's work, but our examination is restricted to his attempted refutation of Mead's characterization of adolescence on Ta'u and her conclusion that the period of adolescence there was one of relative ease. By placing his arguments in the context of Mead's major assertions, it is possible to assess the extent to which Freeman's criticisms are actually as well documented and well reasoned as they appear at first glance.

Before examining Freeman's criticisms, however, it is important to consider just what forms of evidence are acceptable in a controversy of this magnitude and importance, particularly since this controversy entails one person claiming to have conclusively refuted another person's major research findings. Freeman makes the very strong claim that he has scientifically *refuted* Mead's coming-of-age thesis. Therefore, the standards of proof in science place the onus on him to provide *irrefutable* evidence; if there are other plausible interpretations of the evidence he gives, then his conclusions cannot be considered any more definitive than Mead's, and the controversy becomes simply that of one interpretation against another. His evidence must also be "hard" to the extent that it cannot be dismissed by fiat. Poorly validated evidence cannot reasonably be considered in a critique that claims to constitute a refutation. Thus, innuendo, rumour, results of personal conversations, and quotations of material that are taken out of context or put together to form a "creative collage," are all unacceptable. Others have commented on the standards of evidence needed to resolve this controversy (Bock, 1983; Goodale, 1984; Patience and Smith, 1986; Yans-McLaughlin, 1984; Young and Juan, 1985).

Freeman's criticisms of Mead's treatment of biological factors

Freeman has referred to Mead's conclusions regarding adolescence in Samoa as "preposterous" (1985a, p. 910) and "egregious" (1987, p. 930). When the basis of this strong condemnation is examined, however, it appears that Freeman has misconstrued Mead's conclusion. From his reconstructions of her writings, Freeman appears to be attempting to portray Mead as claiming that "biology" has no relevance for adolescent behavior or disturbances in behavior during adolescence. In one place he "quotes" her as saying that " 'we cannot' . . . 'make any explanations' in terms of the biological process of adolescence itself" (1985a, p. 910) and in another as saying that " 'we cannot make any explanation' of the 'disturbances' of adolescence other than 'in terms of' the 'social environment'" (1987, p. 930).

The reader will note that these are not direct quotes; rather, they are a collage of passages. In fact, Freeman does this throughout his book and he provides all of the references from each paragraph in single endnotes, making it appear that the quoted passages are from one source (this technique produced over fifty pages of endnotes). More often than not, Freeman is not quoting from Mead's *Coming of Age*, but from other sources, published for vastly different audiences over her fifty year career. The result is problematic because it is very difficult for the reader to judge the validity of Freeman's reconstructions of Mead's thoughts. As Rappaport (1987a) notes, "Professor Freeman seems to have combed Mead's corpus for phrases and sentences that can be construed in ways convicting her of his charges" (p. 304). (See McDowell, 1984, for a thorough critique of Freeman's writing and referencing style.)

What is most interesting, however, is that when we turn to Mead's actual conclusion from *Coming of Age*, she simply said that because the biological processes of adolescence are the same among individuals in different cultures, her finding that adolescence is an easier one in Samoa than in the United States would mean that difficulties experienced by American adolescents must be attributed to characteristics found in American culture but absent in Samoan culture. This reasonable conclusion was stated as follows by Mead:

> If it is proved that adolescence is not necessarily a specially difficult period in a girl's life – and proved it is if I can find any society in which that is so – then what accounts for the presence of stress and storm in American adolescents? First, I may say quite simply that there must be something in the two civilizations to account for the difference. *If the same process takes a different form in the two different environments, I cannot make any explanations in terms of the process, for it is the same in both cases.* But the social environment is very different and it is to it that I must look for an explanation. What is there in Samoa which is absent in America, what is there in America which is absent in Samoa, which will account for the difference? (Mead, 1928, pp. 197–198, emphasis added)

Interestingly, in his original critique, Freeman does not paraphrase Mead's conclusion, but rather provides it verbatim. After doing so, he states the following:

In other words, any explanation in biological terms of the presence of storm and stress in American adolescence was totally excluded. . . . Instead of arriving at an estimate of the relative strength of biological puberty and cultural pattern . . . Mead dismissed biology, or nature, as being of no significance whatsoever in accounting for the presence of storm and stress in American adolescents, and claimed the determinism of culture, or nurture, to be absolute. (Freeman, 1983, p. 78)

Freeman's interpretation of Mead's conclusion raises questions about his understanding of both research design and biological research on adolescents. Mead had, in principle, a sound research design: American society constituted the control group and Samoan society the experimental group; the independent variable was cultural institutions governing adolescence (known to differ) and the dependent variable was the ease/difficulty of coming of age. If a difference were found on the dependent variable, it would be attributable to cultural institutions, because the biological processes of adolescence were held constant. In practice, however, Mead's actual research is problematic in terms of being a *rigorous* quantitative experiment because her findings are largely anecdotal and qualitative, and she did not repeat her observations on American adolescents; rather, she relied on her common sense knowledge as a native of American society. Her research design is also potentially problematic because race might be considered a variable. Although some of Freeman's supporters have suggested this possibility (Appell, 1984; Buchholz, 1984), they should heed Sprinthall and Collins (1984), who state that "racial and ethnic differences in puberty are minor" (p. 74) (See also Zuckerman, 1990, for a discussion of problems associated with research that attempts to make claims about racial differences in behavior without employing adequate controls for social differences.)

Freeman goes on to criticize Mead for not paying sufficient attention to biological variables, and accuses her of not being "scientifically equipped to investigate the subtle and complex interaction, in Samoan behavior, of biological and cultural variables" (1983, p. 75), but these criticisms are unconstructive because of their vagueness. He never specifies just what she should have done to assess biological variables, particularly given that in 1925 the state of knowledge regarding the biology of adolescence was totally theoretical and there was virtually no technology available to measure relevant physiological variables. He also claims that she did not carry out "any systematic comparison of hereditary and environmental conditions" (p. 76), despite the fact that she gathered a sample representing pre-puberty ($n = 11$), puberty ($n = 14$), and post-puberty ($n = 25$), and she noted that there were no major characterological or psychopathological differences among these three groups. If puberty is responsible for adolescent storm and stress, such differences should have been observed among her groupings of informants. This evidence, however, is apparently insufficient for Freeman. Again, just what he expected her to do is unclear, as is what he would expect of someone conducting such research today with current knowledge and technology.

In view of these considerations, Freeman's "meta-critique" of Mead's treatment of biological factors affecting adolescence is weak. And if we assume that he is not being obtuse in his reading of Mead, we might conclude that he is naive regarding the difficulties of understanding and documenting the interplay between biological and cultural factors. Moreover, at no time in her career did Mead dismiss the relevance of biological factors (compare Rappaport, 1987a, b). If she were able to participate in this debate today, she would probably clarify her position by arguing that cultural factors can stimulate certain biological reactions in adolescents that are part of a chain of causation. She was simply implying that in the absence of certain cultural factors, these biological reactions are not stimulated, and therefore the storm and stress can be considered neither natural nor inevitable. Thus, she would probably not have argued that biological factors are "of no significance in accounting for the presence of storm and stress in American adolescents" (Freeman, 1983, p. 78), but rather that they constitute intervening not independent variables. Thus, as Rappaport notes,

> Mead clearly recognized the biological character of puberty, never claimed that biological factors had nothing to do with behavior, and simply stated that differences in the emotional and cognitive correlates of "the same [biological] process" in "different environments" are to be accounted for by environmental differences. *Hardly preposterous*. (1987, p. 160, emphasis added)

Ironically, recent research undertaken with state-of-the-art theory and technology supports Mead's conclusion that biological factors do not *directly* affect most adolescent behavior or disturbances (Adams et al., 1990; Montemayor et al., 1990). As argued by Sprinthall and Collins, biological changes [associated with puberty] seem to influence psychological development through the subjective meanings that the changes have for adolescents themselves and for adults and peers around them. ... [thus] the effects of the primary physical changes of adolescence are *socially mediated* by the reactions of self and others. In this view one's self-image and self-esteem reflect one's own and others' subjective reactions to biological maturation. And these reactions are determined by socio-cultural standards, norms, and expectations about physical characteristics that are widely held in a society or culture. (1984, p. 79)

Furthermore, in comparison to the socializing effect of culture on the adolescent, biological factors are minor in comparison, as noted by Montemayor and Flannery in a recent review:

The evidence ... indicates ... that pubertal effects, by themselves, account for a relatively small proportion of the variance in early adolescent behavior. For example, in a recent study, hormone levels explained 4% of the variance in girls' negative affect while social factors accounted for between 8% and 18% of the variance in depression and anger respectively. (1990, p. 294)

Finally, in specific reference to the Mead/Freeman controversy Muuss argues that:

[Freeman's] argument for a synthesis between biological and cultural determinism seems to come too late to have a major impact. The synthesis has already taken place. Although proponents of culture or biology may emphasize one more than the other, most contemporary theorists view development as an interaction between nature and nurture. Adolescent turmoil, storm and stress, and crises are no longer considered inevitable, not even for adolescents growing up in the United States. And regardless of whether or not Mead was correct about Samoa, other anthropologists have observed societies in which adolescence is not turbulent. Thus, the physiological changes of puberty and sexual maturation alone are not categorically responsible for adolescent difficulties. Anxieties, insecurities, social pressures, social expectations, and cultural, educational, and family factors may all contribute to adolescent stress. (1988, p. 142)

When critically examined, Freeman's criticisms of Mead's treatment of biological factors amount to straw arguments. As Rappaport notes, "The conclusion that Freeman asserts was Mead's is indeed preposterous, *but it verges on the preposterous to attribute it to her"* (1987, p. 304, emphasis added).

Freeman's critique of Mead's conclusion regarding the ease of Coming of Age

The above straw arguments created by Freeman to discredit Mead's research were augmented by several forms of counterevidence that he believes refute Mead's conclusion that the adolescence she witnessed was one of relative ease. One is based on the argument that she contradicts herself in her own work; a second is based on statistical arguments that crime and delinquency are, and were, rampant in all parts of Samoa; and a third is based on his conversations with "highly educated Samoans."

Contradictions in Mead's work?

Freeman believes he has caught Mead in a contradiction in claiming that she actually identified several informants who were exhibiting problematic behavior. Indeed, Mead discussed in detail seven individuals who exhibited various forms and degrees of deviance. Four of these were potentially classifiable as "delinquent" or "downward deviants," while three were classed by Mead as "upward deviants" (Freeman, 1983, p. 171). Freeman argues that if there were four "delinquents" out of Mead's twenty-five postpubertal adolescents, then the "delinquency rate" in Ta'u would have actually been "about ten times higher than that which existed among female adolescents in England and Wales in 1965" (1983, p. 258). Taken at face value, it would appear that Freeman has found contradictory evidence in Mead's work. But let us consider this matter further, first by looking at what Mead actually wrote and then by applying current social scientific knowledge regarding adolescence to the supposed contradiction.

Throughout *Coming of Age* Mead describes various social and personal unpleasantries that she witnessed in Ta'u (contrary to the mythology that she painted a *simple* idyllic picture; compare Feinberg, 1988). Included in these descriptions are instances of adjustment problems experienced by the seven informants mentioned above. Freeman argues that these cases are examples of adolescent storm and stress. Upon examination, however, they more closely resemble conflict-produced adjustment problems that might be found in any culture. That Mead documented these cases so carefully attests to the credibility and thoroughness of her research. Had she really been intent on presenting a distorted image of Samoan adolescence, she surely would not have devoted a full chapter to these problems.

Instead, she showed us how individuals with certain "temperaments" found it difficult to come to terms with the constraints of Samoan culture, a culture limited in terms of the range of temperaments it could accommodate (see Mead, 1969, pp. 80–86). Moreover, she argued that these adjustment problems never became serious enough to constitute severe psychological disorders or symptoms of adolescent storm and stress. Indeed, the three cases she described as "upward deviants" appear to have had the temperamental capacity to move "beyond" their culture as with the "wish to exercise more choice than is traditionally permissible" (p. 171). Furthermore, this desire to make nontraditional choices was "encouraged by the educational system inaugurated by the missionaries" (p. 171), and it would therefore have been less common in precontact Samoan culture. In any event, these three individuals were apparently managing adequately within their community by utilizing the options available to them. Two others were identified by Mead as potential delinquents, one of whom was eleven years old, but they too were managing.

This leaves only two cases out of fifty in which individuals exhibited what might be considered serious behavioral problems. Again, though, Mead cited their problem as an incompatibility between their temperaments and the constraints of the culture, a problem exacerbated by a labeling process that stigmatized them. On the other hand, Mead found the culture to be very tolerant of certain forms of behavior and she noted that deviant individuals were not usually stigmatized unless they had few qualities that were recognized as socially redeeming. In reference to these two individuals, Mead speculates about their "temperamental handicaps":

> Lola and Mala both seemed to be the victims of lack of affection. They both had unusual capacity for devotion and were abnormally liable to become jealous. Both responded with pathetic swiftness to any manifestation of affection. At one end of the scale in their need for affection, they were unfortunately placed at the other end in their chance of receiving. . . . So it would appear that their delinquency was produced by the combination of two sets of causal factors, unusual emotional needs and

unusual home conditions. Less affectionate children in the same environments, or the same children in more favorable surroundings probably would never have become as definitely outcast as these. (1969, p. 180)

Of these two individuals whom Mead classed as "delinquent," one had just reached puberty but had experienced problems since childhood, while the other was two years past puberty but had manifested behavioral problems for at least four years (1969, p. 177). Strictly speaking, then, these were not symptoms of adolescent storm and stress (caused by hormones or some other biological "affliction" in adolescents), but problems of childhood that persisted into adolescence (Freeman appears to consider adolescence to be the postpubertal period). In fact, Mead did not report any serious behavioral problems that began after puberty. As for the delinquency rate at the heart of Freeman's critique, this would be more reasonably two out of fifty (Mead's entire group of study). But even when recast in this manner, we are ignoring that Freeman's statistics are for *indictable offenses*, whereas Mead's cases involve mainly the violation of social mores, which in England and Wales (Freeman's reference point) would likely not have evoked the reaction of the justice system (compare Young and Juan, 1985).

Freeman's use of official statistics therefore ignores the well-established finding that far more crime takes place in Western societies than is reflected in indictment statistics. For example, in the criminology literature it is commonly known that

> not all offenses result in a charge being laid; and not all charges result in a conviction. Indeed, only about one known victimization in 100 comes to a conviction, if attention is confined to crimes against persons such as assault or rape, only one victimization in ten is reported to the police and only one such report in ten results in a conviction. (Tepperman, 1977, pp. 7–8)

Thus, Freeman's statistical argument would indicate something close to the *minimum* estimate for one culture, while Mead's account would represent something close to the *maximum* estimate for another. The differences between their accounts become clearer when we see that Mead defined the "delinquent" as an "individual who is maladjusted to the demands of her civilization, and who comes definitely into conflict with her group, not because she adheres to a different standard, but because she violates the group standards which are also her own" (1969, pp. 171–172). That a small minority of her sample engaged in some delinquency by this generous definition stands in stark contrast to Gold and Petronio's (1980) observation that "[o]ver 80% of American adolescents admit to committing one or more delinquent acts . . . in the course of a few years of adolescence" (p. 523).

Rather than consulting crude delinquency statistics to gauge adolescent storm and stress, Freeman should have examined contemporary work that *directly* assesses the difficulties that adolescents can encounter in coming of age. For instance, Offer and Offer (1975) found that some 56 percent of a sample of American adolescents experienced a variety of serious conflicts over a six-year period (they classified 21 percent of their sample as experiencing what they termed "tumultuous" growth while 35 percent were classified as experiencing "surgent" growth). Only 23 percent of their sample were classified as experiencing conflict-free, "continuous" growth, comparable to that described by Mead. Similarly, other researchers have found that in samples of American young people a majority at some time have problems in terms of developing and sustaining a sense of commitment and belief (e.g., Marcia, 1980). In addition, up to two thirds of Canadian young people are estimated to have experienced problems with parental conflict, a lack of a sense of direction in life, and an uncertainty of belief (Côté, 1986). Mead's identification of two informants with serious problems and five with minor problems would put the range of difficulties experienced by her entire group of 50 informants at 4 percent to 14 percent from *all causes*, none of which appear to have had their genesis in adolescence (defined as the postpuberty period).

In evaluating this aspect of Freeman's "refutation" of Mead's work, therefore, it is clear that his evidence is itself easily refuted and his argument is poorly conceived: he does not define the concepts of adolescence or storm and stress, he does not offer a theory of adolescence that accounts for biological factors, and he does not evaluate Mead's research against the vast repertoire of theory and research on youth and adolescence that has accumulated since she carried out her pioneering work.

Rampant delinquency?

Freeman goes on to present several other statistically based arguments in his attempt to refute Mead's claims that the adolescence she witnessed was one of ease. But much of his position rests on the tenuous assumption that Ta'u in 1925 would not have been significantly different in terms of day-to-day life from Western Samoa in the 1960s, and that *all* of the islands in the Samoan archipelago have been plagued with high rates of crime and delinquency for some time. As argued above, such a contention is problematic given the historical, geographical, and political differences among the Samoan islands.

Freeman cites data that he collected in Western Samoa documenting 746 convictions for crimes of violence committed by persons aged twelve to twenty-two between 1963 and 1965 (he does not explain, however, the methodology he used in collecting these data). In discussing his results he stresses that the peak age for these convictions is sixteen, but he does little more than imply that there is some sort of biological cause for the association between age and conviction rate. His evidence for this inference is a citation of Katchadourin's (1990) *The Biology of Adolescence* and the argument that "the attainment of puberty is marked by steady and rapid improvement in physical strength, skill and endurance, and this development is also marked by involvement of adolescents in aggressive encounters of various kinds" (Freeman, 1983, p. 260).

To state that physical development is "marked by" aggressive encounters is both vague and problematic, as is the suggestion that the "attainment of puberty" is related to these aggressive encounters. Had he consulted the available literature on the topic before publishing his book, he would have encountered a literature review stating that "[a]n explanation of . . . delinquent behavior in terms of the onset of puberty seems weak . . ." (Gold and Petronio, 1980, p. 523).

Curiously, Freeman does not entertain the very plausible hypothesis that his conviction statistics might be related to the social structure of adolescence in 1960s Western Samoa. He should be aware that, in traditional Samoan society, males would have undergone their rites of passage (tattooing and entry into the *'aumaga*) at age sixteen and would be subsequently engaged in a meaningful participation in Samoan society (e.g., Turner, 1986). By the 1960s, however, as economic, religious, and educational forces continued to transform Samoan society, many males no longer had the opportunity to experience these rites of passage. And with no substitute for them, the traditional basis for developing a sense of identity was undermined, and the transition to adulthood was becoming increasingly ambiguous and prolonged. If we assume that Freeman's statistics are valid, then at least part of an explanation of them must include factors associated with the social disorganization affecting the time and place producing his statistics. Further, given his own call for an "interactionist anthropology" that takes into account the interaction between culture and biology, Freeman must be willing to entertain the question of how the social environment can produce biological reactions such as aggression. The deleterious effects of this social disorganization on Samoan youth are analyzed by a number of social scientists (Baker et al., 1986; Côté, 1994; Leacock, 1987; MacPherson and MacPherson, 1985; O'Meara, 1990; Pitt and MacPherson, 1974; Yusuf and Peters, 1985), and are characterized by Albert Wendt in several fictional accounts of the impact of Western culture on Samoan society and Samoan youth (Wendt, 1973, 1977, 1979).

Finally, Freeman presents statistics that he compiled from Western Samoan police records (again he provides no discussion of his methodology other than to say that he selected a random sample of 2,717 convictions). The offenses include "assault and other crimes of violence; the 'provoking of a breach of peace'; theft and other offenses against property; trespass; rape and indecent assault; abduction; obstructing the police; uttering threatening, insulting, or indecent words; drunkenness; and perjury" (1983, pp. 264–266). He then compares these figures with those published by Cyril Burt in 1925 for crimes in England, figures that exhibit similar characteristics, especially a peak rate at age sixteen with the highest rates occurring during ages fifteen to nineteen years.

The last source of evidence reveals just how strained Freeman's delinquency argument is. In effect, Freeman is claiming that the small island of Ta'u, with its small population living in closely knit villages, was as crime ridden as Western Samoa in 1965 and England in 1925. Clearly, most of the crimes he lists are irrelevant to a community based on communal sharing where there was virtually no private property or consumer items, no local police or courts, and no alcohol. This would leave only offenses of violence, which of course would be highly disruptive in such a setting if they existed on anything but a small scale. Notwithstanding the conditions that likely made 1920s Ta'u a time of peace and accord (as mentioned above), traditional Samoan society also had numerous mechanisms for preventing excessive community disruptions, some of which can still be found (see Filoiali'i and Knowles, 1982, for recent examples from the island of Ta'u). While some violence undoubtedly occurred, it was likely restricted to disputes between *aiga* (extended families) and neighboring villages – both of which were dealt with quickly by the *matai* – and sanctioned domestic violence (compare Holmes and Holmes, 1992). In any event, isolated acts of violence would not necessarily have had any direct relevance in terms of coming of age, the focus of Mead's book.

Expert Samoan opinion?

Freeman's third source of evidence is clearly the weakest. This evidence comes from his account of conversations he has had with "highly educated Samoans" (1983, p. 259). As mentioned above, this type of evidence is really inadmissible in a scientific controversy of this nature. Indeed, any court of law would dismiss it as "hearsay." Nevertheless, it must be addressed here because some observers have apparently been swayed by it (e.g., Muuss, 1988, p. 142, writes that this evidence "devastates Mead's conclusions"). Freeman claims that he has never met "a Samoan who agrees with Mead's assertion that adolescence in Samoan society is smooth, untroubled, and unstressed" (1983, p. 259). To substantiate his claims, Freeman cites conversations with four Samoans. Interestingly, one of these sources wrote a review of Freeman's book, but certainly did not endorse it. Her comments are quite illuminating:

> I have seen days (and nights) like Margaret Mead's and moments of mayhem like Freeman's. No one who has lived in Samoa long could doubt the existence of both. My only problem is with people who, like the blind men and the elephant, feel for one aspect or another and draw conclusions about what Samoans really "are." (Ala'ailima, 1984, p. 91)

Freeman also cites this source as having recorded "that Samoan adolescence is a period of 'Sturm und Drang'" (Freeman, 1983, p. 259). In fact, in her book (Ala'ailima, née Calkins, 1962) about her adventures in adjusting to Samoan life (she is an American who married a Samoan in the 1950s), she muses that Mead must have been wrong because of several episodes involving some of the young people she had dealt with in Western Samoa. It is ironic for Freeman's argument, though, that most of the incidents she describes involve the attempts of these young people to engage in sexual liaisons without their adult custodians finding out.

While I am reticent to engage in hearsay, because Freeman makes the claim of an absolute consensus of opinion on the matter, it should be noted that I informally asked similar questions in Samoa, but got different answers. The consensus of these answers was that young people in Samoa are no different than young people elsewhere. This should be no surprise given the extent of Western influence, especially in American Samoa, which now has strong ties with Hawaii and California. If anything, there is now a concern about the importation of gang mentalities from these US communities, and an increase in violence as a result. In Western Samoa, the concern tends to be with the lack of jobs available to the young when they graduate from high school, and with the inability of some young people to find a place in Samoan society because of *recent* economic and social change.

To conclude this examination of Freeman's evidence, in the final analysis, Freeman's "refutation" of Mead is itself easily refuted. His criticism that Mead ignored biological factors is not only erroneous, it is empty, because he himself does not suggest ways in which she might have examined such factors any more than she actually did. His contention that 1925 Ta'u can be understood with observations and statistics collected elsewhere during the 1960s is dubious to begin with, and his arguments meant to support that contention disintegrate upon critical examination. Finally, his contention regarding a consensus among Samoans that adolescence is characterized by "storm and stress" is based on unreliable evidence.

The plausibility of Mead's Coming of Age thesis

In view of the fact that Mead cannot contribute to the controversy and account for her position, several things should be kept in mind when judging the overall merit of her work.

First, we cannot go back in time to the Ta'u of 1925–1926, a period when Mead was the only record keeper. Furthermore, it is fruitless to try to assess her thesis today with ethnographic or quantitative social/psychological measurements because life on Ta'u is so transformed. In fact, it now resembles small town USA, replete with a high school, television, modern European houses, air service twice a day, local stores, and pickup trucks. Therefore, in evaluating her claims about that time and place we must rely on inference and plausibility as well as on corroboration from other observers, particularly those closest to her research site in time and place. Indeed, corroboration for the majority of her observations can be found in the writings of either missionaries (e.g., Williams, in Moyle, 1984 (1830–1832); Stair, 1983 (1897); Turner, 1986 (1862)) or other anthropologists (e.g., Holmes, 1987; Schoeffel and Meleisea, 1983; Shore, 1983).

Second, it is unrealistic to expect her study to be flawless, especially given the pioneering nature of her research. The recognition that some of her observations cannot be verified or that some of her conclusions are tenuous does not justify a conclusion that "anyone who can read with a discerning mind would have seen that Mead's *Coming of Age* was just plain rubbish" (Appell, 1984, p. 205). It is this type of unreasonableness that has generated more "heat than light" (Feinberg, 1988, p. 656) in this controversy. Thus, with very little prior research to go on, it is understandable that she might have overlooked some matters and overemphasized other matters.

Finally, it must be remembered that what is at issue here is ethnographic research, a research technique that can be high in internal validity (accuracy), but low in external validity (generalizability). As Bernard (1988) notes, two of the principal weaknesses of ethnographic research are that "(a) it is difficult for other researchers to replicate an ethnographer's findings . . . ; [and] (b) whatever an ethnographer learns about one village or island may have little to do with other villages or islands in the same general cultural region" (p. 146). Mead's research is vulnerable to both weaknesses, but it is hardly appropriate to hold her personally responsible for the shortcomings of a research method.

Given my earlier criticism that Mead inappropriately generalized to other parts of Samoa, but also having found Freeman's critique of her coming of age thesis to be weak, it is appropriate to now turn to an examination of that thesis. Hence, we can now consider whether the structures and processes governing adolescence in 1925–1926 Ta'u could have plausibly provided the ease of coming of age that she claimed. Perhaps the best way to assess her claim is to consult the anthropologist most familiar with the island of Ta'u – Lowell Holmes. Holmes conducted his doctoral research on Ta'u in the 1950s and his primary goal was to assess the results of Mead's 1925–1926 research. Holmes recently published what is to date the most extensive evaluation of the controversy in *Quest for the Real Samoa* (1987). In it he states that he finds "the validity of her Samoan research remarkably high" and that he can "confirm Mead's conclusions that it was undoubtedly easier to come of age in Samoa than in the United States in 1925" (p. 103).

I leave it to the reader to consult Holmes's book, in which he provides a convincing argument in support of Mead's conclusion (see also Holmes and Holmes, 1992). Of course, Freeman has been harshly critical of Holmes, and employs the familiar tactic of questioning the competency and intellectual integrity of those who disagree with him (Freeman, 1987).

Conclusion

Mead's thesis

With respect to Mead's conclusion that coming of age on the island of Ta'u in 1925–1926 was accomplished with relative ease, there is little in Freeman's critique that constitutes an actual refutation. Not only are Freeman's arguments regarding adolescence easily refuted themselves, there is also sufficient corroboration of Mead's conclusion from other sources. Furthermore, there is little reason to doubt that she reported accurately what she saw during her study, to suspect "fudging" on her part, or to assume a "duping" on the part of her informants. Nevertheless, it appears that she popularized parts of her account, capitalizing on romantic notions about the South Seas and sexual stereotypes about Polynesians to make her book more marketable. She also seems to have engaged in some unsubstantiated speculation regarding why coming of age was accomplished with ease, and she had insufficient grounds for assuming that all of her observations and conclusions could be generalized to all of Samoa. Thus, while her main thesis appears supported by the evidence, she did not exercise what is now considered the appropriate scholarly restraint expected of an academic in presenting and interpreting findings. On the other hand, she did write the book for "teachers, parents, and soon-to-be parents" (preface to the 1973 edition), and she was ostensibly trying to convey a message to that audience.

Freeman's critique of her coming-of-age thesis appears to have merit only to the extent that Mead popularized and overgeneralized her account. Unfortunately, Freeman has squandered an opportunity to make a constructive contribution to the literature because he has sought to personally discredit her rather than to improve upon her work. It is unfortunate as well that the controversy has focused on a few passages from her book, to the exclusion of the vast proportion of it that has been described as a "rich and sensitive ethnography" (Feinberg, 1988, p. 656). With its faults and limitations, if it is read in the context of a semipopular, pioneering study with cross-cultural implications, it can be appreciated as a valuable historical document and a landmark study. Not only did her book advance the understanding of adolescence in its time by demonstrating that adolescence was not inevitably a time of storm and stress, it also anticipated later developments in the field, such as the concept of the moratorium period and the forces prolonging youth and adolescence.

The impact of the controversy

Finally, forgotten throughout much of this controversy are Samoans themselves. Freeman bases some of his evidence against Mead on conversations he has had with Samoans, and he has left the impression that there is unanimous agreement among Samoans that she was wrong. This does not appear to be the case at all. Indeed, there is considerable resentment toward Freeman for blowing the affair out of proportion and for portraying Samoans in such a negative fashion (Ala'ailima, 1984; Levy, 1984; Wendt, 1983; F. Wendt, 1984).

In both Samoas, there is a wide range of opinion about Mead, with most of the negative opinion being based on the mythology that has emerged there about her work. Most Samoans apparently have not read her book, but rather rely on rumor and local consensus. The images and information they have of it often do not correspond with her work (e.g., there are beliefs that she spent only two months there, that she could not speak Samoan, that she was teased and duped, that she really described her own sexual exploits, and so forth), and there is the impression that the book was primarily about Samoan sexual behavior. Of course, the belief that she portrayed Samoans as sexually promiscuous does not sit well among devoutly Christian Samoans, who constitute the majority of the population in both Samoas. Undoubtedly, conservative Samoans would like to see her soundly discredited and the whole thing forgotten (compare F. Wendt, 1984).

In this "bible belt" of the South Pacific, the notion that one's elders and grandparents were promiscuous "animals" (as one Samoan in the documentary film put it) or engaged in "free love" is not entertained lightly (compare F. Wendt, 1984). In fact, the denial that their ancestors had anything but a "Christian" attitude toward sex could almost be called a national obsession. Indeed, if we are to believe the accounts of the missionaries who made the earliest records there (e.g., Turner, 1986, pp. 90–91), it would appear that a massive "cover-up" has taken place in an attempt to rewrite history (compare Gerber, 1975). As a scholar of Samoan culture recently noted after reviewing the journals of John Williams, the first missionary in Samoa, Williams' "assessment of sexual mores seems closer to that of Margaret Mead . . . than to that of Derek Freeman" (Schoeffel, 1986, p. 63).

In American Samoa, there appear to be mixed opinions about *Coming of Age*, ranging from a feeling that much of what she wrote is plausible, to the belief that she has nurtured stereotypes that are harmful, particularly in the current Christian culture where chastity is the ideal. On the island of Ta'u, however, where the elders' youthful "personal habits are recounted to the public at large," feelings about Mead and her book tend to be "petulant, irritated, and contentious. . . . Mention of her name is a touchy subject, and her book is treated as if it were best forgotten quickly" (Cranberg, 1983, p. 182).

In the final analysis, there are grounds for Samoans to be annoyed with all of the publicity directed at them, beginning with Mead's "exposé," but also as stirred up by Freeman, who has only added to the stereotypes created by social scientists about Samoans; his addition being a negative one, presenting them as "a race of sex-starved rapists" as one Samoan has put it (Levy, 1984) or as "violent, competitive, extremely puritanical, delinquent, rape and suicide prone, Jehovah dominated, and rank-bound people" as another Samoan put it (F. Wendt, 1984, p. 95). The grounds for complaint extend to the inordinate amount of attention paid to this small population of people by social scientists. As an exercise in role taking, readers are asked to imagine their own "hometown" or neighborhood being so closely scrutinized and publicized, and the behavior of one segment of the population – the sexiest or the most violent segment – coming to represent the worldwide popular image of their community, and by implication them personally. This problem perhaps was best expressed by someone who, ironically, was cited by Freeman to support his case against Mead:

> . . . in the relentless pursuit of knowledge and each other, don't anthropologists consider what their pronouncements do to the people they

study? . . . [Freeman's] unmaking of the myth makes me wonder how I escaped alive! Derek Freeman's book may bring him fame and fortune but it will hardly make life easier for thousands of Samoans struggling to gain acceptance in Honolulu, Auckland, and Carson City. For them it may operate more like a stereotype than a great intellectual discovery. I am not sure they will continue to thank him (Ala'ailima, 1984, p. 92)

References

Adams, G. R., Montemayor, R., & Gullotta, T. P. (Eds.) (1990). *Biology of Adolescent Behavior and Development.* Sage, Newbury Park, CA.

Ala'ailima, F. (1984). Review of Margaret Mead and Samoa. *Pacific Studies,* 7: 91–92.

Appell, G. N. (1984). Freeman's refutation of Mead's Coming of Age in Samoa: The implications for anthropological inquiry. *Eastern Anthropology,* 37: 183–214.

Appell, G. N., & Madan, T. N. (Eds.) (1988). *Choice and Morality in Anthropological Perspective: Essays in Honor of Derek Freeman.* State University of New York Press, Albany, NY.

Badock, C. R. (1983). [Review of] Margaret Mead and Samoa: The making and unmaking of an anthropological myth. *British Journal of Sociology,* 34: 606–607.

Baker, P. T., Hanna, J. M., & Baker, T. S. (Eds.) (1986). *The Changing Samoans: Behavior and Health in Transition.* Oxford University Press, New York.

Baker, T. S. (1984). [Review of] Margaret Mead and Samoa: The making and unmaking of an anthropological myth. *Human Biology,* 56: 402–404.

Baldauf, R. B., Jr., & Ayabe, H. I. (1977). Acculturation and educational achievement in American Samoan adolescence. *Journal of Cross-Cultural Psychology,* 8: 241–255.

Bernard, R. H. (1988). *Research Methods in Cultural Anthropology.* Sage, Newbury Park, CA.

Bock, P. K. (1983). The Samoan puberty blues. *Journal of Anthropological Research,* 9: 336–340.

Brady, I. (Ed.) (1983). Special section: Speaking in the name of the real: Freeman and Mead on Samoa. *American Anthropologist,* 85: 908–947.

Buchholz, T. G. (1984). [Review of] Margaret Mead and Samoa: The making and unmaking of an anthropological myth. *Commentary,* 77: 78–80.

Calkins, F. G. (1962). *My Samoan Chief.* University of Hawaii Press, Honolulu.

Caton, H. (1984, March). Margaret Mead and Samoa: In support of Freeman's critique. *Quadrant* pp. 28–32.

Caton, H. (Ed.) (1990). *The Samoa Reader: Anthropologists Take Stock.* University Press of America, Lanham, MD.

Côté, J. E. (1986). Identity crisis modality: A technique for measuring the structure of the identity crisis. *Journal of Adolescence*, 9: 321–325.

Côté, J. E. (1994). *The Mead/Freeman controversy and its context: Western influence and the cultural disenfranchisement of Samoan youth.*

Cranberg, L. (1983). Ta'u revisited. *Human Organization*, 42: 182.

Crocombe, R. (1989). *The South Pacific: An Introduction* (5th ed.). University of the South Pacific, Suva, Fiji.

Ember, M. (1985). Evidence and science in ethnography: Reflections on the Mead-Freeman controversy. *American Anthropologist*, 87: 906–910.

Erikson, E. E. (1968). *Identity: Youth and Crisis.* Norton, New York.

Feinberg, R. (1988). Margaret Mead and Samoa: *Coming of Age* in fact and fiction. *American Anthropologist*, 90: 656–663.

Filoiali'i, L. A., & Knowles, K. (1982). The ifoga: The Samoan practice of seeking forgiveness for criminal behavior. *Oceania*, 53: 384–388.

Freeman, D. (1983). *Margaret Mead and Samoa: The Making and Unmaking of an Anthropological Myth.* Harvard University Press, Cambridge, MA.

Freeman, D. (1984). "O Rose thou art sick!" A rejoinder to Weiner, Schwartz, Holmes, Shore, and Silverman. *American Anthropologist*, 86: 400–405.

Freeman, D. (1985a). A reply to Ember's reflections on the Freeman-Mead controversy. *American Anthropologist*, 87: 910–917.

Freeman, D. (1985b). Response to Reyman and Hammond. *American Anthropologist*, 87: 394–395.

Freeman, D. (1986). Rejoinder to Patience and Smith. *American Anthropologist*, 88: 162–167.

Freeman, D. (1987). Holmes, Lowell D.: Quest for the real Samoa: The Mead/Freeman controversy and beyond. *American Anthropologist*, 89: 392–395.

Gerber, E. R. (1975). *The cultural patterning of emotions in Samoa.* Unpublished doctoral dissertation, University of California, San Diego.

Gold, M. G., & Petronio, R. J. (1980). Delinquent behavior in adolescence. In Adelson, J. (Eds.), *Handbook of Adolescent Psychology.* John Wiley & sons, New York.

Goodale, J. (1984). [Review of] Margaret Mead and Samoa: The making and unmaking of an anthropological myth. *Pacific Affairs*, 57: 180–182.

Goodman, R. A. (1983). *Mead's Coming of Age in Samoa: A Dissenting View.* Pipperline Press, Oakland, CA.

Handler, R. (1984). Review essay/Ruth Benedict, Margaret Mead, and the growth of American anthropology. *Journal of American History*, 71: 364–368.

Hanson, F. A. (1973). Political change in Tahiti and Samoa: An exercise in experimental anthropology. *Ethos*, 12: 1–12.

Heimans, F. (Producer) (1988). *Margaret Mead and Samoa.* Brighton Video, New York.

Holmes, L. D. (1980). Factors contributing to the cultural stability of Samoa. *Anthropological Quarterly*, 53: 188–197.

Holmes, L. D. (1987). *Quest for the Real Samoa: The Mead/Freeman Controversy and Beyond*. Bergen & Garvey, South Hadley, MA.

Holmes, L. D., and Holmes, E. R. (1992). *Samoan Village: Then and Now* (2nd ed.). Harcourt Brace Jovanovich College Publishers, Fort Worth, TX.

Hooper, A. (1984). [Review of] Margaret Mead and Samoa: The making and unmaking of an anthropological myth. *Oceania*, 55: 224–225.

Hunt, T. L., & Kirch, P. V. (1988). An Archaeological survey of the Manu'a Islands, American Samoa. *Polynesian Sociology Journal*, 97: 153–183.

Katchadourian, H. (1990). Sexuality. In S. S. Feldman and G. R. Elliott (Eds.) *At the threshold: the developing adolescent*. Cambridge, MA: Harvard University Press.

Kuklick, H. (1984). [Review of] Margaret Mead and Samoa: The making and unmaking of an anthropological myth. *Contemporary Sociology*, 13: 558–562.

Kuper, A. (1989). Coming of age in anthropology. *Nature*, 338: 453–455.

Laing, P. K. (1987). [Review of] Holmes, Lowell D.: Quest for the real Samoa: The Mead/Freeman controversy and beyond. *American Anthropologist*, 89: 395–399.

Leach, E. (1983, March 24). The Shangri-la that never was. *New Society*, 63: 477–478.

Leacock, E. (1987). Postscript: The problems of youth in contemporary Samoa. In Holmes, L. D. (Ed.), *Quest for the Real Samoa: The Mead/Freeman Controversy and Beyond*, Bergin & Garvey, South Hadley, MA.

Leacock, E. (1988, July). Anthropologists in search of a culture: Margaret Mead, Derek Freeman, and all the rest of us. *Central Issues Anthropol.* 8: 3–23.

Levy, R. I. (1984). Mead, Freeman, and Samoa: The problem of seeing things as they are. *Ethos* 12: 85–92.

MacPherson, C., & MacPherson, L. (1985). Suicide in Western Samoa: A sociological perspective. In Hezel, F. X., Rubenstein, D. H., & White, G. M. (Eds.), *Culture, Youth and Suicide in the Pacific: Papers from the East-West Center Conference*. East-West Center, Honolulu.

Mageo, J. M. (1988). Malosi: A psychological exploration of Mead's and Freeman's work and of Samoan aggression. *Pacific Studies*, 11: 25–65.

Marcia, J. E. (1980). Identity in adolescence. In Adelson, J. (Eds.), *Handbook of Adolescent Psychology*, Wiley, New York.

McDowell, N. (1984). Review of Margaret Mead and Samoa. *Pacific Studies*, 4: 99–140.

Mead, M. (1928). *Coming of Age in Samoa: A Psychological Study of Primitive Youth for Western Civilization*. Morrow Quill Paperbacks, New York.

Mead, M. (1969). *Social Organization of Manu'a* (2nd ed.). Bernice P. Bishop Museum, Honolulu.

Meleisea, M. (1987). *The Making of Modern Samoa: Traditional Authority and Colonial Administration in the Modern History of Western Samoa.* Institute of Pacific Studies of the University of the South Pacific, Suva, Fiji.

Montemayor, R., Adams, G. R., & Gullotta, T. P. (Eds.). (1990). *From Childhood to Adolescence: A Transitional Period?* Sage, Newbury Park, CA.

Montemayor, R., & Flannery, D. J. (1990). Making the transition from childhood to early adolescence. In Montemayor, R., Adams, G. R., & Gullotta, T. P. (Eds.). *From Childhood to Adolescence: A Transitional Period?* Sage, Newbury Park, CA.

Moyle, R. (Ed.). (1984). *The Samoan Journals of John Williams 1830–1832.* Canberra: Australian National University Press.

Muensterberger, W. (1985). [Review of] Margaret Mead and Samoa: The making and unmaking of an anthropological myth. *Psychoanalytic Quarterly,* 54: 101–105.

Murray, S. O. (1990). Problematic aspects of Freeman's account of Boasian culture. *Current Anthropology,* 31: 401–407.

Muuss, R. E. (1988). *Theories of Adolescence* (5th ed.). Random House, New York.

Nardi, B. A. (1984). The height of her powers: Margaret Mead's Samoa. *Feminist Studies,* 10: 323–337.

Offer, D., & Offer, J. B. (1975). *From Teenage to Young Manhood: A Psychological Study.* Basic Books, New York.

O'Meara, T. (1990). *Samoan Planters: Tradition and Economic Development in Polynesia.* Holt, Rinehart and Winston, Fort Worth, TX.

Patience, A., & Smith, J. W. (1986). Derek Freeman and Samoa: The making and unmaking of a biobehavioral myth. *American Anthropologist,* 88: 157–162.

Paxman, D. B. (1988). Freeman, Mead, and the eighteenth-century controversy over Polynesian society. *Pacific Studies,* 11: 1–19.

Pitt, D., & MacPherson, C. (1974). *Emerging Pluralism: The Samoan Community in New Zealand.* Longman Paul, Auckland, New Zealand.

Rappaport, R. A. (1986). Desecrating the holy woman: Derek Freeman's attack on Margaret Mead. *American Scholar,* 55: 313–347.

Rappaport, R. A. (1987a). Reply to Freeman. *American Scholar,* 56: 159–160.

Rappaport, R. A. (1987b). Reply to Freeman. *American Scholar,* 56: 304.

Reyman, J. E. (1985). Some comments on the Freeman-Mead controversy. *American Anthropologist,* 87: 393–394.

Scheper-Hughes, N. (1984). The Margaret Mead controversy: Culture, biology, and anthropological inquiry, *Human Organization,* 43: 85–93.

Schoeffel, P. (1986). [Review of R. Moyle] The Samoan journals of John Williams 1830–1832. *Oceania* 57: 63–64.

Schoeffel, P., & Meleisea, M. (1983). Margaret Mead, Derek Freeman and Samoa: The making, unmaking and remaking of an anthropological myth. *Canberra Anthropology,* 6: 58–69.

Sherif, M., Harvey, O. J., White, B. J., Hood, W. R. & Sherif, C. W. (1961). *Intergroup Conflicted Co-Operation: The Robber's Cave Experiment.* Norman Institute of Group Relations, University of Oklahoma.

Shore, B. (1983). Paradox regained: Freeman's Margaret Mead and Samoa. *American Anthropologist,* 85: 935–944.

Sprinthall, N. A., & Collins, W. A. (1984). *Adolescent Psychology: A Developmental View.* Addison-Wesley, Reading, MA.

Stair, J. B. (1983). *Old Samoa or Flotsam and Jetsam from the Pacific Ocean.* R. McMillan, Papakura, New Zealand.

Stanner, W. E. H. (1953). *The South Seas in Transition.* Australasian Publishing Co., Sydney.

Swaney, D. (1990). *Samoa: Western & American Samoa.* Lonely Planet Publications, Hawthorn; Victoria, Australia.

Tepperman, L. (1977). *Crime Control: The Urge Toward Authority.* McGraw-Hill Ryerson, Toronto.

Tribe, K. (1984). [Review of] Margaret Mead and Samoa: The making and unmaking of an anthropological myth. *Sociological Review,* 32: 398–401.

Turnbull, C. M. (1983, March 28). [Review of] Margaret Mead and Samoa: The making and unmaking of an anthropological myth. *New Republic* pp. 32–34.

Turner, G. (1986). *Samoa: Nineteen Years in Polynesia.* Western Samoa Historical and Cultural Trust, Apia, Samoa (John Snow, Paternoster Row, London, 1861).

Wendt, A. (1973). *Sons for the Return Home.* Penguin, London.

Wendt, A. (1977). *Pouliuli.* Penguin, London.

Wendt, A. (1979). *Leaves of the Banyon Tree.* Penguin, London.

Wendt, A. (1983). Three faces of Samoa: Mead's, Freeman's and Wendt's. *Pacific Islands Month.* 69 (April): 10–14.

Wendt, F. (1984). Review of Margaret Mead and Samoa. *Pacific Studies,* 40: 92–99.

Yans-Mclaughlin, V. (1984). Derek Freeman. [Review of] Margaret Mead and Samoa: The making and unmaking of an anthropological myth. *ISIS* 75: 410–411.

Young, R. E., & Juan, S. (1985). Freeman's Margaret Mead myth: The ideological virginity of anthropologists. *Australian and New Zealand Journal of Sociology,* 21: 64–81.

Yusuf, S., & Peters, R. K., Jr. (1985). *Western Samoa: The Experience of Slow Growth and Resource Imbalance.* The World Bank, Washington, DC.

Zuckerman, M. (1990). Some dubious premises in research and theory on racial differences: Scientific, social, and ethical issues. *American Psychologist* 45: 1297–1303.

Index

Note: Page references in italics indicate figures and tables